About The Author

Ian Wishart is an award-winning journalist and author, with a 26 year career in radio, television and magazines, a #1 talk radio show and three #1 bestselling books to his credit. Together with his wife Heidi, they edit and publish the news magazine *Investigate*.

This book is dedicated to the people who have the courage to speak out. Journalists may write about it, but you live it.

Ian Wishart
#1 bestselling author

Absolute POWER

The Helen Clark Years

HOWLING AT THE MOON PUBLISHING LTD

First edition published 2008
Howling At The Moon Publishing Ltd
PO Box 302-188
North Harbour
North Shore 0751
NEW ZEALAND

www.helenclarkbook.com
email: editorial@investigatemagazine.com

ISBN 978-0-9582401-3-0

Typeset in Adobe Garamond Pro
Cover concept: Ian Wishart, Heidi Wishart, Bozidar Jokanovic
Book Design: Bozidar Jokanovic
Cover photo: Jane Ussher/Presspix

*To get another copy of this book airmailed to you anywhere in the world, or to purchase a fully text-searchable digital edition,
visit our website:*

WWW.HELENCLARKBOOK.COM

Contents

"The Prime Minister Has No Recollection Of The Pot"

"Power tends to corrupt, and absolute power corrupts absolutely. Great men are almost always bad men." – **Lord Acton, English jurist**

AS BOOK TITLES GO, *ABSOLUTE POWER* tells the story of the Helen Clark years pretty well, but I did briefly flirt with an alternative title, *High Crimes and Misdemeanors*. Unfortunately, US columnist Ann Coulter had already turned a book of that name into a bestseller on the Clinton presidency, but no one in New Zealand can deny that Labour's reign has been dogged by more immoral and illegal behavior than any other administration in a century. Yet despite its crimes, no one within the Government has ever been prosecuted.

What you are about to read, however, will go further than anyone has gone before – digging up a Prime Minister you didn't even know existed, and exposing genuine, Queensland-style corruption in the country that keeps priding itself on being corruption-free.

Frankly, if I'm not up against a wall in handcuffs being read my rights by the end of the first week of this book's release, I'll be pleasantly surprised. If Police Commissioner Howard Broad thought he had problems with a chicken sex movie last year, he's in for a surprise in these pages but it won't be so pleasant.

Deputy Police Commissioner Rob Pope will have some fresh questions to answer as well, and they won't be pleasant either, and Police Minister Annette King and Prime Minister Helen Clark will face equally sticky questions over what they knew and when, and what they did when they found out.

Education Minister Chris Carter will face questions over whether he deliberately misled a police investigation, Heather Simpson is caught dead to rights interfering in the independence of a government department in breach of the rules, and you'll find out why one of the Prime Minister's media team was forced to utter this classic line, "The Prime Minister has no recollection of the pot."

And that's just a snippet, a trifle, of the revelations in this book. Then there's Labour's connections to a Caribbean tax haven tycoon with alleged links to the New York mafia, described as "a sugar-daddy to a coked-up black hostess"; a tycoon whose right hand man got pinged in a massive fraud case involving a murderer and a bank robber.

Let's not forget Helen Clark herself – the child who suffered social phobias and panic attacks yet grew up to be Prime Minister. That in itself is an amazing story, but trying to tell it is like scaling the walls of Camelot, only to find the whole thing's made of cardboard. The Helen Clark we see today is a carefully manufactured, airbrushed brand. She is a woman who makes all the right noises at all the right times, and delivers her lines seamlessly. She has an intellect like a bear-trap – sharp and lethal. But she is also a chameleon, an actress or, as even her first biographer put it, a "control freak". Many see Clark as a leader with a dangerous agenda.

"She wants to busy herself with what goes on in the homes of the nation in areas which families regard as their own responsibility, and I think she's going over a very dangerous line."

There are also many other views of what Clark has done. The Helen Clark who emerges from these pages is a Helen Clark measured against her own words from years ago. While her *actions* suggest she has remained true to her core principles and has carefully introduced policies to reflect those, the news transcripts show Clark has been prepared to *say* anything to anyone if she thinks it will advance her agenda.

Case in point? That quote above about interfering "in the homes of the nation" was not someone talking *about* Clark. It *was* Clark! She was trying to paint her opponent Jenny Shipley as the devil incarnate of the "Nanny State". Vote for Shipley, warned Clark, and you'll have "Nanny State" poking its nose into your family's life and how you bring up your kids! Somewhere between entering the polling booth on election day 1999, and waking up the next morning as Prime Minister-elect, Clark's views shifted 180 degrees.

No one, not even the earlier biography by Clark's own media advisor, Brian Edwards, has done the comprehensive trawl back through thousands of old news stories that *Absolute Power* encapsulates, in search of the authentic Helen Clark. These, too, are revealing. Only in Clark's more candid appearances, such as her essay in Virginia Myers' *Head & Shoulders*, published in 1986, does the future Prime Minister let her guard down and give vital hints of what really drives her. Clark, who'd actually given the interview in late 1984 only months after being rejected for a Cabinet position in the Lange administration, was angry at the time (a little like John Tamihere's infamous interview 21 years later when he'd just been cleared by the SFO but told he could not return to his cabinet post), and the resulting essay under her byline was all the better for it.

The contents of that interview have become defining statements for Clark, such as this intense comment about children:

"I've never had any intention of having a child. I definitely see children as destroying my lifestyle. It's inconceivable that I would become pregnant."

By the time of the Edwards book, a very positive portrait published just ahead of the 2002 election, Helen Clark's earlier candour had become far more spun – fuelling an emergent mythology about Clark, with repeated references to Helen Clark and Peter Davis' sexuality.

For reasons that are shrouded in mystery, some of the things that have been written about Clark in her official biography are not true. Or if they are, then Clark has lied elsewhere on the public record. For example, her stated addresses on the electoral roll in various years differ from claimed addresses in her book, and in one election she is registered to vote in two different electorates, simultaneously.

During the course of researching this biography, I made a conscious decision to avoid, for the most part, rehashing people's current memories surrounding past events. As an investigative journalist, one often finds our memories and recollections can be tainted or tilted by both hindsight and our current worldview, let alone tricks of the memory over time. So wherever possible I have sifted through official documents, interviews and news reports contemporaneous with the events in question. It is often said that journalism is the first draft of history, and this biography draws heavily on those first draft accounts when it comes to quotes and context.

Brian Edwards' work, *Helen, Portrait of a Prime Minister*, is without footnotes or index. It was also, as Edwards himself notes, based not so much on the historical record but on face to face interviews with colleagues and friends of Helen Clark. Nonetheless it has been invaluable, and I am indebted to Edwards for laying the groundwork. As his own publisher anticipated in the blurb to *Helen*, "His [Edwards'] authoritative account is the first book to be published on Helen Clark and will provide the indispensable foundation for any future biography."

Absolute Power, on the other hand, is not just about what happened publicly and what played out on the news each night. It is much more about what was going on behind the scenes – the power plays, the dirty tricks, the Machiavellian maneuvers. The bits the daily media missed.

This book concludes that New Zealand's political system is at a dangerous constitutional crossroads, that the power of the Executive has evolved too rapidly for checks and balances to keep up, and that abuses of that power are now becoming more frequent. I call, like former Prime Minister Sir Geoffrey Palmer did in his seminal work, *Unbridled Power*, nearly 30 years ago, for a much wider public debate around what we want our democracy to reflect, and what we are prepared to tolerate from our rulers.

The lessons of *Absolute Power* are drawn from the actions of the fifth Labour

Government, but they are universal political lessons and whoever wins the next election would do well to ponder them, lest they end up in a similar predicament.

As a former Labour cabinet press secretary in the fourth Labour Government, who grew up and worked in Wellington, I am acutely aware of the heart that beats inside that city and the blood that flows through its veins. I am, like Edwards, a sometime practitioner of the dark arts of media advice by virtue of that political baptism.

I am nonetheless apolitical, supporting individual policies rather than ideological packages. When National was voted out in 1999, I applauded like many others to see Clark take the podium and promise a brave new future, free of the corruption and sleaze that had dogged politics for what seemed like forever.

So when critics accuse me of being anti-Labour, they are painting a convenient two dimensional portrait of a three dimensional issue. The analysis I bring to *Absolute Power* is the same that I brought to the Winebox investigation: scrutiny by the Fourth Estate of the activities of the Executive, in the interests of informing the public. Nothing more, nothing less.

Finding The Rough In The Diamonds

Sir Humphrey: "But it is the truth, Minister."
Jim Hacker: "I don't want the truth. I want something I can tell
Parliament!" – **Yes, Minister**

THERE IS A STORY TOLD by an old schoolmate of Helen Clark's, of the time when they were both 15-year olds in the Waikato farming settlement that the Clark family called home. One of the local girls had just become the proud owner of a litter of kittens, and invited the other teenagers around for a look.

"Ugh," was 15 year old Helen Clark's response when she saw so many squirming kittens trying to feed from their mother. "How horrible. There's too many. You should just drown them."

It certainly left an impression on those in the room.

As a patron of the Family Planning Association in later life, and the architect of radical laws to allow abortion clinics to perform abortion surgery on 11 year old girls without parental knowledge or consent, one can only wonder what part the kittens played in fashioning Clark's attitudes to parenting.

There are some who say you can divorce the private life and the private past of a politician from their performance in the actual job; that all that matters is what you see in the 9-5 workday, not what they do after hours, not what they privately believe.

For a number of major reasons, this is utterly, totally and fundamentally wrong. It is a political lie that's been told for so long and so regularly that the news media have come to believe it, and through the media they have conditioned you – the public – to believe it too.

It may be true of an ordinary person in a professional or working class job, where the employer sets the tasks for the day and you are paid to complete them. Politicians are a different breed: we are their employers, but they often don't do what we tell them – unless it is election year.

Politicians want your money – nearly 40% of what you earn on average by the time fees and GST are included. Labour's tax take has increased a whopping 37% since they came to power. Politicians, once they get your money, exercise enormous power over your life. Sudden access to all that cash, tens of billions of dollars, makes those politicians dream about all the pet projects they have *privately* fantasized about all their lives. They can now put those schemes into place.

The voter's only defence to political ambush of the kind we've seen in the past two decades is to encourage the news media to do more in-depth digging of those who have the power to tax, to legislate and to enforce police action against those who defy the regime. We, the people, have a right to know what really makes our politicians tick, and what they do in their private lives that may impact on their public duties or the legislation they support.

After all, the laws they make affect your life. With absolute power should come absolute scrutiny.

How far should the media go into the lives of public figures? It is an age-old ethical question: is the issue sufficiently relevant to be in the public interest? Contrary to popular misconception, the news media knows far more about most public figures than it ever publishes, because it correctly deems that much of that information has no bearing on how the person does their job.

For example, the fact that a politician may be gay is irrelevant to whether they're a good Minister of Transport or Minister of Finance. The fact that another politician is a strong Christian is irrelevant to their performance as Minister of Health. It is particularly where one's private life intersects with their public duties that issues of relevance and/or the voters' "right to know" surface.

Take those two previous examples: that same gay politician chooses to champion a bill favouring gay adoption of children, but without disclosing his own sexual preferences. The image presented to the voters is of a straight politician rising above prejudice and emphasizing tolerance and acceptance. This sends a powerful message to voters about their own biases. But the message is untrue. It might be valid from someone else, but not him. The politician is not straight, he is a member of a community whose members stand to benefit from a law change. In other words, he has an undeclared conflict of interest.

Voters should be able to see whether an MP has a personal, rather than professional, interest in any issue. By choosing to become involved in a political issue dear to his heart and which challenges the boundaries of social acceptability, *the politician makes his private life relevant*. Likewise, a strong Christian appointed as Minister of Censorship might make decisions that many agree with, but his beliefs are indeed relevant to how he performs in that particular portfolio and should be disclosed. On the flip side of that coin, the same applies to raging social liberals occupying powerful positions. The top two appointees in the Office of the Film Censor are, for example, gay. Likewise, we now have a gay Education Minister, while the head of the

Ministry of Education is lesbian. So if it was valid for the news media in 1984 to continually highlight (and often ridicule) the Christian conservatism of then Education Minister Merv Wellington, it must be equally important for the public to know the backgrounds of others in public office. Anything else would be hypocrisy on the media's part.

Likewise, if leading campaigners to abolish smacking were themselves parents whose kids drifted into trouble because of a lack of discipline, isn't that relevant to the political debate?

As you proceed to unravel the real story of the Helen Clark government in the pages that follow, you will be confronted with this dilemma from time to time: have our politicians tried to persuade the public by hiding their real intentions, or who they really are? And do you have a right to know?

The New Zealand media regard politicians' private beliefs and lives as largely out of bounds, but I've taken the trouble of including leading international views on the problem, to help you better understand - because this book will certainly push boundaries.

In the essay, "Can Public Figures Have Private Lives?", Harvard University's Frederick Schauer[1] has contributed significantly to the debate.

"In most of the debates about the issue of disclosing facts about the lives of candidates or office holders that those candidates or office holders would wish to keep secret, the issue is framed around the question of the relevance of the fact at issue.

"Typically, as with the debates about the extramarital sexual activities of President Clinton or about past drug use or other allegedly "minor" crimes that took place in the distant past, it is alleged that the facts ought not be disclosed because they are irrelevant to the performance of the job. Regardless of whether people want the information, the argument goes, information that is not relevant to job performance has no place in the public electoral discussion.

"Such claims of irrelevance mask a host of deeper and more difficult issues. Chief among these are contestable issues about what the job actually is, and equally contestable empirical issues about the relationship of some fact to that job."

Illustrating that point, Schauer raises the example of US judge Douglas Ginsberg, whose nomination to the US Supreme Court was spiked in 1987 after reporters, using unnamed sources, disclosed that Ginsberg had been a frequent user of marijuana in the past. Leaving aside the medical argument over whether marijuana would have dulled his wits sufficiently to make him a liability on the Supreme Court bench, Schauer concentrates more on the fact that as a person supposed to uphold the law in one of the supreme positions available under the US constitution, Ginsberg simply couldn't measure up:

"The fact of past disobedience to law was material to Ginsberg's qualifications".

---

1 http://www.ksg.harvard.edu/presspol/research_publications/first_amendment_series/schauer2.PDF

Just as it was, of course, in the fall from grace of New Zealand's Attorney-General David Parker, after he was caught by *Investigate* filing false returns to the Companies Office.

"My point here," Schauer continues, "is that a claim of 'irrelevance' presupposes some standard of relevance...denials of relevance often mask narrow conceptions of the positions and its responsibilities, conceptions with which others might reasonably disagree."

This is one of Professor Schauer's central points: that even if a majority of voters might believe something is "irrelevant" or out-of-bounds, a functioning democracy requires that the interests of a minority who might want to hear that information be protected.

"When such disagreement does exist, however, the issue becomes more difficult, because there is now the question of when it is appropriate to make widely available a piece of information that some voters might think relevant to their voting decision, under circumstances in which the information is indeed relevant to their voting decision based on criteria that they take to be relevant."

Schauer uses the Monica Lewinsky affair to illustrate the problem:

"The claim that marital infidelity is irrelevant to the office of President of the United States presupposes that the role of President should not include the role of being an exemplar of marital fidelity. For many people it should not, but for many others it should, and debates about relevance to the job are commonly smokescreens for debates about just what it is that the job really entails.

"It is widely known that President Clinton cheats at golf. Although it is clear that playing golf is not part of the job description of President...many people believe that maintaining certain high standards of veracity are indeed part of that job description. And if that is the case, then the empirical question is presented whether evidence of cheating at golf is some evidence of (or relevant to) a likely failure to maintain high standards of veracity in public pronouncements."

This of course is precisely the credibility problem Helen Clark has during this election year: does she have a flawed character that, while it might be forgiven once, is now showing a clear pattern of behavior? If readers are suddenly sensing a merging of Paintergate, Speedogate, Doonegate and Pledgegate, read on:

"It is possible that the answer is no," continues Schauer, "and that there is neither a causal relationship or even a correlation between the existence of the trait of cheating at golf and the existence of the trait of being abnormally dishonest in one's public and political dealings. But it is also possible that the answer is yes, and that a cheater at golf, holding everything else constant, is more likely to be dishonest in public statements. And if this latter alternative is in fact the case, then the argument that golf behaviour is 'private' or none of the public's business becomes a somewhat more difficult one to maintain."[2]

---

2 The NZ media, in publishing details of Don Brash's rumoured affair (still not proven, incidentally but the media felt justified in raising the issue in principle), adopted a similar

Cheating, however, is a personality trait that many people can agree is relevant. What about the grey areas of sexuality? After all, we all have sex lives.

"No less real is the example of the disclosure, against the presumed wishes of the candidate, of the sexual orientation of a candidate for public office. Although many of us believe that sexual orientation is both immaterial and irrelevant to job performance in all or virtually all public sector and private sector settings, it is unfortunately (from my perspective) the case that not everyone agrees.

"For a not insignificant proportion of the population in most countries in the world, having a gay, lesbian or bisexual orientation is immoral, and having a heterosexual orientation is not only morally commanded, but is also a necessary qualification for holding public office."

Schauer's view is that like it or not, you can't have a meaningful public debate on these issues in a general sense but only on a case by case basis – the circumstances of each politician being different. Voters may decide that sexual behaviour is irrelevant in one case but exceedingly relevant in another, because of the different personalities or responsibilities of the politicians in question.

"It may turn out that disclosure of traits that some deliberators believe to be morally immaterial or empirically irrelevant will nevertheless properly be part of the process by which [the public] decides collectively…what its moral criteria will be."

And again, the Harvard professor returns to the checks and balances necessary in a democracy. Even if only ten percent of the electorate believe that private life information should be disclosed, he says, and the other 90% believe it shouldn't be, publication is justified.

"Under these circumstances, it is tempting to conclude that the majority should prevail, and that disclosure should be deemed inappropriate. But given that we are discussing the topic of the information necessary for exercising [the vote]…*there is something deeply problematic about majorities deciding that information relevant to the voting decisions of a minority ought in some formal or informal way be made unavailable to that minority.*" [author's emphasis]

Although Schauer hears the argument often used in New Zealand politics – that raking over the coals of politicians' private lives will discourage good people from standing for election – he disagrees with it.

"There are moral arguments on the other side as well," he acknowledges. "Chief among those is the argument that control over the information about one's life is itself a central part of what is sometimes referred to as personal autonomy, and that there is no good reason why a person should be required to relinquish that right simply to enter the public domain.

"Yet if personal autonomy is the basis for the countervailing right of non-disclosure, it may be hard to distinguish this right from all of the other

---

line, that revealing Brash's action was a matter of public interest, however distasteful it may have been for all involved, including the media.

autonomy rights that one must forgo to enter the public arena.

"One has the right to speak or to remain silent, to live where one pleases, sometimes to work where one pleases, and a host of other rights that are commonly and properly thought relinquishable by one's voluntary decision to stand for public office or to operate in the public domain more generally."

In other words, what makes a public figure's right to privacy sacrosanct when they may give up a whole lot of other rights as part of standing for office?

Naturally, Professor Schauer is not alone in his assessments of the reduced right to privacy of public figures. In a major editorial early 2005, Britain's *Guardian* newspaper tackled the issue in the wake of the David Blunkett affair.[3]

"The awkward truth is that the way people live their private lives does tell us things that can help to make judgments about them as public people...this is not the same as saying that the world will only be put to rights if it is run by certified saints. This country was seen through two world wars by leaders who would certainly not qualify on that score; but whatever the human failings of a Lloyd George or a Churchill, they did not include an inability to get the job done."

It's a comment that echoes the earlier ones on relevance. Are the personal failings relevant to the particular job they have?

The *San Francisco Chronicle's* test in regard to public figures is this: "Personal conduct may have a bearing on public roles and public responsibilities. The degree to which a public figure voluntarily conducts his or her life in public or the degree to which private conduct bears on the discharge of public responsibility should guide the publication of personal information."

Journalist turned lawyer Hal Fuson, now the chief legal officer at America's Copley Newspaper Group, told a panel discussion that journalists should not pull back from disclosing facts about elected officials just because of their own worldviews.

"Worry about the facts, folks, and let the truth take care of itself. Truth is like beauty, it's in the eye of the beholder. And facts depend on verifiability. Verifiability depends upon being able to get your hands on lots of information that people don't want you to have, because they want to shape their stories to suit themselves, not to suit the interests of society, and certainly not to suit your desire to inform your communities."

The American Press Institute has published an ethics "checklist" for journalists weighing up publishing private information on politicians. They include:[4]

Does this matter affect the person's ability to do his job?

Does this matter reflect on the person's conduct in office?

Does this matter reflect on the person's character?

Does the matter reveal hypocrisy?

"Character matters for public officials," says the Press Institute. "They

3   http://www.buzzle.com/editorials/11-30-2004-62334.asp
4   The American Press Institute missed one: Does the matter reveal a hidden agenda?

publish family pictures on campaign brochures and proudly reveal private matters that reflect positively on their character. Private matters that reflect negatively on their character matter to readers as well."

The Institute concludes:

"Don't look for easy answers. Many stories involve consideration of more than one of these questions. However you decide, you can't ensure that you will please all your readers. If you write the story, some readers will say you are prying into matters that should be private. If you don't, some readers will say you are covering up for people in power...Sometimes the proper decision is to publish the story along with an explanation of your reasons for publishing and your consideration of various factors. Most readers understand that these are not black and white decisions.

"You might decide that a long-ago consensual affair between adults is no one's business, and some readers will decide that you're covering up. Or you might decide that criminal conduct is newsworthy whenever it occurred and some readers will think you are dredging up mud about youthful mistakes because your editorial page opposes the candidate."

Australian political reporter Peter Cole-Adams was quoted in one ethics discussion this way:

"Elected parliamentarians were, he said, the paradigm of the public figure: each chose to enter politics; was paid by the public; spent public money; lived by publicity; enjoyed perks; and had the right to defame anyone he chose from the sanctity of the parliamentary privilege...in this sense, the public, as the hirer and firer, has a right to know what its representatives are up to. 'If they are not going to be honest...they should be careful'."

The questions the press has to ask are: is it true? Is it interesting?

Is it in the public interest to disclose? He noted Lord Northcote's dictum: 'News is what someone wants to suppress. Everything else is advertising."

Those who say we should ignore the private beliefs and activities of politicians overlook one other thing as well. Should the Catholic or Anglican churches be required to hire an atheist as Cardinal or Archbishop, on the grounds that their beliefs are irrelevant to how they perform their job? If a politician was secretly a huge believer in the policies and ideas of Adolf Hitler, shouldn't the public have a right to know before giving them the keys to our Treasury chest, police force, army and laws?

If a cabinet minister allegedly role-played adult child sex fantasies as part of a bondage and discipline session in his own time, is that truly private behavior and therefore "out of bounds", or is it something voters are entitled to consider, in case such a politician was ever responsible for children's welfare policies?

The answer, in all these cases, is that sometimes private beliefs and private actions are indeed relevant, regardless of whether political supporters or the rest of the news media agree or not.

Armed with this perspective, then, our journey begins on election night, 1999.

Helen's Journey To The Dark Side

Sir Arnold: "Are you suggesting that I give confidential information to the press?"
Sir Humphrey: "Certainly not, Arnold. This is confidential disinformation."
Sir Arnold: "Ah, that is different." **– Yes Minister**

THE VOYAGE FROM POLITICAL INNOCENCE to corruption does not happen overnight. It follows evolutionary steps. Helen Clark's public journey to the dark side began in her very first week in power. You may think you know about the dismissal of Police Commissioner Peter Doone, but what Helen Clark did behind the scenes to Doone has never been fully documented, until now, and it sets the tone for her entire administration.

For the newly-elected Helen Clark, the seeds for the first test of her leadership (and her first Machiavellian power-play) were being sown on election night, November 27, in Wellington. Police Commissioner Peter Doone – a man named in a news report just days after the election as being on a government hit-list for dismissal – managed to get himself in a spot of bother during a routine police traffic stop. Doone had been in the hot seat over the disastrous INCIS police computer debacle, and a favourite target of Labour during the previous year.

Doone had recently left his wife, Anne, and family, decamping the family home in favour of new digs with Robyn Johnstone, a media advisor at the LTSA head office in Wellington. Whether or not the Commissioner's new arrangements were common knowledge among police rank and file in Wellington is not clear – chances are that although Police National Headquarters staff would have become aware of the office scuttlebutt, the marriage break-up, understandably, probably wasn't the subject of an "All Points Bulletin" to the wider police district.

So when a car driven by Johnstone, with Doone in the passenger seat, was pulled over in Wellington around 9pm on election night in a routine patrol stop, the sensitivities surrounding his new relationship may have been one of the reasons Doone bounced out of the vehicle to greet the approaching officer. It was Doone's new partner – the 'other woman' – who was driving, and Doone was probably hoping to head off one of those embarrassing smirks from a senior colleague. He needn't have worried, as it turned out. While a senior officer remained in the squad car radioing number plate details back to base, the man approaching Doone was rookie constable Brett Main, who'd only been a police officer for three days, and was surprised and – in his own words – "intimidated" when he found he'd pulled over his boss.

The alleged offence was a minor one – Robyn Johnstone had forgotten to turn her headlights on as she pulled out onto one of Wellington's floodlit main roads. It is police policy, however, to stop drivers at night if they're caught without their lights, and talk to them. The logic behind this seems incredibly simple and straightforward: coming from behind, a police car would have no option but to stop the vehicle precisely so they could tell the driver their lights weren't on. In other words, it's not rocket science, and the intention seems to be mainly advisory, rather than prosecutorial – police policy also recording that any subsequent action is at the discretion of the officer.

So at one level, the decision by Doone to talk to the officer did not, in itself, defeat the purpose of the policy: the car had been stopped by police, and the driver – albeit via the passenger – advised that her lights were off. Doone, as you'll discover later, says he didn't even realize a traffic offence had been committed, and he got out of the car merely because he assumed it was just a random stop and he saw it as a chance to greet his "troops".

Whatever, the issue exploded to become the defining symbol of Prime Ministerial power in her first 100 days in office, and an example of her no-nonsense approach to cleaning up the "sleaze" of the previous National administration. At least, that's how she pitched it.

To understand the events that followed, however, and the Prime Minister's central role in them, we'll first retrace the story the way it developed in the news media, because this is the storyline that was given to the public.

The traffic stop happened just after 9pm on election night. News of the event did not reach the public, however, until a brief item on TVNZ's *Holmes* programme on Friday, 3 December 1999. That item referred to the fact that the Police Commissioner had "exchanged pleasantries" with a constable who'd pulled over the vehicle he was in on the previous Saturday night.

Two days after *Holmes* broke the story, the *Sunday Star-Times* carried a front page story on 5 December, with little fresh information except the revelation that Deputy Police Commissioner Rob Robinson had commenced an internal investigation into the incident.

A week later, the *Star-Times* was again back in the fray, this time with a small page 3 story suggesting the internal investigation had become "complicated" because the evidence of the constable differed from the evidence of Doone.

By the 19th of December, the *Star-Times* was in full flight on the story. It had candid front page photos of Doone and Robyn Johnstone, along with details that the pair had been seen at a corporate function at Wellington's overseas terminal prior to being pulled over on election night. It repeated the news that Doone had stepped out to meet the police officer, and that no breath-test was done on driver Robyn Johnstone, the police commissioner's partner.

It was this story that sent the rest of the news media into a feeding frenzy.

"Mr Doone stepped from the car and engaged the constable in conversation before the constable reached the driver's window, an informed source told the *Herald* yesterday," reported journalist Alison Horwood.[5]

"Mr Doone and Ms Johnstone had spent the day at a corporate yachting function before going out to dinner. They were pulled over by a police car containing two constables...as [the rookie] never made it to the driver's window and did not speak to her there was no way he could have performed the routine breath-test for excess alcohol.

"A source close to the inquiry said last night: 'It's a disgrace. If that was a member of the public who got out of the car and talked to the cop, they would be asked to step aside and the driver would be spoken to.'"

Further down the story, Police Association president Greg O'Connor was quoted as saying he'd had to hire lawyers for the two constables involved because "there has been a lot of trauma put on the young constables".

The implication of the news coverage was becoming clear: Police Commissioner Peter Doone had acted inappropriately by intercepting a police officer trying to do his duty, and effectively preventing the Commissioner's partner from being breath-tested. That, in a nutshell, is the allegation the media were dancing around the edges of.

The following day, a *New Zealand Herald* editorial[6] noted Doone was now in the Prime Minister's gunsights.

"The Prime Minister has indicated that Mr Doone's future now depends on the outcome of the Police Complaints Authority inquiry. The authority is investigating whether correct police procedures were followed by the officers who stopped the car in which Mr Doone was a passenger because its lights were not on...

"The authority must decide not only whether the police commissioner's action was contrary to the law but also whether it might have been unreasonable, unjustified, unfair or undesirable.

"Of all public services, the police are perhaps the most important. They give the public not only a sense of security but also the confidence that law and order

---

5   *NZ Herald*, 20 December 1999, "Officer failed to question Doone driver"
http://www.nzherald.co.nz/index.cfm?objectid=106089
6   *NZ Herald*, 21 December 1999, "*Editorial:* Commissioner of Police should quit"
http://www.nzherald.co.nz/index.cfm?objectid=106113

will be upheld impartially. It goes without saying, therefore, that the country's most senior policeman must be above reproach. Such, unfortunately, is no longer the case with police commissioner Peter Doone."

Doone, now the subject of both the Robinson investigation and a Police Complaints Authority investigation, felt hamstrung in his attempts to hit back at the *Herald* editorial.[7]

"Formal inquiries are underway. There is a due process of law in New Zealand under which these matters are judged. The full facts…are not currently in the public domain…Because they are still underway and no issues have been determined, I am unable to enter public debate on the issues at this point. I would ask, therefore, that judgments or comments about these matters are not made until the full facts have been properly considered."

Despite Doone's pleas, the case against him gained momentum over the Christmas/New Year break.

On 30 December, the *Herald* reported,[8] "Prime Minister Helen Clark was last night weighing up the future of beleaguered Police Commissioner Peter Doone. She was handed a copy of the Police Complaints Authority report into Mr Doone's conduct at a police checkpoint [sic] almost immediately on her return yesterday from a three day climbing holiday."

Clark, playing it by the book in her public comments, told the paper, "There will be no precipitate action. We are going to study it very carefully." She added she would be seeking advice from Attorney-General Margaret Wilson and Solicitor-General John McGrath, as well as discussing the matter with Police Minister George Hawkins.

By January 9, the political spin was that Doone was dog-tucker, provided the Government could find a bone substantial enough to beat him with.

"The Government is taking legal advice on how beleaguered Police Commissioner Peter Doone can be sacked."[9]

Two days later, news reports were suggesting news of Doone's demise would probably emerge from the first Cabinet meeting of the year, set down for January 25.

"The Police Commissioner's position is cabinet-approved and therefore if he is to be disestablished the feeling is that it has to be a cabinet decision," a prime ministerial spokesman was quoted in the *Herald*.[10]

The following weekend, however, came a dramatic and decisive new revelation in the Doone affair – an alleged attempt to actually prevent the junior police officer from breath-testing Robyn Johnstone. Up until this

7   *NZ Herald*, 22 December 1999, "Wait for all the facts: Doone"
http://www.nzherald.co.nz/index.cfm?objectid=106461
8   *NZ Herald*, 30 December 1999, "Clark in no rush over Doone"
http://www.nzherald.co.nz/index.cfm?objectid=106866
9   *Sunday Star-Times*, 09/01/2000
10   *NZ Herald*, January 11 2000, "Doone's future goes to cabinet"
http://www.nzherald.co.nz/index.cfm?objectid=109571

point, news coverage had been circumspect, but on 16 January the *Star-Times* went for the Commissioner's jugular, accusing Doone of telling the young cop "That won't be necessary" when the policeman told him he wanted to breath-test the driver.

The reaction to the story is probably more telling than the story itself, so here's how the *Herald* ran it on the Monday morning:[11]

"Police Commissioner Peter Doone yesterday denied a newspaper allegation that he advised a constable against breath-testing his partner. He says he may take legal action over the article.

"Mr Doone, aged 52, has been under intense scrutiny since a Wellington police patrol stopped his car, driven by partner Robyn Johnstone, at 11 p.m. on November 27 for not having its lights on.

"Mr Doone said yesterday that allegations in the *Sunday Star-Times* that the constable tried to breath test Ms Johnstone were untrue and defamatory. 'The allegations that the commissioner told the constable that breath-testing his partner 'won't be necessary' have never been raised, are false and also defamatory,' a statement from his office said. 'I will be seeking urgent legal advice with a view to taking action,' he said."

Perhaps the most intriguing paragraph in the whole story, however, is this one, because it suggests the latest revelation is exactly the golden gun the government was looking for.

"Helen Clark has agreed that it would be hard to remove Mr Doone, but legal sources have said that if the Commissioner interfered with the constable's duties, such a misuse of authority could be enough to get him fired."

The entire story shifted gear with the suggestion that Doone had not merely "exchanged pleasantries", but had used his authority to prevent the officer from carrying out his lawful duty. Radio talkback went wild. Doone had to go, screamed the public.

The *Herald's* political editor, Vernon Small, wrote the following Saturday[12]:

"A Police Complaints Authority report to Prime Minister Helen Clark contests evidence given by police commissioner Peter Doone, government sources say. The *Weekend Herald* also understands that the evidence of an off duty police officer provides a crucial eyewitness account of a late-night incident when Mr Doone and his partner were stopped by a police patrol. A cabinet meeting on Tuesday is due to decide the commissioner's future amid signals from the Beehive that Helen Clark has lost confidence in him."

If Doone's denials of any wrongdoing had carried any weight with the public the previous Tuesday, the weekend media reports were political dynamite with their suggestions that Doone's credibility was in doubt because other

---

11 *NZ Herald*, 17 January 2000, "Doone threatens to sue over breath-test story" http://www.nzherald.co.nz/index.cfm?objectid=111724
12 *NZ Herald*, 22 January 2000, "Surprise Doone witness" http://www.nzherald.co.nz/index.cfm?objectid=113778

witnesses were contradicting his version of events.

By this stage, the first reports of the sequence leading up to the traffic stop were filtering out into the media. Doone had been a guest on a corporate yacht as part of a regatta on Wellington Harbour between 1.30 and 5.30pm. The *Herald* reported that race rules prohibited any consumption of alcohol during the regatta, but that Johnstone had been seen with "at least one drink" from the bar at the Overseas Terminal after the race had ended at 5.30.

"Someone who spoke to her and Mr Doone a few minutes before they left said they appeared sober. 'They were socializing with the Governor-General. No one in their right mind drinks too much in front of him'. The couple left the function between 6pm and 7pm and went to dinner at a Chinese restaurant in central Wellington, Uncle Chang's."[13]

In other words, although Johnstone had been drinking, there was no suggestion from witnesses that she was over the limit.

The following day, 23 January, the *Sunday Star-Times* again hammered Doone.[14]

"Government sources told the *Sunday Star-Times* Doone will be asked to fall on his sword. The request would be made to allow him to salvage some dignity. It was also viewed as preferable to a sacking which could prompt legal action.

"Doone had failed to realise the seriousness of the situation until very recently, one source said. It is understood he has spent about $40,000 on legal advice in the past month.

"Part of the Robinson inquiry findings, obtained by this newspaper, contains evidence from Main's partner which confirms the constable was carrying a breath-test sniffer. Constable Mark Haldane was an acting sergeant teamed with Main. He stayed in the patrol car and used his radio to check the car's licence plate.

"Haldane says in his evidence: 'Constable Main got out of the car to go and speak to the driver. As he got out he leaned back in saying the words `forgot the sniffer' and took it from the centre arm rest between the two front seats'."

The newspaper was using its exclusive access to the Robinson inquiry, "obtained by this newspaper", to effectively bury Doone's denials of trying to prevent a breath-test.

"A lawyer acting for Doone has threatened legal action against the *Sunday Star-Times*, claiming a report last week was defamatory. The letter says: 'At no point in the current investigation has that officer even said anything that suggests that he conveyed to Mr Doone an intention to breath-test Ms Johnstone or that the officer had in fact tried to breath-test her.'

"Last night another lawyer for Doone, John Upton QC, issued a statement, saying: 'The commissioner did not see any breath-testing device on the constable.

13 *NZ Herald*, 22 January 2000, "The day Doone's troubles started"
http://www.nzherald.co.nz/index.cfm?objectid=113776
14 *Sunday Star-Times*, 23 January 2000, "Last chance to resign" by Oskar Alley

Neither was any request or attempt made to breath-test Ms Johnstone'."

The damage was complete. In what would become a trademark form of political murder in the Clark years, Doone had suffered not just an attack on his actions, but on his credibility. Almost invariably, it was this latter type of attack that would prove fatal to Clark's targets. When confronted with allegations or individuals she didn't like, Clark's response was usually for lesser ministers to open fire on the victim with personal attacks designed to ridicule, or lessen the target's credibility in the eyes of the public.

In a final twist of the knife, the *Star-Times* article hinted that Doone couldn't even remember what time the incident had happened. The news media had been repeatedly given an 11pm timing, so when Doone's lawyer wrote to the *Star-Times* suggesting it was earlier in the evening (presumably less time to get 'tanked') the paper challenged the claim:

"The lawyer's letter to the *Star-Times* said Doone and the constable 'agreed that the incident occurred shortly after 9pm'. This is despite earlier reports of it happening about 11pm. Sources also say Johnstone has indicated to investigators the pair was stopped after 10.30pm.[15]

"It is understood Doone claims to have a good memory of the events that night. However, the Robinson inquiry notes that when the media began asking questions he struggled to remember what day the incident took place. 'The commissioner's initial comment when the media interest in this incident was brought to his attention by Mr Player (Police Headquarters public affairs general manager) on Friday the 3rd of December has been commented on above," the Robinson report says. 'In that conversation Mr Doone had difficulty recollecting the exact night this incident took place.'

"Also, he claims he was not standing close to Main when he spoke to him. However, the evidence of the constable and a third witness contradicts that claim."

It's important to remember, here, that at this point the Robinson inquiry had not been publicly released. The newspaper had "obtained" a copy, or at least verbatim quotes from it, from an unknown source. This source was brave enough to leak the information even though it was a report still before Prime Minister Helen Clark for consideration.

The predictions were correct, however, Doone was gone by lunchtime the following Tuesday, opting to resign as Commissioner, be demoted to constable and serve out a six month "sentence" working, ironically, in the Prime Minister's department on a special project. He would continue to draw his $275,000 salary until retiring from the police force in September 2000.

"Prime Minister Helen Clark said the reports raised issues of judgment which in turn raised issues of whether there could be confidence in Mr Doone," reported the *Herald*.[16]

---

15 The radio call on Doone's number plates would have been exactly timed in the police computers. There should have been no controversy over this.
16 *NZ Herald*, 26 January 2000, "Unrepentant Doone forced to step down"

"The incident itself is pretty innocent," Doone told the waiting media, " – it is what people have interpreted from it. Without that [media role] this incident would not have reached the proportions that it has."

Doone would later realize he was laboring under a massive misconception here. He blamed the media for spinning the story, which in turn forced the government's hand. In truth, as he would discover during his court case against the *Star-Times* for defamation in 2005, it was Prime Minister Helen Clark herself who'd been stirring the pot and who had passed damning, false, information about Doone to the media in a bid to crank the story up.

You've seen the version of events the Prime Minister wanted you to see about the downfall of Police Commissioner Peter Doone. Now let's see what really was going on behind the scenes.

THE ALLEGATION: Destruction Of A Man's Career On False Evidence, For Political Gain
THE CULPRIT: Prime Minister Helen Clark

In the supercharged world of New Zealand politics, little is what it initially seems. In the particulars of the Doone case, nothing was as it seemed. The context is really anchored around Doone's involvement in the INCIS computer disaster – one of the Commissioner's pet projects. In reality, Doone was a victim of birthing a good idea before its time: computer technology was advancing so rapidly in the late 1990s (from 386 to 486 to the first Pentiums) that hardware and software providers were having a hard time keeping up. Projects commenced in the mid-90s at vast expense were obsolete by 1999, which is one of the reasons the INCIS project kept having budget blowouts.

Already on Labour's black list, the Police Commissioner's behavior on election night was a political godsend to the new administration. Clark had been looking for a credible public excuse to dump Doone in favour of her own appointee to the crucial constitutional position. Whilst public dissatisfaction over INCIS was running high, it wasn't quite the smoking gun Clark needed. Abuse of power, intimidating a junior officer – these on the other hand were issues that heartland New Zealand could easily understand and disapprove of.

If true, Doone deserved to go. But what if they weren't?

The truth emerged in 2005, before the election. New Zealand's mainstream media failed to appreciate the real significance of the devastating revelations however, so it became the most under-reported political story of 2005. It could, in fact, have changed the result of the election. But while the media were more than happy to savage National over the Exclusive Brethren pamphlets, none were interested in covering court documents revealing Helen Clark had provided false information to the media for political gain.

http://www.nzherald.co.nz/index.cfm?objectid=114200

The details of who was really yanking Doone's chain were revealed in court documents filed by the *Sunday Star-Times* as it tried to defend the defamation action brought by Doone and Johnstone. In a brief of evidence for the court, *Star-Times* journalist Oskar Alley says his own involvement had escalated in mid December 1999, when he was rung by "a senior Wellington lawyer who had some direct involvement in the matter [who] spoke to me 'strictly off the record' saying that 'Doone should be facing charges over this', urging me to keep investigating because there was a very good story in this, saying that in the sources' [note the plural] view Peter Doone had acted highly inappropriately".

Alley does not disclose the identity of the "senior Wellington lawyer" or who, exactly, the lawyer was acting for in order to have some "direct involvement".

However, *Investigate* magazine discovered from a Cabinet briefing paper released on the *Sir Humphrey's* blog site that Labour's incoming Prime Minister had been briefed on 3 December, the same day the *Holmes* programme later went to air with the first media report of the incident. Additionally, the new Police Minister received a full briefing from Deputy Commissioner Rob Robinson on December 10. In other words, Labour was well across Doonegate long before a "senior" lawyer came forward to urge the *Star-Times* to dig deeper.

On 14 December, Alley then attended a police Christmas Party where he spoke to several people "employed at Police Headquarters" who disclosed fresh details to him about the case, such as the fact that the car had been stopped because its headlights were not turned on, and that both the Commissioner and his partner had been at a corporate function that evening and stopped off at a restaurant on the way home. Alley says the police sources he spoke to were adamant that the driver of the car should have been breath-tested as standard procedure.

On the same day, December 14, Rob Robinson's preliminary report had been completed and delivered, and the more in-depth Police Complaints Authority investigation was well underway.

Among those interviewed by the PCA was another police officer who'd seen Doone and Robyn Johnstone at the corporate function:

"It was my impression the last time that I saw them that neither of them were intoxicated or unfit to drive. I do not think that Robyn Johnson had in fact had much to drink and I also gained the impression that she was the designated driver."

The PCA also heard analysis from a doctor about the likely levels of alcohol in Robyn Johnstone's blood (two to three small glasses of wine, with food, over several hours), and found they were likely to be "well below the legal driving limit, at levels unlikely to be associated with any significant intoxication or impairment of judgment or behaviour".

The PCA head, Judge Neville Jaine, concluded, "The only evidence available to the Authority leads to a conclusion that at the time of driving the blood alcohol level of Ms Johnstone did not exceed the legal driving limit."

This latest point is important. It suggests that Johnstone and Doone had nothing to fear from a breath-test, and they had no reason to obstruct one.

If Johnstone was the designated driver (having previously been the mouthpiece for the LTSA's drink-driving safety campaigns) and had only consumed a couple of glasses of wine over four hours, with food, Doone had no motive to interfere with Constable Brett Main in his duties. It cannot have been a factor.

This information was in the Government's hands by December 29. Regardless, the heat really started to go on in the New Year, with that *Star-Times* lead story on January 9 headlined "Labour considers sacking Doone". According to Alley, much of the information for this story was actually provided by the paper's political editor at the time, Ruth Laugeson, who'd interviewed key but unnamed members of Helen Clark's staff.

The following week, Alley published a front page lead of his own, the first story to allege that Doone told the young constable "That won't be necessary" in reference to breath-testing. For Labour, this was the silver bullet with which they hoped to dispatch the Police Commissioner.

"The first information I received about Peter Doone allegedly using the words 'that won't be necessary' came from an *anonymous phone call* to me," says Alley, "on about Tuesday 10 or Wednesday 11 January 2000..[the caller] said something along the following lines: … 'I know the constable involved. Are you aware that Peter Doone said to that constable 'That won't be necessary' on the night in question?'

"Of course, an anonymous phone call on its own is not a reliable enough source," continues Alley's brief, "so that week I contacted a Senior Government Advisor in the Police Sector [who] confirmed that he was told that our information and the words 'that won't be necessary' were correct…[and] he also told me, which was something I did not know at the time, that the constable who spoke to Peter Doone on the night in question was holding a sniffer device, which I understood was [for breath testing]."

A "senior government advisor in the police sector", by the way, is journo-code for one of Labour's political spin-meisters. A genuine police source would be called "a senior police national headquarters official".

Adopting the Woodward & Bernstein three source rule, Alley decided to approach Prime Minister Helen Clark.

"By the time I approached the Prime Minister, both the Robinson and PCA reports into the matter would have been completed, signed off and handed to appropriate government members," says Alley in his brief.

"The Prime Minister made it clear that she had seen both reports."

Alley says he specifically rang Clark – as the person with both reports in front of her – to check whether the claims about the sniffer being visible and

Doone's alleged response – "that won't be necessary" – were included in the report Clark was holding.

"The Prime Minister confirmed that I was correct that the Constable had a sniffer device in his hand to test for alcohol; and included in the comments Peter Doone made to the Constable, with regards to the breath test, Peter Doone said 'that won't be necessary'.

"The Prime Minister specifically said '…you're not wrong'."

In her own brief of evidence, Helen Clark admits confirming the detail, although she suggests she drew attention to the fact that Peter Doone was "disputing" some of those details.

But even if Clark is telling the truth about alluding to the "dispute", in actual fact *nowhere* in the two reports on her desk when she spoke to the *Star-Times* is there any suggestion that the constable had intended to breath test the driver. Nor does the phrase "that won't be necessary" appear in either the Robinson report or the Police Complaints Authority report. That allegation was never "in dispute" because it had not been made by any named source except Helen Clark herself.

The documents released by *Sir Humphrey's* before the election included statements from Mark Haldane – the police officer waiting back in the police car – and two other police witnesses, none of whom mentioned seeing a sniffer device in the young constable's hand as he approached Doone.

Even Brett Main, the constable concerned, says in his brief of evidence for the Doone's defamation case against the *Star-Times* in 2005 that there's no guarantee his sniffer was visible to anyone:

"I have read the article from the *Sunday Star-Times* dated 16 January 2000. The headline for this article is 'Doone case cop was ready to breath test'. This article reported that I had said to the Commissioner that I wanted to breath test the driver of the car. I did not say that to the Commissioner. I know I had the sniffer with me but I can't remember whether it was in my hand or my pocket. When I got out of my car, I had no intention of breath testing anyone at that stage. I only grabbed the sniffer from the car in case I needed it. I recall that I did not even mention EBA (excess blood alcohol) procedures or breath testing to the Commissioner.

"The article also said that the Commissioner said in response 'That won't be necessary'. At no stage did the Commissioner say that to me.

"There is no truth to either of those statements reported in the *Sunday Star-Times*," concluded Constable Main, the officer at the centre of the firestorm.

So what does that mean?

The Prime Minister, then, told a national newspaper that the reports in front of her contained a phrase that was absolutely damning in its implication that the Commissioner of Police had improperly intervened to prevent a breath test. Yet the phrase does not appear in those reports, and is denied by the police officer it was allegedly said to.

Not only did the Prime Minister say it once. She was contacted again by Alley on the 15th of January, and also by the paper's editor Sue Chetwin, and repeated her assertions that Doone used those words, telling the newspaper to hang tough in its hounding of Doone.

"I don't see what more I could have done," reporter Oskar Alley told the court later. "Various credible independent sources corroborated the key facts that appeared in the story. I had no reason to doubt the accuracy of the story or the information provided by my sources."[17]

Naturally, when the *Sunday Star-Times* published on January 16 this hitherto unreleased information leaked to them by the Prime Minister, all hell broke loose in the media and Peter Doone's position as Commissioner became untenable.

It was behind the scenes, however, that the newly released documents disclose how events were falling nicely into place for Labour's plans to oust Doone from his job. For a start, there had been bad blood between Labour and the Police Commissioner for months leading up to the election because of the INCIS computer debacle. Doone and National's police minister Clem Simich had taken the brunt of Labour's INCIS attacks in parliament. Politically, Doone was already seen in Labour circles as a lame duck, long before the alleged drink driving incident happened.

Sir Humphrey's published a cabinet briefing paper dated 21 January – five days after the bombshell *Sunday Star-Times* article now known to have been caused by the Prime Minister's deliberate leak of false information to two journalists.

In the cabinet paper, Attorney-General Margaret Wilson tells her colleagues that "Serious issues of confidence were raised by…the perceptions created by the incident in terms of the wider public perception of the integrity of the law enforcement system."

In other words, *crucial to the issue of whether Doone should keep his job was the amount of media opprobrium bouncing around the case.* And that's why the Prime Minister's decision to up the ante by leaking false incriminating information is directly relevant to the events that followed.

That Labour was making the issue a top priority is confirmed in the briefing paper, with Margaret Wilson acknowledging that she'd been asked by Helen Clark to take over the Government's handling of the matter as early as January 5, instead of leaving it to Police Minister George Hawkins.

Wilson admits that Labour had known as early as December 17 that there were no grounds for criminal prosecution of the Commissioner or his partner, and she admits the Government had also been told at the same time by Deputy

---

17   Of course he had no reason to doubt. Whilst we all know politicians are manipulative and the media like a good scoop as much as anyone, few journalists would suspect the Prime Minister of the nation would cynically and deliberately feed them *false* information to destroy the public life and private reputation of a man. Years later, when Helen Clark began complaining about media scrutiny of her activities and private life, few people knew of the hypocrisy of her complaints.

Commissioner Rob Robinson that "it was the PCA's report, and not his, which would be authoritative in terms of any adverse findings."

In other words, Labour was clearly on notice that it should not rely on the Robinson report if it wanted to criticize Doone.

The cabinet paper reveals just how much knowledge Helen Clark had of this. It says the Prime Minister, Deputy PM Michael Cullen and Attorney General Margaret Wilson met on January 11 with the Solicitor General, the head of the Prime Minister's Department Mark Prebble and the head of State Services, Michael Wintringham.

At that meeting, full copies of the authoritative Police Complaints Authority report, the Robinson report, and submissions made on behalf of Peter Doone, were tabled and discussed, along with their legal implications. The document reveals that public perception of the Doone affair was identified at that meeting as a critical factor in whether the government would be within its rights to dismiss Doone.

This meeting took place three days *before* Helen Clark leaked false and damaging information about Doone to the *Sunday Star-Times*. In other words, knowing the adverse media coverage was likely to be a determining factor, the Prime Minister turned up the heat.

In her briefing paper, Margaret Wilson also acknowledges that the issue was not serious enough, but for the publicity, to warrant sacking:

"A decision to advise the Governor-General to remove the Commissioner is one with considerable personal and financial impact for the Commissioner. His reputation would inevitably suffer. He would also suffer significant adverse financial effects.

"Given the mitigating factors found by the PCA, a decision to recommend the Commissioner's removal would be a severe sanction."

Hold the phone! Attorney-General Margaret Wilson is admitting the story is a beat-up, and the Government would be acting unfairly if it forcibly removed Doone, knowing what they now knew.

The briefing paper released by *Sir Humphrey's* also shows Margaret Wilson gave specific advice to her cabinet colleagues, including Prime Minister Clark, on the basis of the findings of the Police Complaints Authority:

"On account of the findings in the PCA's report, my advice is that Ministers should proceed on the basis that the Commissioner is being truthful, in particular as to the amount of alcohol consumed [very little] and in stating that it was his belief at the time the car was stopped that no road safety issue was involved."

The cabinet briefing paper was dated Friday, January 21, in preparation for the following week's cabinet meeting where Doone's position would be discussed. Before that, the *Sunday Star-Times* had another go at the Commissioner on January 23:

"Last chance to resign, Cabinet ready to ask Doone to fall on his sword," screamed the headline.

"The Government is set to ask beleaguered Police Commissioner Peter Doone to quit this week," it began, quoting unnamed government 'sources' as saying Doone would be asked to fall on his sword.

In the released brief of evidence, Oskar Alley reveals that his 'source' was, again, none other than Prime Minister Helen Clark. He believes he spoke to her on Friday January 21, the same day Margaret Wilson's memo had gone to all cabinet ministers.

Alley says Clark told him that Constable Main definitely had the sniffer device – "she quoted a passage from the Robinson report on that subject" – and she said she "would hang tough on this one if she were the *Sunday Star-Times*."

"I took comfort from the Prime Minister's comments," says Alley. "She had the relevant documents and reports, parts of which she read to me over the telephone…she confirmed that there was nothing to worry about in the story the previous week. In effect, she confirmed that, despite Peter Doone's statement, the 16 January 2000 article had been accurate.

"She also read to me parts of the Robinson Police Inquiry, which were quoted in the story."

One of the pieces of information in the Prime Minister's possession, however, was advice originating from the January 12 legal briefing that she should *not* be relying on the Robinson report. In fact, the cabinet briefing paper from Margaret Wilson specifically says, "I do not propose to refer further to the Robinson report. I suggest Ministers likewise focus on the PCA report."

So what game, exactly, was the Prime Minister playing, by continuing to feed the media titbits from a report her own Attorney-General was backpeddling from?

"I specifically put it to the Prime Minister that they would ask Peter Doone to fall on his sword. It was confirmed to me he might, that that 'was in the plan', and that that was what the Government were going to ask him to do," recalls Alley.

Not content, *Star-Times* editor Sue Chetwin was back on the phone to Helen Clark as well, and came away reassured.

"She encouraged the newspaper to continue its investigation as the matter was reaching its critical stages."

For sheer treachery, double-dealing, lying and destroying a man's reputation for your own political gain, the Prime Minister's direct involvement in the Doone story is almost unmatched in the way it puts her pawprints brutally at the scene of the crime.

While Helen Clark was telling journalists that the reports in front of her showed Doone had tried to block a breath-test with the words "that won't be necessary", an examination of the PCA report shows just how far from the truth Clark's claim was:

"The Constable describes in these words the conversation which followed:

'He said words to the effect, 'why have we been stopped?'. I replied something like, 'because you didn't have your lights on and I would like to speak to the driver'."

So what was Peter Doone's response to this crucial question? In his own words in the PCA report, Constable Main says Doone replied, "Yep, that's okay. I'm just out with a friend on a Saturday night having a meal."

When Main asked to speak to the driver, Doone answered, "Yep, that's okay".

That's a million light years from Helen Clark's version of the story.

It was at this point, however, that Main realized he was dealing with the Commissioner, and he told the inquiry that he became flustered and "felt very nervous...At no stage did he introduce himself or tell me he was the Commissioner...I don't think I said anything in response [to 'yep, that's okay'] but I nodded my head I think in acknowledgement."

A pregnant pause appears to have passed before Doone "then said to me words to the effect, 'We'll be on our way', or something like that."

And that was the end of it. In his confusion, Main had apparently forgotten to make his way to the driver, despite Doone's affirmation, and both parties instead returned to their cars. Nothing more sinister.

Did Doone deserve to lose his job because of a media hatchet job orchestrated by Prime Minister Helen Clark's false testimony? While he was the first public service casualty of the new "squeaky-clean" Labour administration, Peter Doone was by no means the last.

The Rise And Fall Of Howard Broad

Jim: "I want to know the truth Humphrey."
Sir Humphrey: "I don't think you do Minister." – **Yes Minister**

WHAT YOU ARE ABOUT TO read in this chapter is the untold story about Police Commissioner Howard Broad and his Deputy Rob Pope, that we held off releasing in *Investigate* last year. We sat on it, despite being taunted by Police Minister Annette King and various media outlets, because we were determined to see the real lay of the land: could we get an independent Commission of Inquiry into the Police? Would the Police Complaints Authority do a proper investigation of our existing material or whitewash it?

It was our firm belief then, and pretty much set in concrete now after the discovery of more evidence, that the New Zealand Police are systemically corrupt. It is our belief that such corruption may be a factor in decisions not to prosecute over crimes like the $800,000 misuse of taxpayer funds by Helen Clark's second in command, Heather Simpson, to illegally fund the Pledge Card at the last election and other initiatives.

Not one Government MP or political appointee has been prosecuted despite prima facie findings in some very serious cases.

The story isn't quite so rosy for National though, and the prosecution of MP Shane Ardern for driving a tractor partway up the steps of Parliament during a farmers protest over the hated "Fart Tax" is a strong indicator of possible police/government corruption.

Ardern, a farmer with plenty of experience on tractors, carried out the stunt as a political statement. A decision to prosecute him was announced by Inspector Marty Grenfell, who'd enjoyed a close working relationship with the then Minister of Police, George Hawkins, while working in the minister's office.

The Police Prosecutions Service, after reviewing the file, had wanted to drop the case against Ardern, because it was "fraught with difficulties" and unlikely to succeed in court. But an email from Wellington District

Commander John Kelly put paid to that. Kelly told the regional PPS head Craig Tweedie[18] that "In relation to this issue, there are to be no moves to withdraw this matter."

Kelly added that he wanted to be personally briefed on the case:

"If there is to be a review of the charge…then I am to be fully consulted and involved in that process."

The charge was reviewed, by a Senior Sergeant Erasmusen, who recommended throwing out the charge and noted, "it is inescapable that comparisons will be made with other high profile cases where a decision not to prosecute followed." Wellington PPS head Craig Tweedie stood by the recommendation not to prosecute Shane Ardern. He was overruled however by his immediate superior, the national manager of the Police Prosecutions Service, Superintendent Graham Thomas.

Thomas, based at Police National Headquarters, and Wellington commander John Kelly were singing the same song, although as National MP Murray McCully told parliament,[19] Graham Thomas had at least been forced to admit that Kelly's directive not to drop charges was highly irregular:

"Is the Minister aware," McCully asked, "that the head of the Police Prosecution Service, Superintendent Graham Thomas, confirmed on radio this morning that he had seen no other incidents of a district commander issuing a direct instruction to so-called independent prosecution officers; if so, can he tell the House why Mr Ardern was singled out for special treatment?"

Act MP Gerry Eckhoff chipped in:

"What is the point of having a supposedly independent police prosecutions centre, if regional commanders like John Kelly send emails to subordinate officers working at the centre, instructing them to prosecute, regardless of the merits of the case, or was Shane Ardern a special case?"

Struggling to maintain a credible line, Police Minister George Hawkins simply mumbled that the process was fair.

It was only after the political heat became too much, and a district court judge told police they didn't have a snowball's chance in hell of succeeding, that police finally relented and dropped the charges.

When emails were stolen from National's computers and possibly from MPs' homes, the New Zealand Police failed to catch anyone. The emails ended up in a Nicky Hager book.

Former National Party leader Don Brash began to wonder if police were taking political instructions from the Labour Government, which makes this next chapter critical in our growing understanding of the corrupt constitutional dynamic surrounding Labour: is a Government protected by a dodgy police

---

18   *NZ Herald*, 13 May 2004, "National accuses top policeman"
http://www.nzherald.co.nz/section/1/story.cfm?c_id=1&objectid=3566144
19   Questions for Oral Answer, NZ parliamentary Hansard, 13 May 2004
http://www.parliament.nz/en-NZ/PB/Debates/Debates/b/2/3/47HansD_20040513_
00000024-Questions-for-Oral-Answer-Questions-to-Ministers.htm

administration in turn providing its own protection to that dodgy police administration in a symbiotic relationship of mutual support?

The clear impression for many observers was that Labour was indeed telling police what to do, and who to target – one of the first steps towards totalitarianism. As you'll see in this book, there have been several more steps since then, but the underlying stench remains that police top brass are corrupt.

It is bitterly ironic, then, that Helen Clark worked so hard to get rid of Police Commissioner Peter Doone when she took over in 1999, but did so little when confronted with even more serious allegations about Police Commissioner Howard Broad.

Doone, of course, was pinged for distracting a junior officer who *might* have been about to attempt a breath test on Doone's partner. He couldn't really be pinged, of course, because even the rookie Constable admits he didn't discuss breath testing or even take the breathalyzer out of his pocket.

The mere suggestion of improper influence, however, was enough for Cabinet to demand Doone's head on a plate.

So imagine, as a "popular and successful" Prime Minister, how the public would react if they found out the current Police Commissioner had been stopped at a checkpoint, allegedly drunk, and told junior officers to "f*** off!", before driving away – and that the Prime Minister was aware of such allegations.

Imagine if Deputy Police Commissioner Rob Pope had some pretty serious skeletons of his own in his closet that impacted his work as an officer, and that the Government knew about those as well?

Before we get to the main course, however, we need to set the context. It is a story that reeks not only of serious misconduct, however, but also a government cover-up, because when *Investigate* magazine busted open massive corruption in the Dunedin police district last year, most people assumed it was only about whether Broad had watched a chick-porn (poultry, not women) movie at his home – because that's all the news media chose to focus on.

Consequently, the magazine was criticized by some who accused us of trying to besmirch a good man over a trifling incident 20-odd years ago. The Prime Minister and Police Minister Annette King did everything they could to squash the story, too. And little wonder. Labour has relied heavily on Police not to prosecute key members of the Labour government from the Prime Minister down, for offences that could, if proven, have forced an early election.

So, what follows provides hard evidence that Clark and King relied on testimony from corrupt police, who in turn were protecting a Police Commissioner who we now believe to be corrupt, for reasons that will soon be made clear.

When Police Commissioner Howard Broad apologised "unreservedly and unequivocally" to the women at the centre of the Bazley report on police sexual misconduct last year, he suggested the corruption was confined to "a very few officers who have behaved disgracefully. Their actions were wrong and contrary to their oath of office."

That's what Police National Headquarters wanted the public and the news media to believe. It is not, however, the reality.

Who, after all, can forget the media attention that fell on this small portion of a 17 page special investigation in the magazine:

"Howard Broad himself, according to former colleagues, was part of that police culture when he worked in Dunedin in the 1980s. One colleague approached by *Investigate* alleges Broad had bestiality videos at his going away party from Dunedin's CIB in the mid 1980s, a party held at 19 Arawa St, Dunedin.

" 'There was one particular video being shown, of a naked woman holding a chicken while a man had sex with it. The chicken basically expired, and then the woman immediately performed [a sexual act] on the man. I remember it very clearly, because it's the only time I've ever had the misfortune to witness bestiality.'

"Another colleague, former Detective Sergeant Tom Lewis, was Howard Broad's boss in Dunedin, and recalls incidents of indecent assault.

" 'He was a bit of a groper...He didn't take much to get him drunk, and when he got pissed he got a bit of Dutch courage. He was never charged with anything, and I don't know that he was even investigated properly – it might have just been something that was written off. Women had complained about him when he got drunk. But certainly I don't think they ever initiated any proper investigation into him. He might have had a smack on the hand, but that was about all'."

The future police commissioner's actions reflected the police culture he tried to distance himself from when he spoke last year at the release of the Bazley report, before the *Investigate* story broke:

"To the women of New Zealand I say: I have been disgusted and sickened, as you will be, by the behaviour put before the Commission of Inquiry in many of the files that covered some 25 years of our recent history," Broad told a news conference.

"To all New Zealanders, I am truly sorry that a very few of our number have undermined the high expectations you rightly have of your police.

"We are encouraging every staff member to have the fortitude to come forward where they perceive things aren't right. I am personally sponsoring our leadership, management and accountability programme.

"Thankfully, the Commission did not find evidence of any concerted efforts across Police to cover up unacceptable behaviour and I hope the report will provide reassurance that we all take sexual abuse complaints seriously.

"To any victims of sexual abuse who have perhaps been reluctant to make a complaint, please come forward," Broad pleaded.

The Broad bestiality video allegation was, as explained, part of a general introduction to the wider police culture in Dunedin and a much bigger story of corruption involving police in drug dealing, rape, perjury, underaged sex and turning a blind eye to vice crimes like prostitution in return for a piece of the action. In other words, massive corruption similar to that found in New South Wales, Victoria and Queensland. There was a political element to it as well. Senior Labour politicians had helped put out bushfires when it looked like some of the claims were surfacing two decades ago, and more recently senior ministers in Clark's government had been briefed in 2000 about extremely serious allegations of Dunedin police corruption.

For those who missed it, the full story is now online.[20] But it was only the chicken movie story that got coverage in the general media, and many members of the public were left with the impression it was the only allegation in the entire article.

Just to divest you of any misunderstandings in this area, here in fact is a brief extract of the allegations that first special investigation contained:

1. That current Police Commissioner Howard Broad had, and was watching, bestiality videos at his going away party from the Dunedin CIB at 19 Arawa St

2. That current Police Commissioner Howard Broad fondled junior staff whilst stationed at the Dunedin CIB

3. That Howard Broad, when he stated that only a "few" officers were involved in sexual misconduct, either knew or should have known of the extensive sexual misconduct in the Dunedin CIB

4. That Police National Headquarters, Dunedin Police and the Lange Labour Government helped quash an investigation into a child sex, bondage and bestiality ring operating in Dunedin in 1984 run by the father of a police officer and attended by at least one Labour cabinet minister

5. That current Attorney-General Michael Cullen and the current Minister responsible for CYFS, David Benson-Pope, helped run damage control over the child sex, bondage and bestiality case in 1985

6. That current Labour coalition MPs Pete Hodgson, Tim Barnett[21], George Hawkins and Matt Robson were aware of major allegations of police misconduct from 2000 onwards, including the existence of videotapes of police rapes and bestiality involving police officers

7. That by failing to rein in police corruption brought to their attention in the eighties and again in 2000, the Labour government has permitted the culture of corruption to widen in that time, wrecking more lives

8. That former Wellington District Commander and current Police National Headquarters officer, Superintendent John Kelly indecently assaulted a number of women, including the daughter of a previous police commissioner

9. That Dunedin and Christchurch Police had arrangements to turn a blind eye to organised crime – including underage sex and drug dealing – in return for sexual favours from brothels

---

20 *Investigate*, June 2007 issue. http://www.thebriefingroom.com/archives/2007/08/to_serve_and_pr.html
21 To be fair to Barnett, after this article ran he made contact again with the women who had originally come to see him in an effort to move the case ahead, so any criticism of Barnett is withdrawn on my part.

10. That police have maintained files on key politicians and public figures capable of being used to blackmail the government, judges, lobby groups and even police association members into supporting the status quo

11. That Dunedin police officers, former and current, have been involved in multiple rapes of junior female police staff, prostitutes and civilians, drug deals, and conspiracy to pervert the course of justice, including falsifying charges

12. That several of the top officers in the David Bain case were allegedly corrupt police officers

13. That the officer involved in the alleged rape of a court worker, detailed in our May 07 issue and cleared by Police National Headquarters, is also a corrupt officer

14. That the culture of police corruption, far from being localised to the Bay of Plenty or historic, extends to a large number of jurisdictions because of staff movements, and continues to the present day

15. That the only way to weed the bad cops out of the force is a Royal Commission, because the Old Boys Network within the police is currently looking after its own interests and bringing discredit to the many hardworking honest police who do not have the institutional power to bring change

These allegations, although well-supported in the magazine article, were too hard for the daily media to match, so they tried to breathe as much life into Howard Broad's chicken as they possibly could.

Here's how *Investigate* magazine covered the developing story in the following issue:

When Investigate called for a Commission of Inquiry last month, former Dunedin cop Peter Gibbons sprang to the Government's and Howard Broad's rescue. But now we can reveal damning new information about Gibbons and police corruption, in another special report that now implicates the ACC corporation in Dunedin police misconduct as the shockwaves spread:

The political fallout from *Investigate's* special report on police corruption is about to get a whole lot worse, with confirmation that Police Minister Annette King and Prime Minister Helen Clark staked their own reputations on the testimony of a man who now turns out to be a corrupt cop.

When *Investigate's* major story broke last month, the news media were quickly introduced to former Dunedin police officer Peter Gibbons, who told reporters the *Investigate* story about widespread corruption was "rubbish", and that police commissioner Howard Broad had not watched the infamous bestiality movie referred to in the article.

Gibbons – now a Dunedin private investigator – provided information to Police Minister Annette King urging her to name a rival private investigator, Wayne Idour, as the man who brought the bestiality movie to Howard Broad's party in the 1980s.

Chapter 3

Gibbons' testimony created a media firestorm and was used in a massive political offensive to defame and discredit Idour and, by implication, *Investigate* magazine's call for a Royal Commission of Inquiry into the NZ Police.

At the time, *Investigate* already had Gibbons in its sights as an alleged corrupt officer, but our inquiries had not been completed and cross-checked for accuracy. So, for a month, *Investigate* has stayed silent.

Now, however, we can reveal that *Investigate* views Peter James Gibbons as one of the more bent police officers we've come across, based on the evidence assembled here[22], an officer who not only appears to have committed perjury by lying to a judge in a court trial, but who has also been captured on audiotape justifying police corruption and privately endorsing a group of officers who chose to lie to an official inquiry. Gibbons has been accused in affidavits supplied to *Investigate* of behaviour including tipping off drug dealers in advance of police raids, and corruptly obtaining police search warrants from his police constable son-in-law to help him fulfill lucrative commercial contracts as a private investigator working for a major government organization.

The irony – that the government and Police National Headquarters brushed off the need for a Royal Commission by relying on the word of a bent cop – will become chillingly apparent over the next few pages. But first, a look at the substance of Gibbons' spin campaign against Idour and *Investigate*.

The first most people really heard was National Radio's *Morning Report*, when host Geoff Robinson interviewed Police Minister Annette King. Although Gibbons had been interviewed the previous day sticking up for Howard Broad, he had not gone as far publicly as the Police Minister was about to.

"Geoff, yesterday you had a man on your show who stood up for Howard Broad, who worked with him. I spoke to that man yesterday," said King.

"He gave me the name of the person who took the film – it's actually a film – to Howard Broad's house. He gave me the name of the person, the same person, who played the film, and the same person is the person who's been hawking the story around the news media.

"The person, on your show, and I'm quite sure if you were to ring him he would confirm this, is Mr Idour.

"I am told by the same man that was on your show that when Mr Idour played the film that most people walked out of the room in disgust. They didn't want to see it, leaving Mr Idour with very few people but himself to watch it."

That last comment alone should have been enough to sound warning bells in the ears of intelligent listeners – the idea that boozed-up police at a rugby fundraiser walked out rather than watch a porn film that included a bestiality scene with a chicken.

National Radio's Robinson asked the Minister how Peter Gibbons had ended up sticking up for Broad.

"Mr Broad spoke with people that he'd known in Dunedin at the time to go over his memory of events," replied King.

Acknowledging that his question might appear "cynical", Geoff Robinson queried the sequence of events, saying, "Certainly the names [of police prepared to support Broad] were provided to us by Police HQ, which raises the question of whether there was some concerted campaign by Police –"

"I doubt whether Howard Broad would be involved in some sort of concerted campaign," interjected King.

Increasingly, however, that's how it is looking. And if Police National HQ introduced Peter Gibbons to the Minister of Police, then to all practical effect PNHQ set up their own Minister to take an embarrassing fall if the true facts about Gibbons ever emerged.

With Wayne Idour's name publicly besmirched as a bestiality-purveyor by the Minister of Police on National Radio, the media went wild. Peter Gibbons appeared on radio and TV interviews, telling the same carefully-constructed story. Note how the wording is deliberately strong and rehearsed as if to underline his credibility as a witness:

"Wayne Idour played that movie, Wayne Idour put it on, Wayne Idour was watching it. That's what I categorically remember. I and another person spoke to him about it. And I remember it very, very well," Gibbons told *3 News*.

Contrast his rock-solid memory, however, with his comments on National Radio's *Checkpoint* programme:

"I can't remember if it was a movie or a video, bearing in mind I can't even remember which year it was. Wayne put that movie on, or video on, and when people saw what it was, they moved out of the room. What I can tell you Mary is myself and the Vice Captain of the team [Gordon Hunter] actually went and spoke to him and asked him to desist. He wanted to continue watching it and we told him he would have to watch it by himself. He watched it by himself. The party continued in another room."

"Police Minister Annette King stands behind Gibbons," continued the *3 News* report as it led into a video clip of King:

"He told me directly, the person who brought the film to the party was Mr Idour. And Mr Idour played the film."

It didn't occur to many journalists that the likelihood of Wayne Idour tipping off the country's most controversial magazine about the chicken film was nil, if he had in fact been the person who originally brought it along. After all, it was not a private screening but a party attended by about 100 men, many of them police officers.

Police Commissioner Howard Broad himself muddied the waters significantly by revealing that when he found out the movie was playing in his house, that he complained to Peter Gibbons and a fellow detective, Gordon Hunter, about it.

"I moaned about it because I just didn't want that sort of thing being beamed onto the wall of my lounge," Broad told the *Herald*. According to Broad, and

Gibbons, the party was a fundraiser for the police rugby club and the main attraction was movie reels (there were no videos in 1981) of "old Ranfurly Shield rugby games".[23]

One person who doesn't buy that explanation for a nanosecond is Howard Broad's former boss, retired Detective Sergeant Tom Lewis. Speaking from Australia, Lewis has told *Investigate* that the idea of 100 police officers and their mates holding a fundraiser in 1981 by screening "old Ranfurly Shield games" on a projector is a fabrication.

Lewis says commercial film footage of old Ranfurly Shield matches did not exist on home movie format in 1981, and the idea that 100 cops had gathered to watch a fellow policeman's shaky home movie of an entire game is ludicrous.

He's told *Investigate* he was aware of a number of similar fundraisers, and the drawcard was usually the latest pornographic movies seized by police. Like Wayne Idour, he says they were not functions normally attended by women. He recalls on one occasion two of his junior staff, Gordon Hunter and Jim Stacey, discussing the porn movies they'd viewed at a police rugby fundraiser, and he says that may have been the one at Howard Broad's house.

Lewis also scoffs at former Detective Peter Gibbons' claim that everyone left the room when the movie came on.

"Is he expecting people to believe that a hundred people suddenly crammed into Howard Broad's kitchen, and that Broad then asked Gibbons and Gordon Hunter to tell the one person in the lounge to turn the movie off, using his prime authority as the householder, but that the person in the lounge refused and neither Howard Broad nor Peter Gibbons did anything? That's almost an even bigger indictment on their policing and decision making ability than watching the bestiality movie in the first place!"

It is also, says Lewis, impossible to believe.

The gullible Police Minister Annette King, however, fell for it hook, line and sinker.

"Mr Gibbons is well known in Dunedin, I'm told, highly respected. He is prepared to back what he said. I think it's now up to who people believe and I personally believe Mr Gibbons."

King wasted no time upping the ante, either. Under the cloak of Parliamentary privilege she launched a stinging attack on the credibility of Wayne Idour and *Investigate* magazine:

"The modus operandi of that magazine is to base a story on a half-truth, and from that to build an entire menu of fantasies. There was a party in Dunedin in 1981. There was an objectionable pornographic film shown at it. The basis for the story came from information provided about the party by an unknown person. Mr Wishart said that he did not identify the informant at the time, because the informant had a sick family member. When has Mr Wishart ever given a damn about the family members of his targets?"

---

23   *NZ Herald*, 14 May 2007, "Broad: Public can judge me"
http://www.nzherald.co.nz/category/story.cfm?c_id=30&objectid=10439573&pnum=0

For the record, *Investigate* has withheld information about some political figures from publication because of concern for their families, nor did we conduct a major investigation into how Police Minister Annette King's daughter crashed a ministerial vehicle containing illegal drugs. Also, for the record, the "sick" family member King refers to was dying, and the Minister knew it when she chose only to call him "sick". *Investigate* had issued a news release explaining that the man was terminally ill. For the record, Idour's close relative died two days after Annette King's callous attack in parliament.

"His informant was outed," King continued in parliament, "and subsequently Wayne Idour has had to own up. That man was a former police officer in Dunedin. He is the same man who was employed by the Exclusive Brethren to dig up dirt on the Prime Minister and on Labour MPs and their families. He is a proven liar. Wayne Idour lied to TV3 about working for the Brethren, and I believe he is now lying again. I believe he is lying when he says he did not take the bestiality movie to the party. I believe he lied when he said he did not show the pornographic film. I believe he lied when he said he saw Howard Broad watching it."

Again, for the record, Wayne Idour is arguably a "proven liar" only in regard to one event – distancing himself from the Exclusive Brethren. As a matter of historical fact, however, Idour was not hired by the Brethren but by an Auckland private investigator who did not disclose the identity of the clients to Idour until well down the path of the investigation. Nor was Idour employed to follow the Prime Minister or Peter Davis – another common error made by politicians and the media.

Peter Gibbons' dishonesty, however, is far more serious and includes giving false testimony, on oath, to a court, as you will read shortly. The people who ultimately relied on "a proven liar" are the Minister of Police herself, and Prime Minister Helen Clark.

And it's not as if Gibbons' motives were not transparent to others.

"In my view Peter Gibbons has a vested interest," Tom Lewis told *Investigate*. "He's a close mate of Broad's, and he also gets a lot of his private detective work from Dunedin Police. So it's in Gibbons' best interests to support the police on this."

Gibbons' relationship with Dunedin Police is, in literal fact, incestuous. Although Gibbons had to leave the force 10 years ago and set up in business as a private investigator, his daughter Melissa became a police officer and subsequently married another young cop named Andrew Henderson, who transferred to Dunedin.

Investigate stumbled across this relationship during a thorough search of Gibbons' property transactions, which included a number of sales and purchases involving the AW and MA Henderson Family Trust, which Peter Gibbons is a trustee on. Recognising it as a family trust for his daughter and son-in-law, *Investigate* put those documents to one side as irrelevant, until a chance comment from Dunedin man Bruce Van Essen, who's been battling

ACC, suddenly made the Henderson Family Trust centrestage again.

Van Essen had posted comments on the ACCForums website about Peter Gibbons' work as a private investigator for ACC, and when we contacted him he remarked how Gibbons would execute police search warrants on the homes of ACC claimants, even though he was no longer a police officer.

"We think the warrants are really dodgy," Van Essen remarked. "He must have a mate inside the police doing it for him. Besides which, it's always the same cops who turn up to do the searches with Gibbons."

"Really?" the magazine asked. "Who?"

"It's a Sergeant Kindly and a young constable named Andrew Henderson. Every time. And sometimes there's another guy, Graeme Scott, who has now left the police force and is working for Gibbons."

When *Investigate* obtained copies of the police search warrants used by Gibbons to raid homes of ACC victims and seize their property, we found a direct match between the signatures of Constable Andrew Henderson on the warrants, and the signatures of Andrew Henderson we already had on a string of property purchases with Peter Gibbons. The fact that private investigator Peter Gibbons, whose business has a lucrative $172,000 contract with the government ACC agency, is using his son-in-law in the police to draft the search warrants he needs, appears, to *Investigate*, to be a massive conflict of interest, and further evidence of the need for a full Royal Commission of Inquiry into police corruption.[24]

But it gets worse. In an affidavit provided to *Investigate* for review by an eminent legal entity, Van Essen discloses that the police searches were conducted outside standard police operating procedure. For example, it has been common for the police presenting the warrants to play no part in the actual searches, and instead let civilian Peter Gibbons and his private assistants search through the houses with no police supervision at all.

"The cops actually turn their backs, they don't watch," confirms Van Essen to *Investigate*.

Under New Zealand law private investigators working for anyone, including ACC, have no legal authority to search anyone's house, as powers of search and seizure are tightly regulated under ancient common law and the Bill of Rights Act, as well as the Police Act itself.

Section 6 of the Police Act specifically forbids any non-sworn (civilian) person carrying out any of the powers and duties of a sworn police officer without explicit written authority from Police Commissioner Howard Broad, and that written authority must be carried by the civilian at all times and presented to householders if requested, Gibbons had no such authority from his friend, Howard Broad.

---

24 You can read the hard documentary evidence nailing Police Minister Annette King's source – corrupt former Dunedin cop Peter Gibbons – online: http://www.investigatemagazine.com/gibbonsmedia.pdf

Three Dunedin residents have sworn affidavits about Gibbons executing search warrants in the company of Graeme Scott and Constable Andrew Henderson, along with irregularities in the search warrants. On one occasion the ACC corporation replied to a complaint by blaming the irregularity – a reference to a false declaration – on a "cut and paste" error by a police typist.

In case you missed it, the first damning revelation against the man the Prime Minister and Police Minister relied on (apparently at Howard Broad's suggestion), is that Gibbons misused his authority and misused police resources by getting his police officer son-in-law to access information he needed on private investigation cases, and by getting his son-in-law to draft and execute search warrants against people he was interested in targeting for his private investigation business.

This is basic police corruption 101.

But the evidence against Labour's star witness didn't end there:

Peter Gibbons has had a long career in the police, entering in the early 70s and perfing in 1997 for reasons we are still investigating. He is well schooled in the fine arts of giving compelling evidence in court, and training younger cops what to say and what not to say.

Gibbons told NZPA last month that he was telling the truth about Wayne Idour being the man who brought the bestiality movie along.

"I wouldn't have said that if I wasn't prepared to swear an affidavit or go into any court in the land and say it."

But there's strong evidence that Gibbons is a man who is even prepared to lie in court, making his word utterly worthless.

In 1988 an undercover police officer using the name "Brent Stace" testified in the trial of an arrested man that the suspect (who we'll call 'John Doe') had been a "target" for the police operation, codenamed "Sub Rosa", even before it began in early February 1987.

Doe was a second hand dealer who owned a car wrecking yard in Dunedin. The city was undergoing a bit of a car theft epidemic in the mid 80s, and popular wisdom within some in the police was that John Doe must have had something to do with it. In fact, as the evidence you'll read suggests, the real mastermind was a man named Bob Wood, who just happened to be a good friend of a popular Dunedin police officer. And it was Wood that police used to help set up John Doe. Wood would offer drugs and other items to targets, and ask them to onsell them to his mate, undercover cop Brent Stace.

"I was made aware of him [John Doe] at the beginning of the operation...the police were interested in him," Stace told the court, on oath.

"Were you made aware," asked the suspect's lawyer, "that he had no previous criminal convictions?"

"No," said Stace, "because I am sure he has got one."

"So you have seen a list of his convictions?"

"Yes," confirmed the undercover cop.

What's interesting is that the 37 year old suspect, John Doe, had virtually no criminal record at all, just one conviction for a minor theft at the age of 17 – twenty years earlier – for which he received a $30 fine. That offence, in 1968, was the only record listed.

"At the beginning of the operation I saw some people's criminal history," Stace told the Court.

"Can you recall who showed you that?" challenged the lawyer.

"Detective Sergeant Peter Gibbons, my operator. He was the operator who briefed me."

"At that time," continued Doe's lawyer, "were you given the accused's name and address as a target?"

"Yes, I was. He was disclosed to me."

That's the sworn testimony of "Brent Stace" – now a Christchurch businessman using his real name – back in the Dunedin District Court in 1988.

But later in the same court transcript, here's what Gibbons had to say under cross-examination:

"When Constable Stace commenced this operation did you provide him with a list of names?" asked the suspect's lawyer.

"No."

"Did you provide him with the accused's name?"

"No. This accused was not a target at the commencement of the operation," answered Gibbons on oath.

"When did he become a target?"

"When he offered to sell a firearm [on March 31st]."

Two men, both police officers, both with totally contradictory stories. Both giving evidence on oath. Nor is it a matter where faulty recollection is an issue. The trial was taking place less than a year after the arrest, and both police officers had had plenty of opportunity to get their stories straight. But the younger, less experienced Brent Stace was first up on the witness stand and let slip some crucial information. His recall of seeing the suspect's prior conviction, and being made aware the man was a target, when Gibbons briefed him right at the start in early February 1987, is in stark contrast to Gibbons' assertion that he did no such thing.

Why is it important? Because it is one thing to do an undercover operation as a fishing expedition. It is another to carry out what's known as "entrapment", where you attempt to set people up.

It also, of course, casts doubt on the credibility of either Peter Gibbons, or Detective Brent Stace. One of them was lying to the court, and therefore may still be prepared to lie on oath today.

If it was Brent Stace who lied on oath, then question marks now arise over his testimony that saw nearly 80 people prosecuted. Based on the evidence you are about to read in this story however, *Investigate* believes it is Peter Gibbons who lied on oath in the evidence given above.[25]

Again, in case you missed it, you can now add an allegation of perjury – lying on oath to a court – to the list of credibility hits the magazine was stacking up against Police Minister Annette King's star witness, Peter Gibbons.

It is very easy for politicians to stand up on their hind legs in parliament and, under parliamentary privilege, launching stinging and totally false attacks against *Investigate* magazine and its editor. Annette King and Helen Clark have both done this. But by the time the magazine had finished with Gibbons, the credibility of Labour's top female MPs was shredded with him.

Peter Gibbons – in *Investigate's* view – committed the worst form of lying possible: perjury in front of a judge. Forget lying to TV3 about the Exclusive Brethren – Wayne Idour's supposed crime. Lying on oath in court is the ultimate taboo, the sign of a person whose word can never be trusted on any occasion.

And Peter Gibbons, readers will recall, is the Dunedin private investigator who urged Police Minister Annette King to wrongly name rival Dunedin private investigator Wayne Idour as the man who brought a bestiality movie to Police Commissioner Howard Broad's party.

Investigate is aware of threats that as many as 40 former and current Dunedin police officers "are prepared to swear affidavits" contradicting what the magazine has published and that Idour was the source of the bestiality movie.

Given what *Investigate* has now uncovered involving the willingness of police to lie on oath, any affidavits sworn by any current or former Dunedin police are probably worthless in the public eye.

And just to reinforce the lack of police credibility on any of this now, *Investigate* is releasing portions of a taped conversation between Peter Gibbons and former undercover officer Peter Williamson, whose story later featured in the book *Stoned on Duty* by Bruce Ansley.

The two men were discussing an internal inquiry into the police undercover programme by senior police officer Bruce Scott in 1993. As the man tasked with training undercover cops in the South Island, Peter Gibbons could be considered an expert on the topic. On the subject of lying to cover your backside, Detective Senior Sergeant Peter Gibbons is heard justifying the actions of police officers who lied to an official inquiry:

"What you have to then accept is that when those guys got interviewed, their jobs, or they would have perceived their jobs and so on were at stake, so they would not tell the truth when they got interviewed by Scott."

On the subject of stealing official documents, Gibbons admits on tape trying to induce a Police National Headquarters worker to send him an advance copy of the

---

[25] A former colleague and mentor of Stace's in the undercover programme describes the officer as "a very straight-up, honest guy". The mentor has no doubt Gibbons was lying.

Scott report, even though PNHQ had expressly forbidden Gibbons from seeing it:

"I rung Helen, because Helen has done wee jobs for me for years, and I thought I'd slip a copy through the back door and get a look at this thing you see, so I rang Helen and said, 'Look, don't tell anyone, just get me this report and send one down to me'. Well, she must have been ferreting around and someone must have seen her and she got the big handsmack and got told, 'he is not to get that report!'

"So she was told, you do not send that down to Gibbons!"

Further on in the tape, undercover agent Williamson criticizes a senior police figure:

"I suspect he's not an honest man, I suspect he is manipulating this inquiry in the interests of the department."

"Well that's what they're all going to do," admits Peter Gibbons, "that's what you have to accept."

"I call that corruption, that's what," protests Peter Williamson.

"Well," continues Gibbons, "the bottom line is this, and I would say that no matter who runs it...that's always going to be the end result: the department will look after the department first."

"Well I consider people, undercover agents, more important than the department," counters Williamson. "I'm not so naïve as to think that the department can run without any form of corruption Peter, I'm not so naïve as to think that, but when the casualties of that corruption are directly related to cops f***ing up then, I'm, I cannot sit back and accept it unfortunately."

Then follows a priceless line from Peter Gibbons:

"...I'm ingrained into the system and can't see it from an outside perspective, but the bottom line as I see it is the department is always going to whitewash the department."

Classic. "The department is always going to whitewash the department". And this from the man who last month told Police Minister Annette King there was no need for an inquiry into Dunedin Police and *Investigate's* "laughable" allegations:

"The general public shouldn't be asked to believe that sort of stuff. The call should not be for an inquiry into police conduct in the Dunedin CIB in the 1980s because you get some [person] saying that."

So that's Peter Gibbons' view.

On the other hand, *Investigate* has been collecting affidavits of its own on behalf of an eminent legal figure who will review our evidence in favour of a Commission of Inquiry. One of those affidavits is from a contractor who worked on a home belonging to the sister of Peter Gibbons when she lived at 17 Slant Street in Carey's Bay, just north of Dunedin in the early 1980s. Other residents of the house included Peter Gibbons' brother.

"I became aware very quickly that drugs were a feature in this house," says our witness in a sworn affidavit, "as the occupants offered me marijuana and speed called Benzedrine. I declined the offer. I still remember the smell of the house and it stunk of marijuana. They mainly smoked joints. I noticed that their eyes were dilated most of the time.

"There was a flurry of activity and cleaning one day when I went out there in the morning...[Peter Gibbons' sister] said that her brother, Peter Gibbons, had phoned to say the Police were going to raid the house for drugs. The Police subsequently came and searched the house...the afternoon of the same day that Peter Gibbons phoned, and the Police did not find any of the drugs.

"[Peter Gibbons' sister] stated to me on several occasions that Peter Gibbons would phone her and pre-warn her if the Police were going to raid the house for drugs. She told me that Peter Gibbons saved their arse on a number of occasions.

"[The siblings] made comments that it was helpful having a brother on the Police force to keep them out of trouble."

Remember, this is the same Peter Gibbons running Operation Sub Rosa, and the same Peter Gibbons being relied on by Police National Headquarters and Prime Minister Helen Clark to discredit *Investigate's* story last month and our call for a Royal Commission of Inquiry into the police.

It is worth noting that Gibbons' brother Tony was a pro-marijuana reform advocate.

The affidavit continues:

"I saw Peter Gibbons brother on a number of occasions deal drugs to people outside and inside of the house. They would arrive at the house and I saw money and drugs change hands. I also dropped Peter Gibbons' brother into town one day, he told me that he was going to sell marijuana to people who were attending a function."

The magazine has confirmed that the house at 17 Slant St was indeed a drug house, and a former associate of the Gibbons family has also noted that on the *one* occasion police arrested and charged Peter Gibbons' sister on drugs offences some years later, an 'error' in the paperwork resulted in the charges being withdrawn. The same associate, now a respected citizen, also recalls Tony Gibbons discussing Benzedrine, the early form of speed mentioned by our first informant.

Among others we spoke to was another underworld figure, now a businessman, who is prepared to testify to a Royal Commission of Inquiry that police "shorted" drugs seized as evidence, criminal slang for a procedure where corrupt cops seize drugs and either don't enter it into the record at all, or otherwise remove a quantity of drugs from the deal bags before they are submitted and weighed as evidential exhibits.

The drugs are then sold by underworld figures like Bob Wood, controlled by police, with profits split between police and the drug dealer.

"I wasn't any angel myself back then," the businessman, Michael*, told *Investigate*, "but there were the likes of people being busted for marijuana, and like I went up to court myself – I got caught with 13 ounces and I got charged with 10. There was a lot of that going on."

Who was the arresting officer?

"It was a cop called Peter Gibbons," Michael said.

What happened to the missing three ounces of dope?

"It was put back out for supply," says Jack*, another former drug dealer turned businessman who saw a large amount of his seized marijuana vanish without trace between arrest and the typing up of the charge sheet. "The cops had their networks, people they used, and they made a fortune from seizing drugs and reselling them."

"They had their hands out all the time," Michael confirmed to *Investigate*. "I know people who were pulled up with heaps and heaps of drugs but they just left them alone if you fixed them up.

"They'd take all your money, or drugs, whatever, then say 'don't let us see you out here again', but you'd never be charged. That happened to me quite a lot. I got picked up a few times with amounts of pot on me and they'd just take the weed and say 'I won't see you again tonight'."

According to Michael, senior Dunedin Police were running a protection racket where drug dealers would be left alone provided they paid substantial money to certain police officers.

"There was people getting paid under the table. [Name deleted] was a bit of a drug dealer back then but the cops never went around to see him. I was working in with him as well and we never got touched hardly, then this Peter Gibbons would come in.

"I was probably making three or four thousand dollars a week selling drugs and stuff like that, and because they weren't getting anything out of it they were coming around and just ripping people off," recalls Michael.

Furious at being set up during Operation Sub Rosa, John Doe went to the trouble of doing a little research on Gordon Hunter. He hired his own private investigator, who did an asset search and found the detective owned substantially more property and assets than his meager police salary would appear to support.

"Hunter and Gibbons also had accounts at the same bank in South Dunedin, where I banked. One of the staff members there showed me printouts one day. On the statements I saw, Hunter was taking in thousands of dollars a week. The bank executive made the comment to me that Hunter's incomings far exceeded an ordinary detective's wages," says Doe.

Which tallies with information provided to us by Bob Wood's former girlfriend, who has also sworn an affidavit.

"I remember I had to go away and drop money off to Gordon Hunter, but I don't remember why. I had to take money out of an account and give it to Gordon Hunter in cash. It was $1500. I had to meet him, in one of the D cars. He came and met me at Lookout Point, and I was to just park there and sit and wait by the Fire Station, and I can't remember if I was the one to get out of my car or not. I was given all these instructions, do this, do that, do this, do that.

And I had to do it in cash, out of the Westpac branch in South Dunedin. It was a lot of money. It was to be gotten in littler bills, not hundreds. It was a big wad of money."

To give Hunter the benefit of the doubt, perhaps there was an innocent explanation for the city's top car thief paying a police officer $1,500 in small bills at a remote location. But it's hard to think what kind of explanation that might be.

The magazine was also able to implicate Peter Gibbons' partner Detective Gordon Hunter in stealing jewellery from the scene of a central city robbery. But what about the central question that the media had been banging on about, and which Annette King had wheeled out Gibbons to defend Broad over?
There is one final mystery *Investigate* has been able to solve – the identity of the police officer who was obtaining hardcore pornographic movies for the police rugby functions. The officer was a good friend of Peter Gibbons and a member of the police rugby club, which may be why Gibbons was prepared to lie about Wayne Idour supplying movies.

"I know that [the police officer] was going up to [a drug dealer]'s place and getting blue movies and stuff like that. Very early 80s. I was working with [a drug dealer] at the time," says Michael, and [the police officer] used to turn up and I thought, 'this is a bit odd, this is a bit weird' because here was some cop dropping off movies and picking up new movies, and they were all banned ones."

For the sake of the officer's family and children, *Investigate* chooses not to name him. He is named, however, in the documents prepared for independent legal review.

Of course, Gibbons' claim already had credibility running against it. As previously pointed out, if Idour were truly the source of the bestiality movie he had nothing to gain and everything to lose by mentioning the incident to *Investigate*. Yet Peter Gibbons was insistent to the point of overacting:

"Wayne Idour played that movie, Wayne Idour put it on, Wayne Idour was watching it. That's what I categorically remember. I and another person spoke to him about it. And I remember it very, very well," Gibbons told *3 News*.

"I personally believe Mr Gibbons," Police Minister Annette King chimed in, before deliberately vilifying an innocent Wayne Idour.[26]

Like an episode of the cartoon show *Roadrunner*, however, the ground has fallen away beneath Gibbons with these latest revelations, and with them the credibility of the Government's opposition to a Commission of Inquiry.

Howard Broad's chickens have well and truly come home to roost.

Indeed, they have. As you are about to see, there is evidence that the New

---

26 Some months after this article ran in the magazine, we were provided with information that Peter Gibbons was also in the habit of procuring porn movies for functions at the Otago Surf Lifesaving Club at St Kilda. His entire outburst against Wayne Idour, with the connivance of Howard Broad, was a fabrication.

Zealand Police management (not the rank and file) are rotten from the top down. It is evidence that *Investigate* offered to put in front of a Royal Commission of Inquiry into the Police, but the Government refused.

Here's how it unfolded.

The very day that Howard Broad denied there was a problem with Dunedin Police, and asked Peter Gibbons to defend him on the chicken sex video allegation, other former cops who knew more about Howard Broad got in touch with *Investigate*.

"Some more info about Broad on a confidential basis," emailed one former officer that day.[27] "Early to mid 90's while he was Detective Inspector in charge of the Sandston Homicide in Christchurch , he drove out of the central police station carpark one evening completely drunk.

"He was stopped by Senior Constable Wayne Stevenson who was in the traffic branch at the time. Broad said "do you know who I am?" and told the officer to "f*** off" and he drove away."

The email came from a named, and respected, former policeman. It was one of dozens of messages and phone calls from serving and former police, urging *Investigate* magazine to dig deeper into police corruption, and force an inquiry.

As we began following up some of the leads, one of them, a recently retired Senior Sergeant named Colin Campbell, revealed he'd been based at Christchurch and had information about police corruption there.

He'd only just left the force literally weeks earlier, the end of a 34 year career.

"I joined the police as a police cadet in 1973. I served in Porirua, Wellington and finally in Christchurch. I was a CIB detective for seven years, a Sergeant for nine years and have been a Senior Sergeant for 15 years. In my current rank I have been a Christchurch Shift Commander, O/C Christchurch Traffic Unit, O/C Communication Room Shift Manager, O/C Christchurch Watchhouse and O/C Traffic Infringement Unit."

As you've probably guessed, bells were going off everywhere. As head of the police traffic teams, did Campbell perchance recall any incident where Howard Broad was ever caught drunk driving, possibly by a cop named Wayne Stevenson?

"I remember there were rumours that my staff had picked up a senior officer, but they never told me who was involved," he answered, stunned. "Stevenson was one of my staff!"

Bingo!

And it's not just Campbell. While I continued my own inquiries, Campbell – who has experience assisting with PCA investigations – agreed to ask his former team. Retired police officer Dave Jarden, like the first officer who contacted me, can put Broad in the frame as well.[28]

"I was on Group 5, Christchurch Central Police in 1992. I remember the

---

27   Email to author, May 07
28   Statement to Senior Sergeant Colin Campbell, 26 June 2007

incident vividly. We were on swing shift and put up a checkpoint, which we often did. It was a Friday night and was in Riccarton Road or Harper Ave. They are very close to each other.

"Broad drove into the checkpoint and appeared to be drunk. He was driving a plain police car. Wayne Stevenson was the cop in the line who stopped him. Broad told Stevenson, 'do you know who I am? If you want to keep your career you will wave me through', or words to that effect.

"Broad then drove off and was not processed. I don't know if he had to blow into anything but the boys believed he was really drunk. Stevenson was bloody wild. Stevenson had described Broad as being 'pissed' in the sense of drunk.

Jarden says news of the incident made the police radio channels, which is how he heard and why he pricked his ears up.[29]

"All the troops spoke about it and it was even spoken about on the main police radio channel. I was not on the checkpoint, I was working an I-car [incident response car]that evening.

"While in my patrol car I heard a report on the police radio remarking that a senior officer had refused to provide a breathtest at a checkpoint and had driven off. When I subsequently caught up with my colleagues later that evening, they were all talking about the fact that Detective Inspector Howard Broad had ignored a police request to provide a breathtest to Constable Wayne Stevenson.

"I recall there was considerable discussion about Broad pulling rank on Stevenson by making it clear that he was a senior officer and would not be cooperating with the checkpoint team.

"Naturally, the incident caused a lot of concern on the checkpoint. Normally with a 'drive off' a police patrol would be dispatched to pursue and arrest, but the junior staff manning the checkpoint were unsure how they should proceed against an officer of Broad's rank.

"A number of us discussed how the incident should be handled and whether to file an official report, but there were strong fears that it could result in repercussions for any of us who put the incident on the record, particularly as Broad was a high profile senior officer.

"This happened about one year after the merger. I am pretty sure I have the date of it as I kept detailed timings of everything. I had come over to police from MOT (Ministry of Transport) and we did not trust the police, hence the diary," says Jarden.

[Name of serving officer withheld by author for evidential purposes], now based at [withheld] station in [withheld], can verify the basic details of the scandal, but not the identity of the offender:[30]

"I was on Group 5 in 1992 and recall the furore over a high-ranking cop being stopped in a checkpoint and nothing happening. I can't remember who

29 Interview with author
30 Statement to Senior Sergeant Colin Campbell, 2 August 2007

it was but it created a furore. I did not do many checkpoints as I was an I-car cop, and not from the MOT."

Another former officer states:[31]

"I was a cop on Group 5 in 1992. Broad was stopped one night in one of our checkpoints and I think it was Wayne Stevenson who stopped him. I remember the talk that Broad was driving drunk and that he was not charged.

"Broad, I seem to remember, had a gambling problem too. He presented himself as a Salvation Army type but this was not the case at all."

These are explosive and serious allegations to level against New Zealand's top cop, but there seems to be no shortage of officers pointing the finger.

Readers will recall that Howard Broad's former boss, Detective Sergeant Tom Lewis, remembers Broad getting "pissed" and out of control while he was based in Dunedin.[32] So the allegation that Broad was drunk in charge of a police vehicle cannot be written off as impossible. Especially when we have direct eyewitness testimony from another former colleague of Broad's:[33]

"I have seen Howard Broad in action in the Christchurch Police bar. Not a pretty sight as he is not a man who can hold his liquor."

Armed with all this and, in fact, much more, *Investigate* magazine fired a series of questions to Police National Headquarters, initially just laying some groundwork rather than going straight for the jugular.

"A number of senior police and former police have been in touch with *Investigate* magazine offering further information about the activities of the Police Commissioner and his team, and also some historical information that puts other events in context.

"One officer who went through training in 1976 says cadets were shown porn movies as part of their training, and also a bestiality movie called *Animal Farm*.

"We require confirmation from National Headquarters of when the practice of screening porn movies and bestiality movies to police cadets ceased.

"We have also been advised by direct witnesses of shift inspectors in Wellington screening porn movies late at night in the control room and running the sound feed through the headphones of the police operators there.

"Has Commissioner Howard Broad EVER been drunk on police premises? If so, what was the occasion and what penalty if any did he suffer?"

On 17 May last year, police media maven Jane Archibald fired back a "Foxtrot Oscar" letter:

"PNHQ notes that the latest issue of *Investigate* Magazine was prepared without

---

31 [name withheld], statement to Senior Sergeant Colin Campbell, 28 June 2007
32 *Investigate*, June 07 issue, "To Serve & Protect"
http://www.thebriefingroom.com/archives/2007/08/to_serve_and_pr.html
33 Email to author, May 07

any approach or questions to this office prior to publication. *Investigate* has shown itself to be lacking in ethics associated with responsible publications. PNHQ, therefore, declines to answer belated questions from the magazine on policing or any other subjects."

To which the magazine responded immediately:

"Ducking for cover are we Jane...
    "Last time I looked you and the Commissioner were public servants. That requires you to provide information. I suggest you do it.
    "*Investigate* is not required to register itself as an "approved" media outlet with either Police or the Government.
    "I expect a response in an hour."

A chastened Jane Archibald's reply arrived in only half an hour:

"Thank you Ian for your reply. We note your request which will now be given attention under the Official Information Act. This email will be formally registered through our OIA process with the date of registration being yesterday."

By this stage, *Investigate* and one of the magazine's sources for the original article, Wayne Idour, had been viciously attacked under parliamentary privilege by Annette King that same afternoon. With the daily news media running Labour party spin, apparently swallowing it hook line and sinker, the magazine was forced to go public on the least of the information it had corroborated:

Media Release From *Investigate* Magazine, 17 May 2007

Police Minister Annette King has gone heavily into bat for what now appears to be one of the most bent police forces in the Southern Hemisphere, but it's already looking shaky.

Investigate editor Ian Wishart spent much of Wednesday talking to a number of police sources before putting a list of questions to Police Commissioner Howard Broad late Wednesday for his comment before they are released.

"Howard Broad is a drunkard. He has an alcohol problem and engages in what fellow officers have described to the magazine as 'offensive behaviour' and on the basis of the evidence now given to *Investigate* by Broad's colleagues, we believe he is unfit for the job. We are awaiting Broad's response to this and a range of fresh information.

"I had not expected to be looking into Howard Broad's problems in such detail," said Wishart, "but the media's concentration on Broad and refusal to examine more serious allegations in the magazine has actually backfired on the Commissioner: more police have come forward to us with stories about Broad's many indiscretions while stationed around the country.

"While Annette King attacked Wayne Idour in Parliament this afternoon over flashes of porn scenes cut into a training tape by Dunedin's police photography unit," senior police sources revealed to *Investigate* that Police College staff routinely screened porn and a bestiality movie called "Animal Farm" for recruits in the mid-1970s, the time that Howard Broad graduated. This too was apparently for "training" purposes and happened under the supervision of Senior Sergeant Evan Jordan, apparently with the approval of Police National Headquarters..."

...*Investigate's* editor Ian Wishart says significant new information has come to light about Broad and other members of his management team at Police National Headquarters, information that should be put before a Royal Commission of Inquiry into Police Corruption.

While it was chicken sex and the vilification of Wayne Idour playing out on national television and radio broadcasts, behind the scenes World War Three had erupted between *Investigate*, Police National HQ and the Police Minister's office.

On May 18, after another skirmish with police media liaison, *Investigate* responded to police spokesman Jon Neilson, "Good...now you can tell me about Deputy Commissioner Rob Pope's affair with a convicted heroin dealer..."[34]

The magazine had, by this stage been provided with extremely serious allegations about Howard Broad's 2IC, Rob Pope. Readers will recall that Pope was the officer in charge of the controversial Scott Watson case – the murders of Ben Smart and Olivia Hope. Pope had not come out of that case smelling of roses,[35] but nonetheless he was promoted up the ranks.

His former colleagues, however, have a very jaded view of Rob Pope.

"Rob Pope, yes the Deputy Assistant Commissioner, had an affair with a colleague's wife, another officer and should have been brought before the

---

34 The story of Rob Pope's alleged affair with a drug dealer almost leaked out at one point, when a rumour swept the parliamentary press gallery that Rob Pope was taking out an injunction against *Investigate* magazine to prevent us from publishing something. NZPA and the *Dominion-Post* made contact with Investigate, but we did not disclose the detail of what we were working on, and professed no knowledge of any injunction – which was true. There wasn't one. How the media came to find out is a mystery however – the leak can only have come from Police National Headquarters or possible the Minister's office.

35 Apart from widespread allegations of incompetence (see *Ben & Olivia* by Jayson Rhodes and Ian Wishart, Howling At The Moon Publishing Ltd, 1999), it has only recently been revealed that Pope is under investigation for allegedly making misleading statements in a sworn affidavit on the Ben & Olivia case. The *Herald on Sunday* (March 23, 2008) reports that the "investigation" has so far taken four years, which means it is probably just another police cover-up, and that apparently bosses were fully appraised when Pope was promoted to Deputy Commissioner two years ago. Police National HQ has also tried to suggest there is no suggestion of criminality. Police can throw a rope around it and call it a heffalump: last time I looked s108 of the Crimes Act defined misleading a court as "perjury", and s109(2) says that if it is done to secure the conviction of someone like, say, Scott Watson, the penalty if proven is 14 years jail. Section 116 of the Crimes Act, conspiring to defeat justice, might also be relevant. The Government told New Zealanders last year there was no police corruption, and no need for a Royal Commission. I wonder if any of you will still believe that after reading this book.

internal disciplinary system, but never was. Plenty of other officers were brought before the tribunal for the same reason," one disgruntled former officer told *Investigate* in an email.

"Rob Pope was a uniform senior sergeant here in Christchurch" explained another, "late 80s, around 1988. Pope was married. He went on to a shift and had an affair with a very junior policewoman on his shift [name deleted by author]. Her husband was also a senior sergeant. As a result of that the [couple]'s marriage split up and he got in a very distressed state, apparently on the verge of suicide – this is [the fellow senior sergeant, now an inspector].

"Now we were all pretty bloody gutted about that, because shortly after this blew up he [Pope] got promoted."

Another case of Rob Pope not smelling of roses but still being promoted up the ranks.

"During the late 80s or early 90s," recalls another officer, "Pope was in a car and the radio transmission was accidentally switched on. Pope was busy telling the other occupants of his sexual conquests and of further conquests… The control room inspector managed to intervene and when Pope got back to work the tapes were wiped."

Three former police officers allege that Pope had a long running affair with a convicted heroin trafficker, Dale Frances Mulvihill, and that he had managed to get himself special visits at Christchurch Women's Prison, where she was being jailed.

The woman had been the girlfriend of Christchurch detective Wayne Haussman, who after going undercover was later busted for importing heroin for supply and jailed.

"Wayne Haussman's girlfriend also went to jail for being a party to importing heroin," one Christchurch cop told *Investigate*. "Pope used to keep going out to the jail where she was serving time, trying to have sex with her."

"Pope was a dirty letch, and he was looking for women to bonk," explained another, "and Pope's been bonking her on and off ever since."

"You know Pope's got a conviction?" one police officer asked the magazine. "While we were at Trentham [as cadets together], Pope and two others got caught underage in a bar, and got convicted via an offence notice.

"The point that I made is, what it shows is, that we knew at the time that if any of us were caught in a pub it was *instant* dismissal. Yet Pope was prepared to do it – as we all were, I have to be honest – but Pope got caught and he never got kicked out! But what I'm saying is that that shows his propensity, at a very early stage in his career, to be prepared to break the rules."

Normally, the activities of a police officer after hours, unless illegal, would not be the subject of comment[36]. But in Rob Pope's case they interfered with

---

36 Although a good case in point is the former head of the Dunedin CIB, Detective Chief Inspector Peter Robinson. Robinson headed the Bain murder case, but became the butt of police jokes in Dunedin when a rookie cop, apparently acting on someone's

his duties as a senior police officer. Firstly, he disrupted the unity of his force by sleeping with the wife of a fellow officer. Secondly, it wasn't just an ordinary affair – she was also a junior constable under Pope's command; a subordinate. Thirdly, he is accused of maintaining a relationship with a convict – not exactly the character one would expect of a Deputy Police Commissioner.

It is especially not the character of one tasked by Police Minister Annette King with helping set up the new Organised Crime Agency, an agency whose core principles include:[37]

• Prevention of opportunities for organised crime to operate.
• Protecting New Zealand's infrastructure from undue influence, corruption of public officials and serious conflicts of interest. This will further enhance public reassurance and New Zealand's international credibility.
• The provision of leadership for law enforcement investigation agencies.

"I look forward," said Rob Pope the day the new agency under his command was announced,[38] "to working with our counterparts in setting up the OCA and assisting with one of its first tasks – an organised crime strategy to provide a coordinated, whole of government response to organised crime and the activities of criminal gangs."

Now here's the damning catch. Howard Broad and Police National Headquarters knew prior to announcing the OCA (and the fact that it would report to Pope) that *Investigate* had the goods on Rob Pope as well. Either the police top brass were fundamentally and irreparably stupid, or they believe that they are somehow untouchable.[39] And if they really are untouchable, one can only wonder what goods they've got on the Government.

---

mischievous tip-off, raided a brothel only to find Robinson hiding in a wardrobe wearing women's clothing. Needless to say no charges were brought against the brothel, and the young cop got the bollocking of his life from his boss. As an example of Dunedin police corruption in the 1990s it is hard to beat, but for the record Robinson's son, also a police officer, was investigated but "cleared" of the rape of a policewoman, on the grounds that he believed the sex was "consensual". The woman was told her career would end if she complained. She did, and it did. She now lives in London.
37 News release, Annette King, Minister of Police, 11 September 2007
http://www.beehive.govt.nz/release/new+government+agency+will+fight+organised+crime
38 News release, NZ Police, Rob Pope, 11 September 2007, "Working together in fight against organized crime"
39 There is reason for extreme concern about the management team of the New Zealand police. The fact that Clint Rickards nearly made Commissioner despite police knowing his background speaks volumes about the management culture of the police. That Rob Pope made it anywhere near National Headquarters, let alone Deputy Commissioner, given his background, is also inexplicable, and Broad's weaknesses have now been revealed. Then there's Superintendent John Kelly – the former Wellington District Commander whose timesheet practices provoked an official inquiry and who is now in a cushy headquarters role (not to be confused with John Kelly of the police road traffic division). Superintendent John Francis Emile Kelly has nonetheless been promoted through the ranks despite also having allegedly indecently assaulted a number of women including a former police commissioner's daughter (see http://www.thebriefingroom.com/archives/2007/08/to_serve_and_pr.html) . These are the men that Howard Broad has surrounded himself with. John Kelly was also named in Parliament in 2004 as the driving force behind the prosecution of National MP Shane Ardern for driving a tractor up the steps of Parliament.

Whether Howard Broad had alerted his Minister to the existence of our questions about Rob Pope, we don't know, but colleagues of both Broad and Pope suggest the Commissioner and his Deputy are as thick as thieves.

"He [Broad] and Rob Pope investigated the poisoned professor case, and he stuffed that up as well," commented one former officer. "He [Broad] did three big things. The Civic Creche inquiry, which was a stuff up, the poisoned professor case which was a stuff up, and the Sandston case which was a stuff up."

"Both Pope and Broad don't have the moral outlook to hold those positions."

One officer wrote to the magazine:

"I have spoken to a former undercover officer who, while undercover, was approached by two other undercover cops who urged him to supply them with drugs including LSD. The officer declined, and reported them and left the programme.

"Detective Superintendent Larry Reid took a statement off the U/C [undercover officer]. When the officer returned to his former role, another former U/C approached him and told him that he too and been pressure to supply drugs while U/C to these same two staff.

"The U/C believed the whole matter was brushed under the carpet, and the last senior officer to speak to him was Detective Inspector Rob Pope who asked him if his 'little problem was sorted out'."

So, with allegations that the nation's top cop was a drunk driver who refused to obey police instructions at a checkpoint and drove off after intimidating staff, and that the second in command of the police has had an inappropriate relationship with a convicted drug dealer including alleged conjugal visits to a women's prison, and has a conviction to boot, you can perhaps understand why the Government might be sensitive about calls for a Royal Commission into the Police.

Our sources inside Police National Headquarters told us there was rabid panic on the top floor every time *Investigate* made contact. Officially, though, all we got was radio silence:

From: Ian Wishart [mailto:ian@investigatemagazine.com]
Sent: 21 May 2007 15:35
To: 'Jon.Neilson@police.govt.nz'
Subject: No response yet

Am still awaiting response to my query regarding Rob Pope, and other outstanding matters.

And radio silence:

From: Ian Wishart [mailto:ian@investigatemagazine.tv]
Sent: 30 May 2007 09:59

To: 'jon.neilson@police.govt.nz'
Subject: FW: No response yet

Jon, I will be publishing the deliberate lack of response by Police to questions... so I strongly recommend that you turn attention to this matter and the others I have raised.
Ian Wishart

And a failure to comply with the deadlines imposed by the Official Information Act:

From: Ian Wishart <ian@investigatemagazine.tv>
Sent: 22/06/2007 12:20
To <Jane.Archibald@police.govt.nz>
cc <jon.neilson@police.govt.nz>, <kathryn.street@parliament.govt.nz>
Subject RE: Request of the Commissioner

Dear Jane
I note that the NZ Police are now in breach of the OIA time period per my request on 16 May, and have been in fact for ten days now.
I want full answers to my questions under the OIA within two hours please.
Ian Wishart

In the interim, *Investigate* decided to ratchet up the heat under Police Commissioner Howard Broad by disclosing specific allegations to the Prime Minister's office about his alleged drink driving and refusing to stop.

On June 20th, 2007, we sent the following list of questions to Helen Clark:

Questions for the Prime Minister:
1. In accepting nomination to the position of Police Commissioner last year, did Howard Broad disclose to the Prime Minister or the Police Minister that he was picked up on suspicion of drunk driving by a junior police officer in the 1990s, but used his position as a ranking officer to intimidate the junior officer into not breathtesting him?
2. Did Mr Broad disclose to the Prime Minister or the Police Minister that his exact words were, "Don't you know who I am? F**k off!"?
3. Did Mr Broad disclose that he then drove off without being breathtested?
4. Did Mr Broad disclose that he had just finished attending a function at the Police Bar?
5. Is the Prime Minister aware that any attempt by any police officer to put pressure of any kind on the officers prepared to testify to this would be a corrupt practice under the Crimes Act 1961?
6. Does the Government still have confidence in Mr Broad as Police Commissioner?

Investigate magazine awaits your response.

We heard nothing back. Finally, on June 25, a partial response from Police National Headquarters, who chose not to answer some questions.

From: Jane.Archibald@Police.Govt.NZ
Sent: Monday, 25 June 2007 5:27 p.m.
To: ian@investigatemagazine.tv
Subject: RE: Request of the Commissioner

Dear Ian
Police's obligations under the Official Information Act require responses to requests for official information rather than comment on unsourced allegations. That being the case responses to specific requests are as follows:
The screening of porn or bestiality movies has never been part of the curriculum of the Police College. Anecdotal comment suggests that pornographic film material may have been screened as part of operational familiarisation training by guest presenters from the then Vice or similar crime squads.
Anecdotal comment also suggests that pornographic movies may have been shown on occasion late at night in the Wellington Central Police Station some years ago.
There are no records of Police Commissioner Howard Broad ever being drunk on police premises.
Regards
Jane Archibald

The admissions through gritted teeth about animal porn being screened in police college and hardcore regular porn being screened in the Wellington Police Control room in the 1990s must have been hard for PNHQ, which had been desperate to try and claim that *Investigate's* sources were all wrong.

But there are a couple of things about Archibald's response that illustrate the depth of the cover-up. The words "There are no *records* of Police Commissioner Howard Broad ever being drunk on police premises" do not say that Howard Broad has *not* been drunk on the premises, it merely says police did not keep written records. In fact, as the Ombudsmen have previously ruled, the Police answer is wrong under the Official Information Act, because the definition of "official information" includes information in the memories of government officials, not just what is written on paper.

To put it bluntly, Jane Archibald was indeed "ducking for cover".

The second issue is the question police chose not to answer: the circumstances of Deputy Commissioner Rob Pope's relationship with a convicted heroin trafficker. Archibald did not acknowledge the question and used a generic "unsourced allegations" claim as a reason for not answering. Again, the police were breaking the Official Information Act. Information held by Rob Pope is "information" for the purposes of the Act. Rob Pope categorically knows whether he had a relationship with a prison inmate and drug dealer. If the story was not true he was legally required by the Act to issue a straight denial. It was not up to the magazine to provide him with chapter and verse, and the name of a source (or three). Legally, *Investigate* did not have to under the OIA.

By kicking for touch, the Police not only broke the OIA (again) but effectively admitted that the line of questioning was correct.

We firmly reminded Jane Archibald of the settled case law on refusing to provide straight answers:

"Further to my email this morning re my Official Information Request on Howard Broad being drunk on police premises, I thought I would save the taxpayer money and time by retrieving the Ombudsman's established position on the definition of Official Information.

It would be a wasteful use of taxpayer resources if I was indeed forced to bring the Ombudsman formally into this situation merely for him to state the obvious, which is:

"...the fact that information has not yet been reduced to writing does not mean that it does not exist and is not "held" for the purposes of requests under the official information legislation.

"In these circumstances, if the official information legislation were to apply only to information held in documentary form, the purposes of the legislation could be easily frustrated.

"The Crown Law Office has closely considered our approach to this issue recently and expressed agreement with it." – SOURCE: Ombudsmens Quarterly Review, Vol 4 Issue 3, 1998, penned by Brian Elwood and Anand Satyanand.

To save time, please can you ensure, as requested, that Mr Broad answers my specific questions as previously set out."

The Police did not, however. The following day, June 26, *Investigate* sent questions direct to Howard Broad, and cc'd them to the Prime Minister's press secretary Kathryn Street and the Minister of Police:

"Ian Wishart"<ian@investigatemagazine.tv>
To: <howard.broad@police.govt.nz>
26/06/2007 10:30
Cc: <commissioner@police.govt.nz>, <hbroad@police.govt.nz>,
<john.saunders@parliament.govt.nz>, <Jane.Archibald@police.govt.nz>, <jon.neilson@police.govt.nz>, <kathryn.street@parliament.govt.nz>
Subject: Your comment

Dear Mr Broad

We will shortly be publishing a story that you intimidated a junior police officer into not breathtesting you when he suspected you of driving drunk.

We are seeking your comment on this, and you will have been alerted to the existence of our questions by the Prime Minister's office last week.

You have had ample time to consider your response, and given your publicly stated commitment to: "play it straight down the line" and "When confronted by this sort of stuff I'll tell the truth and not try and gild the lilly. I [don't] want to be seen to be ducking or diving or trying to put a spin on it.", I strongly recommend that you end the current ducking and diving that your media section is undertaking on your behalf and simply tell us what happened.

Yours sincerely

Ian Wishart

But Howard Broad's "ducking or diving" continued. This was clearly one question he didn't want to answer directly.

From: Jon.Neilson@police.govt.nz
Sent: Tuesday, 26 June 2007 11:37 a.m.
To: ian@investigatemagazine.tv
Cc: commissioner@police.govt.nz; hbroad@police.govt.nz; howard.broad@police.govt.nz;
Jane.Archibald@police.govt.nz; john.saunders@parliament.govt.nz;
kathryn.street@parliament.govt.nz
Subject: Re: Your comment

Dear Ian
In response to request for comment from the Commissioner:
Mr Broad is aware of the questions you have asked the Prime Minister's Office. Given that course of action the Commissioner considers it is now appropriate for you to await answers from the PM's Office rather than for direct commentary to be provided by him.

Regards
Jon Neilson
Manager Media Relations
Police National Headquarters

We had been in daily contact with the office of Police Minister Annette King, whose staff had promised a statement at the start of the week. One phone call of ours, recorded on tape on June 26, was particularly telling, and we ran it verbatim on our website that day:

Police Minister Annette King's office is this morning refusing to express confidence in Police Commissioner Howard Broad.

In an extraordinary verbal exchange with *Investigate* magazine, the Minister's office says it is preparing a statement in regards to Howard Broad after fresh allegations about the Police Commissioner were forwarded to Prime Minister Helen Clark by *Investigate* magazine last week.

Asked whether Ms King still had confidence in Broad, the Minister's executive assistant John Saunders refused to commit the office to supporting Broad, saying only, "I'm afraid I'll have to stay with the original statement".

"So you can't express confidence at this point?" we asked.

[Silence for 8 seconds]

"John?" we asked

[Silence for 5 seconds]

"John?"

[Silence for 3 seconds]

"Hello?" we asked again.

[Silence for 2 seconds, except for the sound of Saunders breathing]

"John?"

[Silence for 4 seconds, more breathing]

"I can hear you," *Investigate* pressed

[Silence for 3 seconds]

"Why is there reticence to express confidence in Howard Broad?"

[Silence for 3 more seconds, and then finally Saunders speaks]

"I'm afraid I have no comment to make on that".

ENDS

The reason that Annette King's spokesman John Saunders was caught like a possum in the headlights is because the Government was still trying to figure out what evidence *Investigate* might have, and how it should respond.

We pressured the Prime Minister for an expression of confidence in Broad, but it took more than two days to arrive.

From: Kathryn Street [Kathryn.Street@parliament.govt.nz]
Sent: Thursday, 28 June 2007 6:08 p.m.
To: Ian Wishart
Cc: John Harvey; John Saunders; jon.neilson@police.govt.nz
Subject: Re: Questions for the Prime Minister from Investigate magazine

Hello
Please refer all questions on this issue to the office of the Minister of Police. The Prime Minister has confidence in the Police Commissioner.
Cheers

Finally, two weeks later, a formal reply was finally received from Police Minister Annette King.

"I provide the following responses to the allegations that you have made in emails to the Prime Minister and myself," wrote King.

"**Allegation:** In accepting nomination to the position of Police Commissioner last year, did Howard Broad disclose to the Prime Minister or the Police Minister that he was picked up on suspicion of drunk driving by a junior police officer in the 1990s, but used his position to intimidate the junior officer into not breathtesting him?

"**Response:** Commissioner Broad made appropriate disclosures.

"**Allegation:** Did Mr Broad disclose to the Prime Minister or the Police Minister that his exact words were, 'Don't you know who I am? F**k off'?

"**Response:** Commissioner Broad could not disclose this as there was no truth in the allegation in the first place.

"**Allegation:** Did Mr Broad disclose that he drove off without being breathtested?

"**Response:** Commissioner Broad could not disclose this as there was no truth in the allegation in the first place.

"**Allegation:** Did Mr Broad disclose that he had just finished attending a function at the Police Bar?

"**Response:** Commissioner Broad could not disclose this as there was no truth in the allegation in the first place.

"**Question:** Is the Prime Minister aware that any attempt by any police officer to put pressure of any kind on the officer prepared to testify would be a corrupt practice under the Crimes Act 1961?

"**Response:** Yes.

"**Question:** Does the Government still have confidence in Mr Broad as Police Commissioner?

"**Response:** Yes."

On the face of the evidence provided to *Investigate* magazine – a number of police officers prepared to put Broad in the frame for alleged drink driving and absconding from a checkpoint (a criminal, not just moral offence) – and a blanket denial from Howard Broad that any such incident had taken place, only four explanations appear credible.

1. Either Broad is right because the incident never happened. Or

2. Broad cannot remember the events of the night in question and therefore does not realise that it happened. Or

3. Broad remembers, and was prepared to lie to the Minister of Police to save his position and prevent the obvious next step, which would have been a Commission of Inquiry into the Police, given the heat already flying around. Or

4. Broad remembers, and the Government knows, but for political reasons the Government chose to lie to *Investigate* magazine rather than provide massive ammunition for a Royal Commission.

If there is a further option, I can't think of it. Option One appears unlikely. A number of senior staff have put their own reputations on the line to reveal details of the incident. There is no upside for them in this, apart from doing the right thing.

Option two is perhaps the most likely, and would provide an innocent explanation of the blanket denial.

Either way, Prime Minister Helen Clark and Police Minister Annette King have now staked their own credibility on Howard Broad's denial. As you've already seen, however, they also staked their reputations on the credibility of Howard Broad's friend Peter Gibbons – at Broad's recommendation.

Now that Gibbons has been caught as a corrupt cop, Helen Clark and Annette King will have good reason to be looking sideways at Broad for a more credible explanation than he has so far given.

More likely, however, is that police will attempt to pressure witnesses to change their stories – especially serving officers, but the Independent Police Conduct Authority has already been alerted about Wayne Stevenson and the other witnesses. Any pressure, even a wink, will backfire.

You'll recall we asked the Government:

"Is the Prime Minister aware that any attempt by any police officer to put pressure of any kind on the officer prepared to testify would be a corrupt practice under the Crimes Act 1961?

"**Response:** Yes.

Well, despite that assurance, those kind of dirty tricks appear to happen all the time in the NZ Police force, which would make the force corrupt on the basis of the Prime Minister's own admission.

"A retired Detective Superintendent's son in law was caught stealing money," one former officer told *Investigate*, "[but] the accusing cop was then investigated for alleged unauthorised use of a police car. He won that one and a lot of money as well, as he took it to the Employment Authority.

"The same Detective Superintendent's daughter lost a large sum of money while she worked for a bank. It was repaid and nothing happened."

Or take the case of Senior Sergeant Colin Campbell. After 34 years of exemplary service to Her Majesty's Constabulary, he was forced to resign last year. As he told a parliamentary select committee hearing:

"Over the last 34 years I have arrested hundreds of offenders and overseen and supervised the arrest and preparation of criminal charges of thousands more. Yet on the one occasion when I report allegations against a senior Christchurch officer, I am vilified and my career ruined."

What happened, according to his official testimony to the select committee, was simply this: In 2003, Campbell was in charge of the Christchurch Beat Unit, based at Cathedral Square. Underneath him served three Sergeants and 25 police constables. Campbell reported to Inspector Dave Lawry. In the annual staff appraisals given to every officer each year, Campbell's had always been "outstanding" or "commendable". 2003 was no different: "The inspector [Lawry] had just recently issued the highest possible grade in my annual appraisal," says Campbell. "Our relationship was amiable."

But then, trouble struck in the form of a police "teambuilding" evening in a hospitality tent at Jade Stadium in August 2003, where Lawry had gathered some of his senior staff for a knees-up while they watched the rugby. Campbell did not attend.

Within days of the event, gossip was sweeping through police circles that Lawry had become drunk and overly friendly to a young and unappreciative Jade Stadium waitress.

Campbell heard the rumours but paid little heed. However, as Lawry tried to find out who knew and who didn't, he discovered Senior Sergeant Campbell had been present when other staff were discussing the incident. He called Campbell in and told him nothing had happened, and warned Campbell that he needed to know he could trust him.

When a *Christchurch Press* journalist began ringing various officers from Lawry's unit in February to inquire about the alleged incident, Campbell followed the procedure laid out in the police regulations and reported the media inquiry to his superiors.

"I did not know the reporter. She said she was contacting a number of police officers in the course of the inquiry...I explained that I was not present [at the function] and would not comment.

"Under police regulations I was required to report this...irrespective of police policy, I would have thought that senior management would have appreciated being advised that the media were investigating their staff."

Accordingly, Campbell compiled a brief summary of what the journalist had said, and took it to the officer in charge of professional standards for the Canterbury police region, Inspector Banks.

"Much to my surprise Banks told me that he was present at the function and to my disappointment he did not take notes nor ask for a report as is standard police practice," says Campbell.

Instead, nothing was done. Well, almost nothing. Dave Lawry *was* told that Campbell had tried to "formally report" the rumours about the Jade Stadium incident.

Inspector Lawry placed his entire Christchurch Beat Unit under a "secret" criminal investigation, accessing staff fingerprint records for the purposes of some still undisclosed purpose.

"Despite the fact that myself and 19 of my staff were under 'criminal investigation', at no stage was the enquiry reported to the Police Complaints Authority as is a statutory requirement," notes Campbell.

The inquiry dragged on for six months but found "no fault by any person".

Despite this, the staff at the Beat Unit were booted out of the unit after management decided to introduce a new "staff rotation policy" retrospectively.

Four staff, including the unit's 2IC, Sergeant Kerry Joyce, filed personal grievance claims and by the time Campbell testified to the select committee hearing last year two of the four had won substantial damages, with two cases including Joyce's still to settle.

Christchurch Police bosses, from District Commander Sandra Manderson down, made Colin Campbell's life hell, forcing him – as a ranking Senior Sergeant – to do clerical filing work with 17 year old school leavers, or to work in an unheated warehouse during the winter months. Their actions were all the more unusual because Campbell had sustained an injury in the line of duty when he went to the aid of Asian tourists being attacked by a man in the central city one night. The offender and Campbell ended up in a fight, busting Campbell's knee.

Police bosses used the injury as a pretext for "disengaging" Campbell from the force.

"After 34 years of unblemished police service and after being hospitalised as a result of an attack while protecting the public, I was given one week's notice in writing to decide if I wanted to resign. I was stunned. During the court hearing of the offender who assaulted me, the presiding judge praised my courage and bravery.

"My surgeon was surprised that I was facing the prospect of being medically disengaged, and he told me that he had recently performed surgery for two hip replacements and a knee replacement on a West Coast constable. This officer's employment in the police, unlike mine, was secure."

Incredibly, despite the massive conflict of interest, police bosses allowed Inspector Lawry to place "adverse reports" about Colin Campbell on his personal file, with a series of fabricated allegations. Again, in the author's opinion, a classic sign of police corruption – discrediting the whistleblower any way you can.[40]

An ironic twist is that Campbell subsequently discovered from Manderson's aide, Inspector Jury, "that there was an enquiry into the Jade Stadium incident shortly after the event but that the girl at the centre did not wish to complain, and it was *not* reported to the PCA [Police Compaints Authority]. Jury told me that Detective Superintendent Burgess wished to keep the incident and enquiry low key."

Inspector Jury also confirmed that Lawry had been forced to refund $700 taken improperly from the police budget, which had been used to buy alcohol at the incident.

"Yet again," says Campbell, "clear policy was being ignored. Even if the girl did not wish to complain, the matter must be reported to the PCA. There are

---

40 Police were forced to withdraw and destroy the adverse report in September 2006 as a result of a personal grievance action.

still offences under the Police Act and Police Regulations involving drunken behavior by police. The misuse of public money to pay for 'boozing' is a breach of numerous police and Treasury regulations."

The reason for including this brief summary of Colin Campbell's testimony to Parliament is an important one. It shows the lengths a corrupt police administration will go to protect their own, and discredit anyone who dares to testify against them.

Colin Campbell's gutsy willingness to be seriously injured in the line of duty while protecting members of the public, is echoed by his willingness to dig deep for details of the Howard Broad drink driving/abuse of power incident. I have published his background so that people can see for themselves the dirty tricks he has already been subjected to, and how a previously exemplary record has been smeared by those trying to protect their positions.

The story of the Helen Clark years is one of sleaze and corruption. Sleaze and corruption can only exist in a society that tolerates it. New Zealanders, thanks to the malfunctioning moral [and news] compass of many in the news media, tolerate it. The New Zealand police force, who thanks to Head Office are increasingly looking as dodgy as anything out of Australia in the past thirty years, tolerate official corruption because their own bosses are, in fact, corrupt.

When you get a corrupt Government and corrupt law enforcement agencies backing each other up, all hell starts to break loose, as you are about to see.

Parkergate: The Untold Story

Jim Hacker: "Are you saying that winking at corruption is government policy?"
Sir Humphrey: "No, no, Minister. It could never be government policy. That is unthinkable. Only government practice."
– Yes Minister

IF YOU THOUGHT THE LAST chapter contained bombshells, then keep your flak-jacket on because there's more to come – evidence, I believe, that the document used to reinstate David Parker to cabinet two years ago was a forgery, produced with the connivance of a Government agency in a deliberate attempt to pervert the course of justice. This is Parkergate, the untold story.

When news of this book's impending arrival broke in the daily media, journalists immediately made the connection – the journalist the Prime Minister called a "creep" has now written a biography of the Helen Clark years!

The incident that gave rise to the "creep" comment was nothing scandalous or salacious, it was just good old-fashioned investigative reporting, but the events behind the scenes show just how much power Labour wields to get favourable treatment from prosecutorial agencies.

In February 2006, while our coverage of David Benson-Pope was hitting the headlines, *Investigate* was approached by a Dunedin businessman named Russell Hyslop – a former business partner of new Attorney-General David Parker. Before his entrance to Parliament in 2002, Parker was a Dunedin-based lawyer and businessman.

While there's no point re-litigating their personal business dispute, the relevant facts are that a business deal between them went sour, resulting in Hyslop's bankruptcy. Despite that, Hyslop was still listed as a shareholder on the property development company they owned together, Queens Park Mews Ltd, which was still in business.

Every year, companies are required to file "Annual Returns" with the

Companies Office, disclosing up to date director and shareholder information. As part of the return, directors are required to sign off that the shareholders have "unanimously agreed" in writing to waive their right to appoint an auditor to examine the company's books.

Between 1997 and 2005, David Parker or his agents had each year filed those annual returns confirming that all shareholders were agreed there was no need for an auditor.

The only problem was, Hyslop and Parker – both shareholders – were locked in bitter dispute over their company, and what Hyslop claims was the disappearance of $500,000 of his money.

"For at least the past five years," began a report in the April 2006 *Investigate*, "four of them while he was a Labour MP, David Parker has personally filed declarations to the Companies Office where he has answered 'Yes' to the following question: 'Did the shareholders pass unanimous resolution not to appoint an auditor for the current year?'

"The Attorney-General's problem? One of the three shareholders says he hasn't been consulted about the company's affairs since 1997, and certainly has never been asked to approve a 'unanimous' shareholder's resolution each year waiving the right to audit the company's accounts."

If he had been asked, Hyslop points out, he would have demanded an audit.

Now the picture is complicated somewhat because Hyslop's affairs were being managed by the Official Assignee during his bankruptcy, which lasted between mid 1997 and mid 2000. But throughout the period, and right up until April 2006, Hyslop was listed as a shareholder on the official register.

After a lengthy backgrounder on the wider business dispute, *Investigate* finished its article by returning to the false documents that had been filed with the Companies Office by the Labour MP who was now Attorney-General:

The irony is that Russell Hyslop may get the last laugh. He was discharged from bankruptcy in 2000, and as we stated at the start of this article he remains a 33% shareholder in Queens Park Mews Ltd which is still operating and still controlled by Attorney-General David Parker and his father. Hyslop hasn't seen a financial statement from that company since 1997, but the company has clearly completed property development projects and sold houses, so presumably official accounts exist somewhere. As a shareholder, Hyslop is entitled to see those accounts and see if he's owed any money after nine years.

While the dispute over the missing half million dollars may or may not be resolved, and may at the end of the day not be David Parker's problem at all, the Devil in some business dealings is in the detail. And it is in the technical detail that the Attorney-General may be about to come a cropper.

Investigate has obtained documents from the Companies Office confirming that for at least five years, and quite possibly nine years, he has filed official declarations with the Companies Office waiving the need for an audit of his company's accounts on the basis of a "unanimous" resolution of shareholders.

Clearly, with Hyslop saying he has never been contacted for either an AGM or a shareholder's resolution, the documents filed with the Companies Office appear false, on the face of it: either Parker filed the statements knowing he hadn't sought the approval of a hostile major shareholder, or alternatively Hyslop is no longer a shareholder (and so didn't need to be consulted) but Parker has continued to file documents saying he is...so the documents still contain false statements.

It appears Labour's new Attorney-General is in trouble unless he can turn up proof that he contacted Hyslop each year and gained his assent to waive an audit.

Given what we now know, it seems highly unlikely that such a contact was made, let alone agreed to by Hyslop in the circumstances. And the documents held by *Investigate* on Empire Delux show Parker filed the 1996 Annual Return of that company with a declaration of a "unanimous resolution" despite later admitting he hadn't even shown the Annual Return to one of the shareholders, dismissing the problem as merely "a procedural step" that was not "contentious".

Section 377 of the Companies Act states:

"Every person who, with respect to a document required by or for the purposes of this Act – (a) Makes, or authorizes the making of, a statement in it that is false or misleading in a material particular knowing it to be false or misleading... commits an offence, and is liable on conviction to the penalties set out in section 373(4) of this Act."

Section 373(4) of the Act says:

"A person convicted of an offence against [s377] of this Act is liable to imprisonment for a term not exceeding five years or to a fine not exceeding $200,000."

If it was five offences, that's potentially a million dollar fine or prison. If it is nine offences you can add another $800,000, taking the potential fine facing Attorney-General David Parker to $1.8 million for breaches of the Companies Act.

For Attorney-General David Parker, the day the magazine hit the newsstands was the day his life exploded. It was Monday, March 20, 2006, which meant Helen Clark was in the hotseat for her Monday morning interview with Newstalk ZB's Paul Holmes.

"I'm not going to start a public inquiry every time *Investigate* magazine decides to smear somebody, which is every month on average," snarled Clark – overlooking the obvious fact that if her ministers hadn't told porkies they wouldn't be in the media spotlight. Every month.

But events spun rapidly out of the PM's control. Reading the article, Attorney-General David Parker knew what he'd done, and knew it was wrong.

"I'm ashamed," Parker told a packed news conference later that day to announce his resignation as Attorney-General,[41] "I'm certainly ashamed of this particular mistake. With the benefit of hindsight I was a bit glib in the way I ticked the form and sent it in."

TV3 expanded on it, suggesting Parker had been worried for some time that the problem might be raised, but that he was unsure whether he had broken the law and decided not to raise it with the Prime Minister when he was first appointed to cabinet.

In other words, this wasn't some momentary lapse or inattention. Filing a document asserting he had gained the approval of all shareholders, when he knew he hadn't, clearly was gnawing at Parker's conscience and had been for some time.

"I filed the last of these declarations in the middle of last year," added Parker. "I had the relevant resolution signed by myself and my father ... and didn't flick it past either the official assignee ... or Mr Hyslop and that's my mistake and that's why I've resigned."[42]

So far so good. It was an honourable departure, unlike many of the previous scandals involving Labour MPs. Fair cop, guv, ya got me. But the honour was about to disappear as the politician in Parker rose to the surface, and Labour's anti-*Investigate* spin machine swung into action.

At her post cabinet news conference, Prime Minister Clark blamed both *Investigate* and Rodney Hide[43] for Parker's predicament, lamenting an emergent style of politics in which "every little blemish that is possible on every person's character" was under scrutiny.

This, again, was classic Clark spin. Attorney-General David Parker had admitted filing false declarations to the Companies Office. More than that, he knew it and it had been bugging his conscience. In a functioning democracy, lawmakers get no special protection from the laws they create or administer. What's good for the goose is equally applicable to ganders.

After all, *Investigate's* test in this case was proof to a courtroom standard, whereas Helen Clark had once beaten the previous National government around the ears for mere blunders: "...more mistakes by individual ministers and less coordination of Government work – as if there haven't been enough blunders already. The overwhelming image will be of a Government which has simply given up and intends to limp towards the polls with no coherent programme to present to New Zealand."[44]

Indeed.

It is hard to see why Clark would complain about *Investigate's* coverage, when she herself said in a 1997 media interview that "hammering away at the cronyism, sleaze and dishonesty of the Government" was a top priority for

---

41 *NZ Herald*, 21 March 2006, "I'm ashamed, says minister who resigned"
42 *Dominion-Post*, 21 March 2006, "I cut a corner and that was a mistake"
43 Hide had nothing to do with the Parker story
44 *NZ Herald*, 16 March 1999, "Cabinet to meet only fortnightly"
    http://www.nzherald.co.nz/section/1/story.cfm?c_id=1&objectid=3756

those, like herself, trying to keep politics honest.[45]

Whilst Clark could dish it out, however, she had real trouble taking her own recommended dose of medicine. Normally when the news media cover a story, the issue is the story itself, not the journalist behind it. Labour spinmeisters, though, wanted desperately to personalize their attacks on any journalist who dared to challenge their authority. By personalizing it they could divide and rule, separating rogue media lions from the rest of the pride. "Helen Clark vs *The Herald*", for instance, looks like paranoia on Helen Clark's part. But "Helen Clark vs right-wing blogger Fran O'Sullivan"[46] makes it appear that O'Sullivan is out of step. TV3's John Campbell, another facing increasing marginalization, was called "a little creep" for allegedly ambushing the Prime Minister in his Corngate interview. But now, after the Parker story, it was Ian Wishart's turn in a front page *Herald* article:[47]

Helen Clark has labelled another journalist a "creep" – this time targeting *Investigate* magazine editor Ian Wishart.

Mr Wishart this week published a report which revealed David Parker had filed several false Companies Office declarations, forcing him to resign his ministerial portfolios.

Asked about Mr Wishart on Newstalk ZB yesterday the Prime Minister said: "He's a scandalmonger and he'll carry on with that.

"He'll carry on trying to pry into every little nook and cranny of people's lives and all I'd say to people – and I think a lot of people listening would empathise with this – have any of us got nothing in our lives that we'd rather rerun the film on? I don't think so.

"Mr Wishart is the sort of creep who really delights in picking out any little thing that people might have in their background.[48]

"And what it says is if you want to meet the Wishart test of public life, you'd better be one of the Vestal Virgins."

Mr Wishart said he found the comments "astounding".

"Helen is probably under a bit of personal stress ... she's lashing out. I don't take it personally, I find the comments saddening more than anything else."

The media was required to be a Government watchdog. If National was in power it would come under similar focus, he said.

In 2002 the Prime Minister labelled TV3 journalist John Campbell "a little

45 *The Dominion*, 17 February 1997, "Opposition terriers to have their day with some good scraps"
46 *NZ Herald*, 21 October 2006, "Prime Minister, what have you let yourself become?" http://www.nzherald.co.nz/section/1/story.cfm?c_id=1&objectid=10406898
47 *NZ Herald*, 24 March 2006, "Clark labels magazine editor a 'creep'" http://www.nzherald.co.nz/topic/story.cfm?c_id=289&objectid=10374194
48 See Chapter One. There are degrees of relevance, and the new Attorney-General being sprung as a man who knowingly filed false declarations is hardly "any little thing". Clark appears to be arguing that her politicians should be above media scrutiny, even though she regards opposition MPs as fair game.

creep" after an interview with her on the "Corngate" saga, in which she claimed she had been hijacked.

* *Vestal virgin: a virgin consecrated to the Roman goddess Vesta and vowed to chastity, who maintained the sacred fire burning on Vesta's altar.*

Clark's complaints about journalists tracking through MPs' pasts need to be contrasted with her own decision to railroad Maori Affairs Minister Dover Samuels straight out of cabinet in 2000 over allegations that he had done something illegal – not six months earlier as in Parker's case, but two decades earlier. An Audrey Young analysis in the *Herald* highlights the PM's dilemma:[49]

It's unlikely the sordid allegations surrounding Dover Samuels will quickly subside, because whether or not the police investigation into the matter is conclusive, Prime Minister Helen Clark faces an on-going problem.

If the report points to anything illegal, he is gone. End of question. End of political career. End of problem.

If it is any other scenario – and at this stage in a maelstrom of "facts" an uncertain scenario looks likely – the murkiness will linger, even if he is exonerated.

The scandal is a blow to a Government that promised to clean up politics. It follows this week's *Herald*-DigiPoll showing it has more support than it did on election night, and is 11 points clear of National.

If the Minister of Maori Affairs is cleared of an allegation that he got an underage teenager pregnant in the 1980s, the political problem will remain, despite Clark saying he will get his job back...

...She must avoid taking a heavy moral position because it would open up a Pandora's box, and Parliament promises to be a rather large glasshouse if personal morals become commonplace political stones.

References have been made by MPs this week about the morals of the Press Gallery as well, essentially a veiled threat to tread warily.

When Samuels was eventually cleared of any criminal offending, Helen Clark refused to reinstate him to cabinet, saying he lacked "the moral authority to remain a cabinet minister".[50]

So whilst it was OK for Clark to pass moral judgment on the past activities of her MPs, apparently it was not OK for journalists to investigate their pasts.

Bearing all this in mind, let's return to what happened next in the David Parker case. First of all, something had caused Prime Minister Helen Clark to go feral in her Newstalk ZB interview on Wednesday 23 March.

The personal attack had come out of nowhere, a day after David Parker had

49 *NZ Herald*, 24 June 2000, "Samuels affair poser for Clark"
http://www.nzherald.co.nz/section/1/story.cfm?c_id=1&objectid=141380
50 *NZ Herald*, 5 September 2000, "Samuels seeks utu over underage sex claim"
http://www.nzherald.co.nz/section/1/story.cfm?c_id=1&objectid=150213

gone the whole hog and resigned all of his ministerial portfolios, realizing that he couldn't really keep saying to people that while it was bad for an Attorney-General to file false documents, it was OK for ordinary cabinet ministers to do so.

Indeed, the Prime Minister herself told a news conference that if Parker hadn't jumped she would have pushed, such was his error of judgment.[51]

"It probably would have come to that but it didn't need to. He's an honourable person and that's the step he's taken," Clark said. She also revealed there would be a Companies Office investigation into Parker.

But, and it is a very big "but", something was up. The following Monday, March 27, Clark was taking an aggressively different stand. She was now confident Parker was going to be cleared of all charges.

"Prime Minister Helen Clark indicated she will reinstate David Parker to the Cabinet immediately if the Companies Office does not charge him over false declarations made," reported the *Herald's* Audrey Young.[52]

Young noted the huge contrast between Clark's attitude the previous week, and what she now appeared to be hinting at:

"At her post cabinet press conference yesterday, Helen Clark turned what had been acknowledgments of 'mistakes' at the very least by Mr Parker into 'allegations'. And she indicated that if he were not charged by the Companies Office for filing false returns, she would have him back immediately."

Then there was this comment by Clark at her news conference:

"If this set of allegations doesn't stack up then it would not be natural justice to deny Mr Parker a place."

Then, on April 5, came bombshell revelations in Parliament that both Clark and David Parker had been briefed about aspects of the supposedly independent Companies Office investigation:

PRIME MINISTER – COMMENTS ON DAVID PARKER

Hon Bill English (National – Clutha-Southland) to the **Prime Minister**: Why did she make public comments about the possible reinstatement of David Parker to her Cabinet when the Companies Office has yet to complete its inquiry into declarations made by David Parker?

Rt Hon Helen Clark (Prime Minister) : Because reinstatement is an option.

Hon Bill English: Why did she change the view she held on 21 March that Mr Parker had made mistakes serious enough for her to accept his resignation to a view on 28 March that the mistakes he had personally admitted were only "allegations"?

Rt Hon Helen Clark: Those are matters for the Companies Office to determine, and we will be guided by the facts.

---

51   *NZ Herald*, 21 March 2006, "Parker quits all portfolios"
http://www.nzherald.co.nz/category/story.cfm?c_id=30&objectid=10373702
52   *NZ Herald*, 27 March 2006, "PM may reinstate Parker to Cabinet"
http://www.nzherald.co.nz/category/story.cfm?c_id=30&objectid=10374772

Hon Bill English: Did any member of her office or her department, or any Minister's office, seek or receive information, advice, or opinion from the Companies Office in relation to Mr Parker or the matters for which he is currently under investigation?

Rt Hon Helen Clark: Mr Parker has, of course, kept in touch with the leadership of the Labour Party. There has, I understand, been communication from the Companies Office to the head of the Department of the Prime Minister and Cabinet about the pace of the inquiry. I do not want to comment on what may have occurred in those conversations, but I am satisfied that Mr Parker is keeping his leadership in the loop.

Hon Bill English: Is the Prime Minister telling the House that a statutory agency responsible for a decision over whether to prosecute a senior Minister in the current Government has been communicating with the Prime Minister's department over the progress of that investigation?

Rt Hon Helen Clark: Obviously, I have made no request whatsoever for any information from the Companies Office, but—

Dr the Hon Lockwood Smith: Just answer the question.

Rt Hon Helen Clark: Settle down, Dr Smith. The member is very vocal at question time. [*Interruption*]

Madam Speaker: Order, please.

Rt Hon Helen Clark: I am directly answering the question by saying that my understanding is that the head of the Ministry of Economic Development spoke to the head of the Department of the Prime Minister and Cabinet at a very early stage about the likely timing of the inquiry.

Hon Bill English: Can I take the Prime Minister's statement to the House today as confirmation of rumours and allegations that personnel from her department contacted an officer of the Companies Office last week, and that that officer of the Companies Office provided written advice on the Companies Office view of Mr Parker's declaration; and does she regard that as appropriate behaviour for a member of the Prime Minister's department and for a statutory officer responsible for making a decision about whether to prosecute a senior member of her Government?

Rt Hon Helen Clark: I have no advice of any such interaction as the member has referred to.

Hon Bill English: How come the Prime Minister, then, is aware of a discussion between the head of the Prime Minister's department and the Companies Office; and how can anyone not construe that as pressure on the Companies Office from the political leadership of the Government to consider its view very carefully?

Rt Hon Helen Clark: Let me be very clear about what I have already told the member. The head of the Department of the Prime Minister and Cabinet quite correctly reported to me that he had been phoned by the head of the Ministry of Economic Development.

Hon Bill English: Can the Prime Minister now confirm to the House that not only has somebody from the Department of the Prime Minister and Cabinet been discussing these matters with the Companies Office, but those discussions have been reported to her; and how does she think that looks to a Parliament concerned that a statutory agency should be totally independent in making a decision about whether to prosecute a Minister?

Rt Hon Helen Clark: All that I can confirm is that, as I said in the previous answer, the head of the Ministry of Economic Development apparently contacted my head of department at a very early stage. It would have been in the day or two after the matter became public. My head of department quite properly reported that to me.

Hon Bill English: Can the Prime Minister then answer a question I asked earlier as to why she said on 21 March that Mr Parker's actions were "mistakes serious enough for me to accept his resignation", then a week later, after being briefed by the head of her department on discussions with the Companies Office, changed her view to one where she said that Mr Parker's actions were only "allegations"?

Rt Hon Helen Clark: The facts are that on day one Mr Parker said he had made mistakes.

Hon Bill English: And you agreed.

Rt Hon Helen Clark: I accepted his word. Since that time Mr Parker has been in communication with the leadership of his party, as is entirely proper.

What Clark did not explain, because the Opposition ran out of question time, is what was said to herself and Parker that suddenly boosted her hopes. Alone of all the news media, however, *Investigate* magazine found out, and posted details on its website on April 5:

"Sources in Parliament have told *Investigate* this afternoon that a Companies Office official informed Labour – possibly as early as March 23 – that they would take the line that because Hyslop had gone bankrupt, his ownership of the shares lapsed in favour of the Official Assignee and was never returned to Hyslop. Our sources said the Companies Office had given the Prime Minister's Department a copy of a letter signed by the Official Assignee and sent to David Parker back in 1997, soon after Hyslop's bankruptcy, which would be used to establish that fact. For that reason, according to our sources, the Companies Office might be able to find Parker not guilty because he was not required to seek Hyslop's approval from that point on."

This paragraph you've just read is smoking gun evidence of Labour Government corruption, and Companies Office corruption, and here's why – because on <u>April 26</u>, exactly three weeks later, the Companies Office investigation officially "concluded" with this announcement:

"The bankruptcy of Mr Hyslop also affected the status of the 50 shares previously owned by him. By the operation of s42(1) of the Insolvency Act 1967, those shares vested in the Official Assignee for the benefit of his creditors.

Mr Hyslop was automatically discharged from bankruptcy three years later on 30 July 2000. The shares did not, however, re-vest in Mr Hyslop upon his discharge or at any later stage."

That's silver bullet number one. It dovetails exactly with the April 5 *Investigate* tip-off that "because Hyslop had gone bankrupt, his ownership of the shares lapsed in favour of the Official Assignee and was never returned to Hyslop."

Now for the next magic *Investigate* prediction to come true. The Companies Office investigation reports that:

"The Official Assignee wrote to Mr Parker on 10 August 1999, stating, 'Please note that the Official Assignee waives the requirement to seek confirmation on a yearly basis that a unanimous resolution was achieved in respect of no auditor being required for the above company.'

"The wording of the letter is a little inapt," admits a Crown legal opinion, "but its intention is tolerably clear. In essence, the Official Assignee advised Mr Parker that he waived the requirement for his approval of future shareholder resolutions that no auditor be appointed. It appears that Mr David Parker had no recollection of this letter when initially questioned by the media following the *Investigate* article. Now that a copy has been shown to Mr Parker, he does recall it as it is consistent with his subsequent actions in not seeking the Official Assignee's consent on an annual basis to shareholder resolutions that no auditor be appointed for the ensuing year."

And there, folks, is silver bullet number two, predicted three weeks earlier by *Investigate* when we reported: "Our sources said the Companies Office had given the Prime Minister's Department a copy of a letter signed by the Official Assignee and sent to David Parker back in 1997, soon after Hyslop's bankruptcy, which would be used to establish that fact."

But how could *Investigate* magazine know from parliamentary sources on April 5, the legal excuses that would be used to exonerate Parker three weeks later, unless the "investigation" was indeed corrupt, and leaking information to the Prime Minister's office?

It is an extremely serious allegation to be making – that the Companies Office investigation was not independent – but that seems to be the only reasonable conclusion to draw from the facts. And that's how we played it in the next issue of the magazine:

Faced with an ageing cabinet line-up at the shallow end of the gene pool, it is perhaps no surprise that Prime Minister Helen Clark and her advisors moved so swiftly to resurrect disgraced Attorney-General David Parker in the wake of *Investigate's* bombshell revelation that he had filed false documents with the Companies Office.

When the magazine's April issue hit the streets on March 21 with details of a series of false returns signed by David Parker, the Attorney-General firstly quit that post the same day, and the following morning resigned from cabinet completely. The Prime Minister told reporters that if Parker hadn't jumped, she'd have pushed him.

So what happened? Why was Parker then cleared by the Companies Office on 26 April, and did *Investigate* really get its facts wrong, or was the Companies Office investigation politically influenced?

The first signs that something was badly amiss came just a week after Parker's resignation, as a report published in *Investigate's* "The Briefing Room" on April 5 discloses (pay close attention to the dates, and the leaked information to *Investigate)*:

"On Monday March 28 the Prime Minister announced that Parker could be returned to Cabinet soon once the Companies Office had found him not guilty of what she was now calling mere 'allegations'.

"In a bombshell development today [April 5], National MP Bill English gained an admission from the Prime Minister in Parliament that her office had been liaising directly with the Ministry of Economic Development (which oversees the Companies Office) about the course of its investigation into Parker's affairs.

"The Prime Minister also admitted her statement on March 28 directly followed discussions between her officials and the Ministry of Economic Development about the case."

But what made the story even more intriguing was that on March 28, the Companies Office had not even approached Dunedin businessman Russell Hyslop to seek an interview. How could an official investigation send signals that someone would be acquitted, before all the evidence was in?

But it was the next paragraph in our April 5 Briefing Room story that contains the most damaging evidence of a whitewash:

"Sources in Parliament have told *Investigate* this afternoon that a Companies Office official informed Labour – possibly as early as March 23 – that they would take the line that because Hyslop had gone bankrupt, his ownership of the shares lapsed in favour of the Official Assignee and was never returned to Hyslop. Our sources said the Companies Office had given the Prime Minister's Department a copy of a letter signed by the Official Assignee and sent to David Parker back in 1997, soon after Hyslop's bankruptcy, which would be used to establish that fact. For that reason, according to our sources, the Companies Office might be able to find Parker not guilty because he was not required to seek Hyslop's approval from that point on."

Sound familiar? That's the leak out of Parliament on April 5, and apart from dating the OA's letter two years early (1997 instead of 1999) it exactly matched the outcome of the Companies Office investigation that wasn't released until April 26.

Even more incriminating however was this: the decision of the Companies Office and the Crown solicitor in Auckland was not only common knowledge around Parliament three weeks before it was released and allegedly two weeks before the Crown solicitor wrote his legal opinion, but Russell Hyslop still had not even been interviewed by investigators on the morning we were told what the outcome of the official "investigation" would be.

As a matter of record, *Investigate* was tipped off by our parliamentary sources on the morning of April 5. Russell Hyslop was not interviewed until later that day. And surprise, surprise, the Companies Office lawyers adopted the position right from the outset that we'd been told they would:

"Hyslop, who was not aware of the development in Parliament until the magazine told him after we questioned him tonight, has told *Investigate* both lawyers came at him from the perspective that because he was a bankrupt, his shares had lapsed in favour of the Official Assignee and he had no further rights to them. Hyslop said the two lawyers also had the first shareholders' resolution, which was signed by the Official Assignee, and they told him this proved he was no longer the owner of the shares."

In *Investigate's* opinion, the Companies Office investigation sails dangerously close to conspiracy to pervert the course of justice, particularly as the magic letter detailing the Official Assignee's waiver of an audit was only effective for one year, not six. As an experienced lawyer, David Parker should have known that, the Companies Office lawyers certainly knew it, and the Crown solicitor knew it because he admitted as much.

Section 196(2) of the Companies Act forbids shareholders making waivers for future years, and expressly says all waivers must be renewed, in writing, each year, by law. In other words, the Official Assignee acted "ultra vires" or outside his powers and, in fact, outside the law, by purporting to waive the need for future resolutions.

So that's the first big weakness in the Labour Party/Companies Office get-out-of-jail-free card claim: that the letter, in fact, simply didn't work. It was itself illegal.

This is a very important point. Because it was thoroughly overlooked by the news media as they reported Parker's Lazarus-like resurrection to cabinet. Take the *Herald's* John Armstrong;[53]

"David Parker will surely go down in history as the first politician to resign for something he did not do," wrote Armstrong. "Yesterday's report covering the month long investigation by the Companies Office draws the reader to one inescapable conclusion: the former cabinet minister effectively pleaded guilty to the prime allegation made against him by *Investigate* magazine when the evidence overwhelmingly points to his innocence."

John, if you are reading this, I refer you again to s196(2) of the Companies Act above. Please explain to readers how one letter written in 1999 could purport to cover all future years? This one fact should have been enough to ring alarm bells in every newsroom across the country, but it didn't. Instead,

---

53 *NZ Herald*, 27 April 2006, "Govt relief as report clears ex-minister"

every single outlet was publishing stories suggesting Parker was entirely cleared. *Investigate* staff watched from the sidelines, scratching their heads in bemusement wondering – in the infamous words of Lara Bingle's Tourism Australia ads – "where the bloody hell are ya?"

The much bigger story, of apparent corruption in the Companies Office investigation, was missed by every single newsroom, purely because not one of them had actually read the Companies Act. Let's return, however, to the *Investigate* analysis:

Secondly, if David Parker genuinely believed Hyslop was not a shareholder, why did he continue to file returns for years falsely stating that he was? If the returns were not false because Hyslop didn't have to be consulted because he was no longer a shareholder, then arguably they were false by continuing to list Hyslop as a shareholder.

The issue of "honest belief" is central to prosecuting crime. To prove a crime to a criminal standard, prosecutors have to show not only that a defendant broke the law, but that he did so with dishonest intent. When David Parker was interviewed by media in the wake of the first *Investigate* article, he admitted that that he'd felt his conscience twitch when ticking the box declaring there had been a unanimous resolution of shareholders on a given date. This was one of the reasons he resigned – he felt guilty.

In *Investigate's* view, this action, and his continued listing of Hyslop as a shareholder, are evidence of Parker's real state of mind. He didn't even know about the 1999 letter from the OA's office when first questioned. Parker's actions appear to reek of criminal intent.

Thirdly, there's the controversy over whether the shares controlled by the Official Assignee were formally transferred back to the Company or not. Although there were preliminary discussions, no formal transfer actually took place, and the Companies Office investigation admits as much.

If the transfer of shares did not legally take place, and it is agreed they did not, then by virtue of s78 of the Insolvency Act and s89 of the Companies Act it appears the shares did indeed re-vest in Hyslop by virtue of the company continuing to list him as a shareholder after his discharge from bankruptcy. And that means that Parker should have consulted him, so we're back to square one.

Here's how it works.

To us the issues in a legal sense were very, very simple: If Hyslop's shares had not re-vested in him after his discharge from bankruptcy, then why on earth did the company's annual return and in fact its own share register falsely record that Hyslop was the lawful owner after the bankruptcy discharge?

S89 of the Companies Act specifies that the share register is the final proof of legal title, [author's emphasis] barring a specific declaration by the High Court to the contrary. The share register says Russell Hyslop is, to this day, a one third shareholder. By disclaiming any interest in the shares himself, the OA effectively handed them back to the company. But instead of following proper legal procedure, dotting the i's etc, to either cancel them or sell them under s78(5) of the Insolvency Act, the company chose to list Hyslop as the ongoing shareholder.

Like it or lump it, that is an act of the company that goes towards establishing legal and beneficial ownership.

Crown solicitor Mark Woolford hasn't actually tackled this point in his analysis. From what we can see, it hasn't even occurred to him. He hasn't followed the money – the ownership of the shares – through all the logical steps. Sure, Hyslop was bankrupted and the OA took over. Sure, the OA could have sold them, but didn't. Sure, the OA could have expressly legally transferred the shares back to either Hyslop or QPML, but didn't. In the absence of either of those actions, the Insolvency Act appears to suggest the company becomes the lawful owner again, but according to High Court cases in practice it is usually the former bankrupt who picks up the rights.

Here's what Justice Hammond in the High Court judge ruled in *Re Hobbs*, HC Hamilton, b407/98:

> Sometimes an *Official Assignee* will become legally saddled with property that he or she does not want, it being thought to be worthless.
>
> In practice, commonly a bankrupt or former bankrupt takes over the proprietary rights in property which has been so abandoned by the *Official Assignee*. It was common ground by all counsel before me that this represents the present law..

This High Court ruling[54], and others like it, were not referred to by the Crown solicitor, but clearly are material in determining whether Hyslop is in fact the rightful owner of the shares.

Clearly in the 1993 case, all counsel on both sides agreed that the former bankrupt took up the reins again, and that "this represents the present law".

This in our view is probably reflective of Parker's own understanding in 2000 when Hyslop was discharged as a bankrupt, and would explain why he made no attempt to excise Hyslop from the share registry.

The NZ Court of Appeal has likewise, in *Edmunds Judd v Official Assignee*, agreed that property abandoned by an OA can re-vest in the former bankrupt who owned it, even without the extra help of having the ex-bankrupt's name placed on the annual return as the owner for five years.

Now either of the two scenarios above work for us: either Hyslop could own the shares by virtue of abandonment, as per the High Court opinion, or he could own the shares because legally they became the company's property at

---

54   As a 1998 High Court ruling from a Judge, this judgment trumps the 1993 "Master's ruling" quoted by the Companies Office investigation. A Master is not as highly ranked as a High Court judge. The Crown solicitor quoted two Masters rulings. Those rulings are not only less authoritative, they appear to be wrong.

s78(5) of the Insolvency Act but that the company legally gave them back to Hyslop by continuing to name him in the share registry and in annual returns.

No matter how you look at it, Labour's brightest legal mind remains in a quagmire of his own making. A mere Crown solicitor's opinion does not, of itself, determine ownership of Hyslop's shares. From *Investigate's* perspective, we think Hyslop still owns them, and we think Parker thought that too, right up until the Companies Office investigation told him otherwise.

That was the conclusion *Investigate* magazine reached in June 2006, but now there's even more light we can shed on it: there is reason to believe the August 1999 letter claiming to waive the requirement for future audits may be a forgery. If so, it would turn the circumstances surrounding the investigation of David Parker and his subsequent reinstatement to cabinet into a crime of Watergate proportions, unprecedented in New Zealand parliamentary history.

There appears to be evidence of this, firstly with some major forensic discrepancies in the letter itself. For 1997 and 1998, an Alistair Moore of the Dunedin lawfirm Anderson Lloyd can be seen corresponding with the Official Assignee Rhys Cain to obtain shareholders' resolutions. In his letters there is no mention of David Parker. Instead, Moore says each time, "We act for Queens Park Mews Limited".

Whenever Rhys Cain has responded, on the legal file released as part of the investigation, he has addressed his correspondence to Alistair Moore.

Yet, on this mysterious letter that was so crucial to absolving Parker of responsibility, the letter is addressed direct to Parker, rather than the designated point of contact for all correspondence, Alistair Moore. There is no apparent reason for this.

Secondly, and extremely unusually for a government agency, there is no letterhead. The August 1999 letter is printed on blank paper, even though it purports to be not just an official document but a document of record for the purposes of the Companies Act. In my journalistic career – and indeed my brief time as a civil servant – I have never seen an official government document go out without letterhead. If the letter were a hastily-crafted forgery, the lack of letterhead would be deliberate – government logos change frequently, and in 2006 no 1999 letterhead would have been available. Use of a modern letterhead would have instantly destroyed the document's credibility, so a forger would opt to leave out letterhead entirely.

Thirdly, there is no return address. Normally, even without a printed letterhead, a document purporting to be an official declaration would carry the address of the agency making the declaration. There is nothing. Only Parker's address appears on the document. The sender purports to be the Assignee and therefore shareholder by proxy – but what on his document proves this? Assignee of what? Which department? Which region?

Fourthly, the signature of Assignee Rhys Cain, whilst genuine, differs from

ABSOLUTE POWER

the style he used on a provably genuine document just two weeks earlier, on 29 July 1999, and an earlier one in 1998. Did someone cut and paste Cain's initials onto this new document?

Fifthly, there is no draft of the letter disclosed in Rhys Cain's files as supplied in the document bundle for the Companies Office investigation. Instead what we have is a signed original, and nothing else.

Sixthly, the letter is typed in the Arial font. Of around a dozen letters sent by Rhys Cain during the same period and obtained by Russell Hyslop, all were printed in the Times New Roman font (as in the November 1998 example pictured). An Arial font was however in use in May 2006, when Cain sent Russell Hyslop a letter relating to the Parker case, a week after the Minister had been cleared.

In all cases, incidentally, the letters we've seen from Rhys Cain are all signed in full, and all carried an official letterhead.

Seventh and finally, why on earth is the signed original, addressed to David Parker, found sitting in Companies Office records? How did it get there? Why doesn't Parker have it? There is no mechanism in filing Annual Returns for attaching extra documents. The Companies Office doesn't want extra documents. Shareholders' resolutions are required to be held at the registered office of the company concerned, by law.

Even Prime Minister Helen Clark admits the appearance of the document is a miracle:

"It just so happens that he's very fortunate that the Companies Office has kept the documents which would clear him. I understand in the normal course of events the Companies Office would not normally keep records going back this far, but its dealings with Mr Hyslop have been such that it has kept those documents."

Er, not so fast, Prime Minister. The Companies Office should not even have *had* this letter. It wasn't part of Hyslop's file. It was addressed to David Parker. If the letter is genuine, the Companies Office must explain why it has the letter and not Parker. Where is the "date received" stamp common to official documentation? Where is the covering letter it came with? And why is the letter in the Hyslop file? And if the letter is genuine, why was no draft discovered in Rhys Cain's files?

Forensically, the August 1999 letter simply does not stack up as genuine. It reeks of fraud in my opinion.

Then there are the circumstantial discrepancies with the August 1999 letter. Firstly, it does not comfortably fit with the other correspondence around it.

On 26 July, 1999, Alistair Moore at Anderson Lloyd had written to Cain, enclosing the annual shareholders' resolution and asking him to sign and return it.

On 29 July, 1999, Rhys Cain emailed Alistair Moore with the following message:

10 August 1999

Mr David Parker
C/- Anderson Lloyd
Private Bag 1959
Dunedin

Queens Park Mews Ltd

Please note that the Official Assignee waives the requirement to seek confirmation on a yearly basis that a unanimous resolution was achieved in respect of no Auditor being required for the above company.

I reiterate my offer to sell Mr Hyslop's shares to the other shareholders. If I am unable to sell the shares I will formally disclaim them.

Thanks you for your assistance with this matter.

Rhys Cain
Deputy Assignee

Ministry of **Economic Development**
Manatū Ōhanga

4 May 2006

Mr Russell Hyslop
5/B Aberfeldy Street
Dunedin

Dear Russell,

Firstly, I am not going to enter into discussion or debate with you in respect of your dealings with David Parker, nor am I going to comment on David Parker's actions to you or your actions to him.

Secondly, in respect of the aircon (your description) trans clearly that I will not specifically comment about it as I

Rhys Cain
Official Assignee
Insolvency & Trustee Service
Private Bag 4714, Christchurch

The top letter, allegedly written in Dunedin in 1999, bears a striking resemblance to the style of a 2006 document from the Christchurch Official Assignee's office, except that the top letter has no letterhead and no contact details. All the other letters we have from the OA's Dunedin office, as recently as 2002, all had letterhead and all used a Times New Roman font (see next page) **INSET**: the signature on the 2006 letter.

ABSOLUTE POWER

NEW ZEALAND INSOLVENCY
AND TRUSTEE SERVICE
Level 6, 300 Princes Street
PO Box 407, Dunedin, New Zealand
Telephone 0-3-477 3722
Facsimile 0-3-477 5932

Link Centre, 44 Don Street, Invercargill
Telephone 0-3-214 9191

MINISTR. OF COMMERCE
Te Manatū Tauhokohoko

16 March 1998

Mr R E Hyslop
C/- 28a Moreau Street
Dunedin

Your Affairs

As part of the normal administration of the bankruptcy, an investigation has been carried out into your business involvement with the Parkside Development. At this stage nothing of major concern has been discovered, however, there are some questions to which the Official

---

**V ZEALAND INSOLVENCY
D TRUSTEE SERVICE**

Level 1, 300 Moray Place
P O Box 407, Dunedin, New Zealand
Telephone (03) 955 2500
Facsimile (03) 955 2508

New Zealand Insolvency and Trustee Service

CAUTION: The information contained in this facsimile message is legally privileged and confidential. If the reader of this message is not the intended recipient, you are hereby notified that use, dissemination, distribution or reproduction of this message is prohibited. If you have received this message in error, please notify us immediately and return the original message to us. Thank you.

TO: **Russell Hyslop 4790204**

FROM: **Rhys Cain**

PAGE of: **1 of 1**

DATE: **19/07/02**

SUBJECT: **Section 112, Insolvency Act 1967**

We act for Queens Park Mews Limited, for which you signed the Annual Shareholders Resolution last year on behalf of the Bankrupt.

We enclose this years Resolution and ask that you sign it and return it to us, so that we can then file the company's annual return.

Yours faithfully
ANDERSON LLOYD

Per:

Alistair Moore
Partner

Signed + returned. Rhys 29/7/99.

TOP, A 1998 letter from the Official Assignee, with letterhead, in Times New Roman. MIDDLE, a 2002 fax from Cain to Hyslop. BELOW, A portion of the shareholder's resolution letter for 1999 that had literally just been signed, quite happily, by Cain and returned on 29 July 1999. As you can see, there was no logical reason for Cain to raise the issue again just two weeks later.

"Dear Alistair,

"I have received your letter dated 26 July 1999 regarding the shareholders' resolution for Queens Park Mews Limited. I will sign this and return to you in today's mail. I am in the process of winding up the administration of Mr Hyslop's bankruptcy and would like to dispose of his shares in this company. Please forward a copy of the Annual Accounts for QPM Ltd and ask the other shareholders if they are prepared to make an offer for Mr Hyslop's shares.

Thank you,

Rhys Cain, etc

The intent of this letter is clear enough: Cain was planning to "dispose" of the shares. End of story.

Now, given that Cain had just thrown the ball back into Alistair Moore's court, there is no credible explanation for his purported letter two weeks later, direct to David Parker, of 10 August 1999, claiming to waive the need for future shareholder's resolutions specifically relating to audits. Why would Cain raise this with Parker for the first time ever, instead of his usual contact Alistair Moore? Why would Cain raise it at all?

That last question is more significant than you possibly realize. In his July 29 email, it is clear Cain fully expects to be rid of the shares soon. Therefore, he wouldn't need to send a waiver for future audit resolutions – *he wasn't expecting there to be any!* By the time next August rolled around, the shares were to have been sold long before and Hyslop was scheduled to have already been discharged from bankruptcy.

Cain had only just signed the latest audit return and sent it back on 29 July 1999. The next one wasn't due for a year.

The only *new* information in the 10 August letter is the alleged waiver of future audits – which just happens to be the crucial issue that Parker needs this precise letter for, years later. The other information is almost identical to what Cain had sent two weeks earlier. And as a point of fact, paragraph 2 of the letter contradicts paragraph 1, because if the Assignee sold or disclaimed the shares as set out in para 2, there would not be any future audits for him to waive in para 1.

The letter of 10 August simply doesn't fit the existing documentation chronology. It is as if someone has dummied up a letter recently, to deal with Parker's specific problem in the past. If true, that is not just fraud, but conspiracy to pervert the course of justice.

There is more strong circumstantial evidence to support the forgery line. Among the documents released as part of the Companies Office investigation is a letter to Rhys Cain, from David Parker, dated 27 March 2000. Parker is *not* responding to the August 10 letter supposedly sent to him by Cain, but to the July 29, 1999 email addressed to Alistair Moore.

That email, you'll recall, told Moore that Cain was wanting to sell Hyslop's shares, and to ask whether the other two shareholders (Parker and his father) were interested in buying them. The email also asked for copies of the company accounts to be forwarded to Cain.

David Parker's letter to Cain reads:

"You enquired some time ago as to whether I or my father would be interested in purchasing Russell Hyslop's shares in the above company. I enclose copies of
 1. The accounts for the company to 31 March 1999..."
 ...Thus, as I mentioned on the telephone, there is no doubt that the liabilities of the company exceed its assets and that the shares are of no net value.
 Assuming that the Official Assignee is wishing to dispose of the shares, I enclose a share transfer. Please let me know if you require any further information.
 Yours faithfully...

This is the only documented response, and it is responding to the last known genuine letter – the July 29 email. It is not responding to the alleged letter of August 10. In fact, it is as if the August 10 letter did not even exist.

Another piece of damning circumstantial evidence is the illegality of the letter. Are we to really believe that an experienced Assignee (who now also carries out company liquidations) would be so incompetent as to write a letter that would break the law if it were used? Specifically, s196(2) of the Companies Act makes it very clear that waivers _must_ be renewed in writing _every_ year, and that existing waivers in writing lapse, every year. Rhys Cain could not, and to give him the benefit of the doubt would not, produce a document that breaches the very laws he was required to administer.

The idea that signing a shareholder's resolution waiving an audit once a year was so onerous that it required Rhys Cain to write a letter about it is ridiculous – the Official Assignee's offices up and down the country deal with shares belonging to bankrupts all the time. They deal with annual company returns all the time. It is routine, not special.

It wasn't even difficult – the Anderson Lloyd lawfirm had already drafted the shareholders' resolution and posted it to Cain. All he had to do was sign on the dotted line, lick a stamp and send it back. Which he did, quite happily, the very day he received Anderson Lloyd's request, July 29, 1999.

Even if you don't believe a word I've just written about the document probably being a forgery, you can't escape the inconvenient truth that the letter is legally worthless to Parker. It was valid for one year only, because no shareholder, not even the Official Assignee, can break the legal requirement to _renew_ the waiver in writing each year.

Could it be that the outcome of the Companies Office "investigation" was pre-determined from the moment it began: to clear David Parker at all costs. The fact that *Investigate* magazine knew, and published, the specific outcome of the inquiry on April 5, three weeks before it ended and *two weeks before the*

Crown solicitors were even asked to provide an opinion,[55] suggests this was an inquiry straight out of *Yes Minister.*

The Prime Minister's comments at her post-Cabinet news conference on 26 April 2006 also suggest some kind of dodgy inquiry:

"Mr Parker kept me appraised, and within a relatively short time of his having stood down as a minister, he did advise Dr Cullen and me that there did appear to be information in the Companies Office records which would exonerate him."

If the letter was found in Companies Office records by the inquiry team, as claimed, why did the "independent" inquiry immediately alert Parker, instead of checking the bona-fides of the letter first?

Then there's a strange comment made by Acting Registrar of Companies Adam Feeley the Tuesday that Parker resigned. He told the *Herald* the inquiry would probably only take "days":[56]

"Days, possibly a small number of weeks, certainly not many weeks or months."

The inquiry had barely begun just a couple of hours earlier. How could Feeley already know it would be short?[57] Additionally, he was already publicly playing down the seriousness of it:

"Every day people break the road code...If we fail to stop at a stop sign completely...a traffic officer will say 'Well, technically I could prosecute this person or fine them. I've got to use my judgment about whether any public interest is served by doing that."

In other words, there were very strong signals coming from the Companies Office that it would adopt the police tactic in Paintergate – prosecution is not "in the public interest".

There's one final, very suspicious twist to the mystery letter, and Wellington's *Dominion-Post* referred to it – the speed with which the letter turned up:

"It appears [Parker] found out just hours after quitting his other portfolios [on the Tuesday] that the letter that would exonerate him existed."

Investigate magazine had already been digging around in the Companies Office archives in the lead-up to running the story. Those files were archived in storage vaults. They were not instantly accessible to anyone, not even the Companies Office. Yet this crucial letter, with its inexplicable reference to waiving the requirement for a shareholder audit an entire year away, even though the Official Assignee had just indicated he was going to dispose of the shares (and therefore rid himself of the problem anyway), turns up "just hours" after Parker resigned.

---

55 The Crown solicitor's opinion dated 26 April 2006 states, "Thank you for your instructions of 20 April 2006. You have sought my advice as to whether an offence has been committed..."
56 *NZ Herald*, 22 March 2006, "Parker inquiry likely to be swift"
http://www.nzHerald,co.nz/topic/story.cfm?c_id=109&objectid=10373838
57 It is now obvious that some kind of heads-up went from the Companies Office, probably via Parker, to the Prime Minister, and this was the news that inspired Clark to launch her personal "creep" attack the next day.

Who knew where to search for it? Why was it in the Companies Office, and not at the home of the man it was sent to? There are far too many convenient coincidences involved here, and again, it should have rung alarm bells for every one of my Press Gallery colleagues.

The document trail tells the real story, I believe. It suggests that while the lawfirm Anderson Lloyd was representing Queens Park Mews Limited, the paperwork was kept up to date. When David Parker took over filing the details himself, it appears he didn't bother to contact the Official Assignee for a shareholder's resolution, and assumed that with Hyslop out of bankruptcy the shares had reverted back to him (as was established common law practice according to the High Court ruling we cited).

Parker knew that if he contacted Hyslop, Hyslop would demand an audit. So it was easier not to contact Hyslop. *That* is the reason Parker suffered those twinges of conscience every year. Because he knew he was doing wrong.

That is also the reason he didn't initially remember the August 1999 letter – because it is a fake that he'd never seen before, origin unknown but worthy of an independent investigation.[58]

Maybe Prime Minister Helen Clark painted it during her "artist" phase.

Or perhaps it was a cover-up masterminded by the Companies Office.

Either way, the biggest unreported story of 2006 appears to be a criminal conspiracy involving unnamed officials within either the Ministry for Economic Development or its subsidiary unit the Companies Office, to pervert the course of justice by forging a document to get a high-flying Labour cabinet minister responsible for one of their own portfolios off the hook.[59] The press gallery should be looking sheepish for taking the Prime Minister's word at face value, and not questioning the provenance of the miracle letter enough. Maybe we missed it, but *Investigate* was unable to find one media report where a journalist even went so far as to question the lack of an official letterhead.

As the Prime Minister herself admitted[60], the issue involved very high stakes:

"Those particular allegations, if they had been true, carried a potentially heavy penalty, that penalty being that he would have had to vacate his seat in parliament. In addition, given that he was Attorney-General and must uphold the law, given

58   If Parker had seen that letter, ever, he would not have forgotten it. It was so crucial to his actions in ticking the appropriate box every single year. Years, incidentally, that he told the media he had cut corners on and felt twinges of conscience about. Years where he knew he was in dispute with the shareholder whose name was starting up at him from the company document he was signing. In 2001, he would have easily remembered the letter. Then in 2002 as he sat down to file the return again and tick the same box, he would have remembered the letter. But he didn't. The reference in the Crown Solicitor's report to Parker allegedly recalling it when shown a copy is more likely attributable to adrenalin, tricks of memory and not looking a gift horse in the mouth. Parker qualifies it by saying he recalls it as it is consistent with his actions – which is really a chicken and egg argument. Does he really remember the letter, or does he merely think he remembers the letter because that would explain why he repeatedly ticked the box?
59   If this matter ever ends up in court, a good QC would rip the credibility of that letter, and whoever stands up to defend it, to shreds in about 30 seconds.
60   Post-cabinet news conference, 26 April 2006

that he was a Minister within the Ministry of Economic Development, where the Official Assignee is, and given I understand that personnel who had worked in the energy area, who were working in the Official Assignee area, it didn't seem to be a particularly good idea for a minister to be hanging on while this was being looked at."

So again I say, when the Companies Office (part of Parker's portfolio) miraculously then trots out a letter whose opening line is:

"Please note that the Official Assignee waives the requirement to seek confirmation on a yearly basis that a unanimous resolution was achieved in respect of no Auditor being required for the above company."

My response is, "Yeah, right". It didn't even begin "Dear Mr Parker". Wasting no time getting straight to the point, a random letter allegedly sent out of the blue without even being requested, on August 10, 1999, just happens to focus immediately on the very problem threatening one of Labour's top ministers seven years later, and we're told the Coincidence Fairy is alive and well?

It is remotely possible, in my view a less than one in 1000 chance, that the August 1999 letter is a genuine document from the time period claimed. Personally, I don't believe it is. But even if it is legit, it did not for one second provide David Parker with the exoneration and vindication he claimed, because it only applied for the year to March 2000, not the years through to March 2006. The Crown Solicitor's legal opinion admits that the letter probably was not legally effective, but argues that this was beyond David Parker's competence to know. Parker, however, was a practicing lawyer and consultant to the South Island's largest lawfirm. You would be hard-pressed to find a jury who would believe a senior commercial lawyer did not understand the clear terms of s196(2) of the Companies Act.

And if Parker couldn't recall seeing the letter, let alone acting on it, even while reading the original *Investigate* article taking him right back to the events in question, how on earth can its claimed protections have any bearing on his state of mind?

It's yet another whitewash, in a long list of strange legal decisions surrounding Labour MPs.

TIMELINE:
Monday, March 20, 2006 – *Investigate* magazine publishes company records showing Attorney-General David Parker filed false documents

Parker resigns as Attorney-General, but says other portfolios tolerate a lower standard of behavior, so he refuses to resign his other cabinet positions

Tuesday, March 21, 2006 – Parker tells National Radio's *Morning Report* he has no intention of quitting other portfolios, despite the public backlash that filing false documents is incompatible with any cabinet position

10.45am. After discussions with Prime Minister, Parker quits all remaining portfolios. A Companies Office investigation commences

"Just hours" later, Parker is reportedly told the Companies Office have located a letter that will exonerate him in full. Parker, and possibly the head of the Ministry of Economic Development, passes this information on to Deputy PM Michael Cullen and Helen Clark

Wednesday, 22 March 2006 – Armed in private with news that Parker will be exonerated in full by the Companies Office investigation, Clark decides to go on the offensive in public against *Investigate* magazine and its editor, hoping to dent the magazine's credibility in the eyes of the public

Companies Office acting general manager Adam Feeley tells journalists the 'independent' inquiry may only take "days", and plays down the likelihood of any prosecution

Friday, 24 March 2006 – David Parker reportedly has a copy of the Official Assignee's letter in his hands

Monday, 27 March 2006 – Prime Minister goes on attack at her post-Cabinet news conference, telling the media David Parker could be returned to cabinet, but not disclosing the information that had been leaked to her

Wednesday, 5 April 2006 – 10.00am. *Investigate* magazine is tipped off from within Parliament that the Companies Office "investigation" will find that the shares no longer belonged to Russell Hyslop, so he did not have to be consulted, and secondly that a letter exists from the Official Assignee to David Parker which will clarify his position and exonerate him

2.00pm. The Prime Minister is forced to admit to Parliament that her office received communications from the Companies Office "investigation"

4.00pm. Shareholder Russell Hyslop is finally interviewed by the Companies Office "investigator", who is accompanied by a Ministry of Economic Development official. Both men tell Hyslop as far as they are concerned he did not own the shares, and did not need to be consulted

Thursday, 20 April 2006 – The Companies Office seeks a legal opinion from the Crown solicitors in Auckland

Wednesday, 26 April 2006 – The Companies Office releases the result of its investigation, finding Parker has no case to answer. It also releases the legal opinion from the Crown Solicitor, which states (based on a couple of minor Master's rulings) that Hyslop did not own the shares, and did not need to be consulted. It releases a copy of the letter allegedly sent by Official Assignee Rhys Cain on August 10, 1999, which claims to waive the need for any shareholders' resolutions on audits for future years. The Crown solicitor says that while the letter is legally useless, it would have given Parker comfort that he could file returns without contacting the shareholder

6.00pm. News media describe it as an "emphatic" clearing of Parker

SUMMARY OF PROBLEMS WITH THE LETTER
1. The document, despite purporting to be an official declaration, has no official letterhead.

2. There is no sender's address or contact details on the letter.

3.The document uses a typefont that the Official Assignee was not using in 1999, but was using in 2006 when the issue blew up.

4. Although the letter is signed, and addressed to David Parker, it mysteriously turned up in Companies Office records with no explanation as to how it got there, or why Parker did not have it.

5. The August 10 letter is addressed to David Parker, when all previous letters on the same specific point (including one just two weeks earlier) had been addressed to Alistair Moore at the Anderson Lloyd lawfirm

6. The document does not fit the context of other correspondence between the Official Assignee and lawyers acting for Parker's company. It is also out of sequence. The last genuine letter from Parker's lawyers is dated 26 July 1999, and the last genuine communication from Rhys Cain is dated 29 July. The first genuine communication after the "August 10" letter is dated March 20, 2000, and is a response to Rhys Cain's communication of 29 July. In other words, there is no correspondence leading up to the August letter asking the OA for a waiver, and there is no indication in correspondence afterward that anyone had received or knew about the alleged "August 10" letter.

7. There is no draft of the letter disclosed in Rhys Cain's files released by the Companies Office investigation. It is a signed original but, as explained in point 4, has turned up in Companies Office records, not Parker's.

8. There was no legitimate reason for the Assignee to write the letter in August 1999. He had just licked the stamp and posted the latest resolution, and by the time the next one was due he was fully intending to have sold off the remaining shares. His email of July 29 1999 indicates he was already preparing to sell them.

9. The August 1999 letter contradicts itself. In its first paragraph the Assignee purports to be executing a waiver of all future audit resolutions, even though none were due, while in the second paragraph he says he plans to sell or disclaim the shares, which would remove the need for him to be consulted on audit resolutions anyway.

10. The timing of its "discovery" was nothing short of miraculous

David Parker appears to be a nice guy. I genuinely don't have a problem with him, and I don't believe he was aware that the investigation clearing him was dodgier than Al Capone's tax returns. Nor do I believe, if the magic letter does indeed turn out to be forged, that Parker knew or had any involvement in it. But the issue of filing false documents pales into insignificance compared with the possibility that an entire official investigation into the incident was corrupted by a forged document in a misguided and ultimately criminal display of loyalty by one of the staff in his ministry. It turns the issue from Mickey Mousegate into Watergate in one fell swoop.

If New Zealand had an Independent Commission Against Corruption, I would have raised this issue there. But we don't. We only have the Police, and for reasons already explained, the New Zealand Police Force can no longer be trusted at National Headquarters level. The Government is disbanding the Serious Fraud Office and building a new division inside the Police which will ultimately report to Deputy Commissioner Rob Pope who, for reasons already explained, cannot be trusted.

Welcome to your very own Banana Republic. Without the bananas. Although you're about to meet someone who could possibly paint some.

The Artful Dodger

Sir Humphrey: "You told a lie."
Jim Hacker: "A lie??"
Sir Humphrey: "A lie."
Jim Hacker: "What do you mean a lie?"
Sir Humphrey: "I mean you ... lied. Yes I know, this is a difficult
concept to get across to a politician. You ..... ah yes, you did not tell
the truth." **– Yes Minister**

YOU MAY THINK YOU KNOW the "Paintergate" story, but as you're about to discover, you don't know the half of it. Apart from Helen Clark's signature, there is now good evidence, in my view, to believe that MP Chris Carter – now Education Minister – lied to the police investigation and may have provided false information to the police investigation, which would be a major breach of the Crimes Act, punishable by up to seven years' jail.

For reasons that are probably now becoming apparent, Carter – like Clark – was not challenged or charged, despite police doubts about the conflict of evidence. Nonetheless, regardless of the police whitewash, the public is entitled to know, and the Paintergate incident itself of course is part of a growing mountain of evidence in regards to Clark's honesty. Here's how the whole thing unfolded:

In November 2000, almost a year to the day after winning the 1999 election that brought her to power, Prime Minister Helen Clark attended a charity auction in Auckland to raise money for training unemployed youth in New Zealand via the Prince of Wales Trust.

As the name suggests, the charity's patron is Prince Charles and the event was looking to raise $75,000 to cover job-skills courses for youths. Top-billing on the 57-item auction was reserved for a lithograph copy of an original watercolour painting by Prince Charles of a landscape at his English country estate, Highgrove.

"He's a very keen painter indeed and a watercolourist of some merit," Kerikeri-based artist Sue Dalison-Ryan (a trustee of the charity and friend of Prince Charles) told the *NZ Herald*.[61] The lithograph, one of only ten in existence, carries the Prince's personal signature as artist.

Even before the auction began, a bid of $10,000 was received for the Prince Charles original. So Prime Minister Helen Clark would have been in no doubt that even charity donors like Charles paint their own work, and then sign it.

One can only speculate whether the fine detail of this registered with Clark on that Saturday night in November: the idea that artwork donated to charity auctions and signed by the celebrity artist actually needed to have been painted by the celebrity artist.

Whatever, there is no question that – listening to the auctioneer – Clark must have known. Which makes the set of events that dogged her two years later almost inexplicable.

It was a *Sunday Star-Times* article on 14 April, 2002, that first broke the story of Paintergate. The journalist writing the story is none other than Oskar Alley, who'd previously been led up the garden path by Clark over the Doonegate reports.

"Prime Minister Helen Clark has admitted misleading an animal welfare group by submitting an artist's painting as her own work for a charity auction," wrote Alley. "Clark was asked to do a painting to raise funds for Save Animals from Exploitation (SAFE). Instead her office commissioned an artist to paint it. Clark signed the painting, creating the impression the work was her own.

"Clark is blaming time pressures for her actions, but says while she has 'bent over backwards' for charity groups, she has decided she will no longer contribute art to any fundraising venture. She said she believed the practice had been going on for years, with other ministers from previous governments guilty of the same sort of behaviour.

"Clark is also the minister for arts, culture and heritage.

"The man who bought the painting – Auckland businessman Henry van Dijk – said he was appalled at the deception. The painting had been framed and took pride of place on his living room wall.

" 'She should never have signed that painting if she didn't do it,' van Dijk said. 'I feel I've been misled. It's a rip-off and to me this is like a forgery case.'

"Auckland criminal lawyer Barry Hart said the matter was reprehensible. 'To be perfectly honest it's got all the hallmarks of a conspiracy to defraud under the Crimes Act.'

"SAFE says it feels Clark misled the charity, because it always believed she had painted it herself.

---

61 *NZ Herald*, 2 November 2000, "Prince Charles' art adds colour to youth charity auction"
http://www.nzherald.co.nz/section/1/story.cfm?c_id=1&objectid=157931

"The prime minister was forced to confirm the matter after this newspaper learned of the incident and located the real artist.

"The saga dates back to February 1999, when, as leader of the opposition, Clark agreed to submit a painting. Lauren Fouhy – who describes herself as a 'recreational' artist – confirmed she was asked by a member of Clark's office to paint the art work. She said she was chosen because she had a relative who worked in the office. When confronted Fouhy said: 'I don't want it to turn into anything that's going to cause embarrassment to anyone. Talking to you could backfire on me.' She said she knew it was for Clark to submit to a celebrity auction."

For her part, Helen Clark admitted to the newspaper that she had commissioned an outside artist to do the work because of "time pressures", and urged the public to accept that celebrity items donated to charity auctions were often dodgy:

"Normally these are novelty events where no one takes it very seriously. Let's not get too precious here. The only thing I can be accused of is trying to be helpful when I didn't have time. We thought it was a good cause and something was put in."

In truth, however, Clark was being deliberately disingenuous here. Whilst she stood to make no money from the art forgery, and ostensibly it was for "a good cause", the inherent value in the artwork lay in a buyer's belief that Clark had genuinely painted it. The original buyer may have gone on to sell it later – at a higher price as is usually the case with art – and some other poor sucker would have paid good money for a forgery.

Additionally, as Minister for Arts and Culture, looking to ingratiate herself both with the art world and the wider public, Clark used the publicity from her celebrity art excursion to generate goodwill leading up to the 1999 election. In other words, there was a substantial political pay-off for Clark in passing off Fouhy's work as her own. Especially as it wasn't just a doodle, but a full-blown oil painting.

Certainly, there was extensive news coverage of the original auction in March 1999 and Helen Clark's painting.

"Labour leader [Helen Clark] swapped politics for a paintbrush to produce a painting," the *Sunday Star-Times* had reported in February 1999[62], when Clark's painting went on display at Sky City in the run-up to the auction.

The auction co-ordinator for SAFE, Gary Reese, told journalists he was unsure whether the work was a mountain or a gully.

"It all depends on which way up it goes. I should really call her to ask her what it is."

Perhaps if Reese had done that, Helen Clark would have coughed up to the deception at the time, and told him, "Oh Gary, don't take it so seriously. It's

---

62 *Sunday Star-Times*, Feb 21, 1999, "Celebrities Brush Up On Talents"

just a charity work I had commissioned for your auction. I'll ask the person who painted it what it is supposed to be."

Or she might have given the same answer that the *Sunday Star-Times* later reported when breaking the Paintergate story[63]:

"She said she suspected the painting in her name was 'awful'. 'If I'd done it myself it would have been equally awful if not more awful. But it's really a question of time, it's just not worth it'."

Gary Reese, however, did not phone the Labour leader to ask, and despite the extensive media publicity at the time, Helen Clark did not offer to clear-up any confusion about the artwork.

"I really love it. It's a great painting," enthused Reese to reporters, before heaping more praise on the Labour leader's painting skills. "It's hard for non artists to do something expressive and I think she has been very courageous and it has worked well."

On the day after the celebrity art auction, NZPA noted how popular the celebrity art was:

"Celebrities outsold professional artists at a fundraising auction for an animal welfare group in Auckland. Labour leader Helen Clark chose a mountain scene, actor Sam Neill his back yard and *Shortland Street* star Angela Bloomfield a much-loved cat as subjects for the paintings they donated to Save Animals from Exploitation."

At no point, in the midst of all the beneficial publicity about both her generosity and art skills did Clark once put her hand up and say, "It wasn't me". The Prime Minister was prepared to bask in the media glory, and say nothing.

Little wonder, when confronted with the Prime Minister's deception in 2002, the SAFE charity was unimpressed.

"Helen has been very naughty. I can appreciate that she was busy, but with hindsight it put us in a bad light," noted SAFE spokesman Anthony Terry. "We feel we have been misled." Terry added that SAFE had actually provided Clark with a mounted canvas for her to do the painting on.

As news of the deception broke, Helen Clark's ninth floor Beehive press team rapidly tried to extinguish the fires before they gained sufficient strength to burn her re-election chances that year.

"Putting my name to a painting I did not do was an error of judgement I deeply regret and I apologise," Clark said in a prepared statement that Sunday afternoon.[64] "Politicians are under a lot of pressure to be helpful to a charity, and to my certain knowledge, I am far from being the only MP to have assisted with a contribution of this kind. It should be a salutary lesson to all."

As apologies go, this one didn't seem genuine to the media. Whilst the general consensus was that Clark did indeed "deeply regret" getting caught,

63   *Sunday Star-Times*, Apr 14, 2002, "PM in Fake Painting Row"
64   *NZ Herald*, 14 April 2002, "Prime Minister apologises over fake charity painting"
http://www.nzherald.co.nz/section/1/story.cfm?c_id=1&objectid=1392098

her attempt to blame the practice on other politicians was seen as a slight on other MPs.

"Other politicians have contributed work not done by them," continued Clark. "Over many years, people, staff and families have helped with such things."

If true, this was news to art auctioneers. Dunbar Sloane, with 35 years' experience under his belt, told the *Herald* he had never come across a celebrity painting that was fake. His auction experience included a number of works donated by previous Prime Ministers, which were usually quite simple, as you'd expect.

The reaction from lawyers was equally scathing. Prominent barrister Barry Hart called the Prime Minister's forgery "reprehensible".[65]

"I mean people get charged in criminal courts all the time for being involved in things like this. It's an agreement to commit an illegal act, to deceive the public. If the truth had been known and the auctioneer had said `look it says painted by Helen Clark but, hey, we all know what goes on', nobody would have bid 50c.

"The issue of intent could be said to be missing but there is a conspiracy to defraud here. A person of her standing should know better. The public should not be duped, it's reprehensible all the way through."

Wellington lawyer Robert Lithgow warned the offence could carry a ten year jail term if proven.

National Party leader Bill English accused Clark of trying to smear other politicians in her bid to wangle out of direct responsibility, and called her claims "calculating dishonesty".[66]

Interviewed further by reporters, Paraparaumu-based artist Lauren Fouhy made an admission that further dropped the Prime Minister in it.[67] "I had been asked to do it from her office, so I knew there was a bit of skullduggery involved – I just didn't know how or why or what." Fouhy added that she knew Clark was putting her own name to the painting.

Clark's normally sensitive political antennae seemed to have deserted her, however – perhaps because the crime itself was hers, not another minister's. First, even though by Tuesday she'd been forced to admit signing not one but possibly half a dozen fake artworks (which would negate the momentary "error of judgement" defence), Clark tried to widen her initial circle of blame not just to other MPs but to other celebrities in general.

"I'm not naming names but I'm well aware that this is not a practice that's unique to either MPs or other so-called celebrities," she snapped during Parliamentary questioning.[68]

65 *Sunday Star-Times*, Apr 14, 2002, "PM in Fake Painting Row"
66 *NZ Herald*, 15 April 2002, "PM admits art faking – but says others do it too"
http://www.nzherald.co.nz/section/1/story.cfm?c_id=1&objectid=1392240
67 Ibid
68 *NZ Herald*, 17 April 02, "Paint-flinging PM suffers splashback"
http://www.nzherald.co.nz/section/1/story.cfm?c_id=1&objectid=1442271

"I have never seen such slithery dishonesty from a leader of our country," retorted National's Bill English from across the chamber.

Winston Peters – at that stage still independent of Labour – joined the fray with a warning that Clark was making unsubstantiated claims of criminal fraud against other members of parliament.

"She has implicated every other MP as potential criminals and yet is not prepared now today to say who she is talking about."

The *Herald's* Francesca Mold (now with TVNZ) wrote of the debate[69]:

"It was one of the few times Helen Clark has appeared distinctly uncomfortable in the House. She looked down at her papers and shook her head yesterday as Opposition MPs attacked her credibility and accused her of dishonesty."

By the end of the day, Clark had been forced to make two embarrassing back-downs. One was an admission that she knew of no current MPs who'd provided fake artwork to charities, and the second was having to admit she'd been wrong earlier that day in blaming Act's Rodney Hide for tipping off the media about Paintergate.

International media,[70] less intimidated by Clark than those in NZ who John Roughan would later refer to, compared the actions of the New Zealand Prime Minister to the false claims of people like Ugandan dictator Idi Amin or jailed British author Lord Jeffrey Archer.

The most scathing of the international press, *The Scotsman* in Edinburgh, labeled Clark as one of history's "Great Pretenders".

Back home, however, Clark was trapped in a swamp of scandal largely of her own making. After acting swiftly and decisively against other ministers at the merest whiff of opprobrium, Clark's administration was suddenly a possum in the headlights. National's Bill English kept hammering away, reminding Clark that she was failing to live up to her own standards and that she could not credibly continue as Minister for the Arts after admitting art forgery.

Clark, however, apparently thought she could.

Among the half dozen or so fake artworks credited to the Prime Minister were a doodle of the Beehive, actually drawn by her private secretary Alec McLean, which had sold for $1,300, and a terracotta plant pot purchased at a charity auction by a Dunedin couple, Julie Allen and Jeff Broad, who'd been told Clark had painted the pot, as well as signed it.

"The Prime Minister has no recollection of the pot," confirmed one of Clark's media team, "but she has been informed by staff that she was given a painted pot to sign."

In the United States, of course, "The President has no recollection of the pot" has an entirely different connotation; only in little old New Zealand could such a phrase about one in high office refer to a gardening implement.

---

69 Ibid
70 *NZ Herald*, 17 April 2002, "PM's charity painting hits international stage"
http://www.nzherald.co.nz/section/1/story.cfm?c_id=1&objectid=1442317

"It really was a shocker," wrote the *Herald's* John Roughan.[71] "As my wife remarked after reading the story, it's not as if she simply put her name on somebody else's painting, she actually commissioned it. This was no momentary lapse of judgement; it was a deliberate, patterned response to a request for personal work.

"When a second bogus Helen Clark turned up this week, the Prime Minister admitted she had probably done it half a dozen times. For all that, I don't believe she was, or is, intentionally dishonest. Rather, she honestly believed dishonesty was standard practice," explained Roughan, perhaps overlooking that being dishonest simply because you believe everyone else to be, remains *intentional* dishonesty on your part.

Roughan preferred to think of it as "a deeply ingrained, all pervasive cynicism" about politics.

"Cynicism is dangerous in a Prime Minister, particularly an absolutist leader like this one, not so much because it is unattractive but because it breeds assumptions that can lead the Government astray," he wrote, somewhat prophetically.

But Clark's failure to truly take the rap for art forgery set the scene for her indecisiveness in dealing with errant Ministers in later years. As Roughan figured it, Clark's leadership was compromised by the painting fiasco:

"She has suspended several ministers merely for political embarrassment. Even unproven accusations, she argued, could affect their credibility in their particular portfolio. She would have sacked any other Minister of Arts, Culture and Heritage by now."

If only we'd realized back in mid 2002 just how compromised her leadership really was.

As any watcher of New Zealand politics knows, the Clark administration has never been slow to return fire when under attack. From her office at the top of Mt Doom (the Beehive), deep in the heart of Middle Earth, a very dark Clark turned her withering gaze northward to focus on the small businessman whose decision to go public the previous Sunday had dropped her in it. By the end of the first week, the newspapers were full of innuendo stories[72] emanating from the Clark-supporting art and glitter set about the background and intelligence of the businessman who'd originally purchased the Clark forgery, Henry van Dijk.

"He should be happy to have got Helen's signature for only $1,000," sniped Otago artist Grahame Sydney.

Auckland art dealer Anna Bibby told the *Herald* it was "a myth" that artists had to create their own work, citing grand masters like Michelangelo who had delegated portions of their work to juniors.

---

71 *NZ Herald*, 20 April 2002, "Clark's deception reveals deep, abiding cynicism"
http://www.nzherald.co.nz/section/1/story.cfm?c_id=1&objectid=1592327
72 *NZ Herald*, 20 April 2002, "Art world has little sympathy..."
http://www.nzherald.co.nz/section/1/story.cfm?c_id=1&objectid=1592461

"A lot of art these days is subcontracted out."

Only two problems wrong with Bibby's claim: Helen Clark is no grand master, and if modern artists are regularly passing off other people's work as their own, then people should have grave doubts about purchasing art off a dealer ever again.

Another, Auckland Art Gallery director Chris Saines, cast doubt on van Dijk's claim that he had a Diploma in Art Retailing, because it was mandatory back home in the Netherlands.

"I've never heard of an art retailing diploma in my life," Saines told the *Herald*. "I think he exhibited a remarkable lack of savvy about the way the art market operates for someone who's done a course in art retail."

If the *Herald* had checked, the paper would have found that Diplomas are *indeed* compulsory in the Netherlands, for art retailers and in fact all retailers of all descriptions. Van Dijk was telling the truth. One news story still on the web details how the Dutch government was trying to close down a condom shop in Holland in 1992 because it did not have a Diploma in Condom Retailing:[73]

"Amsterdam officials are threatening to close it down because its owners are not officially qualified to sell condoms. A spokesman for the Economic Affairs Ministry said, 'Under Dutch law, you need a diploma to get a license to go into retail. They haven't got one, so they must get one or close.' But the ministry concedes that there is no formal training for condom sellers in the Netherlands. The shop's owners argue that if there were training, they would be the ones running the course. Ricky Janssen, who co-founded the business, said, 'We've been selling condoms for more than five years'."

If you had to be formally trained in how to sell condoms, how much more training would you need to be allowed to sell art in Holland? It was also unfair for supporters of Labour's arts policies to defend the Prime Minister by suggesting, effectively, "buyer beware". The artworks had been positively sold as authentic works of Helen Clark, and signed by her accordingly. It could not be defended by saying this is the way "the art market operates".

As political writer Vernon Small joked, it was obviously "Helen Clark's post-modernist approach to painting – taking the artist almost totally out of the work!"[74]

Another one doing the rounds was "TAFKAC" – The Artist Formerly Known As Clark – borrowing from a phase that musical giant Prince went through in the early 1990s when he renounced his pop royalty and began referring to himself as The Artist Formerly Known As Prince. He eventually shortened it to just "The Artist", although it is doubtful Helen Clark would now have the confidence to go that far.

---

73 http://www.aegis.org/news/ads/1992/AD922215.html
74 *NZ Herald*, 20 April 2002, "Delegation – it's the art of power"
http://www.nzherald.co.nz/section/1/story.cfm?c_id=1&objectid=1592460

Despite their teasing of Clark, however, most journalists did not really appreciate the bigger issue: dishonesty in an elected official. John Armstrong's commentary illustrates this.

"As so often in politics, it is not the initial indiscretion that does the damage, it is the subsequent mishandling of it…Helen Clark was pinged on Sunday for passing off a painting she signed and submitted for a charity auction as her own work. *That should have been the end of the matter…*" [author's emphasis]

The media, by and large, saw the scandal as entertaining but not job threatening, as if it was just another day at the office, catching the Prime Minister in a fraud.

So what is the international standard? In 2000, London's *Economist* wrote a feature on corruption in European politics, and noted how a signature also killed the future of one high-flying politician:[75]

"Last year a Swedish cabinet minister who might well have become prime minister resigned when it was disclosed that she had bought her child a modest toy on an official credit card."

Hold the phone – that's all it took? A $39.95 child's toy?

The magazine also noted how quickly corruption takes root if voters are prepared to "tolerate dishonesty":

"Italians still have low expectations of their public servants: witness the readiness of many Italians to vote for Silvio Berlusconi, the right-wing opposition's leader, despite his convictions for fraud. His supporters say that the judges who sentenced him were biased – which means, sadly, that Italians either mistrust their courts or tolerate dishonesty among their political leaders."

In a glorious analogy, one business analyst has compared the dishonesty problem to "rats":[76]

"If a farmer never sees a rat, he has only a few. If he seldom sees a rat he probably has a population in excess of 50. If he usually sees rats as he goes about his chores, then he has a severe infestation… As with rats, if you tolerate dishonesty, it's the same as encouraging it."

Since the first "rat" appeared on the New Zealand political scene during the Clark years, how big has the infestation grown?

The voters of Norway, taking that advice to heart, clearly don't tolerate rats in their political environment. In February this year, a Norwegian cabinet minister was forced to resign after being caught lying.[77]

And we shouldn't overlook the British reaction to Prime Minister Tony Blair being interviewed by police:[78]

---

75   *The Economist*, 29 Jan 2000, "Is Europe Corrupt?"
http://lis.ly.gov.tw/npl/hot/sdi/sunshine/benefits/periodical/english/pap7.htm
76   http://contractormag.com/columns/schmitt/cm_column_227/
77   http://www.aftenposten.no/english/local/article2257982.ece
78   *The Daily Mail UK*, 14 December 2006
http://www.dailymail.co.uk/pages/live/articles/news/news.html?in_article_id=422775&in_page_id=1770

ABSOLUTE POWER

Blair first PM to be interviewed by police

By BENEDICT BROGAN, STEPHEN WRIGHT and JANE MERRICK Last updated at 23:27pm on 14th December 2006

The simple fact that a Prime Minister has had to answer formal police questions in an ongoing criminal inquiry is a devastating blow to Mr Blair's reputation

Tony Blair's integrity lay in ruins last night after he became the first serving Prime Minister to be interviewed by the police over a criminal matter.

An unprecedented event in British political history was marked by bitter accusations of Labour spin as Downing Street used every trick in the book to "bury" the news of Mr Blair's final humiliation...

So that's how the rest of the world sees things like this. Now let's return to little old Godzone.

Wrestling with the issue of whether Clark's fake painting was really serious or not, the *Herald's* John Armstrong painted his own picture of Clark's dilemma.[79]

"But how damaging is it? Remember her objection to the boarding-house being built around the corner from her Auckland home, the secret payout to John Yelash to settle his libel suit, and her husband's work-related emails being routed through her office?

"Those sideshows lie forgotten in the vapour-trail of her soaring popularity, largely because most people judged that they were irrelevant to the main act – her running of the country. Given that the painting was signed and sold three years ago, the same logic should apply. But this incident cannot be dismissed quite so easily.

"The ethics of signing a painting you did not do are so black and white that they cannot be fudged – they are something everyone can instantly grasp. There is zero upside for Clark.

"Instead, she is the butt of jokes and comparisons to Idi Amin and Jeffrey Archer.

"Clark has confirmed she is capable of the same sleight of hand as any manipulative politician. But then she has never pretended to be Miss Goody-Two-Shoes. Her tough exterior and ruthless instinct are part of her appeal.

"Neither is there anything pompous about this Prime Minister when compared with the demeanour of Shipley and Jim Bolger.

"If Clark has fallen off her high horse, the horse was not that high. Even so, she is the Prime Minister, and the cavalier use of her signature will come as a shock to those who have placed her on a pedestal since she took office.

"National has sought to exploit the disappointment of voters who feel let

---

79   *NZ Herald*, 20 April 2002, "Paintergate dents Clark's armour"
http://www.nzherald.co.nz/section/1/story.cfm?c_id=1&objectid=1592340

down, particularly as Clark has made a special virtue of rebuilding trust in Government.

"Bill English wants voters to think that because she cannot be trusted with a painting, she can no longer be trusted with a Government. But this ploy falters because he cannot demonstrate a link between a bit of personal naughtiness and any aspect of Government policy."

With respect to Armstrong, that's the Achilles Heel of the NZ media. The issue is not one of proving any actual criminality or dishonesty in regard to a Government policy – it is whether the *potential* for such arises as a result of flawed character. Leaders are supposed to be held to a higher standard than the public, because they have far greater powers. It is a thesis of this book that a continued willingness by the media and the police to let Labour off the hook on a range of misdemeanours has actually seriously weakened New Zealand's democractic process and given the Government a dangerously inflated sense of its own power – witness the Electoral Finance Act.

And when you look, in hindsight, at Armstrong's comment about failing to prove a link between personal "naughtiness" and policy, you see the Pledgecard criminality and the theft of nearly $800,000 by the Labour Party via illegal acts that followed. It may never have happened if, instead of making excuses, the media had pushed for Labour to be accountable to the law. A prosecution for art fraud, and a minor slap on the hand penalty, would have sent a message that, apparently, escaping censure failed to do.

If Helen Clark thought the teasing in regard to Paintergate was tough, however, she was in for a rude shock.

Businessman Henry van Dijk decided to re-auction the painting for charity, this time with a reserve price of $5,000. A *Sunday Star-Times* report on May 5 recorded it had been sold to a secret buyer, and "will be given to someone as a joke present at a party today".

A *Herald* report the next day provided more detail, with auctioneers Webb's insisting that the buyer was planning to give it as a present "because he thinks they're going to find it very, very funny".

The buyer of the painting wasn't laughing for very long, however. That same day, Monday May 6, he was contacted by Webb's, advising that the police were after him. The buyer, you see, was Auckland lawyer Simon Mitchell, a Labour Party functionary and lawyer for Helen Clark's electorate secretary Joan Caulfield. It soon emerged that Mitchell, apparently acting for Caulfield, bought the painting for $5,000 and handed it to Caulfield on that Sunday.

"On 5 May 2002," notes the police report, "Mr Mitchell gave the painting as a gift to Miss Clark's Auckland Executive Assistant, Mrs Joan Caulfield. He had previously discussed the purchase with Mrs Caulfield. Mrs Caulfield sought advice from Miss Clark as to what she might do with the painting. Mrs Caulfield states she was told to do with it as she liked. Miss Clark has not commented on this matter in her statement to Police.

"Mrs Caulfield, acting on her own initiative, destroyed the painting with the assistance of her husband. The painting was partially destroyed on 5 May 2002. The destruction was completed the following morning when the canvas was burned."

What is odd is that the painting was destroyed the very day the police finally decided to obtain it. I say it's odd, because the official police file shows they'd received a formal complaint way back on April 15. It was now May 6, and only *now* did the police try and get the painting. They were too late by hours.

What is also odd is that police appear to have lied to the news media about their investigation. On May 7, the *Herald* stated the police investigation had only begun the day before. By May 9, the *Herald*[80] said "Police confirmed they had received a complaint from an unnamed member of the public in Wellington two weeks ago." In fact, it was nearly four weeks earlier.

"Helen Clark is understood to be angry that police did not warn her they were investigating a complaint into fake artworks signed by her," the article stated. "The normally media-friendly Prime Minister yesterday refused all interviews on the issue after she returned from a trip to Indonesia. A spokesman said Helen Clark first heard about the complaint from the media on Tuesday."

The following morning, Friday May 10, the *Herald* revealed a stunning new twist:[81]

"Prime Minister Helen Clark is understood to have threatened police with legal action unless they release further details of their investigation into the painting saga."

In a functioning democracy, where justice must be seen to be done without fear or favour, the spectre of a Prime Minister at the centre of a criminal investigation threatening police in order to influence the conduct of their inquiry was unprecedented. Not only was Helen Clark the first New Zealand Prime Minister in the modern era to be a suspect in a police investigation, she was also the first to blur the line between the Executive and the independence of a police investigation.

"NZPA understands lawyers acting for the Prime Minister have given police a deadline later today to release details of their investigation," continued the *Herald*. "If they do not, legal action by Miss Clark could ensue."

The details Clark was specifically seeking included the name of the person who'd laid the complaint – as if this was somehow relevant to whether she had forged a painting. Can you imagine the police handing over the name of a complainant to the Mongrel Mob if the Mob threatened legal action?

Compare, for a moment, Clark's actions with those of former Police

80   *NZ Herald*, 9 May 2002, "Police inquiry upsets Clark"
http://www.nzherald.co.nz/section/1/story.cfm?c_id=1&objectid=1844224
81   *NZ Herald*, May 10 2002, "PM has threatened police with legal action"
http://www.nzherald.co.nz/section/1/story.cfm?c_id=1&objectid=1844508

Commissioner Peter Doone two years earlier. His crime was to engage in conversation with his "troops" and in the course of doing so inadvertently distract a rookie cop from doing his job. For that, Doone was railroaded out of office by the Prime Minister herself. Clark's position at the time was that whilst Doone's actions may not have been illegal, they were unwise and arguably a misuse of his authority as a senior figure.

Pot, meet kettle.

The Prime Minister's bullying of the police worked, however. The force rolled over and coughed up the name of the person who'd laid the complaint, Wellington doctor Graham Sharpe. Sharpe had been stung into action after hearing the Prime Minister dismissing the significance of her actions.

Sharpe was not immediately named to the media. Instead, Monday morning's papers reported Police were defending themselves "against allegations that the Prime Minister's Office heavied them into naming the person who complained about her signing other people's paintings."[82]

A police spokeswoman tried to convince the media that giving suspects in criminal investigations access to the names and addresses of complainants was not just routine, but "required".

"The police spokeswoman said the Privacy Act required that a person who had a complaint made against them was entitled to know who had made it. However, if the safety of a complainant was at risk an officer might in exceptional circumstances look at holding that information back".

Naturally, we checked the Privacy Act to see if the Police Headquarters claim was true, or just a little white lie to get the journalists off their tails. There is no "requirement" for police to cough up anything. Instead, the Privacy Act specifically allows police to refuse to release personal information where it might

1. ... prejudice the maintenance of the law, including the prevention, investigation, and detection of offences, and the right to a fair trial; or

2. (d) To endanger the safety of any individual.

As an author and journalist, I am personally well-acquainted with police refusing to hand over information on the grounds that it might prejudice an ongoing investigation. Whilst there is no doubt that an accused person has a right to face their accuser in court, there's a lot of investigative water that must travel under the bridge before that scenario arises. And handing over the names and addresses of complainants to suspects in the early stages of a police investigation is – in my experience – unheard of.

The Monday papers only identified the complainant as "reportedly from Lyall Bay (Wellington), a member of the public who is unknown to Ms Clark."[83]

By Tuesday, however, Sharpe's name was all over the broadcast media and on Wednesday morning the *Herald* had an interview with him.[84]

82 *Christchurch Press*, 13 May 2002, "Police defend fake art naming"
83 Ibid
84 *NZ Herald*, 15 May 2002, "Frivolous signing spurred complaint about painting"

"Wellington doctor Graham Sharpe says he complained to police about Prime Minister Helen Clark because she was 'frivolous' about signing art she did not paint," began the *Herald* story.

Embarrassingly for Clark, Dr Sharpe was no National Party stooge but a former member of the Labour Party in the 1970s, at the same time Clark was cutting her political teeth. Sharpe told the paper it was an issue of integrity.

"I firmly believe that if another member of the public had acted in a similar way they would be in a degree of trouble."

Thursday May 16 brought with it fresh allegations of foul play, this time with somebody complaining to the Serious Fraud Office about a Fay Richwhite donation to National in 1996.[85] As red herrings go, it was a desperate one, but the tit-for-tat use of law enforcement agencies highlighted the ridiculousness of the police decision to name Dr Sharpe, because of the precedent it had set.

"Where and when," asked the *Herald* editorial[86] that morning, "did leading politicians acquire this assumption that they have a right to know their accusers in a criminal investigation? Twice in recent weeks we have heard political panjandrums loftily lambasting the law enforcement authorities for failing to identify a complainant.

"First it was the Prime Minister, who demanded to know the name of person who had the temerity to complain to the police about her passing off a painting as her own for a charity auction. Now it is the president of the National Party, who has written to the Serious Fraud Office insisting it disclose the identity of the complainant behind its investigation of the handling of a Fay Richwhite contribution to its 1996 election campaign.

"Since the police duly gave the name to the Helen Clark's lawyer, Michelle Boag argues she has a right to know National's accuser. If the matter ever comes to a criminal charge against anyone, that person would certainly have a right to know his or her accuser. But at this stage of an investigation there is no such right. And the police should have said so, right at the beginning, to the Prime Minister and her lawyer.

"The reason for not identifying the complainant during an investigation should be obvious. People who witness suspicious behaviour might not approach law enforcement agencies if their identity was likely to be made known to those they are reporting. And many investigations could be stymied if those under investigation knew who had made trouble for them."

The newspaper was also concerned to discover that the Serious Fraud Office had earlier discussed its decision to investigate the National Party with Labour's Attorney-General Margaret Wilson.

"It seems decidedly unhealthy that the Serious Fraud Office should have

http://www.nzherald.co.nz/section/1/story.cfm?c_id=1&objectid=1845294
85 See the chapter, "Labour's Mafia Connections" to see just how hypocritical Labour was being on the Fay Richwhite issue
86 *NZ Herald*, 16 May 2002, "Editorial: Political rivals not above the law"
http://www.nzherald.co.nz/section/1/story.cfm?c_id=1&objectid=1942411

alerted the Attorney-General, Margaret Wilson, to the inquiries it has begun into the National Party's affairs. Yesterday the director of the office told a parliamentary committee that he also approached the heads of the State Services Commission and the Prime Minister's Office seeking advice and guidance on this case.

"It is for the police and other enforcement agencies to decide whether to follow up any complaint. And they must not be discouraged from doing so by an obligation to inform the subject when that person happens to be in politics. Nor should they routinely need to inform the Prime Minister or the Attorney-General when they are about to conduct a politically sensitive inquiry. Yet that seems to be the practice. It is hard to see a need for it."

Although the *Herald* has recently rediscovered its fishing tackle, back in 2002 its journalists and editor were too prepared to give the Prime Minister the benefit of the doubt. The above editorial notwithstanding, collectively the NZ media failed to grasp that the events surrounding Paintergate and the other scandals were not minor, "out of character" slip-ups, but a rare piercing of the corporate veil of the Government allowing us to glimpse, even if only briefly, major, institutionalized dishonesty and – arguably – full blown corruption. If only the media had realized what they were dealing with, and reined the Government in even then, the Electoral Finance Act of 2008 would never have been allowed to come to pass.

In this respect – the deliberate, intentional dishonesty – the police investigation into Clark's artwork is damning, and provides exactly the evidence of corruption within the Government I'm talking about.

But what of Education Minister Chris Carter, where does he fit into all of this?

In February or March 2001, Ponsonby Primary School instigated what it called "The Maggi Two-minute Doodle" – a celebrity art competition to raise money for the school. One of the parents, Chris Money, was friendly with Labour MP Chris Carter and asked him if Helen Clark could provide a quick doodle for the school to auction. Carter agreed to arrange it.

"A pack containing a piece of paper, a pen and instructions on what was required was given to Mr Carter to pass on to Miss Clark," explains the police report on the matter.

"The original pack was apparently lost after it was given to Miss Clark at a caucus meeting in Wellington. A second piece of paper and pen were delivered to Miss Clark's office. In due course a sketch of the Beehive, signed by Miss Clark, was delivered through the mail to Mr Money. There was no accompanying correspondence with the drawing.

"The item was subsequently featured in media coverage of the auction as a work completed by Miss Clark. Again there appears to have been no rebuttal from Miss Clark's office.

"On 28 June 2001 this item was auctioned as lot 6 of 42 items included in the live auction. 86 other items were sold by silent auction. The Clark item fetched $1,300 and was purchased by Mr and Mrs [name deleted by police]. Mr Money rang Mr Carter that night, advised him of the result, and asked him to pass on his thanks to Miss Clark. Mr Carter apparently agreed to do so, commenting at the time that Miss Clark 'will be amused'. Cellphone records on Mr Money's account verify a call to Mr Carter. Mr Carter cannot recall this call, or the conversation referred to by Mr Money," says the police report.

There is strong evidence in my view that Labour's Chris Carter was lying to police, and we'll come to that shortly. But Money recalled Carter's bizarre comment that Clark "will be amused" about the fact that her "doodle" sold for $1,300. Were Clark and Carter getting some kind of perverse kick out of defrauding suckers who purchased the Prime Minister's charity items? Most ordinary people would feel deeply ashamed about passing someone else's work off as their own, especially if they knew that other ordinary people were paying out hard-earned cash to buy those items.

Now, here's where the cover-up begins. According to the police report, one of Clark's private secretaries, Alec McLean, took it upon himself to do a quick sketch of the Beehive on Helen Clark's behalf, because "the item had remained unattended in his office for some days. He said he completed the drawing without Miss Clark's knowledge or consent. Mr McLean gave the completed drawing to Miss Clark to sign, apparently without any discussion. Mr McLean states that he told Mr Carter or his Secretary about the process used to manufacture this drawing."

This little story is important, because someone in this scenario is lying. You've just seen McLean tell police he drew the item because the sketch-pad and pen had been hanging around "unattended in his office for some days". McLean says he drew it, and then he gave it to Clark to sign.

Well, how do we then treat the testimony of Chris Carter's secretary Serge Sablyak?

"Mr Carter's secretary, Serge Sablyak, has stated that he took a piece of paper and a pen to Miss Clark's office, and returned within thirty minutes to uplift a drawing. He states that he had no knowledge of how the drawing was completed."

Sablyak and McLean cannot both be telling the truth. Either the sketch had been hanging around for days on McLean's desk in the Prime Minister's office, or it had been sitting on Sablyak's desk in Chris Carter's office and only visited Helen Clark's office for "thirty minutes". It could not have been in both places. Stunningly, the police failed to more deeply investigate the blatant inconsistencies in the stories they were collecting from within the Beehive.

Sablyak claims that after picking the drawing up from Clark's office (where'd he'd taken it only half an hour after earlier for the very first time), that he then personally "delivered the drawing to Mr Carter and then overheard a telephone conversation between Mr Carter and someone called

Chris. He states that in that call Mr Carter said Miss Clark had been too busy and a staff member had done it. Mr Sablyak assumed that call was to Chris Money."

Major lie number two: Sablyak had just told police a moment earlier that he delivered the clean sheet of paper to Clark's office, and took away the completed drawing half an hour later. Specifically, he told police that he had "no knowledge" of how the drawing was completed.

Yet he is now telling police that as soon as he got back to the office and gave the drawing to his boss, Chris Carter, that he overheard Carter then make a phone call explaining that someone else had drawn the picture, not Helen Clark. Further, we are supposed to believe that Carter himself was so exercised by this that he felt the immediate need to get on the phone to Chris Money from Ponsonby Primary and confess that whilst the picture had been done, it was not a Helen Clark original.

Carter, who is now New Zealand's Education Minister, appears to be an inveterate liar, judging by his confused and incriminating statements to police:

"Mr Carter states that he gave the initial pack with materials and the request for the doodle to Miss Clark at a caucus meeting. He followed this up with a series of telephone calls to Mr McLean. He was told at some point that Mr McLean could not find the pack. He confirms that he and his secretary then purchased paper and a pen, and that these were delivered to Mr McLean.

"Mr Carter's initial recollection was that he followed this up with a telephone call to Mr McLean the following day, and later that day received a call to say the item was complete. When Mr Sablyak's timings for completion of the item were put to him Mr Carter agreed they might be correct, however his recollection was that the completion of the drawing took place over a time span of a day.

"Mr Carter confirms Mr Sablyak's assumption, stating that he then made a telephone call to Mr Money asking where the doodle should be sent and telling Mr Money how the item was completed. He states that he made a joke of it. Mr Carter initially stated that he said, "Alec was a lousy artist". Later in his statement he said that he told Mr Money that a member of Miss Clark's staff had done the drawing, that "he" was a lousy artist, but did not identify who this person was to Mr Money."

If cabinet minister Chris Carter was telling the truth, surely his friend Chris Money at Ponsonby Primary would back up his version of events? Apparently not:

"Mr Money accepts that there was a call to obtain instructions on where to send the item," notes the police report. "He disputes any conversation about someone other than Miss Clark completing the drawing. He is adamant he would have recalled these comments, particularly if they were expressed in the manner described by Mr Carter.

"He further states that if he had been aware of the true manner in which the drawing had been completed he would not have sent it on to the school, but would instead have retained it himself. Mrs Money, who took the drawing to the school said that she would not have done so if she had known it was completed by anyone other than Miss Clark."

The Moneys, like most reasonable people, would have been horrified at the idea of knowingly being part of a fraud. The only reasonable conclusion, in my view, is that MPs and staff within the Labour Government were prepared to give perjured evidence in order to protect their positions.

The question for New Zealand voters is, should a political party that is prepared to lie not just to the public but also to a police investigation be trusted to run the country?

The police report paints an extremely grim picture of the Minister of Education's ethics:

"Mr Carter states that he rang the school on 15 April 2002 [as news began to break of Paintergate] in his role as a Party Whip, to discuss this item. Mr Carter states that the purpose of this call was to determine the price the item sold for, and the views of the school. He states that the principal, Mrs Malcolm, expressed the view that she thought a' number of the items offered for sale were not completed by the person who signed them. His recollection of this conversation is substantially different from that of Mrs Malcolm. Mrs Malcolm is adamant that she made no comments to that effect and points out that the one item the school knew had not been completed by the person associated with it had been given away for nothing.

"She recalls Mr Carter asking how the school would feel about Miss Clark releasing information that the doodle had been completed by someone else and signed by her. Mrs Malcolm states that her response was that she would be disappointed, or words to that effect, but that the school was happy to have paid for their new hall. Mr Carter recalls the latter comment but not the former.

"Mr Carter also states that he rang the school on a second occasion. He states that either then, or in the earlier conversation, he and Mrs Malcolm discussed how upset the purchasers were with the media comments. He also states that they discussed that Mr Money was concerned about how these events reflected on him in the school community.

"Mrs Malcolm has no recollection of a second call from Mr Carter and nor has her secretary. The conversation described by Mr Carter could not have taken place during the call Mrs Malcolm does recollect, as there had been no media interest at that stage.

"On the 15 April 2002 Mr Carter also rang Mr Money. He states that he rang him on this occasion to find the amount paid for the doodle at auction. Mr Money and his wife recall a conversation about the price of the item during a call with Mr Carter. They state that could have been on 15 April 2002 but cannot recall where in the sequence of calls this occurred.

"Mr Money states that he received a call about 3.00 p.m. on 15 April 2002 from Mr Carter, in. which Mr Carter asserted that he had advised the school, through Mr Money, that Miss Clark had only signed the work in the auction. Mr Money states that he told Mr Carter he would discuss the issue with Mrs Malcolm and call him back, without at that point agreeing or disagreeing with Mr Carter's assertion.

"Mr Money states he then rang Mr Carter back. His initial recollection was that this call was about 3.30 p.m. on 15 April 2002. This second call appears to be the call recorded on Mr Money's telephone records at 18:52 hrs on 15 April 2002. During this conversation Mr Money states that he told Mr Carter that he had no prior knowledge of the fact that Miss Clark had not drawn the doodle. This allegedly led to a discussion described by Mr Carter as "robust", and by Mr Money as "heated".

"Mr Carter's recollection was' that both these calls took place on 16 April 2002 with the later call being received on his cell phone in the evening as he walked home from Parliament.

"Mr Carter was asked to provide telephone records relevant to the enquiry to help clarify the timings of these calls. He declined access to the records on the basis that they were confidential."

Carter, of course, was only a junior whip at the time (although a close ally of Clark's), but has subsequently been promoted extensively. He appears on the face of the evidence uncovered by police to have been as dishonest as David Benson-Pope – perhaps worse, as he shows a clear willingness to lie on oath (the inevitable consequence of his actions in lying to a police investigation).

It is surprising that police chose not to pursue Carter or other Beehive staff for conspiracy to pervert the course of justice. But then, there are a lot of surprising things about all the police investigations into Labour MPs.

Why, for example, had it taken so long for police to get their backsides in gear after receiving the original complaint on April 15?

"On receipt of the complaint," says the police report, "background material about the reported incidents was obtained. That process was accompanied by a formal approach to the Solicitor General to advise on constitutional matters that might arise in any enquiry involving Miss Clerk. (sic)"

This is an important point. One of the first steps from police was to get some early legal advice from the Solicitor-General's office. But the next paragraph shows the Solicitor-General was apparently very slow replying, and in fact was so late in doing so that Labour party officials had enough time to purchase the painting and destroy it.

"*Prior* to that [Solicitor-General's] advice being received," says the police report, "media reports suggested that an unknown purchaser had bought the SAFE painting for the purpose of destruction. Those media comments were attributed to the vendor Mr H van Dijk, At that point police enquiries were made in Auckland to locate the painting."

From reading between the lines of the police report and published news stories at the time, it appears as though the Solicitor-General's office tried to run interference in Helen Clark's favour. Firstly, as already noted, the Crown Law Office delay in responding had effectively left the police inquiry in limbo. That's why police had failed to secure the painting. Secondly, the Crown Law Office appears to have finally come back with some kind of draft opinion that let Clark off the hook on the basis that her signature was an "authorization", rather than a claim of authorship:

"Early legal advice," noted the police report, "suggested a…view that Miss Clark, by signing the document, "authorised the making thereof', and that the document may not have therefore constituted a false document.

"According to this view of the law a signature on a canvas or parchment is what turns a painting or drawing into a "document", and in this case the penned signatures are clearly genuine. This view suggests the authorisation of the painting can occur after the event through adoption of the work by the person signing it."

The precise origin of this early advice is not specified in the police report, we are merely told of its existence. But there is reason to believe the police can only have been referring to Crown Law office "early legal advice", because that's who police were dealing with in the early stages, and that particular legal defence they referred to had never been run in public. We know the police asked Crown Law for advice. It's a safe bet this was it.

But there's another huge constitutional questionmark here: the police had not asked Crown Law for an opinion on whether Clark had acted illegally or not. How could they? Their investigation had not even begun. Instead, they *had* asked for an opinion on the constitutionality of investigating the Prime Minister. So it appears that this "early legal advice" emanating from Crown Law and suggesting a get out of jail free card for Clark was generated at the whim of Crown Law, and not a police request.

Who, within Crown Law, had decided to give advice to police that Clark might be innocent, and what was their motivation for doing so? Crown Law is supposed to make decisions based on the facts presented in a police file. They had not even seen the police file. They had no idea how strong the evidence against Clark was.

But there is something even more sinister: Clark – the woman at the centre of the police investigation, may have known of this Crown Law office advice – or at least her office did. Questioned by the media soon after news of the police investigation initially broke, a spokesman for the Prime Minister told journalists a Crown Law office opinion had cleared Clark.

For more than a week various media outlets carried the story that a leaked Crown Law report was stating Clark had no case to answer. The main culprits appear to have been wet-behind-the-ears radio journalists who hadn't even paused to consider the impossibility of Crown Law providing a proper opinion before the investigation had even completed.

Regardless, the media and the Prime Minister's media spokesman were spinning the yarn for all it was worth.

Someone, somewhere, with a bucketload more braincells than either the journalists involved or the PM's spokesman, realized however that any suggestion of a pre-emptive Crown Law opinion clearing Clark was an incredibly bad look, and Crown Law then told journalists on Friday May 17 that the story was not true – there was no such legal opinion in existence.[87]

"The Crown Law Office said today it hadn't tendered advice on whether Prime Minister Helen Clark had committed fraud by signing the picture she didn't paint – despite earlier reports an opinion existed," wrote the *Evening Post's* Ruth Berry.

"There were several media reports during the week alleging Crown Law had provided an opinion that Miss Clark should not be prosecuted as she had not committed fraud. One said police had been advised of that by Crown Law and another said copies of the report had been leaked to the media.

"A spokesman for Miss Clark today initially confirmed to *The Evening Post* that the report existed, but said Miss Clark's office didn't have one."

Now, just for a moment put aside all the denials, because here is one undeniable fact: we know from the final police report when the investigation concluded that "early legal advice" did indeed clear Clark. We know this as an absolute fact. We know this "early legal advice" had not been provided to police by the time the painting was destroyed on Monday May 6th, because the police report says so. But we do know that on Friday May 10th details of an alleged Crown Law office opinion clearing Clark were leaked to the news media. These are indisputable facts.

All of which makes the following series of published denials even more questionable.

First of all, Police National Headquarters media liaison officer Jon Neilson told journalists police had neither asked for nor been provided with any advice or opinion from Crown Law over "Paintergate".[88]

This was either a blatant fundamental untruth from Neilson, or he simply wasn't in the loop and should never have made the comment to reporters. Because, for the record, here's what police later disclosed in their official report on Paintergate:

"On receipt of the complaint [on April 15] background material about the reported incidents was obtained. That process was accompanied by a formal approach to the Solicitor General to advise on constitutional matters that might arise in any enquiry involving Miss Clerk. [sic]"

What part of "formal approach to the Solicitor-General" did Neilson evidently not understand? Clearly, police had "asked for" advice from Crown Law. And received it.

---

87 *Evening Post*, 17 May 2002, "Crown Law did not clear Clark"
88 Ibid

Secondly, there is this denial from Crown Law itself:

"We haven't done an opinion on the complaint over the prime minister's paintings," a Crown Law spokeswoman told journalists on 17 May.[89] But her statement was not strictly true. As police would later confirm, by now they had "early legal advice" exonerating Clark. The police must also have received an answer to their "formal approach" to the Solicitor-General regarding the constitutionality of investigating the PM, because by this time they were locked in dialogue with Clark's legal counsel.

For those reasons alone, the "official" Crown Law office line being spun to the news media was utterly misleading.

So what about this "early legal advice" – did it actually stack up? The police soon discovered it didn't, for obvious and time-honoured reasons:

"A closer analysis of the issues has established that this early advice is not supported in law. This latter view supports the proposition that the person signing a painting is deemed to be the artist. Where the person who signs the painting did not complete the body of the painting, the painting becomes a false document."

It's not rocket science, really.

Clark's "painting" complete with her signature on the back and the front of the picture, went on display at Sky City for ten days prior to the charity auction. As police themselves noted, there was extensive media interest including newspaper stories and coverage on both TV1 and TV3.

"The pre-event publicity by SAFE specifically referred to the fact that Miss Clark had completed the work herself.

"There does not appear to have been any rebuttal of this information by Miss Clark or anyone from her office. Miss Clark states that she has no recollection of any media reports about the charity auction and that reports of this kind would not normally have been included in the media summaries prepared by her staff while she was the Leader of the Opposition."

Again, a credibility issue arises here. In her "authorized" biography, *Helen*, by Brian Edwards, Clark tells how desperate she was for media attention in the lead-up to the 1999 election:

"In opposition you have to work very hard for media coverage…we had to work to be noticed."[90]

It beggars belief that having gone to the trouble of generating such positive publicity, Clark ignored it. Additionally, Clark trades on a one-on-one relationship with journalists: she stays across issues, knows what journalists have written about her, and is not afraid to correct them. Even her colleagues call her a "control freak".[91] The idea that Clark could be in the dark is ludicrous, so ludicrous that in my view (as one who used to provide a cabinet

89 *The Dominion*, 18 May 2002, "Paintergate: Crown Law had no opinion"
90 *Helen: Portrait of a Prime Minister*, by Brian Edwards, Exisle, 2001. p335
91 Ibid, p342

minister with exactly these kind of briefings), Clark must have deliberately lied to police.

When the story finally broke that the painting was a fake, Clark – the Minister for Arts and Culture – indicated to police in a statement that she was unaware passing off someone else's work as your own was illegal:

"Miss Clark states that she sent a personal cheque to the person reported to have obtained the painting without being aware that there was any suggestion of a breach of the law."

Oh really? As a university lecturer before she became a politician, how would Clark have viewed a student who passed off another's thesis as his own? Additionally, Clark could not have failed to read the front page story in the *Sunday Star-Times* several days before she posted van Dijk his cheque, and in particular these paragraphs:[92]

" 'She should never have signed that painting if she didn't do it,' van Dijk said. 'I feel I've been misled. It's a rip-off and to me this is like a forgery case.'

"Auckland criminal lawyer Barry Hart said the matter was reprehensible. 'To be perfectly honest it's got all the hallmarks of a conspiracy to defraud under the Crimes Act.' "

So the Prime Minister told police she sent the cheque to van Dijk without being aware there was even a "suggestion" of a breach in the law?

The police report indicates Clark instead had a very novel reason for paying Henry van Dijk back the $1,000 he'd spent purchasing her "painting" in the first place:

"She states she sent the cheque because it was unacceptable to her that anyone should feel aggrieved by her conduct."

On that basis, the 71% of New Zealanders who do not prefer Clark as Prime Minister should presumably expect to see cheques in the mail sometime soon.

The police report also reveals criminal intent – *mens rea* – in a conspiracy to defraud involving Dawn Bush – a staff member in Clark's office – in cahoots with the artist Lauren Fouhy and Clark herself:

"It seems compelling, on an objective view of the evidence, that there was an intention for the completed painting to be acted upon as if it were genuine," says the police report.

"Prior to the painting being completed Mrs Fouhy states she was instructed to make it look amateurish. There is some dispute about how that instruction came about. Mrs Bush states that she did not give that instruction but when told the painting would not be very professional she confirmed that it "would not want to be professional, amateur would be fine". This tends to suggest an intention, at least by Mrs Bush, to pass the work off as an amateur effort by Miss Clark.

"The act of signing the painting is further evidence that it would be passed off as a work completed by Miss Clark and joins Miss Clark to the

92 *Sunday Star-Times*, Apr 14, 2002, "PM in Fake Painting Row"

offence. Miss Clark does not recall signing the painting. She states she has no recollection of any discussion or instructions about the painting. She further states she' did not recognise that signing a painting might have a different legal effect to signing other items.

"She said had she known she would not have signed the painting. She states that her error was to fail to recognise the different character of this matter."

Again, the Prime Minister has a serious credibility issue here. Not just was there an original lie (the painting fraud), but now Clark was piling further deceit on top by asking police and voters to believe she didn't know about plagiarism.

The signature might have happened back when she was leader of the opposition, but Clark's ongoing dishonesty with police and the public was happening in the here and now, whilst she was Prime Minister of New Zealand.

The findings of the police report, after weighing up the various excuses, are damning:

"Despite the intention to assist a charity, and the explanation that those involved did not recognise the effect of their actions, it is considered that those actions amount to forgery.

"By signing the painting Miss Clark, who had prior knowledge of the request for the painting, has created the false document with knowledge of the use to which it will be put. The discussion at the time the document was signed, as reported by Mrs Bush and Miss Leicester, appears to be evidence of this knowledge. It is therefore argued that knowledge of the falsity of the document and an intention that it should be passed off as genuine, were present at the point that the painting became a document.

"The evidence establishes that Mrs Bush has then passed the painting on to SAFE as an original work completed by Helen Clark. That was what the organisers had requested and she took no action to dissuade Miss [name of SAFE employee deleted by police] from that view when she advised her that the painting was on its way.

"There was widespread media coverage including items on TV1 and TV3. Media commentary was quite specific about the alleged origin of the painting. Miss Clark states that she has no recollection of any media reports about this matter.. She states that such reports would not normally have been brought to her attention by way of media summaries prepared by her staff at that time. Mrs Bush states that she had no knowledge of any media commentary prior to the auction. It is however considered unlikely that Miss Clark or her staff were unaware of this coverage. There appears to have been no action taken to set the [record straight].

"The organiser's brochure promoting the auction states that all works are the original contributions of the individual personalities. The SAFE staff members involved in the promotion are adamant that they were given to understand that the work was completed by Miss Clark. The auctioneer also shared this view.

"On the face of it, despite their assertions that they were trying to help a charity, there is evidence that Miss Clark and her staff member, Mrs Bush are liable for the offence of forgery."

The report also found evidence of a clear intention to defraud:

"On an objective view of the facts it is suggested that all parties must have been aware that attaching Miss Clark's signature to the work would increase the value of that work. It is also argued that those involved must have known that potential purchasers would be deceived into believing the work was completed by Miss Clark, and would therefore pay an inflated price for the item. Indeed it appears to have been the intention of Mrs Bush and Miss Clark that the work be passed off as Miss Clark's.

"It can also be argued that the apparent absence of any rebuttal of what must have been widely known media reports describing the painting as Miss Clark's own work supports this interpretation of the facts.

"Potentially this reaches the threshold of prima facie evidence necessary to establish a fraudulent intention."

The police stopped short of making such a finding, however, after taking into account the intention to help the charities and the remorse apparently shown by some of Clark's staff, as well as the testimony of Labour MP Chris Carter.

But given that Carter appears to have lied to police, one wonders whether the force was too hasty to give the benefit of the doubt. Additionally, not enough weight was placed by police on the positive PR benefits for the Prime Minister in being seen to assist charities – especially whilst she was leader of the Opposition in 1999 and, by her own admission, desperate for positive media coverage. Those who argue that Clark acted for pure, charitable motives obviously don't know many politicians.

The *Herald's* John Roughan, after watching an Australian TV journalist politely but firmly interrogate the Prime Minister about Paintergate, argued the media let her off too lightly in 2002. You can make your own call on that.

LABOUR'S POLITICAL STRATEGY: SUMMARY

Attack the messenger: Labour's tried and true pattern of attacking the complainant is in evidence in this case, with Henry van Dijk targeted as a troublemaker.

The "outrage" defence: Clark attempted to get media and her supporters onside by suggesting her critics were engaged in "gutter politics"

The "Winebox" defence: Repeated appeals to "I cannot recall", or just plain silence on key points

Hypocrisy factor: *"A misdemeanor on that scale should merit dismissal from all portfolios"* – Helen Clark commenting on then Immigration Minister Tuariki Delamere's alleged short-cut of process to help 21 immigrants.[93] Clark's harsh

---

93 *NZ Herald*, 25 November 1999, "Clark jumps on 'weak' gesture"

judgment was merely over the morality involved; unlike Clark, Delamere was not being accused of a crime.

LEGAL MAIN POINTS: SUMMARY
"People have got to know whether or not their President is a crook. Well, I'm not a crook!" – US President Richard Nixon, shortly before his resignation for lying about the Watergate cover-up[94]

Forgery: Clark was found to have reached a prima facie threshold of forgery. In legal terms, prima facie means literally "on the face of the evidence", and barring a particularly creative defence it is hard to see any legal argument that could negate the facts of the matter. The real thrust of Clark's defence of her actions was one of mitigation, by de-emphasising the personal gain and over-emphasising the altruistic motive. This might be relevant to sentencing and possible discharge without a formal conviction being entered, but it would not be relevant to the *fact* of a crime of forgery being committed.

Intention to defraud: There is a mistaken view in some circles (and the Winebox corporates suffered from this) that to be convicted of fraud you actually have to dress like and think like a Beagle Boy; that your dishonesty must not just be dishonesty on the face of it, but with a particularly evil motive as well. As the Court of Appeal and Privy Council pointed out in the Winebox cases, you don't have to form an intention to act criminally in order to be a criminal, you merely have to form an intention to carry out an act which is in itself deceptive or against the law. It is the intent to commit the act, not an intent to be dishonest, that is the test. And as the Crimes Act itself spells out, "ignorance of the law is no excuse".

On the facts as laid out, a strong case can be made that the Prime Minister happily and knowingly went along with plans to sign artwork that she knew was not hers, for supply to various charities looking for Helen Clark originals to auction. The intent to sign any such item, knowing it would be sold for money and possibly onsold again, and with reckless or negligent disregard of the downstream financial impact on a buyer, is sufficient to meet the criminal threshold, regardless of how warm and fuzzy Clark thought her motives were.

As the Court of Appeal noted in one of the Winebox cases,[95] "Where a person makes a positive representation of some kind and is silent as to other matters which would qualify or alter the impression made by that positive representation, the combined effect of the representation and the silence may be to mislead."

Lying to police, Helen Clark: Only in countries like Italy is this sort of moral standard tolerated in Prime Ministers. Clark refused to be directly interviewed by police (in itself odd behavior) and instead issued a statement

---

94 Richard Nixon, televised news conference, November 17, 1973
95 *Peters v Davison*, Court of Appeal, ruling 17 November 1998

to police containing what she wanted to tell them. That statement included claims that she did not know signing someone else's artwork as your own was against the law. Given that most seven year olds know the morality of this, and that Clark had previously been a university lecturer, and that she was Minister for the Arts, she can only have been lying to police in my view. The alternative is too horrible to contemplate, because it means the Prime Minister of New Zealand is too incompetent to understand basic societal principles and is therefore unqualified for the job. If a Prime Minister lies to a police investigation, how much more likely is he or she to lie to the public?

When National's Bill English accused Clark of "slippery deceit" by not telling police all she knew, and equating a failure to disclose everything with telling a lie, Clark threatened to sue him and any news media that ran the comments for defamation.[96] But applying the Court of Appeal ruling above, it is clear that staying silent on material facts can be seen by the court as an intention to mislead.

Clark backed off her defamation threat when she saw it wasn't working, and instead resorted to her old faithful – "It is simply gutter politics and I find it absolutely contemptible" – hoping to get public sympathy by playing the outrage card.

Lying to police, Chris Carter: The evidence from Carter, now Education Minister, so utterly contradicts the evidence of independent witnesses and other corroborative evidence in police files that, in my view, there is no question that this future Labour cabinet minister was also lying to police. Developing that line of reasoning, in many ways Carter's dishonesty was even worse than Clark's on this specific point, because while she was lying about her state of mind, Carter was lying about the facts, and thus giving police false or misleading information in the course of a police investigation. Had the matter gone to court and Carter appeared as a witness repeating the statements he made to police, he would have perjured himself.[97] The relevant law is Section 111 of the Crimes Act: **False statements or declarations**

• Every one is liable to imprisonment for a term not exceeding 3 years who, on any occasion on which he is required or permitted by law to make any statement or declaration before any officer or person authorised by law to take or receive it, or before any notary public to be certified by him as such notary, makes a statement or declaration that would amount to perjury if made on oath in a judicial proceeding.

---

96 *NZ Herald*, 8 July 2002, "PM threatens to sue over 'Paintergate'"
http://www.nzherald.co.nz/feature/story.cfm?c_id=774&objectid=2050846
97 Which is probably why Carter refused to sign his police statement. Incidentally, he also stands accused of lying to protect Clark over the John Yelash affair. Yelash says Carter rang him looking for "dirt" on Dover Samuels at the time of Samuels' fall from grace. Carter denied it, and Clark said she'd rather take the word of Carter than a convicted murderer. She was then forced to pay $55,000 for defamation, because Yelash was not a convicted murderer. After Carter's help with this and Paintergate, he was promoted months later to Cabinet, where he asked to be "judged on my deeds". *NZ Herald*, 12 August 2002, "Judge me on my deeds"
http://www.nzherald.co.nz/feature/story.cfm?c_id=774&objectid=2349077

And also section 108: **Perjury defined**

- (1) Perjury is an assertion as to a matter of fact, opinion, belief, or knowledge made by a witness in a judicial proceeding as part of his evidence on oath, whether the evidence is given in open Court or by affidavit or otherwise, that assertion being known to the witness to be false and being intended by him to mislead the tribunal holding the proceeding.

And the punishment for perjury is: "every one is liable to imprisonment for a term not exceeding 7 years who commits perjury".

Conspiracy **to pervert the course of justice:** The fact that Carter's secretary Serge Sablyak was singing the same song as Carter implies what the late Justice Mahon would have called "an orchestrated litany of lies", in other words, a conspiracy to pervert the course of justice. Carter's and Sablyak's testimony helped tip the balance in Clark's favour during the police inquiry. Whilst a witness is entitled to tell police whatever they like, the flipside is that evidence found to be false testimony can be treated as perjury, and where two or more people are involved a conspiracy is present in legal terms. The relevant law is Section 116 of the Crimes Act: **Conspiring to defeat justice**

- Every one is liable to imprisonment for a term not exceeding 7 years who conspires to obstruct, prevent, pervert, or defeat the course of justice in New Zealand or the course of justice in an overseas jurisdiction.

Accessory after the fact: Helen Clark's electorate secretary Joan Caulfield, and Caulfield's lawyer Simon Mitchell (also a Labour Party member), conspired to procure the painting at the centre of forgery allegations. Caulfield and her husband then destroyed it, after consulting directly with Helen Clark first. Section 71 of the Crimes Act says:

- An accessory after the fact to an offence is one who, knowing any person to have been a party to the offence, receives, comforts, or assists that person or tampers with or actively suppresses any evidence against him, in order to enable him to escape after arrest or to avoid arrest or conviction.

Contrary to the police view that decided the threshold had not been met because Caulfield and co were unaware of the police investigation, as you can see from the excerpt above the test is not awareness of a police investigation, but awareness of an offence. Caulfield and Mitchell were certainly aware Clark was being accused of forgery, and that prominent lawyers like Barry Hart and Robert Lithgow had already given opinions that a prima facie crime appeared to have been committed.

Parties to an offence: **Parties to offences**

Chapter 5

- (1) Every one is a party to and guilty of an offence who –
    (a) Actually commits the offence; or
    (b) Does or omits an act for the purpose of aiding any person to commit the offence; or
    (c) Abets any person in the commission of the offence; or
    (d) Incites, counsels, or procures any person to commit the offence.

(2) Where 2 or more persons form a common intention to prosecute any unlawful purpose, and to assist each other therein, each of them is a party to every offence committed by any one of them in the prosecution of the common purpose if the commission of that offence was known to be a probable consequence of the prosecution of the common purpose.

At the time, the police decision not to prosecute Clark was generally seen as the right one. In hindsight, a decision to clip Clark's wings by making her answerable to the same laws as everyone else might have significantly changed the course New Zealand took between 2002 and 2008.

Clark and her biographer Brian Edwards had worked so hard in *Helen: Portrait of a Prime Minister*, to paint an image of integrity, with Edwards even going so far as to include quotes on this point from Helen's father, George Clark:[98]

"I always tell people, 'At least you've got a Prime Minister who's honest', because when they were young, if they'd sworn at me, it wouldn't have worried me because I swore at the dogs. But if they ever cheated or lied, I'd have been down on them like a ton of hot bricks. So at least she's a hundred percent honest."

Edwards himself writes, "Honesty was at a premium in the Clark family."

Presumably, Clark got a big telling off from her Dad in the wake of Paintergate.

Perhaps the final ironic word belongs to Clark herself, in this exchange with Brian Edwards just months before her art fraud was discovered, at the end of a self-congratulatory poke at the alleged dishonesty of Jenny Shipley:[99]

BRIAN: "So not telling the truth doesn't work?"
HELEN: "No."
BRIAN: "But is it possible to be totally honest in politics?"
HELEN: "It's possible never to tell a lie."

---

98 *Helen*, p57
99 *Helen*, p279

Hoist On Your Own Petard

Jim Hacker: "Humphrey, do you see it as part of your job to help Ministers make fools of themselves?"
Sir Humphrey: "Well, I never met one that needed any help."
– Yes Minister

THE PAST FEW CHAPTERS HAVE served to illustrate what happens when the checks and balances in our society and legal system start to fail. They show that power, after a while, tends to corrupt, and absolute power corrupts absolutely. In other words, where a government or regime is so politically strong it can get away with anything, it generally does get away with everything.

Clark's administration did not begin this way of course – at least not in the public brand it was selling to the electorate in 1999. The Labour government people voted for was pitched as a shining beacon of honesty, hope, integrity, and careful government.

These are good, strong, positive warm-fuzzy messages – what voter doesn't want this? But history will test the Clark administration objectively, not on its self-promotional spin. Did Helen Clark walk the talk, or were they just more cynical election promises?

ITEM ONE: WASTAGE IN THE PUBLIC SECTOR
Jim Hacker: Of course we do what we can, but there's many calls on the public purse you know, inner cities, schools, hospitals, kidney machines.
Lady 1: Tanks?
Lady 2: Rockets?
Lady 3: H-Bombs?
Jim Hacker: Well we can't really defend ourselves against the Russians with a performance of Henry V.

When Clark kicked off her 1999 election campaign, she told voters that

Labour would clean up what she claimed was massive wastage of public money by government departments. Soon after Labour's victory, the *New Zealand Herald* published a "hit list" of public servants rumoured for the chop. As we've seen, Police Commissioner Peter Doone was on that list. So too was a tall, leggy blonde named Christine Rankin.

Rankin's was a rags-to-riches, girl-from-the-wrong-side-of-the-tracks-makes-good-story; a former welfare beneficiary who'd risen above her circumstances to end up running Work and Income New Zealand (WINZ). As a former client, she knew the need for welfare first hand. As the chief executive of WINZ, she knew the need for strong stewardship of its multi-billion dollar budget and a return on the taxpayers' investment.

Her sin was her flamboyance. Forty-six year old Rankin was tough, but known for her large earrings and penchant for the corporate mini-skirt. She had hit the headlines in 1999 for chartering an Ansett Whisper Jet to ferry staff to a team-building conference in Taupo. According to some reports that received wide media coverage, Rankin appeared at the conference in a glitzy promotional video wearing a silver space suit.

The truth was a little more down to earth, as one news website, WYSIWYG News reported at the time:

"The latest allegations of lavish spending by WINZ have fallen flat on their face. An anonymous manager today went public claiming the video presentation at an April conference was a glitzy one – featuring WINZ boss Christine Rankin in a silver suit – associating with yachting notary Sir Peter Blake. But our political staff has seen the video – and says it has a shoestring budget. The scenes featuring Sir Peter Blake were taken from a commercially available video. The tape then cuts to a home video quality shot of Christine Rankin – wearing one of her own coats – being escorted down a pier by two co-workers dressed in orange civil defence overalls."

What wasn't down to earth, however, was the price WINZ paid for its charter flights: $165,000.

"The boss of WINZ has admitted to authorising part of the expenditure for the hire of jets to ferry staff to a conference in Taupo," reported WYSIWYG. "Christine Rankin says she was misled by a staff member as she signed off the travel costs which totalled one hundred and sixty five thousand dollars. She says this is all she has to say on the matter while the investigation into it continues."

The employee responsible was later suspended.

"I certainly knew we were going to charter some flights. I had assurances around the costings of those flights that were not correct," Rankin told *One News*.

The then Opposition welfare spokesman, Steve Maharey, released an "anonymous" staff letter criticizing WINZ for being run "by someone who dresses like a cocktail waitress with earrings longer than her skirts."

Just before winning the election later that year, Helen Clark let it be known she was out for blood, turning golden handshakes and perceived extravagance in the public service into an election issue.

"The party is over for the senior management of [Work and Income NZ] and of all those other Government organizations who have wasted public money," she exclaimed to rapturous applause from a 1200-strong crowd at Labour's launch rally.[100] "To those in the public sector who have forgotten how to spell the words 'public service', I say get ready for change. The party is over."

There would, she said, be a new era of "moderation, frugality and integrity in the public sector".

In her bid to gain power, a calculating Helen Clark ran the sums and knew the public would back her attack on the "countless millions...squandered on consultants" as just one example.[101] The Labour leader, like the rest of New Zealand, couldn't understand why Government agencies were spending so "much on consultants to provide routine policy advice".

Why on earth, for example, would the IRD need to spend $4 *million* on outside consultants and contractors in 1999?

And there were glaring symbols of wastage that Clark used to tremendous effect – the $165,000 spent by WINZ to hire some Ansett jets to fly staff to a corporate retreat in 1999. These things, promised Clark, would never happen under her Labour team.

"What can be more fundamental than advising a Government?" she asked, when confronted by WINZ expenditure on policy advisors.[102] "And you have to get consultants in to do it? What is going on at WINZ?

"You might expect it of a small agency which doesn't have many staff, but for heaven's sake, this one would be the largest government department!"

Fair comment, undoubtedly. So how have the Helen Clark years shaped up in terms of wasting taxpayer money? In its first nine years of government, Labour failed to deliver a cut in personal taxes, insisting that the billions and billions of dollars in surpluses were needed for rainy days. Based on the figures you are about to read, evidently it rains a lot in the public service, presumably to fill the feeding troughs.

While the IRD spent a whacking great $4 million on consultants under National in 1999, recent figures[103] show they spent $27.8 million under Labour in the 2006 financial year! To put that particular feat in perspective, that's like chartering a further 169 passenger jets *a la* the WINZ scandal, in just one year, in just one department.

The figures reveal the IRD hired 73 consultants in the 1999 year at an average cost of less than $55,000 each. In 2006, a staggering 324 consultants

100 *NZ Herald*, 1 November 1999, "Clark's mission: clean up govt"
http://www.nzherald.co.nz/section/1/story.cfm?c_id=1&objectid=17101
101 http://www.national.org.nz/article.aspx?articleid=11179
102 http://www.national.org.nz/article.aspx?articleid=10877
103 http://www.national.org.nz/article.aspx?articleid=9986

shared the $27.8 million between them, for an average payout each of nearly $86,000.

The IRD, incidentally, is presided over by United Future's Peter Dunne.

As National's Associate Finance spokesman Craig Foss wryly noted, Labour has been more successful hiring tax-gatherers (an increase of 1,212 extra since 1999), than it has in its bid to hire 1,000 more police to protect the public from robbers.

What about WINZ? Now part of the Ministry of Social Development, figures released last year[104] showed that spending on consultants had ballooned from $5 million in the year ending June 04, to $17.2 million in the June 06 year. All up, nearly $40 million was spent on consultants in the three year period.

"And if the $15 million spent on promoting Working For Families is included then the expenditure surges to nearly $55 million," warned National's Welfare spokeswoman Judith Collins. "But it is likely the actual expenditure is much higher because the Financial Review required MSD to only include contracts worth more than $5,000."

Despite the massive increase in spending on consultants however, there was also a big increase in the number of salaried staff working on policy and media spin, from 126 policy advisors in June 2001 to 320 by April 2007, and from 23 media staff to 54 over the same period.

Collins threw a Steve Maharey quote back in the former Minister's face:[105]

"Steve Maharey once described Work and Income as a gravy train for consultants. On this rare occasion, it appears he is right!"

Former WINZ boss Christine Rankin says Labour has been hypocritical:[106]

"I was the first CEO ever, and it started the day I was appointed, no one had ever debated the salary of a CEO before but Labour at the time went in and said 'it's disgusting, how can she earn $230,000 running a welfare agency?' The current CEO – and good on him – earns something like $430,000 under their regime. They said public service salaries had got out of control and they were going to fix it. Take a look at them now!

"The second tier in Social Welfare, the Ministry of Social Development, I know that they earn in excess of $300,000, some of those people. The second tier! They have a hard job, fine, but how come, how come, all of that was OK? And it certainly never would have happened to a grey-suited man. Never."

Over at the Corrections Department, things were equally rosy, with $19.4 million of taxpayer funds shelled out to private consultants in the year to June 2007 – nearly double the $10.1 million spent in the 2006 year.[107]

National's Simon Power, who'd dug the figures out of Corrections, noted that they came on top of a $490 million blow-out on the prison construction budget.

104 http://www.national.org.nz/article.aspx?articleid=10648
105 http://www.national.org.nz/article.aspx?articleid=10877
106 Investigate, January 2006 issue
107 http://www.national.org.nz/article.aspx?articleid=11671

Latest figures suggest an even bigger payout is looming in the current financial year, with consultancy fees averaging over $2 million a month for July and August 2007 alone.

When you look at the detail of some of the consultancy contracts, you can see why taxpayers are being bled dry through their mortgage rates.

One news release in 2007 revealed Corrections was planning to pay $180,000 for a contractor to "watch staff at Auckland Women's Prison chatting with prisoners, and prisoners moving around the grounds".[108] One would have thought that a permanent staff member could be hired for far less to carry out that kind of observation.

Strange things have been happening at Housing New Zealand as well.[109] Although Labour has only increased the number of state houses by around 12%, the number of full time staff in HNZ has rocketed from 682 in 2002, to 1005 four years later, a 47% increase.

Money spent on consultants nearly doubled, from $6.7 million in 2003 to $12.6 million last year.

"Housing Minister Chris Carter needs to reconcile Helen Clark's earlier promises with the double whammy of an explosion in HNZ consultants and the rocketing number of staff on the HNZ payroll," argued National's Phil Heatley.

It is worth remembering at this point that Helen Clark's 1999 election campaign speech opened with a claim that she'd "lost count of the number of people" who'd told her they wouldn't mind paying more tax if it was spent on "health and education".

Nine years down the track, would those optimistic taxpayers of 1999 have been quite so generous if they'd realized the money they turfed across to Labour went not into extra surgery, but towards more bureaucrats?

"Fewer kiwis are getting elective surgery on a population basis since Labour came to office," accused National's Health spokesman Tony Ryall. "Labour has bought bureaucrats instead of operations."[110]

Backing up his claim, Ryall released figures showing that while nearly 2000 extra hospital administrators had been hired, only 1200 doctors had been added to the rosters.

"The health bureaucracy is growing out of control," noted Ryall just before Christmas, while far too many patients are forced to wait and wait for operations and specialists' appointments. When thousands and thousands of patients have been culled from hospital waiting lists, this massive bureaucracy is an appalling indictment on Labour's policies."

A cynic might argue that dead patients don't vote, but living bureaucrats do and generally vote for bigger government.

One wonders, too, whether those taxpayers willing to donate more of their

108 http://www.national.org.nz/article.aspx?articleid=9764
109 http://www.national.org.nz/article.aspx?articleid=11179
110 Tony Ryall, National Party news release, 9 January 2008, "Cut bureaucracy..."

hard-earned cash to Labour in 1999 for health and education were happy with the report released in February 2008 about the shocking level of mishaps, often fatal, in the health system.[111]

"Sentinel events," wrote the *Dominion-Post's* Richard Long.[112] "What wonderful words. They were used by the Health Ministry to describe such occasions as patients falling off operating tables, out windows, having the wrong limbs amputated and the wrong teeth pulled – and that's largely the non-fatal ones.

"Altogether it is enough to encourage the mildly healthy to keep away from hospitals. But I still can't get over the sentinel bit. In the newspaper industry the equivalent errors would be described as cock-ups. In other industries they would be listed as mistakes, failures, miscalculations and blunders.

"But the Health Ministry's public relations people manage, brilliantly, to come up with the word sentinel, with its images of watchman and sentry. There is nothing ominous or threatening in that term. It invokes safety, comfort and protection.

"This just goes to show the value of stacking Government ministries with more public relations and communications people than the journalistic staff of this newspaper, Radio New Zealand and Television New Zealand combined.

"Taxpayers might be paying through the nose, but at least they're reassured that all these stuff-ups are not terminal: they are just sentinel events."

So where have your health tax dollars under Labour gone?

According to figures published in November,[113] in the past six years the payroll at the Ministry of Health has risen 55%. Staff numbers increased by 24%.

Opposition leader John Key, in a major speech in mid March 2008,[114] gave an overview of how Labour has spent money on advisors, not frontline staff to deal with public waiting lists:

"Over the past eight years the bureaucracy has grown out of all proportion to those parts of the state sector that actually serve the public. How do we know that? Here are some examples:

• Since 2000, the number of teachers in state primary and secondary schools has grown by 12%. But over the same period, the number of people employed in the various education bureaucracies has grown by 40%.
• Since 2000, the number of nurses and doctors employed in district health boards has grown by 28%. But over the same period, the number of people employed in the Ministry of Health has grown by 51%.
• Since 2002, the service delivery part of MSD, namely Work and Income and

111 *NZ Herald*, 20 February 2008, "Report reveals scale of hospitals' worst mistakes" http://www.nzherald.co.nz/section/story.cfm?c_id=204&objectid=10493561&pnum=0
112 *Dominion-Post*, 26 Feb 2008, "A saga of sentinel proportions" http://stuff.co.nz/dominionpost/4416203a26342.html
113 http://www.national.org.nz/article.aspx?articleid=11536
114 http://briefingroom.typepad.com/news24seventv/2008/03/keynote-speech.html

Child Youth and Family, has grown by 23%. But over the same period, the policy analysis, research, and corporate units of MSD have grown by a whopping 109%.

• Treasury reports show that between 2000 and 2006, employment in government departments that mainly provide services grew by 34%, while employment in policy departments grew by 72%.

"To get a picture of the whole state sector we need to look at survey data from the Quarterly Employment Survey. This shows that since 2000 the number of bureaucrats has grown from 26,200 to 36,000," said Key.

And many of those are based at the Government's head office, Wellington.

In making the Wellington region a Labour election stronghold, the Government has dangled some very large carrots. The number of Housing New Zealand staff earning more than $100,000 a year has jumped from 39 to 80 between 2002 and 2006. At the Corrections Department the $100k Plus Club now measures 76, triple what it was in 2002, while the number of people earning more than $140,000 has leapt from four to 17 over the same period – quadrupling.[115] Similar figures are being reported by other departments.

Little wonder, in October 2007, that news broke of incomes in Wellington rising 21% in just one year as a result of huge pay increases in the civil service and big fees being given to private consultants.[116]

Echoing Helen Clark's own rage against wastage in the machine nine years ago, National's Bill English claims high mortgage rates and inflationary pressures can be blamed on "large increases in spending by the Labour Government."[117]

Then there's the thorny issue of accountability. What was it Clark had said again back in 1999?

"The party is over for the senior management of [Work and Income NZ] and of all those other Government organizations who have wasted public money," she exclaimed to rapturous applause from a 1200-strong crowd at Labour's launch rally. There would, she said, be a new era of "moderation, frugality and integrity in the public sector".

Fast forward to November 2007:

"Agriculture Minister Jim Anderton needs to explain why valuable contracts at the Ministry of Agriculture and Forestry are not being tendered on the open market," exclaimed National's Associate Agriculture spokesman, Nathan Guy.[118]

Contracts being awarded without going to open public tender? That would appear to be a recipe for disaster.

115 http://www.national.org.nz/article.aspx?articleid=10675
116 http://www.national.org.nz/article.aspx?articleid=11180
117 Ibid
118 http://www.national.org.nz/article.aspx?articleid=11428

"MAF's 2006/07 financial review reveals that there is no formal unit within the Ministry that oversees contract monitoring," continued Guy. "That was confirmed by MAF officials who were speaking at the Primary Production Select Committee.

"To make things worse, the Director-General of MAF, Murray Sherwin, acknowledged that MAF had not stuck to the policy of tendering for contracts worth over $50,000 on the open market.

"It appears there are some cosy consultant arrangements being conducted and the taxpayer deserves to know why these contracts were not put out to public tender."

National found a $170,000 contract to a private consultant that wasn't tendered, and another for $119,000.

"MAF is overrun with staff that now number more than 1,700," said Guy, "but no one is tasked with monitoring how much is being spent on consultants and whether the taxpayer is getting value for money."

Similar dodgy awarding of contracts, possibly to friends of staff, was also found in the Ministry of Health in 2006:[119]

"More than $13 million has been paid out by the Ministry of Health in the past financial year in untendered contracts, the National Party has revealed. National's Associate Health spokesman, Dr Jonathan Coleman, told Parliament's Health Select Committee today that despite an Auditor-General's report being severely critical of such practices, the Ministry of Health paid out $13.1 million in untendered contracts during the 2005/06 financial year.

"Many of the contracts were worth hundreds of thousands of dollars.

" 'This is outrageous and poor financial practice,' says Dr Coleman. 'The Ministry was told by the Auditor-General that it was unacceptable for contracts to be awarded on a sole-provider basis, yet in the 2006 financial year we find $13 million worth of just such contracts. Spending public money is a huge responsibility, and tendering processes ensure that the public gets the best possible value for money. We already know from the pledge card rort that Pete Hodgson feels entitled to ignore the Auditor-General. Now it's clear that he's running his Health Ministry on the same basis,' says Dr Coleman."

In March 2007, a similar stunt in the Department of Labour surfaced during parliamentary question time.[120] National's Paula Bennett pinged the department for spending nearly $19 million on consultants the previous year – including *$16 million* on untendered contracts. Bennett called the revelations a breach of Cabinet's Mandatory Procurement rules, and highlighted 11 contracts each worth more than $100,000 which never went to open tender.

---

119   http://jonathancoleman.co.nz/index.php?/archives/81-13m-in-untendered-contracts-at-Ministry-of-Health.html
120   http://briefingroom.typepad.com/news24seventv/2007/03/national_invest.html

Bennett argued taxpayers would want to know the contracts were "squeaky clean".

In May 2007, long after audit concerns had been raised about untendered contracts in general, it was Te Puni Kokiri's turn for scrutiny.[121]

"Can the Minister confirm that four of the 10 largest contracts Te Puni Kōkiri let to contractors in 2005-06 were let without tender, including one to a Nicky Birch for $100,000 because she 'was known to the Ministry'?" asked National's Tau Henare.

When Maori Affairs Minister Parekura Horomia admitted it, Henare followed through:

"How can the New Zealand taxpaying public have confidence in Te Puni Kōkiri's financial responsibility when one-fifth of all its contracts are let without tender and for such reasons as 'the contractor used to work at TPK', and 'the contractor knew people at TPK'?"

Horomia's response, that the contracts were awarded to the best people available, rang hollow. After all, in a string of government agencies it now appears as though taxpayer funds have been treated as slush funds, with few or no checks and balances in place.

The government's checks and balances even came under attack from within. Labour MP John Tamihere, chairing a select committee investigation into the Waitangi Fisheries Commission in 2002, remarked that it seemed like a massive money-making scheme for select Maori leaders, with some of the nominated Commissioners allegedly being paid up to six times for "doing essentially the same job".[122]

Tamihere, commenting on just released figures showing $11 million in fees had been paid to commissioners over the 11 years from 1990 to 2001, claimed it was the tip of the iceberg, because in addition to those fees, some commissioners may have been paid consultancy fees , or for serving on advisory sub-committees to the main board, or as directors of subsidiaries to the Fisheries Commission, of which there were 44 in existence in 2002.

"There's a major issue over conflict of interest," Tamihere told NZPA.

"I still wonder how you can in the morning be the director awarding the contract, and in the afternoon run around and sign it as a contractor. Some of them make Susan Bathgate look like Mother Teresa."

The fees document, released as part of Tamihere's select committee investigation, showed the then Chairman of the Fisheries Commission (now Labour cabinet high-flyer Shane Jones) had been paid $984,000 in fees between June 1993 and September 2001.[123]

---

121 http://theyworkforyou.co.nz/portfolios/maori_affairs/2007/may/10/001

122 *NZ Herald*, 17 May 2002, "Tamihere says fisheries commissioners may have been paid six times"
http://www.nzherald.co.nz/section/1/story.cfm?c_id=1&objectid=1992550

123 Shane Jones is one to watch, if his political career continues. When elected in 2005 he initially refused to give up his $70,000 a year job on the board of another company,

However, telephone number fees paid out to consultants and friends of the government are somewhat esoteric. There is a truism in politics that the voting public are more scandalized by the small things than the big things. Tuku Morgan's $89 underpants, Christine Rankin's dangly earrings – these are much easier for the average punter who pays $19.90 for a five-pack of Jockeys to understand.

Thus, when Prime Minister Helen Clark criticized WINZ for spending $9,000 on consultants back in December 1999, she was able to get plenty of political mileage. Nine thousand dollars was something a voter could relate to.[124]

"Work and Income New Zealand wrote its own post-election briefing papers," reported Wellington's *Evening Post*, but paid consultants...$9,000 for 'editorial assistance', the Government has revealed.

"The revelation...outraged Prime Minister Helen Clark, who said it was 'simply extraordinary' that WINZ did not have the capacity to prepare its own briefing papers.

"Mr Maharey said he had told Mrs Rankin this was unacceptable," reported the *Post*.

What is "simply extraordinary", however, is how $9,000 spent on consultants in 1999 could outrage Clark, whilst the same Ministry spending $17.2 *million* on consultants in 2006 did not raise a media or government eyebrow.

Let's look at another example of Clark's gung-ho public statements in 1999:

"New revelations of spending on consultants by a government department have sparked a hunt for more offenders by Prime Minister Helen Clark," reported the *Christchurch Press*.[125]

"Ms Clark said yesterday that she wanted to know how widely outside help was being used, after a report that consultants were paid more than $30,000 by Treasury's Crown Company Monitoring and Advisory Unit to prepare briefing papers for the incoming government."

Thirty thousand dollars was enough to spark a witch-hunt, back when Labour still had integrity, back when the Prime Minister's word still meant something.

A *Herald on Sunday* investigation by David Fisher[126] discovered much the same. In the mid 90s, he noted, "Clark accused parts of the public sector of increasingly lacking a corporate memory because of the over-use of private consultants. Addressing Victoria University's Master of Public Policy programmes, she said departments relied too heavily on consultants to provide routine policy advice."

Fisher quoted another Clark statement from the mid-90s: "responsible

claiming there would be "no conflict of interest". He was later persuaded to see the error of his ways by Helen Clark, but left to his own devices his own moral code did not see a problem. NZ Herald, 4 October 2005, "New MP wants to keep $70,000 private job", and 6 October 2005, "Jones u-turns on fisheries job"

124   *Evening Post*, 24 Dec 1999, "WINZ paid $9000 for 'editorial assistance' "
125   *The Press*, 23 Dec 1999, "PM questions spending"
126   *NZ Herald*, 8 April 2007, "Tax dollars spent on high paid consultants"
http://www.nzherald.co.nz/index.cfm?objectid=10433104

positions in departments can be held by people recruited from private sector backgrounds and with no long-term commitment to the public service. For them, policy advice is a theoretical game to be engaged in for a short time as a career move."

In a later address to social workers, Clark compared their low wages to "the countless millions of dollars that have been squandered on consultants."

Yet fast forward to the 2003-2004 financial year, a random survey of 25 government departments by the *Herald* found $131 million was spent on consultants. Two years later, spending by those same departments had risen to $180 million a year.

That's a lot of social workers. And that's just a random survey of less than half the government departments. The Ministry of Health, alone, for example, was spending around $200 million a year on consultants.

One of the worst offenders, in terms of percentage increase, is the NZ Qualifications Authority. Its consultancy spend more than tripled over three years, and new chief executive Karen Poutasi has been working hard since May 2006 to wind back the spending to more realistic levels.

"We want institutional memory. We want people who know the context. Personally, as chief executive, I do want people in permanent jobs," Poutasi told the *Herald*.

Over at the Ministry of Education, there are more people in its media and communications area – 18 permanent or contract staff – than most major newspapers have journalists.

The government now collectively employs more journalists in spin mode than the combined newsrooms of all the major media organizations.

So was Labour's attack on overspending in 1999 real, or just for show?

Ironically, media commentators could already see the worm turning even as Labour had just taken possession of the Treasury benches in Parliament:[127]

"Steve Maharey, who had before November 27 never served as a minister," noted the editorial writer of *The Daily News* in Taranaki, "is typical of the opposition politician who seeks to change the world by making all the right noises for a vote or two while in opposition, yet fails to deliver the goods when given the opportunity to do so."[128]

Maharey's crime, in the eyes of the paper, had been to incessantly bag WINZ boss Christine Rankin by calling for the National Government to sack her, and then acknowledge after winning the election that "his actions, in his view, were all part of politicking. Not only can Mr Maharey not sack her, he has done an about turn to the embarrassing extent of praising Ms Rankin."[129]

---

127 *The Daily News*, 27 Dec 1999, "Accountability and honesty come in for renewed scrutiny"
128 Ironically, when the *Herald* published its investigation on consultants, Maharey was responsible for both NZQA and Education.
129 In an interview with *Investigate* magazine, January 2006, Christine Rankin says Maharey admitted it had all been a political game: "But in effect he was controlled by

That was 1999. Imagine the surprise of political commentators, then, to see the ghost of Christine Rankin summonsed once more by Helen Clark in 2008. It came during parliamentary debate on National's plans to review the number of pen-pushing desk jockeys in the public service, and to switch the emphasis away from hiring advisors and towards hiring doctors, teachers and social workers; frontline staff, not bureaucrats.

Recognising John Key was making political capital, Clark told parliament that Christine Rankin was now a National Party member and might end up standing as a candidate at the forthcoming election.

"The conclusion Clark was wanting people to draw," wrote the *Herald's* John Armstrong[130], "was that regardless of what National was saying now, it was still capable of being loose with taxpayers' money. But it was a very long bow to draw. The Rankin episode is so old, it creaks. It illustrates Labour's difficulty that the longer it is in power, the further the distance back to when National was last in power. That was 1999 too. Memories fade. Younger voters have no memory of such events."

"Yesterday's attempted haymaker from Clark was so off target it risked knocking her out instead," concluded Armstrong.

If one had to put Rankin's $9,000 spend-up on PR consultants in 1999, up against the $17.2 million the Ministry managed to spend on consultants in 2006, one would have to conclude there was probably an extremely good case to be made for bringing Christine Rankin back from next Monday to run the show, and pay her whatever she asks!

Little wonder the commentators found Clark's attempted joke at Rankin's expense flew like a cement duck – they'd heard it before in 1999. While they might have fallen for it then, nine years of intergalactic overspending by bureaucrats have put the good old days of a charter flight, a $9,000 PR report, dangly earrings and a silver suit well and truly in perspective. And all of it from a Prime Minister who promised a new era of "moderation, frugality and integrity in the public sector".

ITEM TWO: A REVIEW OF MMP

Jim Hacker: "But you see, it's the public will. This is a democracy, and the people don't like it."
Sir Humphrey: "The people are ignorant and misguided."
Jim Hacker: "Humphrey, it was the people who elected me."

Heather Simpson and Helen Clark, and had it been left to him – what he said to me in our first meeting was 'It's over now', he rang me actually and said 'It's over, go and tell your people they've got nothing to worry about it was just a political game, it's all over' – I believe that was his truth, I believe that that's what he wanted, but he wasn't allowed to do that."

130 *NZ Herald*, 13 March 2008, "Rankin reference rebounds on Clark" http://www.nzherald.co.nz/section/story.cfm?c_id=280&objectid=10497830

In 1999, Opposition leader Helen Clark was adamant she was there to listen to the will of the people:[131]

"Labour leader Helen Clark is promising referendums on ending MMP if a parliamentary review of the electoral system finds a strong public mood for change," reported the *Herald*. "She says the electoral system belongs to the voters, who should have the final say on dumping MMP."

When push came to shove, however, it was a broken election promise from the Prime Minister. Labour members on the committee reviewing MMP, allied with smaller coalition parties the Greens and the Alliance, blocked attempts to get a public referendum on the issue, despite a strong public mood staring them in the face:

"According to the committee's own commissioned research," wrote the *Herald's* Audrey Young,[132] "76 per cent of voters were in favour of a binding referendum and 17 per cent opposed. National and United argued that there was a strong public expectation of one."

The report of the review committee notes that Labour, Alliance and Green MPs "considered that as there have only been two elections under MMP, more time is needed to gain experience of it before major change is contemplated."

Helen Clark's words in 1999 were: "If the public mood against MMP continues to be adverse then it seems to me highly likely the select committee report will reflect that, and then we will be bound to go down the road of more referenda."

Given that the review committee's own poll showed 76% of voters wanted a further referendum on MMP, and of course the 81% who voted to cut MP numbers in the 1999 referendum, and that the only thing in the way was the vetoing inside the committee, it is hard to see how Helen Clark's promise could have been swept aside.

Additionally, Clark's comment that the electoral system "belongs to the voters" is a stark cry from Labour's draconian attack on public free speech via the Electoral Finance Act, which was passed without meaningful public consultation and without a referendum.

The MMP system was the darling of the Left – thanks to better lobbying it ended up the preferred option, instead of the Australian STV system which appears to work more reliably. Additionally, MMP came with flawed credentials – it was invented after World War 2 specifically to prevent one party in Germany holding too much power. What no one factored in was the tail wagging the dog scenario, where minor parties do, in practice, have more influence than their numbers entitle them to.

131   *NZ Herald*, 29 September 1999, "Clark to ensure MMP review"
http://www.nzherald.co.nz/section/story.cfm?c_id=543&objectid=14957
132   *NZ Herald*, 9 August 2001, "MPs disagreement the only agreement"
http://www.nzherald.co.nz/section/1/story.cfm?c_id=1&objectid=205978

With poll ratings for NZ First and the Greens slipping, it is possible the electorate is coming to the conclusion that they don't need minor MMP parties adding to the tension this election.

ITEM THREE: THE WAKA-JUMPERS

Sir Humphrey: To put it simply Prime Minister certain informal discussions took place involving a full and frank exchange of views, out of which there arose a series of proposals which on examination proved to indicate several promising lines of inquiry which when pursued lead to the realisation that the alternative courses of action might in fact in certain circumstances be susceptible of discrete modification, leading to a reappraisal of the original areas of difference and pointing a way to encouraging of compromise and co-operation, which if bilaterally implemented with appropriate give and take on both sides might if the climate were right would have a reasonable possibility, at the end of the day of leading rightly or wrongly to a mutually satisfactory resolution.

Jim: What the hell are you talking about?

Sir Humphrey: We did a deal.

In the late 1990s, a series of defections by MPs from their parties made voters collectively grind their teeth in frustration. Left-wing Alliance MP Alamein Kopu's defection to support the conservative National Government led by Jim Bolger in 1997 was perhaps the most egregious example, with Alliance leader Jim Anderton telling journalists her actions in jumping ship "breach every standard of morality and ethics that are known".

When the split between coalition partners New Zealand First and National occurred in late 1998, a number of NZ First MPs opted to remain supporting National, prompting further scorn from both their former leader Winston Peters and also Helen Clark.

"This serves to remind everyone what a shambles the National minority Government, propped up by party hoppers, has been," said Clark.[133]

Leading into the 1999 election campaign, Clark and Anderton promised a "clean-up" if they became government.[134]

"MPs entering Parliament at the next election would have to quit if they left their parties under a Labour-Alliance government," the *Evening Post* reported. "Labour deputy leader Michael Cullen last year introduced a member's Bill requiring MPs to quit if they left their parties, but it was defeated. Yesterday Miss Clark and Mr Anderton said similar legislation would be a 'top priority' for a centre-left government."

Clark and Anderton told journalists that "Voters feel badly let down", and added that their proposed new law would apply to all MPs and ensure that they

---

133 *NZ Herald*, 25 November 1999, "Clark jumps on 'weak' gesture"
http://www.nzherald.co.nz/section/1/story.cfm?c_id=1&objectid=103870
134 *Evening Post*, 26 Aug 1998, "Make Rebel MPs Quit"

had to leave Parliament if they quit the party they originally belonged to.

"You now have the bizarre situation of list MPs who were elected on the basis of their party's vote, propping up the Government," stated Clark on another occasion.[135]

"Our mission is to clean up Government and to clean up Parliament too," Clark shouted to enthusiastic supporters at the formal opening of the 1999 election campaign.[136] "We want the defectors out!"

Clark told the crowd Labour would "reclaim the country" and her Government would not be "propped up by a ragtag mob of defectors and opportunists".

Within just a couple of years, however, Clark's own Government was reliant on the waka-straddling skills of a man regarded at the time as the ultimate hypocrite – Jim Anderton. And wouldn't you know it, the scandal blew up in the middle of Helen Clark's Paintergate nightmare.

Clark had just finished taking questions about signing the artwork, but her torture in the debating chamber wasn't over. The next questions of the day related to how Labour was handling the split within the Alliance Party, which was now being led by Laila Harre whilst Jim Anderton – having announced he was setting up the Progressive Party – still insisted he was also the leader of the Alliance in Parliament. Anderton had to maintain this charade in order to avoid invoking the provisions of the waka-jumping laws, the Electoral Integrity Act.

The *Herald's* John Armstrong called it "surreal":[137]

"There is the Helen Clark painting that isn't. Then there is Mr Anderton, the leader of the Alliance who isn't. Or who won't be from next weekend when Laila Harre formally takes over. But who will still be because he will still lead the Alliance "grouping" in Parliament despite leading a new rival party – a convenient fiction designed to avoid triggering his resignation from Parliament under the anti-party-hopping law.

"That fiction was made more obvious yesterday by Ms Harre's choosing to seat herself as far away as possible from Mr Anderton and her old benchmate Matt Robson.

"For Act leader Richard Prebble, the whole thing resembled a script from the *Goon Show*. For National MPs, it was an embarrassment of riches which – for once – they made the most of.

"For the Prime Minister, there was the political necessity of arguing black was white when challenged to explain why she had not asked for Mr Anderton's resignation, given all the horrible things she had said about party-hoppers while in Opposition.

"But the non-artist slipped, at one point saying she had not 'brushed up'

---

135   *The Taranaki Daily News*, 13 Aug 1999, "Defecting MPs To Go"
136   *NZ Herald*, 1 Nov 1999, "Clark's Mission"
137   *NZ Herald*, 17 April 2002, "PM Pasted in Surreal Session",
     http://www.nzherald.co.nz/section/1/story.cfm?c_id=1&objectid=1442257

on one particular aspect of the Electoral Integrity Act, provoking hoots of laughter from across the chamber.

"Bill English opened a bigger wound when he asked how she could say that Labour was now in a three-way coalition with the Anderton and Harre factions when the Alliance was supposedly still one entity.

" 'Easily,' she replied dismissively.

"Mr English then wondered aloud whether it was just as easy to reconcile that inconsistency as it was to sign a painting she did not paint....It was all distinctly surreal," Armstrong pointed out.

ITEM FOUR: GOLDEN HANDSHAKES
"A sorry tale of ministerial incompetence, corporate greed, cronyism"
– Labour leader Helen Clark, Feb 18 1997

One of Labour's big policies leading into the 1999 election was a ban on golden handshakes, and transparency so the public could see the facts. Clark told journalists there is a "legitimate public interest" in disclosing how much managers or directors were paid when they quit state sector jobs after falling out with their ministers.[138]

"Whenever National gets into strife, it tries to buy its way out of trouble with large dollops of taxpayer money," scoffed Clark on one occasion.[139]

Clark, and her media minders, had carefully crafted the image of a Prime Minister in waiting who would act responsibly and for the good of all, a leader who was honest, a straight-shooter, a woman whose word you could trust.

So let's test the theory.

On August 7, 2000, National's Murray McCully asked questions in Parliament of Local Government Minister Sandra Lee. Was it true, he wondered, that the Chief Executive of Local Government New Zealand, Carol Stigley, had quit because of a falling out with the Minister and Prime Minister Helen Clark?

Utter rubbish, suggested Sandra Lee, describing her relationship with Stigley as "constructive and compatible" and telling the House she had never had a cross word.

The following day, all hell broke loose:[140]

Local Government Minister Sandra Lee has been politically embarrassed by a leaked letter which contradicts her public assurances that she had no problems working with a key lobby group's top official.

---

138 *NZ Herald*, 24 June 1999, "One rule for all insists Shipley"
http://www.nzherald.co.nz/section/1/story.cfm?c_id=1&objectid=8843
139 *NZ Herald*, 26 May 1999, "Secret deal costs fire head dear"
http://www.nzherald.co.nz/section/1/story.cfm?c_id=1&objectid=7304
140 *NZ Herald*, 8 August 2000, "McCully lays ambush for Lee and Clark"
http://www.nzherald.co.nz/section/1/story.cfm?c_id=1&objectid=147073

The Prime Minister, Helen Clark, is also trying to avoid being tarred by the affair after she was also quick to dismiss National Party claims surrounding the resignation of the chief executive of Local Government New Zealand, Carol Stigley.

In a classic sting operation, National's Murray McCully waited for denials from Sandra Lee, Helen Clark and Local Government New Zealand before releasing a leaked letter and memo revealing problems between the Government and the ratepayer-funded lobby group, which speaks on behalf of the country's 86 local bodies.

It is thought Ms Stigley resigned with a payout close to $140,000.

The memo released by Mr McCully says the golden handshake negotiated by her lawyer was in recognition of "humiliation, distress, [and] extreme stress" plus legal costs and lost earnings.

The documentation in McCully's possession included a letter to Stigley essentially blaming her for a breakdown in "the relationship between yourself and some parliamentarians, in particular the Minister of Local Government (and to a lesser extent, the Prime Minister)."

The letter has other references to the Prime Minister's involvement, while "Beehive sources" spoken to by the *Herald* laid part of the blame on "interference" by the Prime Minister's office – a claim denied by Clark.

There is no doubt, however, that Carol Stigley received a payout that the Government had failed to disclose, despite the Prime Minister's huffing and puffing about transparency and an end to golden handshakes.

In 2004, Prime Minister Clark, struggling to deal with claims that Labour MP John Tamihere had taken a $195,000 golden handshake from the Waipareira Trust, re-defined the meaning of 'golden handshake' as: "people being paid large sums of money to leave the public sector". As Tamihere hadn't left the public sector, it wasn't an issue.

But in 2005 another one was. Claire Austin, the CEO of United Future's pet social engineering project, the Families Commission, walked the plank in undisclosed circumstances.[141]

Chief families commissioner Rajen Prasad refused to talk about the breakdown, only saying that "governance and operational" models had not lined up. "It's really important that these things do line up ... and despite best efforts on this occasion they didn't."

There had been a golden handshake, but he refused to disclose it – his position backed up by cabinet minister Steve Maharey – despite Clark's pre-election claim that the public had a "legitimate public interest" in knowing the details of all payouts.

When the debacle over the performance of the NZ Qualifications Authority

141 *NZ Herald*, 21 April 2005, "MPs demand golden handshake details"
http://www.nzherald.co.nz/topic/story.cfm?c_id=189&objectid=10121558

exploded in May 2005, NZQA chief executive Karen van Rooyen quit, in return for a three month contract to do "project work" from home, worth $50,000.

It was a creative solution to not calling it a "golden handshake".[142] But Labour had borrowed the idea from someone else.

Clark had used a 1999 golden handshake paid by WINZ to a senior executive, to pillory Christine Rankin as part of her election campaign. The background, according to one employment newsletter, was this:[143]

"According to *The Dominion*, WINZ agreed to pay the executive $100,000 in return for his immediate resignation. When the department realised that such a payment was unlawful and exceeded chief executive Christine Rankin's authority, it put together a deal which meant it would not need to seek ministerial approval."

That deal involved a lump sum payment of $50,000, which was below the cabinet threshold, as well as staying on the WINZ payroll for another six months on study leave. The total value of the severance, after holiday pay and performance bonuses were factored in, was $106,000.

"This is a case of stunningly inept personnel management at the top of a major government department," trumpeted Labour's Maharey. "Several cases like this have been reported to me verbally, but WINZ has always managed to hush them up with confidentiality agreements. This is one that got away..."

Maharey urged State Services Commissioner Michael Wintringham to "reopen inquiries into Christine Rankin's management practices" reported the newsletter. "Helen Clark says Christine Rankin was wrong in sanctioning the payout, and has pledged an inquiry into the department after the election."

Indeed, Clark gave Rankin a pounding in that final week before the 1999 election.

"Ms Rankin and WINZ continue to lead the field as examples of how not to run a government agency. In her haste to pay off a senior executive, she made an illegal payment..."

Under Labour, of course, "gardening leave" became standard practice, and suddenly the government wasn't angry about it at all.

ITEM FIVE: JOBS FOR THE BOYS (AND GIRLS)

Jim Hacker: "How do people know they are on this [honours recommendation] list anyway? This file is marked strictly confidential."
Bernard Woolley: "Oh Minister..."
Jim Hacker: "Silly of me."

In 1999, Helen Clark waxed lyrical about the evils of political cronyism – criticizing National's appointment of political mates and friends to positions

---

142   *NZ Herald*, 17 May 2005, "Van Rooyen receives $50,000 to 'work' from home"
http://www.nzherald.co.nz/topic/story.cfm?c_id=133&objectid=10125889
143   http://www.jobsletter.org.nz/jbl11300.htm "Payout Fiasco At WINZ"

of power and influence. All this would change under Labour, she promised. At Labour's election campaign opening, Clark was quoted as slamming parties who governed "in the interests of the few, not the many".[144]

One of the first "crony" appointments to be targeted was advertising agency boss Peter Biggs:

"Labour is attacking possible links between the new chairman of Creative New Zealand Peter Biggs and Prime Minister Jenny Shipley, and warns it may sack him and other 'political' appointments if it wins power," reported the *Herald* that year.[145]

"There is reason to believe," intoned Clark at her conspiratorial best, "that Mr Biggs is very closely identified with the present Government."[146]

As a case study in hypocrisy, however, you don't have to go much further than Labour's appointments to the Land Transport Safety Authority after it took office. In December of 2000, Labour appointed two new directors to the LTSA board – former Labour Prime Minister David Lange, and "family and employment law specialist Simon Mitchell".[147]

Lange could obviously be "very closely identified" with the Labour government, using Clark's own sniff test, much more so in fact than the mysterious "Mr Biggs". But Labour didn't disclose who Simon Mitchell was. Mitchell is a Labour party member and has acted as the lawyer for Joan Caulfield – Clark's electorate 2IC. Mitchell was also the man who paid $5,500 to buy back Helen Clark's forged painting so that Caulfield could destroy it, thus depriving a police investigation of forensic evidence.

In the briefing papers for incoming ministers prepared after the 2002 election,[148] the names of three of the five members of the LTSA board belonged to Labour political cronies[149]: Lange, Mitchell and Louisa Wall. Apart from Lange, whose political heritage was self-evident, the briefing notes did not declare that either Mitchell or Wall were Labour.

"Louisa Wall has a Master of Philosophy, Social Policy from Massey University," noted the ministerial briefing paper. "She has a background in mental health and is currently employed as Kaiwhakahaere Rangahau Hauora, for the Health Research Council of New Zealand. Louisa has represented New Zealand in netball and rugby and sees herself as a role model."

What the biography failed to disclose was Wall's links to the Labour Party.

144 *NZ Herald*, 1 November 1999, "Clark's Mission"
http://www.nzherald.co.nz/section/1/story.cfm?c_id=1&objectid=17101
145 *NZ Herald*, 23 August 1999, "Clark says chair political"
http://www.nzherald.co.nz/section/1/story.cfm?c_id=1&objectid=12358
146 Like much of Clark's rhetoric, her "outrage" was nothing more than dog whistle politics designed to get the public behind her. When Labour came to power, not only did it fail to sack Biggs – it reappointed him as Chairman for another three year term.
147 LTSA news release, December 2000
148 http://www.beehive.govt.nz/briefings/govt_admin_infrastructure/ltsa/11.cfm
149 I use the phrase only generically in regard to Lange, not personally. His background was not hidden, and he was very capable.

She is now the first openly lesbian Maori MP, having entered on the party list in March 2008 to replace the outgoing Ann Hartley.

In 2004, with the decision to turn the LTSA into Land Transport New Zealand, the board still included the Prime Minister's knight in shining armour Simon Mitchell, but also a character named Greg Presland. Presland, it turns out, was the electorate chairman for Labour MP David Cunliffe.[150]

What are the chances, do you think, that someone closely affiliated to Helen Clark's electorate and another to David Cunliffe's should happen to be just the right people for a taxpayer funded job?

Readers of the *Listener* magazine may recall, in the days following the Peter Davis controversy, how it quoted long-time friends of Helen Clark and Peter Davis denying any knowledge of gay rumours. Those spoken to included Aucklanders Jenny Agnew and Phil Harington.[151]

Described as married, and very close friends of the First Couple, it's clear Agnew and Harington were well-connected. A month or two after that very public display of loyalty, however, the Prime Minister's close friend Jenny Agnew was named as one of 12 new appointees to the Government's Small Business Advisory Group. In fact, she headed the list released by Small Business Minister Lianne Dalziel, who noted, "More than 250 applications for positions on the Small Business Advisory Group were received."[152]

Presumably, the appointees were selected on merit, but the Prime Minister must have been delighted that her loyal friend and former Mt Albert Labour electorate worker[153] managed to beat out 238 other people for one of the coveted, fee-paying national spots.

But what about Agnew's husband Phil Harington? He too has a politically-appointed fee-paying role, serving on the Lottery Grants Board that decides which worthy projects will benefit from lottery cash, and which charities will miss out.

Agnew and Harington's appointments are relatively recent, but as the *National Business Review* reported in late 2001, cronyism had already been turned into an art form by a highly cynical Clark administration:

"In opposition, Labour and the Alliance attacked the National government for dubious practices and sleaze. But in power, the coalition's record is looking grubby," wrote journalist Nick Smith.[154]

"Cronyism, graft, greed, sleaze, lies ... in two years the coalition government has accrued a record that might make a Tory politician blush. It is certainly a

150 http://www.cunliffe.org.nz/6.news/articles/detail.asp?id=43
151 *NZ Listener*, "The Silent Type", Sep 30-Oct 6, Vol 205 No 3464
152 Press release, Lianne Dalziel, 20 December 2006, "Dalziel names new small business advisers"
http://www.med.govt.nz/templates/MultipageDocumentTOC____24858.aspx
153 There are photos of Jenny Agnew on pages 201 and 203 of the official biography, *Helen*
154 *National Business Review*, 30 November 2001, " 'Clean and accountable' Labour-Alliance falls prey to corruption of power"

bhsmft

far cry from Prime Minister Helen Clark's promise of open, clean government – a pledge that one year out from an election is looking hollow.

"Some of her ministers' actions could have comfortably enjoyed headlines in the grubbiest of British tabloids: *Sex with Young Charge*; *Official Threatens Police*; *Drinking, Driving and Lying*; *Political Interference in Justice.*

"...Throughout the government's two-year tenure, it has relentlessly pursued a policy of cronyism, politicising the public service appointment process.

"After the election, the coalition moved quickly to fill public service positions with their favourites, many of whom even campaigned for either Labour or Alliance. The Broadcasting Standards Authority, the Employment Relations Authority ... all became the plaything of the government.

"Nowhere was this practice more blatant than at the Human Rights Commission headed by Rosslyn Noonan, a hardcore unionist who had served at executive level on the Council of Trade Unions and was a Labour Party member and an old mate of Attorney-General Margaret Wilson.

"Earlier this year [2001], three new commissioners were ushered in, Warren Lindberg, Ella Henry and Michael Powles, two of whom were candidates for Labour and the Alliance.

"Mr Powles has an extensive foreign affairs background but without strong links to the government. His two fellow inductees, however, stood for Parliament at the last election. Mr Lindberg, who ran the Aids Foundation for a decade, was number 48 on the Labour list, while Mrs Henry stood for Te Tai Tokerau," reported *NBR's* Smith.

The problem with cronies, however, is that often they bring major embarrassment to their positions. Take Ella Henry for example. Only a few months into the job as a human rights commissioner, Henry hit the headlines when her partner was ticketed by police for running an orange light at a school crossing at 8.17am on June 5, 2001.

No controversy there, you might think. But you'd be wrong. Ella Henry was convinced that her partner had been pinged solely because he was "black", not because he was potentially endangering children waiting to cross. She wrote to the Constable who'd given the ticket, explaining that she considered him racist, and enclosing her Human Rights Commission business card. Understandably, police felt she was trying to use her position to intimidate police.

More correspondence ensued, and again Henry enclosed her business card. Police bosses then wrote to Henry's superior, Chief Human Rights Commissioner Rosslyn Noonan, asking the HRC to call off the dogs. Ella Henry was spoken to, and wrote a letter of apology to the police officer – who'd taken particular offence to being called a racist given that he was born in Samoa. When the scandal finally hit the headlines, Labour tried to play it down, with Attorney-General Margaret Wilson telling a journalist that Henry had apologized, "Matter closed".

It wasn't though. Wilson's hands-free style of political management left media with the impression Labour was condoning intimidation of police by senior public servants. Later the next day, Wilson was forced to announce a meeting between herself, Noonan and Henry, and a few minutes later Henry stepped down.

Trying to dig herself out of a hole, Margaret Wilson said she'd actually known about the scandal for a week before it blew up, and "it occurred to me this was the type of action that would require resignation."

The light bulbs apparently burn dimly in the Beehive, because the idea failed to go off before the story did.

Susan Bathgate was another crony whose appointment came back to seriously embarrass Attorney-General Margaret Wilson.

Bathgate – a friend of Wilson's who also had close family ties to Labour – was appointed to a full-time taxpayer funded position at the Employment Relations Authority. But apparently she wasn't content with that. A *National Business Review* investigation[155] found that in addition to her "full time" work, she was "also being paid for being on the Social Security Appeal Authority, assisting members of the Student Allowances Appeal Authority and chairing the Complaints Review Tribunal."

How could she, asked critics, be paid a salary for "full time" work at the Employment Relations Authority whilst she was off, on work time, doing paid work for someone else?

Even though Bathgate was in the wrong, and agreed to repay $16,000 she'd obtained in fees from her secondary employment, Attorney-General softened the blow by paying Bathgate $30,000 to cover her "legal fees" (Bathgate was a lawyer, and probably quite capable of doing most of the donkey-work herself), and allowing her to work out two month's notice on salary, even though she only had one decision to write. That notice period was worth more than $20,000 to Bathgate.

Act leader Rodney Hide was not impressed.[156]

"Wilson has allowed her friend and dinner chum to live high on the taxpayer hog right up until the end," Hide exclaimed. "Her resignation should have been effective immediately."

To add insult to crony injury, one of the very last decisions issued by Bathgate in her capacity as chairwoman of the Complaints Review Tribunal was savaged by High Court judge Rhys Harrison on appeal[157], who ruled that Bathgate had commenced her review with a "predetermined" outcome in mind, and that outcome was essentially "evading performance of its statutory duty to adjudicate on the dispute", said Harrison.

---

155 *National Business Review*, 30 November 2001, " 'Clean and accountable' Labour-Alliance falls prey to corruption of power"
156 *NZ Herald*, 19 December 2001, "Government to give Bathgate $30,000"
http://www.nzherald.co.nz/section/1/story.cfm?c_id=1&objectid=333698
157 *NZ Herald*, 5 June 2002, "Court finds Tribunal prejudged case"
http://www.nzherald.co.nz/section/1/story.cfm?c_id=1&objectid=2045001

Hardly a ringing endorsement of the Labour appointee who'd been earning $100 an hour to adjudicate on both the Complaints Review Tribunal, and the Social Security Appeal Authority, whilst at the same time being paid a salary of $133,000 for full time work at the Employment Relations Authority.

In another review of cronyism three years later in 2004, *NBR's* Corran Lill makes the valid point that while both main parties have engaged in cronyism, at least National's cronies have had the job skills relevant to their positions as directors. Labour's cronies are described as "unskilled":[158]

"Although appointing cronies is not the exclusive domain of either left- or right-wing governments, the boards of New Zealand's burgeoning bureaucracy are increasingly being stacked with what might best be described as "unskilled" friends of the Labour party.

"This isn't to say the appointees have no skills but in many cases they don't have skills pertinent to the positions they're being appointed to.

"The trouble is this government's mates have a tendency to be trade unionists, teachers and former Labour MPs. Friends of more market-driven governments tend to be more market oriented types who bring a wealth of commercial experience: bankers, entrepreneurs, stock brokers and accountants – the types of people you're more likely to find on private sector boards.

"So what is Mai Chen, business partner of [former Labour Prime Minister] Sir Geoffrey Palmer, doing on our Securities Commission? Have you ever heard of Ray Potroz or Louisa Wall? Why is Marilyn Waring on the Reserve Bank? Labour party president Mike Williams on the Transit board? Unionist Ken Douglas on the Air New Zealand and New Zealand Post boards? Are there really not better skilled people out there?," asks Lill.

With some political appointments carrying salaries of $500,000, there are vast sums of money to be had in troughs supplied by the Clark Labour government, which make its attempts to attack cronyism elsewhere ring decidedly hollow.

Arguably, in the spirit of open government, it should be compulsory for Governments of *all* persuasions to openly declare the political affiliations of anyone appointed to public office or awarded a Government consulting contract, so that everyone can see whether the best people are getting the jobs, or whether cronies are.

Some cronies, however, are much bigger than others...

---

158 *National Business Review*, 13 August 2004, "Government pushes cronyism to absurd heights"

Labour's Mafia Connections

Jim Hacker: "Tiny mistake? 75,000 pounds! Give me an example of a big mistake."
Sir Humphrey: "Letting people find out about it." – **Yes Minister**

THE PROBLEM WITH ACCEPTING BIG donations, is that you're so excited about getting the money you might not ask too many questions about where it came from. As you'll shortly read, ex-pat kiwi businessman Owen Glenn is a lot more colourful than the daily media have revealed, and some of his associates allegedly have names like "Guido", "Luigi" or "Tony".

As a party that has waxed lyrical about big business donations and undue influence, Labour's track record exhibits a certain amount of hypocrisy. The publication of Nicky Hager's *The Hollow Men*, for example, gave Labour a chance to taunt National about Sir Michael Fay and David Richwhite allegedly donating to the party through a secret trust at the 2005 election.

Not that Hager himself was certain:

"It is *possible* it was the National Party donors Doug Myers, Alan Gibbs, Craig Heatley and David Richwhite…" (p196)

"Together all these donors *must* exert a strong *but invisible* influence over National Party policy…" (p222)

"…The *identities* of the major donors is *a closely guarded secret*, and it was *difficult to confirm* how much the donations were for or *even whether they were definitely sent…*" (p223)

"…There *appear* in 2005 to have been the following eight high value donors…" (p224)

It was a good effort, but we still can't be sure that any of the big donors in 2005 Hager speculated about are actually big donors, little donors or even donors at all. Nor, for that matter, can we be sure donations were even "definitely sent".

Hager might as well have named the secret donors, Bashful, Doc, Dopey,

Grumpy, Happy, Sleepy and Sneezy, and blamed the whole conspiracy on a "mystery American" eminence grise named Disney. Throw in Mickey Mouse and Bob's your uncle. In a manner of speaking.

Whilst a valid argument can be made for greater transparency, and perhaps his difficulty coming up with anything beyond "possible" illustrates his point about the need for it, Hager's book does not exactly nail National's mystery donors to the wall. None of this vagueness, however, prevented both Winston Peters and Helen Clark having a crack at John Key on the matter last year.[159]

National Party leader John Key is being labelled an apologist for "crooks" following his comments last week about Sir Michael Fay and David Richwhite.

In Parliament New Zealand First leader Winston Peters launched a scathing attack on Mr Key and renewed a call for an inquiry into whether the investigation into the pair was undermined.

Last week's $20 million settlement with the Securities Commission came without an admission of liability, but that has not stopped politicians from attacking the pair in the House...

...It is understood the Government feels an investigation would not be justified without more information.

But Prime Minister Helen Clark was happy to oblige Mr Peters during question time. Asked if any political figures supported the innocence of Sir Michael and Mr Richwhite, she said: "That came from the leader of the National Party who not surprisingly, and consistently with [Nicky Hager's] The Hollow Men, appears to have a closed mind on the issue."

It was a foolish fight to buy into: on the one hand some imaginary hobgoblins who may or may not have donated or not donated to National. On the other hand, there's much stronger evidence (with no ifs buts or maybes) linking those same hobgoblins to Helen Clark's dear friends and colleagues Margaret Wilson and Tony Timms:[160]

Attorney-General Margaret Wilson is refusing to declare a conflict of interest and back out of any further involvement with the Winebox, despite being part of a Labour fundraising team that accepted hundreds of thousands of dollars in political donations organised by millionaire banker David Richwhite.

Richwhite was, at the time, Chairman of European Pacific Group, the company the Government's law enforcement agencies are refusing to prosecute for fraud, despite advice from Crown lawyers and the Court that there's enough evidence to lay criminal charges.

It is not known if Richwhite was one of those considered in the Crown

---

159 *NZ Herald*, 28 June 2007, "Peters labels Key an apologist for crooks..."
http://www.nzherald.co.nz/section/1/story.cfm?c_id=1&objectid=10448343
160 *Investigate*, January 2001

Prosecutor's opinion, but as Chairman of EP he was not directly involved in the Magnum transaction at the centre of the controversy.

Investigate has confirmed that Richwhite – acting as a so-called "bagman" – collected campaign donations for Labour from prominent businesspeople prior to the 1987 election that returned David Lange's Labour Government to power.

Business leaders, including the then Equiticorp boss Alan Hawkins, gave up to quarter of a million dollars each after being approached by Richwhite. In Hawkins' case, the cheque was made out to the Labour Party but hand delivered to Sir Roger Douglas.

Wilson was President of the Labour Party at the time, and the question is: how much did she know?

According to former Prime Minister David Lange, Wilson "almost certainly knew the source of the donations. Even I knew, although I didn't know how much, nor did I care to know."

Former finance minister Sir Roger Douglas was much more reticent, however, when questioned over how much Wilson knew of the donations Richwhite had organised.

"What donations was David Richwhite organising?" challenged Douglas, before continuing "did he?" and then adding "I'm not sure, it's all a long time ago.

"If people wanted to make it known, the headquarters would obviously have known because the cheques would have gone to [party secretary] Tony Timms and been banked.

"There may have been people who, for one reason or another, just sent a bank draft or something."

But did Douglas discuss the source of the donations with Margaret Wilson?

"She was the President, there would have been a committee where there were discussions on those matters."

The then Labour Party secretary, Tony Timms, now works as an advisor to Prime Minister Helen Clark, in her office. When *Investigate* pointed out that he and Wilson would both have known of Richwhite's involvement, Timms' reaction was one of surprise:

"I beg your pardon. What's it got to do with you?"

Timms played down Wilson's role, describing it as "stuff all".

"Nine times out of ten, when we sent out the begging letters they would come back addressed to me and I would handle them, that's basically it," he explained.

"But this wasn't so much a 'begging letter'," we pointed out, "Alan Hawkins donated $250,000, and he has said David Richwhite approached him on behalf of the Labour Party and he was instructed to hand his cheque to Roger Douglas, but made out to the Party."

"Yes, and that in turn was handed to me," confirmed Timms.

But we continued to probe:

"Roger Douglas says there was a Party Committee which included Margaret

Wilson and yourself who would have been up to speed on a regular basis as to the funding."

"Oh, I was, but I don't recall Margaret being involved. I think myself, and probably a couple of others from the executive at the time."

Tony Timms couldn't recall who the "others" might have been.

But when we pointed out that David Lange had said he knew that Richwhite was organising donations and that Margaret Wilson "almost certainly knew" of the source of the donations, Timms agreed.

"Oh, whether one has knowledge of donations – yeah, sure, I mean the NZ Council knew because we had published accounts, but in terms of actual collecting of money, I used to pick them up.

"I was aware that we were getting substantial cheques from a variety of individuals."

Which brings us to Attorney-General Margaret Wilson's strange activities in regard to the Winebox investigation.

When Serious Fraud Office director David Bradshaw made his controversial decision not to prosecute over the Winebox despite three Courts ruling that a prima facie fraud existed, he was called to appear for questioning before Parliament's Law and Order Select Committee.

While being grilled by MPs on the Committee, particularly NZ First leader Winston Peters, TV3's sensitive and well-placed microphone caught the Attorney-General whispering answers to Bradshaw so surreptitiously you could barely see her lips move on camera.

Why would the supposedly objective Attorney-General choose to bridge the constitutional gap that is supposed to exist and whisper answers to the SFO director?

It is a question even Wilson's staff can't answer.

But the situation becomes even murkier. Winston Peters believes Bradshaw may have misled the Select Committee by suggesting that he received legal advice not to prosecute.

The Crown Prosecutor in Auckland, Simon Moore, in fact gave the Serious Fraud Office a legal opinion recommending prosecution over the Winebox, and Peters challenged Bradshaw to put up or shut up by releasing the legal opinions he received on the case.

Bradshaw has refused to do so, threatening to resign as SFO director if he was forced to by the Select Committee.

Attorney-General Margaret Wilson has publicly backed Bradshaw over the issue, again raising questions over whether she has an undeclared conflict of interest and should step aside.

As a precedent, the National Government's previous Attorney-General Paul East declared a conflict of interest over the Winebox and Russell McVeagh's film and bloodstock deals, when TVNZ asked whether it was true that John Lusk of Russell McVeagh was his cousin.

A spokesman for Margaret Wilson says the Minister has only one comment to the public: "There is no conflict of interest" in helping raise political campaign funds from David Richwhite on the one hand, and refusing to prosecute over the Winebox deals.

Why is there no conflict of interest?

"Because the Minister says there isn't", explained her advisor.

It's been revealed, meanwhile, that an official complaint filed with police over the Winebox last year was never investigated by Police. And despite allegations of corruption within the Serious Fraud Office, police refused to investigate that either, on the basis that "there was no evidence of such practices" – this despite testimony to the contrary by former SFO staff at the Winebox Inquiry.

It also goes without saying that normally you don't find evidence until you have investigated something.

"If an investigation of corruption of the Serious Fraud Office was to be instigated at all then it should be at the direction of the Solicitor-General or the Attorney-General, and might well be conducted by persons independent of the police," wrote Detective Superintendent Bill Bishop.

Police National Headquarters, already accused in a Parliamentary report of "contemptuous" behaviour and of mysteriously losing crucial evidence in a case that made police look bad, has joined the IRD, SFO and the Labour Government in refusing to prosecute over the Winebox, despite overwhelming legal advice and Court opinion to the contrary.[161]

If Labour really wanted David Richwhite, he was in their clutches and they let him go, thanks in part to the intervention of Attorney-General Margaret Wilson. It seems a little hypocritical to resurrect him now as a political bogeyman. But there's more on Labour's donations. Soon after *Investigate* published the above article in 2001, we were contacted by a former senior Brierley's staff member who'd physically handled the donation cheques for Labour. The donors definitely included Richwhite, Gibbs, Myers and Brierley, and the secret account Labour set up contained more than $2 million in 1987 dollars![162]

Winston Peters, the same one we all know and love, gave Labour a thumping in September 1987, according to parliamentary Hansard[163]. It was just after Labour had won its second term, Helen Clark had been rewarded with a cabinet position, and Finance Minister Roger Douglas was basking in his success:

"Before the last election," asked Peters, "did he, as Minister of Finance,

---

161 For the record, this was my first inkling of serious corruption inside Police National Headquarters. Commissioner Rob Robinson had been provided with transaction documents, Court of Appeal and Privy Council judgments spelling out a prima facie case, and legal opinions from QCs identifying suspects and specific crimes. In other words, it was join-the-dots easy. Despite laying a formal complaint, however, the police did not investigate. And when the Crown Solicitor in Auckland produced an opinion recommending prosecution, the Government and the police refused to action it.
162 *Daylight Robbery*, by Ian Wishart, Howling At The Moon Publishing, 2001, p88
163 Reprinted in *Daylight Robbery*, p89

make any approaches to corporate bodies for party political funds when Government appointees were part of these bodies?"

"No," replied Labour's then Associate Finance Minister Michael Cullen, the same one we all know and love, running interference on behalf of Douglas.

"Could the Minister then explain the resolution of Trustee Bank Holdings Ltd dated Friday, 24 July, which reads: 'The board decided that an appropriate response to a letter from the Minister of Finance seeking a contribution from Trust Bank for the Labour Party's political campaign was to make it clear that its policy was to make no political contributions'?"

Michael Cullen was at his evasive best:

"The [Trust Bank] board may not be able to tell the difference between the member for Manurewa as an individual member of the Labour Party, and his position as Minister of Finance. The member for Manurewa is certainly capable of making that distinction!"

So evidently the sins of Roger Douglas were not serious enough for Michael Cullen to disown him.

"Is the Minister stating that he wrote to Trust Bank," stammered an outraged National Party leader Jim Bolger, "seeking funds as a Labour Party member of Parliament and sought a distinction between that responsibility and his responsibility as Minister of Finance?"

"That distinction," mocked Cullen, "is well known to every member of the House."

Cullen wouldn't have had to look too far within Labour for evidence of dodgy donation money sloshing around. The woman who later became his wife, East Cape MP Anne Fraser, made an electoral return disclosing she'd received some of the big business money as a disbursement from Labour's parliamentary wing.[164]

Remember, Margaret Wilson, currently Speaker of the House, is said by David Lange to have been intimately involved in collecting these donations from rich, white businessmen. Wilson was part of Helen Clark's women's network and a strong ally and friend, and as a Cabinet Minister Helen Clark chose to accept responsibility for state asset sales to some of these business types at firesale rates after the election, rather than put her hand up in protest. For all of Labour's claims to have exorcised its ghosts from the 1980s, both Cullen and Clark are on record under the collective cabinet responsibility doctrine as supporting all the things the Lange cabinet voted for in its devastating second term. Did Cullen or Clark put their money where their mouths were and walk in protest? No.

And if you are mistakenly thinking this is all ancient history, think again. In the 1999 election that brought Helen Clark's fifth Labour government to power, Labour received $824,375 in anonymous donations. National only received around $600,000 via its secret trust.[165]

---

164 *Daylight Robbery*, p165, citing Hansard, April/May 1990
165 Ibid, p92

Labour had the chance to put the kybosh on large anonymous donations to political parties with its Electoral Finance Act, but it altered the legislation specifically so Labour's donations would not be affected.

So who are Labour's financial backers? A large amount of money – far more than Labour is required to declare under the rules – is funneled in from the huge trade unions who dock their members' pay. One news report carries estimates that the secondary teachers union, the PPTA, spent $373,000 on the 2005 election. The PPTA refused to disclose what it did spend. Leaked account documents supplied to *Investigate* magazine from within the Service and Food Workers Union confirmed around $240,000 of members' money was spent on securing a Labour victory last time around.

If you just take those two figures alone, that's more than $600,000, yet Labour only declared total union donations of $160,000 in its official returns (including only $20,000 from the SFWU).

Some in the SFWU also discovered Labour Party skullduggery:[166]

It was after dark when the key twisted in the lock at the Auckland headquarters of the Service and Food Workers Union, and three shadows flitted through the doorway. Grant Sutton could feel the tightening in his chest as the adrenalin punch kicked in and, for a moment, allowed himself a wry smile at the irony of it – the national president of a major trade union having to break in to his own headquarters to get information. At issue, although he didn't realize the enormity of it at the time: nearly $240,000 of members' funds allegedly siphoned off to help Labour win the last general election; and of course the reason he was actually there himself – a tip-off that a new Labour MP was trying to subvert the democratic processes of the SFWU by allegedly interfering in the election of new union officials.

Sutton, a salt of the earth kind of guy whose day job kept him grounded at Auckland International Airport, had been elected national president of the SFWU last November, head of a union covering some of New Zealand's poorest-paid workers. But his election coincided with a bout of political intrigue inside his union, the like of which is rarely seen in public.

At the centre of the spider's web, newly-elected Labour MP Darien Fenton who – up until October last – had been both the National Secretary and Northern Regional Secretary of the SFWU, working both positions from her desk in the Auckland office. With a husband and kids, Fenton didn't exactly fit the mould Labour was looking for in its list candidates. But what she lacked in politically-correct diversity she more than made up for in her solid trade union background, and it was enough to secure a safe place on Labour's MMP list.

Joining Fenton in the web was her personal assistant, Lisa Eldret, a young British woman who'd gained trade union "qualifications" in England before emigrating to New Zealand several years ago. Gay and strident, Eldret also worked in Prime Minister Helen Clark's Mt Albert electoral organization. Colleagues say she's being shoulder-tapped herself for bigger things.

Part one of the story dealt with a bid by Lisa Eldret, backed by Labour MP Darien Fenton, to take over a top position in the union and thus put herself in the possible hotseat for a future Labour party candidacy, just as Fenton had. After being sprung, the takeover bid failed. Part two of the story dealt with massive election overspending, allegedly authorized by Fenton whilst she was still a union official but also a Labour candidate:

While the Service and Food Workers Union may have resolved some of its problems with the shock defeat of chosen one Lisa Eldret in the northern regional secretary race, financially the union is feeling the pain after former national secretary Darien Fenton allegedly helped the SFWU overspend on Labour's election campaign last year – a campaign that Fenton directly benefited from given that she was also standing for Labour.

Accounting papers leaked to *Investigate* disclosed the union spent a massive $237,000 working to get Labour re-elected. What makes that figure intriguing is that not only is it much higher than the union budget allowed, but it is also far higher than the $20,000 donation Labour has declared to the Electoral Commission as the only money it received from the SFWU.

A financial report prepared by SFWU official Marina Kokanovic soon after the election puts it in black and white:

"Overall, the Union spent $237,364 during the election campaign. Around $100,274 was spent on printing, photocopying, postage, petrol cost, telephone tolls, the delegates' election conference and delegates' expenses. The cost for staff involved in the election activities was $137,090. Our Union dedicated almost 7% of [its] total financial resources as well as one-month labour force for the election campaign."

The documents also disclose that by the end of the election campaign the Union had made a $218,000 loss for the year – money its members would have to stump up with.

Consolidated account statements leaked to the magazine reveal the union had budgeted to spend only $70,000 on the election campaign in 2005. Fenton insists this lower figure is the accurate one.

But *Investigate's* inquiries were not the first time the SFWU's election spending had been scrutinized. In early 2006 (just after the statute of limitations expired for any criminal action against Labour) the results of the police investigation into issues like Labour's 'pledge card' and 'Brethrengate' were released. Buried in the hundreds of pages of files was an investigation of the SFWU's role in the election campaign.

Chief Electoral Officer David Henry referred the SFWU to the police after making a preliminary finding that the union's regular newsletter *Our Voice* should have carried statements by the secretaries of the Labour and Green Parties authorizing the document as 'election advertising' under s221 of the Electoral Act.

That section, in broad terms, essentially says that any advertising in newspapers, periodicals, posters and flyers which encourages or persuades or even merely *appears* to encourage or persuade voters to support a particular party, has to be authorized by the secretary of each party concerned. If the ads, flyers and the like carry no authorization, then the person responsible for putting them out becomes liable for the offence.

The reason for authorization is to bring the promotional spending into official expense accounts. Under the Electoral Act, each party is allowed to spend only a certain amount of money on election campaign advertising. As police pointed out on the Helen Clark pledge card investigation: "Labour was allocated $2.3m. If the cost of the pledge card and leaflet…is added to the total expenditure, then the Labour Party has spent $2.7m, which is $418k over their allocation for election expenses."

All of which makes the $237,000 spent by the SFWU suddenly very interesting.

The account papers in *Investigate's* possession showed the union's $17,000 expenditure on *Our Voice* was not part of the $237,000 in electioneering for Labour. But intriguingly, the union admitted in a letter to police dated 19 January 2006 that "Darien Fenton was a candidate for Labour when she wrote and authorized the *Our Voice* publication." Did that mean that – because of the conflict of interest inherent in Fenton's dual roles as a union official and Labour candidate – Fenton had effectively turned the August 2005 issue of *Our Voice* into one giant Labour party ad?

The police investigation, however, didn't go very deep. It restricted itself only to the *Our Voice* publication and some associated leaflets, and neither police nor the Electoral Office realized the union had spent vastly more on the election campaign than first thought.

Here's what the police decided in regard to the *Our Voice* complaint:

"A SFW Union booklet distributed to members of that union encourages union members to vote for Labour. The booklet is likely to be in breach of s221 of the Electoral Act, as the author did not have written authority from the Labour Party secretary [Mike Smith] to publish the material.

"There appears to be sufficient grounds upon which to base a charge… however the recommendation in respect of this material is that Police issue a warning to the SFW Union as to the implications of their publication in the lead up to a general election and the risk of becoming criminally liable under the provisions of the Electoral Act.

"It is noted," said one police report, "that Darien Fenton was a list candidate for the Labour Party when she wrote and authorized the production of the [*Our Voice*] Election Special 05.

"As such, she had a direct interest in the outcome of the election and potentially stood to benefit personally from any advantage that the Labour Party might gain from this material."

The long and short of all this is that the trade unions are, and will continue to be, a massive slush fund for Labour of undeclared donations that appear to outstrip National's warchest.

While the Electoral Finance Act has made it risky and perhaps even illegal for ordinary New Zealanders to enjoy freedom of speech in election year, major unions will slip through almost unscathed.

Another enjoying special protection is Labour's big business donor, Owen Glenn. If Labour had one overarching message during the Electoral Finance Act debate, it was the need to prevent large donations to political parties from shady business figures. Unless, of course, they were planning to donate to Labour.

Imagine the irony. You're a self-titled "popular and competent" Prime Minister, "a victim of my own success". You have a reputation as a control freak, for attention to the kind of details that would sink lesser mortals than yourself. You know what your enemies are thinking before they even do, and you have a well-oiled publicity and protection team whose 24/7 job it is to keep your nose clear of even the slightest whiff of scandal.

So imagine your surprise when you read in a national magazine that the Labour Party's largest campaign donations at the 2005 election came from a man whose company is the exclusive freight handling agent in Australasia for one of the world's largest tobacco companies.[167]

Yes, the irony is incredible: Labour's biggest election donations have come from the sole customs agent in Australasia for British American Tobacco, Owen Glenn.

But that's not all.

While the rest of New Zealand's media were falling over themselves to call Glenn a "billionaire", *Investigate* magazine – ever cynical – decided to do some digging of its own into the mysterious Mr Glenn.[168]

He's a shipping tycoon without ships – or what is known in the trade as 'a non vessel-operating common carrier'. Basically, his logistics companies book cargo space on real shipping lines and earn their fees from organizing the shipments. Owen Glenn's companies – when we investigated them in early 2006 – are tiny compared to global logistics giants like TNT. In the most recent financial year available at the time, TNT reported a "sluggish" logistics market and profit margins of only 1.4% on turnover.

---

167 OTS Logisitics newsletter, June 2005, http://www.oceanworldshipping.com/ NewsLetter/June2005/OTS_News_June05_GlobalNews.htm

168 *Investigate* magazine, February 2006,
http://www.thebriefingroom.com archives/2008/02/owen_glenns_sha.html

Sealink-USA reports Glenn's empire turned over NZ$500 million for the same period. We did the sums:

"Taking Owen Glenn's global revenues as $500 million and applying a 1.4% profit margin, you're left with a global profit for his companies of only NZ$7 million a year. Hardly lifestyles of the rich and famous.

"Returning to TNT Group as a comparison, TNT's annual turnover is around NZ$21 billion, and the group's net profit is around $1.3 billion (the group includes more profitable divisions than just Logistics). Overall, TNT managed to make a 6.2% profit on its turnover. Assuming this as a best-case scenario for the much smaller Owen Glenn companies, that's a global profit of only NZ$31 million a year."

Owen Glenn is no billionaire on those kind of figures, not even close. Not even after 30 years in business. When the people behind the *NBR Rich List* made contact, saw *Investigate's* story and ran the numbers themselves, they evidently agreed – Glenn was quietly dropped from subsequent rich lists.

Nor is Owen Glenn squeaky clean. Like Helen Clark, he's been pinged for dishonesty and paid a fine of $1.5 million to get out of jail free, so to speak. In 1999, investigators from the Federal Maritime Commission's Bureau of Enforcement (BoE) hauled Owen Glenn and his US-based shipping company Direct Container Line (DCL) into court on three counts of violating the Shipping Act by fraud.[169]

"Respondent DCL is a tariffed and bonded non-vessel operating common carrier that furnishes transportation services worldwide," notes a document on the Commission's website, "including services from US ports and points to ports and points in the Far East and South America. Respondent Owen Glenn is the Chairman and Chief Executive Officer of DCL.

"The Commission initiated two formal investigatory proceedings into the activities of these respondents."

The first investigation, commencing January 1999, "was begun to investigate allegedly unlawful activities by respondent DCL in the South American trade, specifically, allegations that DCL had misweighed and mismeasured cargoes in order to pay vessel-operating carriers less freight than what they were allegedly due, and also that DCL had not properly charged its own shippers the rates filed in its tariff.

"Such conduct violates sections 10(a)(1) and 10(b)(1) of the Shipping Act of 1984."

This alone was bad enough for Owen Glenn. At stake were financial penalties, and the possible suspension of DCL's tariff. But it got worse.

On April 29, 1999, the Bureau of Enforcement opened a second investigation, "to determine if DCL had been receiving rebates in its South American services under an arrangement set up by DCL's principal, Mr Owen Glenn, which

169 Judgment of the court, Federal Maritime Commission, June 29, 1999, Docket 99-01
http://www.investigatemagazine.com/australia/OwenGlenn.htm

arrangement had allegedly been operating subsequent to October 1994."

This time, the Bureau of Enforcement were going for Glenn's corporate jugular, saying they wanted "to determine if DCL's tariff should be canceled or suspended, its license as an ocean transportation intermediary revoked" and whether financial penalties should be imposed.

Was there hard evidence? According to the Bureau files, there was:

"It would introduce evidence in support of the allegations [showing] that DCL misdeclared cargo weights and measurements on bills of lading so as to pay lower rates to two vessel-operating carriers and that its documentary evidence, such as DCL's internal container manifest, would corroborate the fact that DCL routinely restated cargo measurements and weights for the same purpose.

"Moreover, BoE states that it would introduce evidence showing that DCL's "house" bills of lading issued to DCL's shippers show that DCL used higher figures than those on the bills of lading tendered to the vessel-operating carriers, and that DCL concealed equipment substitution practices whereby DCL obtained larger containers than those for which it was charged."

The Bureau also elaborated on what was essentially three years worth of secret kickback payments:

"BoE asserts that it would establish that DCL entered into an arrangement with a vessel-operating carrier for the receipt of rebates and that an officer of another shipping company would testify that in 1996 it was agreed that DCL and the other company would share in the rebates from the vessel-operating carrier.

"BoE asserts that it has documentary evidence to support the testimony. Moreover, BoE states that it would offer testimony of a second witness, a high-ranking sales and traffic manager of another vessel-operating carrier, such testimony showing that DCL and its officer, respondent Owen Glenn, established a rebate arrangement which covered *hundreds* of shipments during the period from 1994 through 1997.

"This second witness, according to BoE, would testify that respondent Owen Glenn suggested the method by which the vessel-operating carrier would pay rebate amounts that had been agreed upon."

According to the BoE documents, DCL received nearly NZ$1 million in "rebates" between 1995 and 1997.

A court judgment in the case records that, "After respondents (that's Glenn and his team) recognized that BoE could submit a compelling case," all parties agreed that it would be in their best interests to proceed to settlement negotiations, "which settlement would include possible violations by DCL with regard to a third vessel-operating carrier…and an agreement that BoE would support dismissal of Mr Owen Glenn as a respondent."

The final terms of the settlement approved by the court were simple: DCL had to pay NZ$1.5 million to the Federal Maritime Commission, in return for the case to be dropped and an agreement that the Commission would not re-open the investigation or widen it or pursue Owen Glenn.

So now there's evidence that Owen Glenn is a dishonest Labour party campaign donor, as well as being a tobacco freight baron. What more do we know about Glenn?

Well, for a start his empire is official run out of a Caribbean tax haven – a phrase not heard often in New Zealand since the Winebox days. That in itself is forgiveable, if again slightly questionable, but *Investigate* found and proved that one of Glenn's key financial officers was implicated in a massive criminal fraud in the US and Canada.

Peter Maxwell Dickson was, in late 2005 while we were writing the original article, still a director on Glenn's NZ subsidiary, Vanguard Logistics. He was simultaneously being investigated for his role in a multi-million dollar fraud involving a Horizon Bank International (HBI) that he was also associated with.

Initially Peter Dickson denied being the beneficial owner of the tax haven bank at the centre of a $20 million fraud, but midway through 2005 authorities felt sufficiently convinced that they revoked HBI's banking licence by way of an official memorandum, cc'd to Peter Dickson.

The international tax haven journal, *Offshore Alert*,[170] meanwhile, had been doing some corroborative digging of its own, discovering: "That HBI used to maintain a now-defunct web-site at http://www.tcn.net/horizon/horizon1. html which, as of October 5, 1999, identified its principal officers and directors as Peter Maxwell-Dickson, Director; Gordon Howard, Director; and William Cooper, Managing Resident Director.[171]

"Mr. Maxwell-Dickson has served at a number of firms including Deloitte, Haskins & Sells and KPMG Peat Markwick (sic)," stated the site. "From 1986 to 1990, he was the executive vice president of the Wraxall Group of companies, a large, diverse international trading and financial services company."

"Research by *Offshore Alert* showed that Peter Maxwell Dickson, a 54-year-old British national, is also a director of Vanguard Global Logistics Limited, formerly known as Direct Container Line Limited [Owen Glenn's company], of Barking, Essex, which was incorporated in England and Wales on January 18, 1982."

But Owen Glenn's right-hand man on the Vanguard NZ board was hanging out with a bad crowd, according to the *Offshore Alert* report. The "William Cooper" referred to as HBI's managing resident director is the same William Cooper sought by the US for the world's largest non-drug-related money laundering prosecution, a US$240 million dollar fraud committed in association with a convicted murderer and armed robber, using an Antigua tax haven bank he'd set up..

---

170   Its articles are available via pay-per-view at http://www.kycnews.com/, and search the archives for Peter Maxwell Dickson
171   Dickson's involvement can also be seen in a government order suspending Horizon Bank's licence, available here – http://www.pwc.com/ca/eng/about/svcs/brs/horizon-002_042805.pdf

Because of Antigua's tax haven secrecy laws, Cooper was not handed over to US authorities despite a four year legal battle by the feds. He remained in Antigua in early 2006, still operating in the tax haven business. And Peter Dickson's Horizon Bank International had been set up in Antigua, by Cooper in 1995.

"*Offshore Alert* has previously reported that Cooper was criminally indicted for money laundering at the U. S. District Court for the Northern District of Florida on April 28, 1999 – less than five months before HBI moved from Antigua, where Cooper lives, to St. Vincent. An attempt by the U.S. authorities to extradite Cooper from Antigua failed.

"Cooper has been implicated in numerous illegal activity involving offshore banks, including American International Bank, of Antigua, which closed its doors in December, 1997 when faced with a criminal investigation and insolvency. HBI listed AIB as one of its correspondent banks on its web-site," reports *Offshore Alert*.

So not only is Helen Clark's biggest donor responsible for handling the imports of most of the cigarettes in Australasia (proof perhaps that money *can* buy you love), but he himself was pinged for fraud and forced to pay a massive fee in the face of what the judge called "compelling" evidence of dishonesty by his company. And now we see one of his right hand men is associated with world class criminals.

Nor is he a billionaire based on both published account information and a comparison with his industry rivals.

In addition to all of the above, which is documented and proven, is an allegation from the US that one of Owen Glenn's "investments" was a joint venture in a California restaurant run by associates of the Mafia.

"He was an investor in a restaurant in California with guys who had NY mafia connections. I knew him then – he was an arrogant jerk. He was a sugar daddy to a coked-up black hostess at that restaurant. Funny thing is – his restaurant partners were ripping him off. A kind of poetic-justice? What, no honor among thieves?"

This particular allegation, from a former colleague[172], has not yet been independently verified, nor does it prove he knew who he was dealing with in the beginning, but given the other information above it cannot be dismissed out of hand, and given his key role in helping the Labour Party there is a strong, or as Clark herself would put it, "legitimate" public interest, even in the mere existence of such a suggestion.

If Glenn is doing business with organized crime, or if he has other income streams from which to make donations, that could explain his apparent generosity despite a lack of obvious value in his wider transport group.

The story then, for Labour, gets better by the minute. A story in February

2008 has put the cat well and truly among the pigeons and again casts a cloud over Prime Minister Helen Clark's credibility.

Owen Glenn returned for a New Zealand visit that month, and to help Clark officially open the new University of Auckland School of Business building named after him. As part of the visit, Glenn's PR company organized a series of media interviews, within set guidelines.

"In Auckland this week," wrote the *Herald's* Fran O'Sullivan,[173] "the billionaire had been supposed to focus on philanthropic matters when a series of interviews with selected journalists were lined up for him by his PR agency Baldwin Boyle Group. This firm's David Jamieson told me Glenn 'doesn't want to talk about the donations issue'. He was here to pump fundraising. But the boisterous entrepreneur didn't stick to the script."

Indeed, he didn't. Whether it was chutzpah, a rush of blood to the head, or whether he was reveling in all the media attention, no one knows. But Glenn gave the *Dominion-Post's* Kim Ruscoe a very incriminating interview.[174]

"The Exclusive Brethren's "sneaky" campaign to oust the Labour government at the last election prompted one of New Zealand's richest men to level the playing field with $500,000," Ruscoe's story began.

Hold the line! As *Investigate* and other media had already recorded two years ago, Glenn met Helen Clark at a tourism dinner in Sydney on July 8, *2004, a full 14 months before news of any Brethren campaign became public* in September 2005. Surely Owen Glenn couldn't be serious? But apparently so.

"There was a little bit of controversy to do with some church that had done something," Glenn told the paper.

"That controversy," wrote Ruscoe, "was a $1 million campaign by the Exclusive Brethren to get National elected, a move that sparked the Government's race to bring in new electoral finance laws before this year's election.

"What really riled Mr Glenn was the "sneaky" way in which the Brethren had reportedly tried to hide the fact it was behind the campaign."

"I thought, 'Poor old Labour; let's make this a little more interesting.' There's a little bit of imp in me."

Privately, as Prime Minister Helen Clark read the *Dominion-Post* that Friday morning, she probably muttered something like, "More chimp, than imp!"

She wouldn't have liked the rest of the interview, either.

"So he settled on $500,000 – because $100,000 was not enough and one million dollars was too much.

"In the past," continued the newspaper, "Miss Clark had tried to lure him back to New Zealand and into the Labour Cabinet, suggesting that, with his background, he would be a sitter for the plum role of transport minister. But Mr Glenn was not convinced, saying that, with all the major transport assets

173 http://www.nzherald.co.nz/category/story.cfm?c_id=144&objectid=10492752&pnum=0
174 http://www.stuff.co.nz/dominionpost/4401616a6000.html

sold off to private owners, there would be little for him to do.

"He had not given any thought to whether he would donate to Labour's campaign again this year, or to any other political party, but believed they no longer needed his help.

"After the last election, he told the Labour Party to ditch the begging bowl and lent the party 'a relatively small amount of money' to employ the services of fundraisers.

" 'From what I'm told, they got some very good advice ... they should be self-supporting now.' The loan has since been repaid."

As an added sting in the tail, after revealing he was offered a powerful cabinet post and that he has loaned more money to Labour, Glenn, who has just coincidentally been given a New Year's honour by the Government with the exclusive ONZM award[175], added that he now wants to see Labour reverse New Zealand's iconic anti-nuclear legislation.

"As for Labour's performance since his controversial donation, Mr Glenn said Miss Clark had done an 'adequate' job, having got a free trade deal with China. But now, for the sake of expediency, New Zealand needed to drop its no-nuclear stance and do a deal with the United States. 'Get the bloody thing. Pump another $4 billion into the country so we can afford another beer and put another ten bucks on the horses'."

Clark, by all reports, was apoplectic by the end of the article.

Having spent the 2005 election campaign insinuating National would kow-tow to shady overseas interests and reverse the anti-nuclear laws, now, here in print, was Labour's biggest campaign donor, with a less than pristine past and an agent for Big Tobacco, suggesting he now wants to see Labour change the anti-nuclear laws.

And who knows, if Labour gets desperate enough for campaign donations after winning the next election, it might change its policies.

The *Herald's* Fran O'Sullivan also sniffed a rat in regard to the interview[176].

"The PM would not have been amused at publicity over the expat billionaire's claim she had dangled the prospect of him ultimately being Transport Minister. A claim which suggested the relationship between Labour and its biggest private donor is close to one of political cronyism.

"Clark would not engage directly on Glenn's claim yesterday. All I managed to extract from her press secretary Kathryn Street was a one liner: "The response from a spokesperson for the Prime Minister is it never happened". But Glenn's recollection of the conversation was sufficiently full that he could relate to reporter Kim Ruscoe just where the conversation took place (Kawau

---

175 As a mark of his respect for New Zealand, Owen Glenn has chosen not to receive his Order of NZ Merit award at the hands of Governor-General Anand Satyanand in Wellington, but instead has made private arrangements to receive his gong at Buckingham Palace from the Queen herself, this coming June

176 *NZ Herald*, 16 February 2008, "Fran O'Sullivan: Public deserves better answers" http://www.nzherald.co.nz/category/story.cfm?c_id=144&objectid=10492752&pnum=0

Island after the Millennium Cup Super Yacht regatta). He also recollected his reasons why he wouldn't want the job (assets like the railways were sold ... Qantas was closing in on Air NZ ... what would he do?) and her rejoinder (these things might not have happened if we had people like you)."

Ouch.

Clearly, Owen Glenn's attempt to justify his massive donations to Labour by linking them to the Exclusive Brethren – even though he gave the money a year before the Brethren campaign even began – begs further explanation. It also forced Labour onto the back foot, with party president Mike Williams conceding to journalists that "Owen is confused about the timing."[177]

"When Glenn's gong was announced Labour Party president Mike Williams was quick to play down any suggestions of cash for honours," notes O'Sullivan. "He said Glenn had not made any donations to Labour since 2005, but he would certainly be approached before the 2008 election.

"The Labour Party president's comments may be literally true," warned O'Sullivan. "But they now appear disingenuous. Yesterday Williams confirmed Glenn had made a $100,000 loan on interest free, not commercial, terms. It has been repaid in full.

"The $100,000 loan Glenn extended Labour would have come at a time when it was cash-strapped after the 2005 election. An election where Auditor-General Kevin Brady later found that Labour had inappropriately plundered the public purse to the tune of more than $800,000."

In saying that Labour Party president Mike Williams' denial of any Glenn donations since 2005 "may be literally true", O'Sullivan was probably being too kind.

Section 21(2) of the Electoral Finance Act 2007 defines a donation thus:

Party donation means a donation (whether of money or of the equivalent of money or of goods or services or of a combination of those things) that is made to a party ... and includes ... where credit is provided to a party on terms and conditions substantially more favourable than the commercial terms and conditions prevailing at the time for the same or similar credit, the value to the party of those more favourable terms and conditions"

In other words, the interest-free portion of the loan was definitely a donation, meaning Williams had given a bum steer to the media when trying to hose down the "cash for honours" scandal breaking at New Year's.

Further embarrassment was heaped on disaster when Glenn let it be known he was expecting to be made honorary NZ consul in the tax haven Monaco. Whilst insignificant, it would have given this big-noter an "in" at diplomatic functions and parties in Europe. In the face of the media glare, Labour backed down from giving Glenn the post.

So while the Electoral Finance Act puts ordinary New Zealanders at risk

177   *NZ Herald*, 16 February 2008, "Clark denies offering post to supporter"
http://www.nzherald.co.nz/category/story.cfm?c_id=144&objectid=10492791

of criminal prosecution for speaking out, it seems big business donations to political parties are totally unaffected. What's more, only the interest-free portion of Glenn's "loan" to Labour is required to be disclosed as a donation. At most, that will be only $8,000 for an entire year's worth of interest, and much less if the loan was paid back faster. Any ordinary voter looking at the donations would not see the businessman's potential influence on Labour with the much larger loan itself, because the loan does not have to be disclosed.

Imagine if a wealthy benefactor gave provided a $2 million "overdraft" facility, of which only the interest portion ($160,000) had to be declared. Would the declared amount under the Electoral Finance Act really reflect the true value to Labour?

Labour was mortgaged to the transport baron who helps import British American Tobacco products into NZ and Australia, and who wants the anti-nuclear laws ditched, and nobody knew. Perhaps that loan is another reason why he received a New Year's Honour.

The latest developments bear a striking resemblance to the "cash for honours" criminal inquiry into Tony Blair's administration in Britain.

"It emerged last year [2006] that a number of large secret loans had been made to the Labour Party before the 2005 general election," reported the BBC[178], "and that some of those lenders had subsequently been nominated for peerages. Scottish National Party MP Angus MacNeil wrote to the Metropolitan Police asking them to investigate whether any laws had been broken. The investigation was later widened to cover the other main parties."

Tony Blair, like Helen Clark, became the first Prime Minister in his country to face police interviews in a criminal investigation. Unlike Clark, against whom a prima facie case of forgery was found, Blair was not being treated as a suspect. A number of his staff and campaign donors were arrested during the course of the investigation, but British police could not find documentation definitely linking a specific donation or loan to a definite promise of an honour.

SUMMARY OF MAIN POINTS:

- Labour's biggest donor meets Clark in 2004, and decides to donate $500,000 leading up to the 2005 election ($200,000 in 2004, and $300,000 in election year). [status: documented]
- Glenn is named as a "billionaire", but inquiries by *Investigate* suggest he is worth nowhere near that amount [status: documented]
- Additionally, his appointee on the board of his New Zealand operations was embroiled in a massive money-laundering case in the US, Caribbean and Canada. [status: documented]
- Owen Glenn was prosecuted for fraud by the US government and made a

---

178 http://news.bbc.co.uk/1/hi/uk_politics/4812822.stm

$1.5 million settlement offer in the face of what the judge called "compelling" evidence[179] [status: documented]

• Labour's biggest donor is the exclusive customs agent for British American Tobacco products across Australasia [status: documented]

• Labour's biggest campaign donor wants the anti-nuclear laws dropped [status: documented]

• Labour's biggest donor claims he was offered a Cabinet post after making his donations [status: documented]

• Labour's biggest donor secretly lent a further $100,000, interest free, to Labour in 2007, at the height of the "pay it back" scandal [status: documented]

• Labour's biggest donor is awarded a prestigious New Year Honour heading into election year 2008, at the same time as Labour party president Mike Williams reveals he certainly intends to collect more campaign funding from Glenn this year [status: documented]

• Labour's biggest donor allegedly was in business with New York Mafia interests [status: under investigation, not proven]

• Labour Party president Mike Williams told the media Glenn had made "no donations" since 2005, when in fact he had [status: documented]

All of this may rise eyebrows among those on the receiving end of Glenn's philanthropic largesse (recipients include not only the Labour Party, but the University of Auckland and the marine research centre at Leigh), but it is Vanguard Logistics' boast that it is now the exclusive customs clearing and handling agent for British American Tobacco that sits most uneasily for some. After all, the Prime Minister is no stranger to fraud herself, but the sight of New Zealand's leading anti-smoking politician accepting money from those involved in shipping cigarettes is anathema to the group Action on Smoking and Health (ASH):

"It's frustrating!" complains ASH director Becky Freeman. "First we find out the government pension funds are invested with British American Tobacco, and now we find out this! It's blood money, and they should have nothing to do with companies that associate with the tobacco industry.

"I would hope now that it's been pointed out that they will no longer accept donations from this particular source."

Yeah, right.

There is one final footnote to this chapter on Labour's secret donors. Apparently, they are not above attempting to bribe minor parties to go into coalition with Labour.[180]

The Maori Party claims a wealthy businessman offered it $250,000 if it would

---

179 http://www.investigatemagazine.com/australia/OwenGlenn.htm
180 TVNZ, 28 September 2006, "Answers wanted over election offer"
http://tvnz.co.nz/view/page/484445/837399

support the Labour Party. The report is the latest in the row over who is secretly backing our political parties.

The Maori Party said it was approached before the last election with an offer of a substantial sum of money, if they would commit to Labour.

"It was pretty clear that we couldn't accept it. We had declared that the Maori Party would look to be a strong and independent voice within parliament," says Maori Party president Whatarangi Winiata.

The party says the potential donor was a wealthy man who also gave money to Labour. But it will not name him.

Labour received 22 donations over $10,000 last election – the largest was $300,000. But it says it knows nothing about the Maori Party offer.

"If we had of heard of something like this, we certainly would not have touched it with a bargepole because it's potentially a breach of the law. Indeed you might go as far to say its a breach of the Crimes Act, which strictly prohibits bribes being offered to people," says Labour cabinet minister Steve Maharey.[181]

The donor's offer was passed on by a third person and there is no independent confirmation that it was conditional on the Maori Party supporting Labour.

Surprisingly, Attorney-General Michael Cullen did not ask the Serious Fraud Office, which has the power to compel witnesses to talk to them, to investigate this. For the record, Owen Glenn denies being behind it.

It seems quite apropos, then, that investigations into the Labour Party's funding reveal a long trail of murk and intrigue, because murk and intrigue have dogged Clark's third term in a spectacular fashion.

---

181 Call me cynical, but breaching the Crimes Act has never proven a moral barrier for Labour in the past

TOP, Labour's controversial donor Owen Glenn (left) is blocked by Trevor Mallard, while Clark, Sir Howard Morrison and Judith Tizard look on (Herald/Presspix). BELOW, The Prime Minister gives symbolic submission to Islam as a woman by donning the hijab. She refused to allow Grace at a State Banquet for Queen Elizabeth, who is the titular head of the Anglican Church. RIGHT, Peter Davis in his University of Auckland office (Herald/Presspix)

LEFT, The Prime Minister and David Benson-Pope enjoying a school visit (Herald/Presspix). **TOP,** Helen Clark once described a Jenny Shipley trip to visit NZ troops as "a fairly thin excuse for wanting to pose in a flak jacket". Nonetheless, Clark seems to enjoy such visits herself (UK Ministry of Defence). **BELOW:** US Defence Secretary Robert Gates escorts Clark into the Pentagon last year. (Defenselink)

The Whipping-boy

Sir Humphrey: "We should always tell the press freely and frankly anything they could easily find out any other way" – **Yes Minister**

AS AN EPITOME OF LABOUR'S problems in its third term in government, you'd struggle to go further than David Benson-Pope. The bombastic former school teacher had entered Parliament in the swing to Labour of 1999, and in his capacity as senior whip after 2002 Benson-Pope helped shepherd the controversial Civil Unions legislation through the House.

But it was his rise to Cabinet in 2004, and promotion to Associate Education Minister, that saw Benson-Pope whacked with a series of allegations in May 2005 that set in motion a fatal chain of events for his career.

Briefly, several former pupils at Dunedin's Bayfield High, where Benson-Pope had taught in the 80s and 90s, came forward to tell their stories of corporal punishment at the Minister's hands. One had been bound with duct tape and had a tennis ball shoved in his mouth, another claimed to have been struck in the face.

"I find such allegations ridiculous and I refute them," a seemingly outraged Benson-Pope told Parliament.[182]

Act leader Rodney Hide stepped up to the plate:

"Did he ever smack a pupil with the back of his hand sufficiently hard enough to make his nose bleed at a school camp in the Catlins and is this the reason along with throwing tennis balls at pupils in the classroom that he has the reputation of being a terrible bully and in fact the students to this day still suffer from his treatment?"

"That is a disgraceful allegation and I refute it completely," the embattled Minister responded, apparently unaware despite his long teaching career that "refuting" something requires more evidence than a mere denial.

---

182   Hansard, NZ Parliament, 12 May 2005

Admitting such behavior would be "clearly illegal", Benson-Pope challenged Hide and National MP Judith Collins to raise the issue with police.

"I have not been guilty or involved in any inappropriate behaviour, nor am I aware of any complaint of any kind."

It was that last comment that would come back to haunt Benson-Pope.

A police investigation was launched, finding (yet again) a prima facie case of criminal offending:[183]

"There was a prima facie case concerning an event where a student's hands were taped to the desk while he had a tennis ball in his mouth and another event involving another student being struck on the face. While there was some conflicting evidence Police concluded there was a prima facie case," noted police.

However, (yet again) police decided it was not serious enough to merit prosecution.

Clearly, the fact that police found a "prima facie" case of assault put heavy pressure on David Benson-Pope's credibility, and raised questions about whether he had misled Parliament in his May 12 statements.

The police file, however, was around 1,000 pages long. Most news journalists had skipped straight to the Executive Summary, assuming the Police would summarise the issue impartially. As all former cabinet spin-doctors know, however, it was a standard trick to write an Executive Summary to emphasise the points you wanted journalists to pick up, and leave the detail buried in the report itself where hopefully it would remain undiscovered.[184]

Buried in the police report were fresh allegations against the Labour cabinet minister, however, and over the summer of early 2006 *Investigate* magazine slowly worked through them. There seemed to be a common thread, and it involved humiliation of children and – according to those interviewed by police – sometimes an almost sadistic pleasure in inflicting pain.[185]

Last year, when the allegations of the MP's brutality first surfaced, he initially claimed his accusers were liars, and school bullies. Ironically, however, one of the themes running through the police file has been bullying by Benson-Pope, that he treated bright students well and the less-academically able badly, or that he simply enjoyed picking on the helpless.

One student told police that when Benson-Pope delivered canings in the

183 Police Southern District News Release, 23 November 2005, http://www.police.govt.nz/district/southern/release/2195.html
184 A similar stunt was pulled by the World Health Organisation in its major 2004 study on condom effectiveness. The Exec Summary ran the line that condoms were the best form of preventing STIs in the medical arsenal, and must be encouraged. The rest of the report however contained study after study showing condoms just don't work. They're better than nothing, but not much better than a kitchen sieve. So most of the world's media missed the big story buried in that report as well. My advice to the media: always read the full report.
185 *Investigate*, March 2006 issue, http://www.thebriefingroom.com/archives/2007/02/minister_of_sle.html

corridor outside the classroom, he did so with apparent relish:

"Mr Benson-Pope would whistle the cane in the air before taking a run up of about 10 feet. I'm estimating the distance but you could actually hear him running up. It was pretty psychologically damning, standing there bent over listening to the run-up. I'm pretty sure it was a run-up for each of the three canes on that occasion. As a result I suffered severe bruising but no bleeding. Obviously very painful to sit for the next few days."

A second boy remembers refusing to jump the vault at PE in the third form because he didn't feel confident. He told police his punishment from Benson-Pope was the cane. He was one of two boys given the cane for non-compliance at PE that day.

"I had to wait outside the school hall while Tony [the other offender] was dealt with first. I could hear screaming and yelling– I still remember it well today because [Tony] was such a tiny boy." A former teacher confirms the incident. "It's a lasting impression because it's the only caning I've witnessed. I remember Tony ran a lap of the assembly hall yelling in pain after the caning."

"When it was my turn," continues the former student who'd refused to jump the vault, "I was brought into the hall. I was bent over and caned once over my trousers by Benson-Pope. I pleaded not to be caned again but was struck once more with the cane.

"I remember Benson-Pope laughing while he caned me – and that's what got me the most. When I got home I realized I had blood on my bum."

These were not the fantasies of errant kids – the police files reveal teachers who not only saw some of these events, but others who were bullied by Benson-Pope themselves.

Then there were the unorthodox punishments, like making students, including girls, stand outside on a winter's night in Dunedin dressed only in their underwear or nighties, while Benson-Pope stood watching them for up to an hour with a torch.

Another student spoken to by police recalled her teacher's "sleazy" approaches.

"Quite sleazy, some of the comments he made used to grate me. The girls, including me, felt that he was always staring at our legs beneath desks…With the girls he was always sleazy if he could be, he seemed to thrive on it."

There was something oddly disquieting about all of these things, but nothing we could yet put our fingers on. Collectively, they lent considerable weight to the original allegations involving tennis balls and assault, and strongly indicated Benson-Pope had lied to Parliament.

When our story broke, however, Benson-Pope tried to brush it off. It was a bad move, because it motivated other students to come forward with their own tales of cruelty. The magazine ran an updated story on its website the following week:

Investigate magazine was inundated with emails and phone calls from former Bayfield students after running a cover story on David Benson-Pope last week. As a result of new information, the magazine contacted more than a hundred former pupils by email in order to corroborate the fresh allegations that had come to light.

Of the latest criminal assault allegation from 1997, one student told *Investigate* David Benson-Pope used a ruler to slap her across her thigh, leaving "a red mark". The student's crime, apparently, was failing to count to ten in German. She told *Investigate* her reaction was one of shock.

"[I thought] Holy s**t!, and I looked around the room to see if anyone else had seen it and people had.

"I seriously would like to have him in a room and tied to a chair so I could knock the living s**t out of him! To be quite honest."

Some of the former schoolgirls contacted by *Investigate* since the magazine came out have distinct memories of what they regard as unacceptable sexual behaviour by David Benson-Pope on school camps.

One woman has told *Investigate* Benson-Pope walked unannounced and uninvited into the girls dormitory while they were getting changed after a mud run.

"He knew we were in there. It was straight after the mud run, he knew we were all in there getting changed and things like that and he just wandered straight on in, and thought he had the right to do that."

The woman says up to twenty-five girls aged 14 and 15 were in various stages of undress, some fully, during Benson-Pope's "visit".

"Girls were naked and in the process of getting changed."

She says the Labour MP lingered, for 30 seconds, before finally getting out because of the pandemonium his presence was causing.

"Screaming and yelling and telling him to get out, and all this swearing."

The woman says it was the second time that day Benson-Pope had attempted to see the schoolgirls undress.

"He walked in on the showers one time, then later on that day walked into the dorm room while we were getting changed. Straight on in."

This incident happened at the fourth form camp in 1997. The woman told *Investigate* she and the other girls were embarrassed and dumbfounded that a senior male teacher felt he had the right to enter the girls' dormitories at all, when it should only have been female staff permitted.

"He's an a******e. He really is. I don't know if any other students did, but me and my parents made a formal complaint about it, but nothing was done about it."

She says they took their concerns in the first instance to Bayfield principal Bruce Leadbetter.

"We were told to write a letter and it had to go in front of the Board of Trustees. But that never happened."

The significance of all this, is that the latest complaints were only a few years old. Whilst the tennis ball incident had happened in 1982, the most recent of these had happened in 1998, only seven and a half years earlier. In other words, it was an ongoing pattern of behavior with this particular teacher turned politician.

Most significant of all, Benson-Pope was Associate Education Minister (and was subsequently promoted to Minister of Social Development, whose responsibilities included CYFS). Voters making a call on the suitability of a cabinet minister were, and are, entitled to know relevant background information.

Additionally, here was the first reference to a formal written complaint – Benson-Pope of course had told parliament there were no complaints. So this aspect was relevant to his honesty – again, vitally important if Benson-Pope were ever to attain even higher office.

The Minister again tried to deny the latest claims, but by now too many students were coming out of the woodwork with stories. Bayfield's former principal, Bruce Leadbetter, who back in May 2005 had told reporters there had been no complaints about Benson-Pope's behavior was now forced to admit there had been, after the school's current principal released copies from his files backing up the *Investigate* version of events.

Then Benson-Pope ran the line that the 1997 complaint wasn't serious because his behavior in entering girls' changing areas was "school policy" at the time, and that it merely resulted in a change to school policies about male teachers going into girls' dormitories.

But according to another female student in an email to *Investigate*, David Benson-Pope again busted in on schoolgirls getting changed on the 1998 fourth form camp, his last year at the high school before entering parliament.

"I do remember one incident involving him when I was in 4th form at a school camp at Tautuku. I remember that the girls were in their dorm getting ready for a tramp and we were all mucking around and taking ages to get changed. BP [Benson-Pope] got quite agitated and just marched on into the dorm without knocking or any warning at all and yelled at us all to hurry up. At this stage quite a few of us were still trying to get changed.

"I'm not sure if anybody reported this incident to the other teachers but it was talked about for a few years after that and it didn't do much for his image with the students in my year!"

The more Benson-Pope tried to dig himself out of a hole, the deeper his hole became. Despite all of this, and despite clear evidence that Benson-Pope had not been honest in his statements to Parliament, Prime Minister Helen Clark was standing by him. Well, almost. As the week wore on even Clark's patience was wearing thin, as the *Herald's* Geoff Cumming reported.[186]

---

186 *NZ Herald*, 4 March 2006, "Operation Benson-Pope"
http://www.nzherald.co.nz/topic/story.cfm?c_id=337&objectid=10370949

Slumped in his chair, he no doubt wishes it would swallow him up. Even team captain Helen Clark gives him a dressing-down and his colleagues offer scant support as the Opposition scores hit after hit.

Since last May it's been a steep descent from a stellar political career for the former Bayfield High School social studies and languages teacher and head of outdoor education.

Student politics, teacher, unionist and city councillor – he bore the quintessential Labour CV and, with powerful friends in the Government, was seen as a future education minister.

But Benson-Pope is a complex character who polarises, as the conflicting memories of former pupils suggests. It's not the allegations themselves, but his inability to extricate himself from them, the suggestion that he misled Parliament, and the implications for a Government with a knife-edge majority.

From the start, Labour's handling of Operation Benson-Pope has been a study in mismanagement – and a curious departure from usual form. The Beehive's ninth floor (the Prime Minister's office) has a reputation for running a tight ship, for being quick to jettison liabilities...

Yes, but not quick enough, as history eventually showed. After two weeks of denying the basic gist of the *Investigate* stories, Benson-Pope was finally forced to apologise and recant. He kept, however, his portfolios as Minister for the Environment and Minister for Social Development.

And there it might have remained, but for a bizarre story that surfaced at the end of 2006. David Benson-Pope, it was alleged, was affiliated with a Dunedin bondage and discipline (sado-masochism) group known as the "Southern Kinx".

A member of the group had let slip details of Benson-Pope's involvement during a select dinner-party with close friends – one of whom contacted *Investigate*.

On tape, the member explained who was involved – names, addresses, phone numbers, special identifying features – the works. A key point, the witness explained, is that duct tape is often used in BDSM (bondage/discipline sado-masochism) sex play, as are balls shoved in mouths. Sure enough, when *Investigate* managed to infiltrate BDSM groups, we found pictures of exactly that.

Suddenly the earlier allegations started to make more sense, and that sense of disquiet was starting to get a name. The driving force behind BDSM is a desire on one person's part to inflict pain for pleasure, and a desire on another person's part to be the victim. Humiliation is a core aspect of this.

Investigate was able to identify other key members of the group, including a prominent young political activist. There were only eight or so people in the particular sub-group that Benson-Pope allegedly interacted with – we had the names of all of them, but named only the ones essential to the story.

There were aspects of the story that were too graphic for general print, and remain so today. More importantly, they are things Benson-Pope's children don't need exposure to. They do however fit the context of the earlier allegations as well.

Most importantly, as a former teacher, and as a Minister responsible for CYFS, the agency dealing with troubled children, the information uncovered by *Investigate* suggested Benson-Pope's private life had a definite bearing on his public actions and duties.

The day the magazine broke the story online, however, Don Brash chose to quit as leader of the National Party. Media attention for the most part was elsewhere, except for the New Zealand *Herald* and the *Otago Daily Times*.[187]

"Enough is enough. You've seen my diary. When would I have time for this?" Benson-Pope told the *Otago Daily Times* senior reporter.

It was the old, "I'm too busy for this" routine. But he refused to deny it. He did everything but. He told the paper he'd instructed his lawyers to contact other news media and warn them. Prime Minister Helen Clark was quoted saying it was "a smear campaign". But Benson-Pope refused to deny it.

It wasn't just a no-comment. The Minister rang one journalist at his home at 10:28 pm that night to ensure the *Otago Daily Times* "does not print a denial".

According to the journalist, Benson-Pope was adamant that under no circumstances was his brief statement to be attributed as a "denial".

Another indicator that the story was bullseye accurate was the swift response from the BDSM community, throwing up scapegoats as sources. It led *Investigate* to issue this public statement:

There has been some speculation in media circles about the identity of our source on the BDSM story. A specific name is being put forward by anonymous members of Southern Kinx.

Investigate's policy has always been to protect its sources where there may be a risk to their safety so we're not confirming or denying anyone or working through lists of "suspects" by a process of elimination

Instead, I make the following comments as a logical argument that can be applied against not just the woman named but against any name put forward by Southern Kinx.

How can Southern Kinx truly know who our source is?

If the story is a fabrication as they claim, how can it possibly be pinned back to a named individual without Southern Kinx being privy to some further information that has not been provided?

Southern Kinx could only actually know our source, if the story was true.

Given that *Investigate* has caught members of Southern Kinx lying on tape about their own involvement in BDSM, is there any reason to believe that its current anonymous "tips" are anything more than a continuation of a disinformation campaign? Given that other members caught talking to the

187   *NZ Herald*, 23 November 2006, "Minister: I'm too busy to join a sex club"
http://www.nzherald.co.nz/topic/story.cfm?c_id=289&objectid=10412063

media have been savaged inside the group over the past 72 hours, is this merely a sign of a group imploding with members looking suspiciously over their shoulders at other members?

One final point: it is routine for *Investigate* to check the backgrounds of everyone it looks into. We know more about the BDSM community in Dunedin and Timaru than their own mothers do.

In fact, media trying to pin the story down were being offered three names as possible sources for the story. All three were on our list of those in the inner circle who were privy to the Benson-Pope information and who had had encounters with him. The fact that such a seemingly outlandish story could be pinged back to three people who we could place in the room with the Minister, was overwhelming evidence of its veracity. If the story had been a fabrication, only the fabricator would have known, and the BDSM group could not have pointed at *anyone* as a suspect – let alone three on our list.

Investigate repeatedly sought comment from Benson-Pope, as did other media, but he never issued a further statement and never issued a denial.

The story raised considerable debate within media and blogging circles about how far it was appropriate to go in digging into a politician's private life. Some argued that private role-playing fantasies about a school situation between consenting adults are out of bounds for media scrutiny, as long as the activity is legal under existing law (which it is). The counter to that argument ran along the lines that mere legality is not a sufficient test of suitability for leadership. It was legal, two decades ago, for men to rape their wives. Would such a man, with a penchant for doing what the law of the time considered his "right", be a suitable character to run, say, the Ministry of Women's Affairs at that time? More to the point, should the media have the right to expose such a background or would it be deemed "private, and out of bounds"?

Those who apply the "it's legal" test and who argue that private morality is irrelevant would be forced to say yes, it's private and has no bearing on how he does the job. The rest of us recognize that life is more complex than that.

But there is one overwhelming argument against a politician's right to privacy that I believe is insurmountable: conscience votes.

You see, politicians are not just administrators running a Ministry. They also get to change laws affecting your life by voting in parliament; sometimes with "conscience" votes. Isn't the background of *anyone* that we give the power of a "conscience" vote to, relevant to voters? Don't the public have the right to know what an MP really thinks?

Of course voters have a right to know, when private beliefs impact on public work, or when somebody exercises a "conscience" vote based on their private beliefs. And don't forget, in Benson-Pope's case, police found prima facie evidence of a bizarre assault that, in hindsight, bore a striking resemblance to BDSM humiliation techniques.

Although, again, David Benson-Pope politically survived this story in late 2006/early 2007, it fatally affected his relationship with the news media. Many organizations, who'd initially been scared into silence by legal threats[188], were frustrated when the Minister pointedly kept refusing to give straight answers to the BDSM questions, so when the Minister next found himself in hot water, no one was cutting him any slack.

---

188 Many, including ourselves at *Investigate*, found the story distasteful. No journalist enjoys writing such articles, but the constitutional role of the Fourth Estate demands it.

Crossfire: The Political Assassination Of Madeleine Setchell

Sir Humphrey: "Bernard, Ministers should never know more than they need to know, then they can't tell anyone. Like secret agents, they could be captured and tortured."
Bernard: "You mean by terrorists?"
Sir Humphrey: "By the BBC, Bernard." **- Yes Minister**

WELLINGTON'S A SMALL TOWN. I know this may come as a shock to many Wellingtonians, but as one who grew up there and worked there I can promise you it is small. Nestled into the port surrounded by mountainous hills that – in a crisp winter – attract dustings of snow, all roads lead to the centre of town, and in that centre stands the Beehive. Wellington, particularly in winter, is not an outdoor city; instead, its heart beats inside the offices and corridors of power. The workforce is heavily dominated by civil servants, and because of generous public sector wage increases it enjoys the highest salaries in the country on average.

It is a power city, but in a different kind of way to Auckland. Where New Zealand's megapolis pulses to a financial and lifestyle beat – the affairs of the capital a distant irritation except where they infringe on the business of making money, Wellington's bureaugnomes thrive on political gossip and power plays.

Because of its smaller size, however, the potential for conflicts of interest arises far more frequently than it does up north. If you're not sleeping with the enemy, you are certainly fraternizing with them on a daily basis. Wellington could not do what it does without recognizing these realities and dealing with them.

In the days of a neutral public service (which is still the legal position, believe it or not), the conflicts were manageable. Civil servants were there to deal with facts; spin was the domain of Parliament and those particular lifeforms who inhabit it.[189] A government department could be expected to spit out a report on, say, the trade deficit that simply told it like it was. How the story was spun by media advisors to the Minister for Overseas Trade was a separate issue.

But increasingly Labour has politicized the public service, sneaking in precedents and pressure through the back door, often because junior officials don't know the rules. Thus, when a PR consultant named Madeleine Setchell applied for a position at the Ministry for the Environment in February last year, she was doomed before she even started.

The Ministry was at the forefront of developing the Government's climate change policy, which meant putting together reports on the latest international data and briefing ministerial policy wonks and hangers on so they could plan accordingly.

It had been a junior ministry, really a politically-correct add-on, similar to the Ministry of Women's Affairs, but the government's decision to turn Kyoto and climate change into an election platform changed all that. By their own admission, the Ministry for the Environment (MfE) couldn't cope with the new pressures during 2006 and undertook a "realignment" – public service-speak for a makeover.

In November 2006 the ministry advertised for a new External Relations Manager. On February 7, 2007, Madeleine Setchell was interviewed by a three member selection panel, who were so impressed she was offered the job later that same day. This was despite the fact that Setchell openly declared a potential conflict of interest: her partner was Kevin Taylor, National leader John Key's chief press secretary.

As the subsequent investigation into the Setchell case headed by Don Hunn found, "It is sufficiently clear from both the interviews undertaken by this investigation and the associated documents , that a potential conflict of interest had been identified by the appointment panel; that they had discussed it in some detail; that the applicant had answered forthrightly all the questions put to her; and that her straightforwardness together with her previous experience convinced the panel that this was not a major issue and that it could be managed."[190]

So far, so good. The start date was set down for 28 May, on a salary of almost $127,000.

---

189 When I and a handful of others were appointed as the first "contract" press secretaries to Labour cabinet ministers in the 84-87 Lange administration, we were demonized as political appointments. Up to that time, all press secretaries had been supplied by the Tourist and Publicity Department, on secondment to Ministers' offices. They were not permitted to be political. As outsiders, I and the others could be more strategic and fully political. The demarcation, however, was clear. The departments remained politically neutral. Until now, evidently.

190 "Investigation into the public service recruitment and employment of Ms Madeleine Setchell", Report to the State Services Commissioner, 12 November 2007

Towards the end of the first week of May, Setchell's appointment, now carrying the title "Communications Manager", was announced to the Ministry for the Environment's comms team.

"Two weeks later," notes the Hunn Report, an MfE staffer on secondment to the Beehive got tipped off on two occasions by other media advisors that Setchell was, in fact, the partner of John Key's chief press secretary. "In the light of what he took to be a potentially damaging rumour...which was likely to end up in the media, he thought it was his duty to warn whom he considered to be the appropriate persons."

Accordingly, the MfE staffer tipped off both a senior manager in the Ministry itself, but also – more tellingly – an adviser to Environment Minister David Benson-Pope, on May 28 – the very day Setchell had commenced in her new role.

Benson-Pope's offsider, trade union official Steve Hurring, felt it was his duty to find out more before alerting his Minister, so he rang MfE chief executive Hugh Logan that same evening to verify whether in fact the rumour was true.

As Logan would later tell a news conference, "In the phone call with [Steve Hurring, he] said that the Minister's office needed to perhaps have confidence in the staff who were visiting the office and there always needed to be an atmosphere where free and frank discussion could take place".

Hunn's report also records that David Benson-Pope had already been told:

"The chief executive is also certain that [Hurring] said at some stage in the telephone exchanges on 28 May that he had told the Minister about the 'rumour': he gained the impression that the Minister was 'exceptionally annoyed'."

Hurring, for the record, disputes this aspect of the conversation, but it appears Logan's recollection is correct. After all, Hurring was already running the line about the Minister needing to have confidence, and he didn't pluck that out of thin air.

Logan was like a possum in the headlights, eyes wide, ears up, paws twitching – this was news to him. He in turn tried to find out from his own staff, but couldn't reach anyone who knew until midway through the morning of May 29.

Naturally, the answer sent his panic level soaring and he "immediately" informed Steve Hurring in Benson-Pope's office: yes, the rumour was true. Logan then phoned State Services Commissioner Mark Prebble, a former head of the Prime Minister's Department and also the brother of politician Richard Prebble.

Prebble remembers Logan spinning out, or, in the more polite "Sir Humphrey" fashion used in official reports:

"The State Services Commissioner gained the impression that the Chief Executive (CE) thought he had made a mistake with an appointment and needed to change things 'rather drastically'."

Quite. Prebble told the MfE boss to slow down, take a deep breath, have a cup of tea, or, in Sir Humphrey-speak:

"Having himself been in a similar situation as [Setchell] appeared to be, the Commissioner said the CE shouldn't rush into things simply because of family connections. The first aim should be to see if the potential conflict could be managed. The Commissioner commented that if he were the CE he would not himself talk to the Minister, in the circumstances."

Hugh Logan, however, having dealt with Benson-Pope on an almost daily basis, was evidently having visions of being strapped to a desk with an apple in his mouth, a sprig of parsley somewhere else, whilst being soundly thrashed by a dominatrix. No amount of soothing from the Commissioner was going to make a shred of difference.

"The CE was insistent that in terms of his 'no surprises' undertakings, he felt bound to speak to the Minister particularly since the inquiry had come from his office."

Logan pointed out he would be trapped in a room with Benson-Pope later that very day, "in circumstances in which the issue could well come up". He already knew Benson-Pope had been briefed and was "exceptionally annoyed".

Yes, pointed out Mark Prebble, but it was "taking a risk involving the Minister in something that was not his business." Prebble added that Logan needed to be "very careful" in his discussions with the Minister, giving that staffing issues were a civil service prerogative, not the politician's.

Sure enough, Logan poured his heart out to David Benson-Pope while they waited to board an aircraft later that day.

"The CE recalls the Minister responding that staff decisions were the CE's to make, but that he would find it difficult to speak as freely as he would with other senior managers, in front of an employee who was in a close family relationship with someone working for the Leader of the Opposition."

Benson-Pope reminded Logan that environment was now a major policy plank for the government, and "it was only to be expected that he would be more cautious in discussion matters of policy and tactics in front of such a person, so that meetings with the senior managers might not be as productive as, desirably, they should be."

It must have added to Hugh Logan's angst, and he certainly told State Services Commissioner Mark Prebble the next day that Benson-Pope had serious reservations about working with Madeleine Setchell.

Prebble tried to tell Logan, politely, to pull his head in:

"If the Government [is] planning a politically-oriented environmental communications programme, the Ministry shouldn't be doing it: if it [isn't], it should be possible to find a way to manage the appointment…[and just] because the Minister might have expressed certain views the previous evening [is] not sufficient reason to do anything dramatic."

The Deputy State Services Commissioner, Iain Rennie, also tried to put the issue into perspective for Logan:

"Well, if the Minister does display concern, just tell him to get over it."

The Hunn Report wryly notes in brackets, "The CE did not find this particularly helpful".

Logan did, however, choose the "dramatic" option. After thrashing through various possible alternatives, Setchell's position soon became untenable and she received a substantial payout for her troubles. Employment elsewhere proved difficult, however. When she applied to go back to her old department, the Ministry of Agriculture, MAF bosses immediately rang their own Minister, Jim Anderton, to see if Setchell was an "appropriate" appointee, as an email in the Hunn Report makes clear.

"I have discussed with [Anderton's Chief of Staff] and he has discussed with the Minister. The answer is a clear 'no'. I can discuss further once you are back."

When State Services Commissioner Mark Prebble – by this time in London on business – heard that Setchell had been bumped from another opportunity because MAF had consulted Anderton, he banged his head Homer Simpson-style.

"This was concerning for the Commissioner," recorded a diary note in its usual understatement, "more so than the MfE issue."

Another employment hope, in the Ministry of Education, fell through as well, but Setchell did eventually find someone in Wellington prepared to give her a go.

As news that Setchell had been effectively dumped from Environment broke in mid July, cabinet minister David Benson-Pope was initially pleading ignorance.

"No, I don't know anything about the detail of that issue," Benson Pope told *3 News* reporter Duncan Garner,[191] "and nor do I think that it's appropriate for me to get involved or actually say anything about employment matters."

If it was a sudden attack of conscience, it was well and truly too late. Where it really mattered, where the line had really been crossed if Benson-Pope was being honest, was back in his discussion with Hugh Logan. After all, that's the constitutional breach, not speaking to a TV reporter.

The following Monday night, in a TV interview with Garner, Benson-Pope was asked if he'd ever had a personal view on Madeleine Setchell's appointment:

"No I don't have a personal view on the matter, it's not for me. I don't employ staff in the Ministry for the Environment, Duncan."[192]

191 *TV3 News*, 18 July 2007, http://www.tv3.co.nz/VideoBrowseAll/PoliticsVideo/tabid/370/articleID/30962/Default.aspx#video

192 http://www.tv3.co.nz/Video/BensonPopeforcedtoresign/tabid/370/articleID/31489/cat/100/Default.aspx

This too, as the Hunn Report makes clear, was a lie.

On Tuesday morning, Benson-Pope took a further spanking at the hands of National Radio's Sean Plunkett.

"I'm not happy that that phone call was made, but it was made and it turned out that the rumour that we'd heard —"[193]

"Hang on, you said 'we'd heard' — had you heard it too? I thought only Mr Hurring had heard it?"

" 'We' is the general term in the office, I hadn't heard it."

"So you're now speaking of the office —"

"Well I'm sorry, I hadn't heard it."

As you can see from the Hunn Report, David Benson-Pope was lying. Just as he had over the assault claims and his treatment of schoolgirls.

He later repeated his denial at a stand-up press conference on his way to parliament:[194]

"Oh I'm sorry. I did not know. Let me repeat that, I've been quite clear on that, OK?"

Prime Minister Clark was forced to defend him with a pasted-on smile.

"As I recall, he said 'we' in the sense of the office. I really don't want to get any further down that track."

But Benson-Pope was now well and truly in everyone's gunsights, including Clark's. The Prime Minister called him into her office that night to ask if there was anything else she needed to know. He coughed to having taken a personal position on Setchell's employment, and effectively it was all over.

Benson-Pope was forced to concede in Parliament on Thursday that he had passed on his views about the hiring of Setchell, a sharp contradiction to his TV3 interview where he'd denied having a personal opinion.

The Minister returned to Dunedin that night refusing to resign, but by the next morning he'd walked the plank.

"I am disappointed because I expect more," Helen Clark told the media. "I expect people to put the full facts out there. I had my chief of staff and another senior minister speak with him last night and make it clear what my expectations were".[195]

Was this the same Clark who, whilst defending Benson-Pope's selective release of facts in late 2005, told Parliament, "It is a matter of judgment by Ministers as to what they put in the public arena."?[196]

"What is the point," challenged National leader Don Brash on that occasion, "in keeping a Minister of the Crown whose actions have been deliberate and deceitful, and whom the media and the public no longer trust?"

193 National Radio, Morning Report, 24 July 2007
194 TV3 News, 24 July 2007
195 TV3 News, 27 July 2007
http://www.tv3.co.nz/Video/BensonPopeforcedtoresign/tabid/370/articleID/31489/cat/100/Default.aspx
196 Hansard, NZ Parliament, 7 December 2005

"I do not accept the assertions in the member's question," scoffed the Prime Minister.

Perhaps if Clark had actually listened to the chorus of media and public voices since 2005 who had questioned Benson-Pope's suitability to be in office, she wouldn't have been faced with the embarrassment of having to sack such a high profile minister heading into election year. Little did she know that her own chief of staff, Heather Simpson, was about to be caught interfering in the same department. The exclusive story is next.

Purple Heather

Sir Humphrey: "Minister I have warned you before about the dangers of speaking to people in the Department." – **Yes Minister**

THE NEXT BEST THING TO catching the Prime Minister red-handed, is capturing her 'Rasputin' – Heather Simpson; 'Robin' to the Prime Minister's 'Batman'. The pair have been strategically inseparable since the late 1980s. When a lame duck Minister has blotted his copybook again, and Clark is left wandering around the Beehive muttering, "Will no one rid me of this turbulent priest?", it is Heather Simpson assembling the firing squad. As you've just seen, it was Simpson, or "H2" as she's known in Parliament, who convinced Benson-Pope to take a walk.

Like all good serial killers, H2 seldom leaves her pawprints at the scene of a crime, but you are about to read how Heather Simpson was caught interfering in a supposedly neutral Ministry, on Prime Minister's orders. This is the first, in-depth, account of what happened – the real story behind the story you read in the daily media.

With one ministerial nemesis out of a job, who would have thought that another – previously pinged by *Investigate* for cutting corners – would be pinged again? No sooner had the dust from the Setchell affair settled, than Climate Change Minister David Parker was in the gun for allegedly directing the Ministry for the Environment to hire a Labour party activist named Clare Curran.

In many respects, the stories were intertwined, because with Benson-Pope out of cabinet and on the outer with Helen Clark, Labour wanna-be's realized they could be in with a chance if they challenged Benson-Pope for his Dunedin South electorate seat. It's such a Labour stronghold that anyone wearing a red scarf on the day would run a good chance of being elected to Parliament. Curran saw an opportunity and announced in October 2007 she would challenge Benson-Pope. She eventually won selection and, barring a landslide to National, will be the next MP for Dunedin South.

However, as Benson-Pope licked his wounds, his opponent Clare Curran suddenly found herself thrust into the spotlight after former Ministry for the Environment consultant Erin Leigh went public alleging David Parker had made a political appointment to the Ministry.

"I was told she was being employed to look after David Parker's personal political agenda, and I could not work in those circumstances professionally or ethically. As a result of her appointment I resigned. I felt the situation was untenable," Leigh told the *Herald*.

Erin Leigh had been working for the Ministry for nearly a year on a range of projects as a communications advisor, including climate change. The Government at that point, despite signing the Kyoto Protocol years earlier, still hadn't come to grips with precisely what it needed to do not only to comply with the protocol, but also to sell it to the public.

To understand the story, however, you first have to understand something that many bureaucrats do not: government departments are supposed to be politically neutral. The reason for this is simple – if they do not maintain neutrality, then each time the government changes all the senior and mid-ranked staff in a department would have to be fired, so the incoming government could appoint its own political lackeys. There's another reason too, perhaps an even better one – only a politically neutral government department can offer the best independent advice. In theory, the ministries are supposed to be a check and balance on the enthusiasm and rogue behavior of ministers. In practice, that line is getting increasingly blurred.

For all of her tough 1999 election talk about supporting a neutral public service, Helen Clark's government has gone out of its way to appoint like-minded people inside government departments.

The Education Ministry, for example, is currently headed by Karen Sewell – formerly the principal of arguably New Zealand's worst secondary school, Green Bay High in Auckland. Under her deputy leadership of the college from 1980 to 1984, and leadership from 1985 through 1997, it was repeatedly in the news headlines in Auckland for having some of the worst academic achievement, worst discipline and biggest social problems.[197]

---

197 Comments from former pupils on the Oldfriends site are a testimony both to the school and its high literacy standards: "Seem to remember been at this school ... smoking buda sticks, hmm ohh yer I was here in person, just not in mind :)." Another says, "Green Bay was always a fairly layed back school. I spent a lot of my time on the driveway or at a friend's place," while another writes, "once the boys all got our licenses we spent a lot of time at Piha". One girl laments a comment on her school report: "Leigh would benefit by attending more often". My personal favourite is, "I luved school. All i really remember is smokin heapsa weed down by the pine tree. cruzy school eh! thought sewell was false...got suspended twice. won talent quest in my 7th form year. learnt nothing scholastic but heaps about people and got a hunger for the arts at Gree ba hi choo .what a motley bloody lot!!"
In truth, parents would bus their kids out of the area in desperate efforts to avoid having to send them to Green Bay under Sewell's watch. Only in politically-correct New Zealand could the principal of such a school wind up running the Ministry of Education, and helping mastermind the government's major new education curriculum.

Yet Sewell was well-connected in the Labour-affiliated teachers union, the PPTA, and served as head of its secondary principals' division. Her sexual orientation may also have been a political advantage. Sewell, soon after leaving Green Bay (the school eventually slid into statutory management in 2004), was appointed to a senior position in the Education Review Office in 2000, before taking up the reins at the Ministry of Education two years ago.

When Sewell took the job, her partner, Frances Salt, took over as Acting CEO of the Education Review Office.[198]

"Ms Salt is presently ERO's National Manager Reporting Services," said State Services Commissioner Mark Prebble, who presumably did not think there was a conflict of interest in two government agencies being run out of the same household.

Inside the Education Ministry's head office you will find Heather Church, a former National Radio journalist and partner of Helen Clark's former chief press secretary Mike Munro. Church is a special advisor reporting directly to Sewell. You will also find media mavens Julia Craven, formerly the press secretary to the ex-Minister of Social Development, David Benson-Pope; and Helen Corrigan, the former press secretary to Labour's George Hawkins.

Education, Social Policy, Climate Change – these are all touchstone portfolios for Labour's ongoing agenda if it wins another term in office, and they are portfolios where the tentacles from the Beehive have spread.[199]

But it is the antics surrounding Climate Change policy, and the Ministry for the Environment, that have thrown up the biggest unreported story of Ministerial interference: Helen Clark herself.

The story begins with Erin Leigh's decision to blow the whistle on Labour activist Clare Curran's appointment to the Ministry for the Environment. Curran, a PR consultant, produced a Labour Party newsletter for Climate Change Minister David Parker's electoral region (Parker is a list MP but broadly represents Labour interests in Otago).

As the *Herald* reports, news that Curran was being appointed to oversee Erin Leigh's work, on the personal recommendation of Parker himself, was a blatant slap in the face to Leigh's independence:[200]

Ms Leigh – who has worked in communications for 20 years and worked for eight different Government departments – had worked on four climate change

198   State Service Commission media release, 19 October 2006
http://www.ssc.govt.nz/display/document.asp?NavID=113&DocID=5584
199   One of Labour's big agendas, which I covered in more detail in the book "Eve's Bite" last year, is sex education, so it wasn't a huge surprise when new ERO boss Graham Stoop came out last year in one of his first major pronouncements and declared that the Education Review Office didn't think schools were doing enough sex education. As one Rotorua high school principal retorted, leave schools to teach real subjects, and leave parenting to parents. NZ Herald, 29 August 2007, "Patrick Walsh: Stay out of our lunchboxes" http://www.nzherald.co.nz/topic/story.cfm?c_id=337&objectid=10460366
200   *NZ Herald*, 22 November 2007, "Activist was minister's watchdog"
http://www.nzherald.co.nz/section/1/story.cfm?c_id=1&objectid=10477645

contracts for the ministry over a year-long period, and then as a subcontractor. Ms Leigh said a permanent position was under discussion, but Ms Curran's appointment meant she could not stay.

"I had never heard of her ... but I made sure I was gone before she started because I didn't want to be tarnished with that. My ethics and my profession are important to me, and my integrity."

Ms Leigh said two senior staff members had convinced her Ms Curran's role would be as a watchdog to ensure Mr Parker's agenda was being "looked after".

"My advice to the ministry at the time was to push back on the minister and that I thought it was possibly illegal. The response of the person I discussed this with, who was a senior member of staff, was that they felt there was no choice."

Ms Leigh said she was under no illusions about the reaction her disclosures would incur, and she expected her personal and professional integrity to be attacked.

"As a person who has worked in communications and PR for so long, and knowing the workings of government so well, I have no doubt in my mind that I will be blacklisted. I did at the time consider making a complaint to the State Services Commission, however I knew the consequences to me personally and professionally were going to be quite profound."

You've read enough of this book by now to know the answer to her last prophetic suggestion. Yes, Labour was again out to shoot the messenger.

Trevor Mallard, who Prime Minister Helen Clark had promised would lay off personal attacks after his actions led to the outing of her husband, was up on his hind legs the following day in Parliament tearing strips off Erin Leigh for incompetence:[201]

"Erin Leigh had repeated competence issues. The piece of work that she was employed to do had to be fixed up six times by her after complaints from senior officials from a number of departments," Mallard told New Zealand.

"As a result of that someone had to come in and fix up the mess. Clare Curran was appointed to do that."

The parliamentary Hansard of what followed is illuminating:[202]

Gerry Brownlee: If Miss Leigh was the person who, according to the Minister, had mucked up the "fart tax"[203], had caused the carbon tax to be dropped, and had caused the need for change, then why did they phone her after she resigned to explain why the Minister wanted Clare Curran there and ask her to come back?

Hon Trevor Mallard: The last record of contact that the ministry had with Erin Leigh was when she came in, in an agitated state, for a quarter of an

201 *NZ Herald*, 23 November 2007, "Mallard's blow-torch on whistleblower" http://www.nzherald.co.nz/section/1/story.cfm?c_id=1&objectid=10477856&pnum=0
202 Hansard, NZ Parliament, 22 November 2007
203 Erin Leigh had done no such things, this was just standard Labour shoot-the-messenger PR.

hour in order to clear out her desk. It is my understanding that the last non-physical contact was when she sent an invoice to the ministry for that quarter of an hour.

Gerry Brownlee: Did the Minister misunderstand my question? I did not ask when her last contact was with the ministry, I asked him this question: why did staff in the Minister's office phone her after she left, ask her to come back, and say they wanted to explain why David Parker wanted Clare Curran in the ministry?

Hon Trevor Mallard: No.

Gerry Brownlee: I raise a point of order, Madam Speaker. I just want to clarify with the Minister whether he is denying that the Minister's office phoned Erin Leigh, asked her to come back, and asked for an opportunity to explain why David Parker wanted Clare Curran appointed to the ministry.

Hon Trevor Mallard: Speaking to the point of order, Madam Speaker, I say to the member the question asked whether I misunderstood the question. I said "No".

Madam Speaker: That has clarified it.

Gerry Brownlee: Does the Minister still wish to claim that New Zealand has a politically neutral public service when it is now evident that the Minister had insisted on Clare Curran being appointed in order to fix up and put a Labour spin on ministry documentation, and then, upon becoming worried about what the effect of that might be, attempted to explain to Erin Leigh why he insisted on the appointment of Clare Curran; and does that not indicate that we do not have a politically neutral public service, we have public servants whom Ministers want?

Hon Trevor Mallard: Ministers have the right to insist on competent advice. That has been established for a long period of time. When something comes to them six times and is criticised by officials not only from the Ministry for the Environment but also from other Government departments, I think that any reasonable chief executive would look for someone who could do the work. When there is someone available to try to fix up the mess who did climate change strategic work for the Australian Liberal Government, I can understand why the ministry employed her.

Later in Question Time, under further attack, Mallard rejected suggestions that Parker had directed Curran's appointment in any way, and called Erin Leigh "a sad person":

"To date, no person who has been in a meeting with David Parker has suggested that he directed the ministry. Someone who is a sad person, who had six attempts at doing a piece of work, and who was replaced on that job is the only person – other than Opposition members – who has suggested that."

In a letter to Deputy State Services Commissioner Iain Rennie, a furious Erin Leigh let rip.

"Although I told you over the phone that I would not be speaking to the media about this matter any further, I have changed my mind. Over the weekend I have had a chance to reflect on the events of the past week and the comments made by Trevor Mallard in Parliament, and have decided I am more determined than ever for the truth to be told.

"I can not, and will not, sit back and watch my career go up in smoke when all I am doing is telling the truth in response to questions put to me. I think the tax payer deserves to have honest public servants working for them and I at least owe it to them to live up to these expectations.

"So, although I won't talk about Clare Curran's appointment to the media, I will publicly talk to them about all of the points that Trevor Mallard commented on in Parliament last week. I notice the parameters of your Terms of Reference are broad enough for me to respond to everything that Trevor Mallard has said in Parliament (as he has attacked me both personally and professionally). I think if you were me, and it was your reputation on the line, you would probably take exactly the same action.

"Some people are wondering why I would stick my neck out over this when I have nothing to gain except to have my personality and my professional competency ripped to shreds in public. The reason why I am speaking up is not because I am some incredibly brave crusader with a political agenda. It's simply because I was asked questions about her appointment by the media and I answered them honestly. What was I supposed to do? Run into hiding? Lie? Say 'no comment' which, from my experience, just encourages the media to dig further into the issue as they know that you are covering up something. In my professional experience it's far better to just be open and honest right from the start.

"Remember, I have not said anything about this for 18 months and have had plenty of opportunities to speak up – especially when the Madeleine Setchell case became public. However, the reason I didn't speak up was simply because I was scared and, at the time, I put my own career before what I thought was right. Also, how could I complain to the State Service's Commission when the boss is David Parker?

"So I'm not really a whistle blower – I'm a wimp. I feel ashamed that I remained silent for so long and watched, in the wings, as Madeline's credibility was questioned and when, all along, I knew there were a lot more questions about political interference that needed to be answered. I don't know Madeline Setchell and haven't spoken to her but I do sympathise with her. However, although I feel guilty about not coming forward earlier, I am determined to put that right.

"I think it is important you understand my background from a political viewpoint since that is what this issue is all about. I truly am completely politically neutral. Interestingly enough, I have only worked in PR for a Labour led government and for Labour MP's. I have never done any work for any political party, activist group, or any other organisation with a political agenda. I have never worked for, or with, the National Party and have absolutely no ties to them."

A little further on (it's a 16 page letter) Erin Leigh lambasts Labour's predictable kneejerk response of smearing anyone who dares to speak out:

"As a PR consultant I knew the Government would launch a smear campaign against me as soon as I went public – and the very next day they did – just as I predicted. However, I did not expect the smear campaign to be completely based on fiction and to be so personal and also done within the confines of Parliament where I can't do anything about it legally. I have, through the media, asked Trevor Mallard to say his defamatory comments outside of Parliament where he is not protected by the parliamentary privilege law – but he has refused to respond to this challenge. Therefore, I feel I have every right to rebuttal and will do so through the media – which is the only democratic channel of communication I have right now.

"If I make a public release of this letter to you it may temporarily encourage the Government to stop making completely false statements about me. However, I know them too well and know that, whilst *they* may stop attacking me personally and professionally they will find someone else who will continue the smear campaign on their behalf. It has been my job to predict these types of actions in the past which is why I can say it with such certainty (yes – they are that predictable). This smear campaign will continue for as long as possible until they either break me, until people are sick of it, or until people actually believe it and lose their faith in my integrity."

It's understandable that Erin Leigh was furious, and mortified. Furious, because the six drafts were in fact the handiwork of none other than Helen Clark's 2IC, Heather Simpson, and mortified because Mallard had just tried to destroy Leigh's reputation.

"I was never ever going to mention Heather Simpson's involvement at all, but then Mallard stands up in Parliament and talks about these six drafts of the document in my final couple of weeks there. And I was like, 'F you, if you're going to blame me for those six drafts, I'm going to have to explain why there were six drafts and what the cause of those six drafts was, and it had nothing to do with the level of my competency'."

The drafts, it now turns out, existed mostly in name only. That's because Heather Simpson was continually changing her mind about what to say in the cabinet briefing paper Leigh was tasked to work on. The document existed on Leigh's computer in electronic form, and Leigh would simply type in the text that Simpson had instructed her to write.

When Leigh was instructed to send the penultimate draft to other government agencies under her own name, she balked, and explained her reasons why in the letter to the State Services Commission:

"When I was asked to send the document to different government departments for feedback, I asked [general manager] Dave Brash to do this himself because I was embarrassed by the paper and didn't want people to think I wrote it (as it wasn't written like a communications strategy at all – it looked like some type of strange policy document that didn't really make much sense from a communications perspective). However Dave Brash was very insistent that it was me, not anyone else, that sent the paper out. I did so, but was so embarrassed and worried that people may think I wrote it, I sent a follow-up email to all the recipients of the paper a few days later to state I didn't have much say in its drafting and that it wasn't actually my own piece of work (in case they presumed I had written it). You should receive copies of these emails when you OIA it," Erin Leigh told the Commission.

"So I then spoke out about it, but because there's been so much other stuff going on with this story, that hasn't been picked up on. That's the gold – they're going on about political interference with Claire Curran, but wait a minute – this is political interference from Helen Clark's chief of staff, dictating through the channel down to the lowest comms [communications] advisor what to write. You can't get more political interference than that!"

In other words, once again, Trevor Mallard's decision to go hunting in the off-season backfired, leaving him one seriously politically-wounded duck. He had taken aim at Erin Leigh, and managed to shoot the inimitable H2 right between the eyes.

Little wonder media reports suggested Mallard's outburst had "caught the Beehive by surprise".[204] I'll bet it did. Mallard, Clark and Simpson could only hope that no one in the media followed up the Simpson angle, because catching Helen Clark's lieutenant dictating how an independent government department should present facts on climate change is nothing short of outrageous, and a clear breach of conventions.

To illustrate just how serious, consider this. The official State Services Commission (SSC) investigation into the appointment of Clare Curran found there had been breaches, which we'll come to shortly, but the SSC breathed a massive sigh of relief when it reported, "There is no evidence that Ms Curran brought her politics into the job and there is a consistent picture that Ms Curran was very professional and produced work of good quality."

In other words, if there'd been evidence that the Curran documents were political, there could have been blood and feathers on the floor.

Meanwhile, Heather Simpson was certainly bringing "her politics into the job" by *dictating the very scripts* of departmental briefings on climate change, via MfE officials, to Clare Curran's predecessor.

What might a State Services Commission investigation make of *that?*[205]

---

204 *Dominion-Post*, 26 November 2007, "Parker inquiry to be widened" http://www. stuff.co.nz/4287822a6160.html

205 Shockingly, the State Services Commission knew, but chose not to investigate. They knew, because the copy of Leigh's letter to the SSC, released to the media, had blackout portions where she discussed who was really behind the drafts. Iain Rennie was on notice, but strangely felt no compulsion to go there.

Ministry for the Environment staff Dave Brash and Julie Iommi were summonsed to the Beehive for meetings with Heather Simpson and occasionally Helen Clark herself in the Department of Prime Minister and Cabinet. Climate change was set to become a vitally important and strategic election policy for Labour, and they didn't want the facts getting in the way of a good story.

Loaded up with the latest changes, Iommi or sometimes Justine Daw – David Parker's private secretary for the MfE portfolio – would phone Leigh to get them made. The irony was Heather Simpson wasn't even working off Erin Leigh's document – she was making changes apparently from memory. Leigh refers to it as "Heather Simpson's brain dance" – a stream of consciousness as H2 struggled to get her head around climate issues, and failed miserably.

Civil service sources have confirmed that Erin Leigh at one stage sabotaged an MfE political attack against National's climate change spokesman Nick Smith. They say Leigh was told to write a rebuttal for Labour against National, and her protestations about neutrality were overruled. But there was hilarity in some sympathetic corners of MfE when they discovered Curran had delivered the text of the document in "wing-dings" – a nonsense and unreadable type font available on computers, so the rebuttal could not be used. MfE bosses may not have been amused, but others were. Leigh laughs, but refuses to comment.

In her letter to State Services, Erin Leigh says it is imperative that public servants are brought up to speed on the need to be politically neutral.

"My…advice is for the Chief Commissioner of the State Services Commission to tell every public servant they have nothing to fear about answering questions honestly when asked about political interference. They need to have their faith restored. This needs to be communicated to all of them in the form of a public announcement, an email, and as an agenda item at team meetings for open and honest discussion with their managers. Every public servant should also receive a briefing about political neutrality and how they can ensure they don't get drawn in to politics as they go about their normal working day."

After receiving a copy of her letter, along with TV3 and the *Dominion*, we asked Leigh how bad the problem was.

"I had people who didn't know that we were supposed to be politically neutral, and these were managers there! No idea that we were supposed to be politically neutral."

In Parliament, it became increasingly embarrassing for Trevor Mallard. Far from being "sad", or having major "competency issues", Erin Leigh was able to produce references where a range of top civil servants, including Clark's own press secretary Kathryn Street, had praised her work.

"The best comms person I ever worked with," said MfE communications manager Neal Cave.

"She is very competent," agreed Ross Vintiner, a former media advisor to both David Lange and Helen Clark.

There were many more, but still Mallard refused to apologise. Helen Clark, challenged in parliament, initially backed him up:[206]

"My understanding is that the Minister spoke on advice. Having read the *Hansard*, I consider it rather mild by his standards."

However, both Mallard and Clark were about to be undermined by MfE chief executive Hugh Logan, who decided to issue a correctional statement and apology. Logan said he was "concerned" that briefing material he had provided to the Minister in response to a request for information about Leigh had led to a reflection on her work "that was not intended" by the Ministry.

"Ms Leigh, a professional communications consultant, was contracted in 2005 by the Ministry. Her contract was renewed three times. In May 2006 she notified the Ministry that she was ending her contract and ceased work. At the time the Ministry accepted this without seeking any further explanation, and paid all contract fees billed to it.

Logan added that Leigh's "media work was professional and of good quality" and that the climate change material she was working on when she left "was not yet concluded and was subsequently completed by others".

"Both personally and on behalf of the Ministry I apologise for what has occurred, and I regret the public attention which has been generated."

Mallard, one of Clark's most seasoned MPs, was being roasted over a slow burning flame, not just over his clearly unfounded attack on Erin Leigh but also because he was being prosecuted in court for assaulting National MP Tau Henare.

Clark expressed disappointment that the Ministry for the Environment had let her down, "in a nutshell"[207], but the writing was on the wall. The same day that Mallard pleaded guilty in court to a minor disorder charge, he stood up in Parliament and apologized to Erin Leigh:[208]

"I now believe it was not wise to make those comments. I apologise to her," he said.

The following day, the State Services Commission released the results of its own investigation into the appointment of Clare Curran.[209] It released an email from Justine Daw in David Parker's office to the Ministry, describing Curran as David Parker's "right hand woman" and seeking an appointment from Curran with Hugh Logan. The SSC, in very measured tones later described by commentators as a "whitewash", suggested the email "did not appear wise".

206 Hansard, NZ Parliament, 4 December 2007
207 *NZ Herald*, 11 December 2007, "Environment Ministry keeps letting me down" http://www.nzherald.co.nz/section/1/story.cfm?c_id=1&objectid=10481588
208 *NZ Herald*, 19 December 2007, "Mallard starts to clean up his act" http://www.nzherald.co.nz/topic/story.cfm?c_id=124&objectid=10483189
209 "Investigation into the Engagement of Clare Curran by the Ministry for the Environment", report to the State Services Commission, 19 December 2007, http://www.ssc.govt.nz/display/document.asp?docid=6335

No indeed. Another email from Daw to senior staff at MfE said, "The Minister has suggested that you both meet (preferably together) with Claire (sic) Curran...he wondered if there was a prospect of potentially engaging Claire to help with the comms work now that Erin is close to departure. Can you please let me know how you get on in terms of arranging a meeting."

Curran was hired on a short term contract to provide 200 hours of assistance to the Ministry for $24,000 – not bad for five weeks' work.

"The standard contracting process for contracts in the $20,000 to $50,000 range is to seek three quotes for the work," concedes the State Services investigation. "In this case, the Ministry did not...Overall, the process used was not appropriate for a situation where the Minister had initiated consideration of a contractor...[it appeared] as if it was a scramble to hire someone suggested by the Minister."[210]

Curran's advice included not just communicating facts but also offering some political spin, to counter possible objections from the Greens or their supporters.

Climate Change Minister David Parker, whose cutting of corners got him into trouble as Attorney-General, should have realized that having his staff make suggestions like this to a weak and malfunctioning Ministry was a recipe for disaster.

Although the inquiry cleared Parker of acting improperly, the *Herald's* Fran O'Sullivan has her own take on events:[211]

After closely studying the State Services Commission's whitewash investigation into the Clare Curran affair, I've now come up with an alternative hypothesis to Deputy State Services Commissioner Iain Rennie.

To recap: the SSC investigation released into the dead zone (Thursday afternoon before Christmas) was remarkable for Rennie's failure to draw obvious conclusions.

Curran is the Labour Party activist who was hired by the Ministry for the Environment after a nudge from Climate Issues Minister David Parker. But despite her advice that the ministry should marginalise critics such as the Climate Science Coalition, minimise the risk of negative comment from the "Greens", and time events to dominate the media agenda, her actions were not considered to overflow into the nakedly political realm by Rennie or SSC boss Mark Prebble because planned announcements did not take place.

My alternative hypothesis based on the report's timeline and emails from Parker's private secretary is different. It's my opinion that Parker (champing at the bit after sitting on the sidelines while Pete Hodgson ran his portfolio) injected close political ally Curran into the Ministry for the Environment in late

210 Ibid
211 *NZ Herald*, 27 December 2007, "Fran O'Sullivan: reading between the lines"
http://www.nzherald.co.nz/section/3/story.cfm?c_id=3&objectid=10484320&pnum=0

May 2006 to make sure he got the spin he wanted on the Government's climate change agenda.

Parker had been frustrated at the ministry's efforts on that front. But he crossed the line by promoting Curran to senior officials then getting his private secretary to follow through with those officials.

He did not canvass the issue directly with the acting CEO, nor did he wait to discuss this important role with incoming CEO Hugh Logan who took up his appointment just two weeks later.

Officials fell into line with Parker's nudge and got Curran on board. But some in the ministry became uncomfortable with Curran's direct line to Parker, with whom she had discussed climate change issues outside of normal reporting lines. And that she used her connections with Parker to try to get an off-the-record meeting with Logan.

There have been suggestions, again not deeply traversed in Rennie's report, that Curran's style of tactical management, as evidenced in her written reports, caused discomfort.

My sense is that Logan, a long-time public servant with an unblemished record to that date, would not have been comfortable with Curran's role and would have taken behind-the-scenes action to restore normal reporting lines and minimise the perception among his officials that she was a ministerial appointee.

Another top former civil servant who backs up allegations of a Labour take-over of the public service is former WINZ boss Christine Rankin, who says the Prime Minister rules with absolute power:

"Oh God, one of absolute fear of Helen. She was 'it' and everybody did what she wanted. It was bullying and extremely vindictive, and it still is. People are afraid and public servants are very afraid. The free and frank advice went, the moment they came in the door. I remember Helen Clark addressing chief executives and telling them what she expected of them, and it was literally 'Do what we tell you to do!' and 'There will be no backchat!', I mean, to give contrary advice to anything they wanted was quite a frightening process.

"I've never seen manipulation of parliamentary questions like I saw from them. We had to increase the number and change the kind of people that we had in that particular area in Welfare, and now apparently they've got a very big team. They just would not accept any answer that they did not want to get out [in public], they'd send it back and tell you to 'change it, change it, change it!' until it said what they wanted you to say!

"Something would have gone wrong and it would cause embarrassment for the government, and so you'd answer the question honestly. Well, they'd send it back, and say 'that answer's not acceptable, describe it another way, come up with something different from that'. Because they did not want anyone to know what the real situation was. So the answer would be very cleverly manipulated to hide whatever it was. I was astonished by it, because I had never ever seen that, in the time I'd worked in the national office, I'd never seen that happen before, and it's a very dangerous thing."

Wishart: And this was Maharey?

Rankin: "Yes, and his office. They'd go crazy if we answered a question in a particular way that looked bad for him. There was no way that that was allowed to happen. And there's a lot of hiding of spending and things that goes on in there. People used to come and talk to me about it for a long time, and they were shocked by the level of spending. They spent a million dollars on doing up a floor once. I had so many calls from people after that saying 'how could this happen? *You* couldn't spend *anything!*'. And they were talking to me about how they'd hidden the spending so that if any questions were asked the Minister could say 'well, that's the Chief Executive's responsibility'. And no one can ever track it because of the way it's coded – well they can, if they know what they're asking. But things like that are so incredibly dangerous. It encourages people to find ways to hide things, and then if they are exposed the Minister denies any knowledge.

"Public servants would be terrified to tell you that they're terrified, they'd be sent out to say 'They're great' and 'No, we have no problem working for them' – they wouldn't dare to say anything else. But the regime has changed them dramatically."

Now, that interview was done in December 2005 for our January 2006 issue. Contrast Rankin's last statement with this passage from the SSC's Curran report in December 2007:

"The Manager – Communications is adamant that his resignation, written on 22 May, and subsequently withdrawn on 20 June, did not reflect a concern about any improper influence from the Minister...I have found no evidence to support the view that [he] resigned on the basis of concerns about the Minister's involvement."

So has the Civil Service been brow-beaten into a state of abject fear and cowardice in the face of Ministerial pressure? Do Labour's tentacles really reach so deep? Rankin suggests they do:

Rankin: "Ha! Everywhere! I have to say with National there was a line they never crossed, and they genuinely did not cross that line. It was like a gentlemen's agreement, I don't know how else to describe it. Labour jumped across that line with both feet, and they got a long way over that line. They have created such a culture of fear that there is no turning back unless there is a different government regime."

Wishart: What happens to people if they buck it?

Rankin: "They get tossed, they certainly don't go anywhere. I don't know any rebels in there now, look at the kind of women they've appointed: quiet, well-behaved, non-entities really. I don't think younger women looking at the leaders in the public service, they'd have to say 'I don't want to go there'. And the men are exactly the same: grey, quiet, well behaved, do-what-they're-told public servants."

And Madeleine Setchell is the poster girl example of this – not just booted out of the Ministry for the Environment, but not employable in the Ministry of Agriculture or the Ministry of Education either. Such is Labour's stranglehold over the civil service.[212] Christine Rankin doesn't see much hope ahead.

Rankin: "Absolutely, it is controlled. Helen's a very smart woman and we all know she knows how to play politics very, very well. So it's not going to make any great advances while she's there.

"By and large a lot of the people attracted to the public service are very left wing, they buy into a government's philosophy. And that's what's happening down there now, absolutely. They follow the government policy line wholeheartedly and they stop anything that contravenes that. I think teachers are an example of that. There's some wonderful teachers out there doing a fantastic job, but a lot of teachers have a left wing agenda, and that's this government's agenda. And that's the way they conduct themselves, every day."

Wishart: "What's the danger for our civil service from this kind of capture?"

Rankin: "It's huge. Either they declare that it is a political organization as they do in places like America where the top jobs are politically appointed, or we go back and have it the way it used to be. Because it's a very valuable tool, it's an essential tool to a democracy to have a public service that gives free and frank advice. The way they use public servants now is really dangerous, they just wheel them out with an agreed line on whatever it is, and they would never step away from that – a public servant now would never step away from that."

Once upon a time, it was a very different climate:

"New Zealand 'has been so well served for so long by loyal, incorruptible, and politically neutral state servants that it may be inclined to assume that this is part of the natural order of things"[213], recorded the 1962 Royal Commission of Inquiry into State Services.

And former Prime Minister, Sir Geoffrey Palmer, underlined the need for a neutral public service in his book *Unbridled Power*.[214]

---

212   Helen Clark has said Setchell's conflict of interest was so bad she should never have been hired in the first place. In case you're wondering how National would handle such obvious conflicts of interest: In 1999 **Alison Timms**, the wife of former Labour Party General Secretary, and at the time Helen Clark's advisor, Tony Timms, was appointed by National to run the Fire Service at a time of major political controversy over the Fire Service. National trusted Timms to act professionally, which she did; **Alec McLean** held the top role (senior private secretary) in the office of National's Deputy Prime Minister Don McKinnon, and also cabinet minister Tony Ryall, during the 1990s, even though his partner Dinah Okeby was Helen Clark's private secretary; **Verna Smith** and **Parekura Horomia** – both were senior civil servants (in Smith's case involved in regular Ministerial briefings) while both were openly Labour party election candidates. They were not sidelined, nor banned from ministerial offices, and their careers did not suffer from their politics. (Hat-tip: David Farrar at Kiwiblog)
213   *The State Services in New Zealand*, Report of the Royal Commission of Inquiry, 1962, para 20
214   *Unbridled Power*, by Geoffrey Palmer, Oxford University Press, (2nd ed.) 1987, p80

"Each department of state has a permanent head. In the case of those departments which come under the State Services Act, the permanent head is appointed by a special committee which deals with higher appointments. There is little opportunity for political interference by ministers in the process, and the permanent head continues even when there is a change in government.

"No appointment to the public service, including those at the top levels can be made from outside the service, unless the person appointed 'has clearly more merit' than any officer from within the service, who is qualified and available for the position… ministers have no say in the personnel processes of the public service. Section 10 of the State Services Act lays down that 'in matters relating to decisions on individual employees… the commission shall not be responsible to the minister but shall act independently'.

"The image of an official as the agent of the minister," argues Palmer, "and accountable to the Minister alone, working unseen and anonymously is simply no longer accurate. Officials should be more broadly accountable to the community for what they do."

So to summarise, we are now left with this inconvenient truth: David Benson-Pope intervened to stop someone from being hired by the Ministry for the Environment that he didn't like. Benson-Pope was forced to resign after being caught lying, again.

Climate Change Minister David Parker recommended that someone he *did* like be hired by MfE, and they were! A subsequent SSC investigation found breaches of procedure.

Helen Clark's "right hand woman" Heather Simpson has just been caught actually writing departmental briefing papers intended for Cabinet, in a clear breach of conventions and of the independence of the MfE, and a breach of the neutrality of public service advice to Ministers.

No investigation has been launched, despite the SSC knowing about this on November 26 2007. Yet another case, I suggest, of absolute power causing a breakdown of the legal checks and balances in our democracy.

Given that the SSC has now been pinged for sweeping this under the carpet, it is impossible for the SSC to investigate this issue because its own inaction would have to be part of the terms of reference of any inquiry.

ALLEGED CRIMES: 1. Heather Simpson directed a Government agency on what to include in a factual briefing for cabinet ministers, in clear breach of civil service neutrality rules; 2. The Ministry for the Environment tried to engage in political battle with National MP Nick Smith, in clear breach of civil service neutrality rules

HYPOCRISY FACTOR: In 1999, then-Opposition leader Helen Clark made political hay out of the fact that Government SOE Timberlands (which had a statutory commercial purpose and was thus entitled to take a less neutral stand) had engaged in lobbying against Labour's forestry policies.[215] Timberlands planning manager Kit Richards eventually walked the plank after penning a December 1999 email suggesting lobbyists target Clark in a bid to get her to change her mind. Clark called the decision by the SOE to take a political stance, "guerilla warfare", adding that it didn't meet "the ethical and moral standards" applicable to SOE staff.[216]

The mother of all quotes on this matter came from Clark when she said, "It is hard to think of any precedent for a state-owned enterprise or any crown agency or Government department running a public relations campaign against the policies of an opposition party."[217]

EXTRA-LARGE HYPOCRISY FACTOR: In 1999, Helen Clark mounted a massive attack on National's Tourism Minister, Murray McCully, over suggestions that he might be influencing departmental work for political gain, although she conceded her evidence was weak:[218] "Helen Clark said yesterday that Mr McCully would probably survive the report because he was unlikely to have left a paper trail that showed clear interference for political purposes.[219] But she said he should resign now for the sake of the tourism industry, which he had undermined already."

"This returns the matter to the central issue: was a major project with significant public funding being hijacked to suit the purposes of the National Party?" she probed on another occasion.[220] One could equally now ask whether climate change issues have been "hijacked" to suit the Labour Party's stated policy?[221] The question is, should the Prime Minister resign, if a paper trail of interference in the Ministry for the Environment is produced?

215 Taranaki Daily News, 15 October 1999, "Activist wants PR in politics exposed"
216 NZ Herald, 29 January 2000, "Timberlands manager steps down"
http://www.nzherald.co.nz/section/1/story.cfm?c_id=1&objectid=114802
217 NZ Herald, 18 August 1999, "Shipley defends role in logging"
http://www.nzherald.co.nz/section/1/story.cfm?c_id=1&objectid=12037
218 NZ Herald, 22 February 1999, "Tough time ahead for McCully"
http://www.nzherald.co.nz/section/1/story.cfm?c_id=1&objectid=2821
219 By March 1, after hundreds of pages of documents had been released, Labour hit paydirt: "A Tourism Board member thought the board's international promotion of New Zealand could help Murray McCully to promote prosperity domestically, newly released documents suggest. It is the first evidence, among hundreds of documents made public, of a perceived link between the global promotion and a selling advantage for the National Government, a recurring theme of accusations made by Labour leader Helen Clark." Gee, as scandals go, that was exciting. Sure beats the Winebox and Paintergate. NZ Herald, 1 March 1999, "Notes tell of spinoff for government",
http://www.nzherald.co.nz/section/1/story.cfm?c_id=1&objectid=3120
220 NZ Herald, 25 February 1999, "Roberts gave PM and on the edge briefing"
http://www.nzherald.co.nz/section/1/story.cfm?c_id=1&objectid=2978
221 Embarrassingly, Labour's much vaunted biofuels policy has been hammered as unworkable by the Commissioner for the Environment, because biofuels may actually generate too much carbon in their production and have a negative impact on food supplies as well, so it appears the policy they worked on was seriously flawed. The question people will now ask is who's to blame for badly thought-out policy: Heather Simpson or the Ministry?

So far in this book, you have seen the extremely serious slide in standards under the Prime Minister's watch, but to understand these things in their full context you first have to understand the woman, her beliefs, her vision and her ethics. It is a story that now takes us into Clark's personal life, beginning in the tiny Waikato settlement of Te Pahu…

"A Determined Little Devil Of A Child"

Jim Hacker: "You're not describing politicians as organized crime?"
Sir Humphrey: "No...well, disorganized crime too of course."
– Yes Minister

MENTION THE NAME "HELEN CLARK" to anyone, and usually there's one of two reactions. Adoration or loathing. On the Conservative right, that reaction is almost always a torrent of hissing, muttering and under-the-breath abuse. And funnily enough, it's always been that way, right back to the dawn of Helen Clark's parliamentary career in the 1981 election campaign where she took the seat of Mt Albert.

"It was a difficult campaign," Clark wrote in an essay for the book *Head and Shoulders* back in 1984. "As a single woman I was really hammered. I was accused of being a lesbian, of living in a commune, having friends who were Trotskyites and gays...

" 'If you elect Helen Clark', my political opponents said, 'your whole society will change overnight'..."

Now, 24 years after making that confession, some would argue the Prime Minister's recollection of the warnings given by her opponents has turned out to be highly prophetic in hindsight.

Under the Clark leadership, a sweeping Labour party social engineering agenda is now well in train. Legalised prostitution, smacking outlawed, the simmering proposal to decriminalise cannabis, Civil Unions, the contentious Care of Children Act which breaks down the legal rights of biological mothers and fathers in favour of State control of children, as well as making it easier for casual boyfriends/girlfriends of biological parents to be given "parental rights" over a child in defiance of objections from the other biological parent.

Little wonder, perhaps, that Helen Clark is the most adored and most reviled New Zealand Prime Minister since National's Rob Muldoon lost power in 1984.

So who is Helen Clark? What does she really stand for? The answers to those questions are also likely to provide clues about where the Prime Minister has taken New Zealand, and where she still wants to steer us.

Born in 1950 to farming parents, Clark reports she grew up in a home with "little spontaneous emotion", with a "dominant" father and a "distant" mother.[222] Mother Margaret later told Clark's PR advisor Brian Edwards that Helen was "a determined little devil of a child".[223]

Her father, George, was the only male in a house with four daughters, and politically he represented everything Helen Clark would later come to hate: a National Party branch chairman, a property-owner, a huge supporter of sporting contacts with South Africa, to the point that he flew on supporters tours at the same time as his eldest daughter was manning protest barricades or marching in the streets.

"I think I was equidistant from both my parents," Clark told interviewer Virginia Myers in 1984 for the book *Head and Shoulders,* published in 1986.

The Edwards hagiography also reveals a near miss between Clark and a mattress.[224]

"I remember having a row with my mother when I was a very small child and going into hiding, and she couldn't find me and she searched the house and called my father to the farm and found me virtually suffocating between mattresses. That was when I was about three."

Her father, George Clark, recalls another of his daughter's early rebellions against family discipline.[225]

"Helen had read this story about these parents being bad to their children. And when they got into bed that night there was a hedgehog in the bed – that was how they punished their parents. Well, one night I went to bed and settled myself down and there was something prickly down the bed. It was one of those spiky wire hairbrushes. She'd got the idea out of the story and put the brush in our bed. So I'm just wondering whether perhaps we'd done something wrong."

When Clark started school in 1955, she began to have asthma attacks out of the blue; at least, that's what doctors at the time presumed and which Clark apparently still believes. From the circumstances laid out in Virginia Myers' book, however, there's a very strong possibility that New Zealand's future Prime Minister may have been suffering from undiagnosed panic attacks, triggered by phobias.

"I was terribly shy, because of the lack of contact with other children. There were no others in the area and when I went to primary school I developed a lot of psychosomatic illnesses from having to mix with other kids," Clark told Myers.

222 *Head and Shoulders,* by Virginia Myers, 1986
223 *Helen: Portrait of a Prime Minister,* by Brian Edwards, Exisle Publishing, 2001, p34
224 Ibid, p36
225 Ibid, p38

Her father, George Clark, likewise, attributed it to a fear of school.

"I say a lot had to do with that first teacher. I used to get dogs sent up from a fellow at New Plymouth, and I got this little dog and it was cowed. I found out this dog used to like to nip people, and somebody on the train had belted the dog. He never recovered. And I think something similar happened at that stage in Helen's life."[226]

When I dusted off her 1984 interview for the Myers book, for the first time in nearly two decades, for a profile of Clark in late 2003, Clark's words leapt off the pages, redolent with hints at what is right and wrong with the Prime Minister.

"I had a very narrow social experience. There are still [as of 1984] whole slices of New Zealand I've never been in contact with and don't feel at ease with. Like the business community. I've never had much to do with middle class urban New Zealand."

Clark's social phobias were aggravated when her parents sent her as a boarder to Epsom Girls Grammar. Clark claims she was made to feel like a country bumpkin amidst the fashion-conscious young things from Remuera and Epsom who formed the majority of the school's roll.

A grim testimonial from the headmistress – remarking that Clark seemed adrift and without a sense of purpose in life – galvanised the young student and perhaps laid the path for the ruthless ambition that's become Clark's trademark.

"Quite a knocking testimonial. I really resented it and thought, I'll prove her wrong. I think that's characteristic of me. I developed great stubbornness as I went along."

Another clue to Clark's current agenda also emerges in the book.

"From the time I was 14 or 15, I began to have completely different and more liberal attitudes from my parents through living in Auckland, and my father and I argued a lot.

"My parents were inclined to be rigid on moral and social issues. For instance, I dropped [out of] church, and we clashed over that."

Further rebellion against religion came when Mr & Mrs Clark's eldest daughter point blank refused to play the organ in the local church anymore either – the final straw on a young camel's back.

Flash forward to 2002, and Clark's now infamous comment at the state banquet for the Queen that "New Zealand is now a secular country", and grace would not be said at the meal.

Is Helen Clark's Prime Ministership really just a Freudian working-out of long suppressed child-parent issues? If so, have New Zealanders become forced captive spectators and unwilling participants in a deeply personal "I'll show them!" three-act tragedy? Have New Zealanders become victims of the most expensive psychotherapy programme in the Western world, where the

226 Ibid, p48

patient on the couch gets to literally act out her fantasies using taxpayer cash and with absolute power? Psychologists examining Labour's policy track after investigating the PM's life story could possibly have a field day on that one.

Again, the social phobias came into play with the Epsom Girls Grammar annual ball. As Edwards tells it, the boarders at Epsom House were not looking forward to it, even though it was one of the few chances to mix with boys.

"I wasn't a good dancer," says Clark. [227] "I loathed dancing. Still do. When people ask me to dance, I decline. I've found that men can be very persistent asking you to dance at a function. I find it quite irritating. It's harassment really, and I don't like it."[228]

Exposure in the late 1960s to burn-the bra, flower power, the drug culture and liberal sexuality was given sharper focus when Clark joined Auckland University in 1968 at the height of the anti-Vietnam war protests.

The eighteen year old, wrote Clark years later, "seemed to drift naturally towards the political causes on campus, like the campaign against Omega foreign military bases. That was the first demonstration I went on and I really enjoyed it."

Clark found new strength in the rise of Marxist and feminist thought, and by the age of 20 was trying to pass on her radical views to her younger sisters.

"Helen would give me Simone de Beauvoir's *The Second Sex* when I was in my early teens," sister Jenefer told Brian Edwards. "I may have been 14 or 16. Radical feminist works like Germaine Greer's *The Female Eunuch*. That was the type of literature she was giving her younger sisters."[229]

De Beauvoir's book clearly had a profound impact on the young Helen Clark, with its suggestions that a woman going into marriage was becoming little more than a man's second-rate plaything, so it's worth having a look at what Clark was reading:

"The normal sexual act in effect puts woman into a state of dependency upon the male and the species[230]…this always constitutes a kind of violation,"[231] wrote de Beauvoir.

"From primitive times to our own, intercourse has always been considered a 'service' for which the male thanks the woman by giving her presents or assuring her maintenance; but to serve is to give oneself a master; there is no reciprocity in this relation. The nature of marriage, as well as the existence of prostitutes, is the proof.[232]

227 *Helen*, p73
228 Clark may not have liked dancing with men, but she did do this to get votes in 1999: "Election campaigns can do embarrassing things to party leaders – as Labour leader Helen Clark discovered yesterday when she had to perform the wing-flapping chicken dance with…a human-sized yellow furry cat at an inner-city playground in Wellington." *The Dominion*, 12 November 1999, "Clark does chicken dance".
229 Ibid, p50
230 *The Second Sex*, Simone de Beauvoir, Vintage, 1997, p395
231 Ibid, p394
232 Ibid, p396

It is doubtful Clark's conservative farming parents fully realized or understood the nature of the wisdom being passed on to their 14 year old daughter by an inspired big sister Helen, but it is fascinating to read the views that shaped the future Prime Minister.[233]

In her third year at varsity, Clark found herself swept up in the anti-racism movement sparked by 1970's All Black tour of South Africa.

"I thought a lot about racism and joined Trevor Richards' Halt All Racist Tours committee. During those years I had a sense of finding my identity through being politicized," Clark told Myers.

Her father joined the National Party and Clark claims he used to bail her up during visits back home "like a vulture preying on something". Her relationship with her parents, she says, became more conflict-ridden as a result.

"My parents are racist in the way that many rural New Zealanders are racist. I consciously rejected them at that time and didn't see much of them for some years."

And those intervening years – perhaps the most formative years of all, are where we now head.

---

233 An essay by Clark for her sixth form history class, reprinted in *Helen* on page 68, reveals even then the creep of Marxist thought. She wrote how the Russian peasants had turned to communism to alleviate their plight at the hands of the Russian ruling class, and that "the monarchy had served its feeble purpose in Russia and the people were ready to progress to a higher, more democratic form of government in which they could all share". Her teacher has corrected this with margin notes, pointing out that the revolution was not supported by the peasants at all (instead of course it was instigated by a liberal middle-class quasi-military Marxist group known as the Bolsheviks). At the end of the essay the teacher writes: "Sketchy and inaccurate. Did you do any reading at all?"

The Elephant In The Room

"The bulk of better reporting consists of information that does not meet the courtroom standards of proof. Journalism is not a court of law; it is a process of weaving together, often from necessarily anonymous sources, the strands of history. If legal standards were applied to news reporting, the public would have learned nothing of the Watergate scandal and President Nixon would not have resigned in disgrace." **– William Pinwill, National Times on Sunday, 1988**

LET'S BE BRUTALLY FRANK. THERE'S an elephant in the room when it comes to Helen Clark that everybody talks about, and no-one talks about. It is the subject of gossip at the coffee machine, tittle-tattle on late night radio talkback: the love that dare not speak its name. Is the New Zealand Prime Minister gay? Does it matter? Does anyone care?

The answer depends on where you sit on the political spectrum in many cases, although it is a controversial debate within political factions as well. Within National, for example, is a strong social liberal contingent whose kneejerk response to any question of politics and sex is that none of it is relevant to voters. Conversely, within Labour, there remains a strong social conservative wing who would be disappointed if the politicians they idolize have lied to them.

The idea that we cannot talk about sex and politics is a particularly curious one, given that politicians have given us laws permitting condom-tipped bananas in school classrooms; repealing the laws against adultery, prostitution and the like; and abolishing discrimination on the grounds of whether you are a bloke who likes to wear dresses. So while the rest of the country has been inundated with sexual expressiveness courtesy of the 'love generation' who grew up in the sixties, somehow it remains off-limits to discuss the motivations of those politicians.

The proper test for the news media is not specifically the sexual antics or orientation of a politician, but whether that politician has traded on a deception, made capital out of one thing publicly while doing another behind closed doors (hypocrisy), or even merely supported a law change consistent with their private practices (an undeclared conflict of interest).

"Character matters for public officials," says the American Press Institute. "They publish family pictures on campaign brochures and proudly reveal private matters that reflect positively on their character. Private matters that reflect negatively on their character matter to readers as well."

Additionally, as I pointed out in regards to David Benson-Pope, New Zealand's political system allows MPs to exercise a "conscience" vote. These conscience votes are clearly based on private beliefs and activities. Yet how can voters truly know which candidate will better represent them in a "conscience" vote, if the candidate's real beliefs (or in this case sexual orientation) are hidden?

In these modern times, I seriously doubt whether the sky would fall in if New Zealand had a gay Prime Minister. Having worked extensively with gay colleagues and for gay bosses for much of my career in the news business, it simply wasn't an issue, they were mates. As I wrote in *Eve's Bite* last year, I flatted in a gay household for six months, so contrary to the way my critics would like to paint it – the sexuality itself is a yawn for myself and I'm sure many others.[234]

It is also quite possible that if Helen Clark came out tomorrow and told the New Zealand public that, yes, she was gay, and explained her reasons for not disclosing it earlier (especially given the fact that she entered politics whilst it was still illegal), the public would breathe a sigh of relief, forgive and move on.

It is also quite possible that Clark is not gay at all, and that the nation's collective "gaydar" has been malfunctioning all these years.

The purpose of this chapter then, is not to categorically "out" the Prime Minister (although that may be an inevitable practical result), but simply to lay on the table the evidence that's been swirling around for years. Ironically – and this may come as a shock to many who right now are preparing to accuse me of "muckraking" – much of this evidence was thrown into the public domain by Helen Clark herself in her authorized biography, *Helen*, by Brian Edwards in 2001.

If you thought it was the *Sunday Star-Times* or *Investigate* that first raised questions publicly about Clark's orientation, you'd all be wrong. Helen Clark herself was the first one to put the allegations in print, seven years ago. With the Prime Minister placing it on the public record, the media and the public are entitled to chew it over and debate it. Having discovered that the Prime

---

234 Just to make sure my critics understand the point properly: I don't care about anyone's sexual orientation per se. But as a journalist I do care if a taxpayer-funded politician is hiding something. It really is that simple. Do we all understand the subtle distinction? And I will not be intimidated by political correctness into shying away from investigating that.

Minister has been dishonest in other areas for political reasons, we are entitled to look at other material that may go towards establishing honesty.

The biggest question of all is *not* whether she is *gay*. In fact, the real question is, *has the Prime Minister told the truth?*

As I've just alluded to, a strong case has been made that this administration has not been afraid to lie to cover its tracks, and then have the cheek to take the moral high ground while doing so. The Owen Glenn political donations fiasco is just one recent example.

An equally strong argument can be made that willingness to deceive the public on one issue is often a sign of a more general problem with the politician/s involved.

British law lecturer Kevin Williams, in a major paper for the legal fraternity,[235] argues strongly that politicians do not have the right to privacy, even on issues of sexuality.

"An Anglican bishop put this point forcefully when he said 'private life has a bearing on public office. An invitation to vote is an invitation to trust... character is relevant.'[236]"

Williams noted that politicians, recognizing the damage that could flow from such scrutiny, take the view that such media intrusion is an invasion of privacy. Williams warns such an excuse is unjustified in a true democracy, and a dangerous restraint on the rights of voters to know.

"It is highly questionable whether politicians, at least, should be allowed to dictate what the public may and may not pay attention to when evaluating their representatives or exercising their electoral preferences.[237] [Professor of Public Law Ian] Loveland has suggested that politicians should be deemed to have waived any presumption of privacy over sexual or other matters whenever Parliament debates such questions (see Loveland 1997).[238]

Surprisingly, law lecturer Williams goes further and says the public have a right to know everything about their political leaders, fullstop.

"Arguably politicians should be expected to put their trust in the public to

---

235 "Re-Regulating Free Speech: Privilege, Public Interest and Privacy", by Kevin Williams, Principal Lecturer in Law Sheffield Hallam University. **http://webjcli.ncl.ac.uk/1999/issue1/williams1.html**

236 The Right Rev. James Jones, Bishop elect of Liverpool, *The Guardian*, 12th March 1998, commenting on an extra-marital affair involving Robin Cook, the Foreign Secretary. Contrast the assertion of Lord Irvine LC that reports of the affair were devoid of any 'public interest' and urging that the Press Complaints Commission be given a power of 'prior restraint' to protect the privacy of public figures. These claims were immediately and forcefully repudiated by the Prime Minister's office. See *The Guardian*, 5th and 6th February 1998. Mr. Cook did not resign following the revelations. (Williams' footnote text)

237 Arguably the 'private' lives of other kinds of public figures should not be treated in the same manner, though matters which go to honesty or competence and hence suitability for office stand on a different footing (Williams' footnote text)

238 In shades of New Zealand debates over civil unions, two British MPs were prompted to "put their sexuality on record" ahead of a Commons vote on lowering the age of consent for homosexuals, see *The Guardian*, 11th June 1998. If such a declaration of interest was necessary in Britain, it raises issues of hypocrisy in the New Zealand parliament, where many closet MPs have still failed to declare their interest.

decide what weight (if any) to attach to the matter in hand. After all, *unlike other public figures, they hold office only because they are able to persuade the rest of us to vote for them.* [author's emphasis] Suggestions that questions of private morality are 'none of our business' and must be disregarded as idle gossip or as appealing only to the prurient are patronising and should be subjected to close and sceptical scrutiny. Courts should bear in mind that while the public neither believes nor necessarily expects its politicians to be saints, in a democracy the people are entitled to decide what the 'real' issues are and to judge their representatives accordingly, and by reference to whatever criteria seem to them to be proper.[239]

The New Zealand media are only slowly catching up with international best practice. The political editor for *The Press* newspaper, Colin Espiner, admits as much[240]:

"The boundaries on the publication of stuff that would once have remained private are continually shifting. The private lives of MPs were once considered completely off-limits but this is no longer the case, as Don Brash found out to his cost last year.[241]

"The advent of the internet and the plethora of media outlets has also meant that it's a highly competitive environment, and if only one mainstream media source decides to run a story, the rest will almost certainly follow.

"To some extent, MPs are public figures and they live in a fish bowl. Some are also happy to parade their children when they achieve, although others fiercely defend their privacy.

"The concern I have is that if we are to set the bar too high for the behaviour of not only MPs but their spouses and children as well, there will be very few people of calibre who will put themselves forward for public office.

"That's not to say that their families' activities should always be off-limits. If an MP leading the charge against prostitution law reform had a daughter who worked in a brothel, for example, I'd argue that was a story that was in the public interest. Or if an MP who made a stand on law and order had children

---

239 The public may be more tolerant than the press or politicians credit. There is little evidence that the electorate is politically vindictive or overly moralistic, though dissembling and evasion are disliked. Recent poll evidence, for example, suggests that homosexuality is morally acceptable (56%) and that being openly gay is compatible with holding Cabinet office (52%), though the public continues to doubt whether privacy laws should extend to politicians, as distinct from royalty and celebrities, see *The Guardian*, 10th November 1998. (Williams' footnote text)
240 http://www.stuff.co.nz/blogs/politics/2007/09/26/a-politicians-son-in-the-public-interest/
241 The Brash case is particularly significant. The media argued that Brash allegedly cheating on his wife was a matter of public interest, particularly as Brash and his wife had appeared as a couple at public events and he had talked of the importance of marriage as an institution. They're right, it is a matter of public interest on the definitions above. However, it cuts both ways: Helen Clark has paraded her marriage when politically expedient to do so, and has certainly pontificated about the nature of marriage. It is weak of her to then protest that somehow her private life is off limits, particularly if the media eventually discover that Clark has been allegedly using her marriage to "cheat on the public".

with a string of burglary convictions, that'd be a story, too," says Espiner.

You can see a touch of the inherent liberal worldview of many journalists in that passage; I'd like to think that if a politician leading the charge in *favour* of liberalized prostitution turned out to have a wife or daughter working in a brothel, or that he frequented brothels himself, that journalists like Espiner would also see this as relevant.

"The media has a legitimate role in exposing hypocrisy or falsehood in public figures," continues Espiner, "and at times that will extend to their families. It's not a blanket rule, as [John] Key suggested this morning, but a "public interest" test on a case-by-case basis."

The media don't seem to have too much trouble recognizing alleged hypocrisy and covering it, but they do seem to have a real problem recognizing an undeclared conflict of interest. Conflicts are not restricted to business or financial dealings – you can have a conflicted position on any number of law changes or policies that might benefit you privately in a range of different ways.

Undoubtedly, as this book hits the newsstands, its author will be pilloried by liberal media over the inclusion of this chapter. Let the record, and Chapter One, show however that the weight of international legal and ethics committee opinion is on my side. You, the public, certainly have a right to know if a politician is living a private life at odds with their public image, and if the British ethics papers are correct you have a right to know about their private lives regardless – *because these people are seeking the power to affect your life and tax your income, and they are very well paid for the privilege.*

Even though Helen Clark herself raised the issue of her alleged lesbianism, extensively, in her book, no New Zealand media have ever taken up the challenge. As I said at the beginning, *it is something everyone talks about, but no one talks about.*

Instead, it is left to tourists to comment, like Maria Cawallis, who wrote to *Investigate* in January after seeing news reports about an Australian Meat Board ad calling Helen Clark "a man":

"Having just spent a few days in New Zealand en route to Australia from Chile, I have become a bit of a fan of your magazine. I am also a big fan of the Bay of Islands – a beautiful part of our world.

"While up in the far north the Australian Meat Board's Sam Kekovich stated that the New Zealand Prime Minister could pass for a man, or words to that effect."

Cawallis says she asked her "kiwi friends" about the NZ Prime Minister.

"They all looked shocked and really apprehensive, before one whispered, 'it's rumoured she and her husband are gay'.

"Since that night I have spoken to a number of New Zealanders about the rumours. They all, without exception, believe their PM to be gay but seem too terrified to discuss this charade rationally. One woman actually said, 'You do not understand – we live in Helengrad, not New Zealand. This woman has entered many New Zealanders' minds and emotions, seriously affecting values and relationships'.

"Amazingly, the conversations described were carried out in the ghostliest of whispers, as though the room was bugged!

"While I realize that Ms Clark is a product of the 1950s and 60s, it begs the question – just why is she constraining herself in a prison of her own making? Why on earth in 2008 is she still maintaining the secret? I cannot believe that she and her man have not been 'outed' by the media, as everyone I spoke with believed both to be gay. What is going on in New Zealand? Perhaps it really is Helengrad."

Cawallis is not the only outsider to have raised the issue – Australian ABC TV journalist David Hardaker's questions of Helen Clark during an interview in 2002 about Paintergate and lesbian rumours sparked a walk-out.

"It was an unpleasant, hostile and rude interview," the Prime Minister later complained to the New Zealand media.

Although Clark's minders put it around the press gallery that the sexuality questions were bad form, it was, as the *Herald's* John Roughan noted,[242] a disgraceful red herring that the NZ media had swallowed hook, line and fishing rod:

"When she walked out of the interview," says Roughan, "her people said it was not just over the painting but followed questions about her personal life. We believed that too, despite the fact that she has happily rehearsed all those questions in a book published by the aforementioned Edwards late last year."

Edwards was "aforementioned" because he was reportedly "spitting with rage"[243] at journalists daring to question Clark in a challenging way.

The straw that broke the camel's back for Clark's spindoctor was a TVNZ *Sunday* programme, the night after the 2002 election, which had lined up panelists to grill Clark after playing a segment from her controversial Australian TV interview. As Roughan puts it, "she walked away from questions on the prima facie art forgery. No journalist in New Zealand could watch that item without a collective sense of shame. We had let her off the hook so easily."

As for the issue of whether the ABC interview was harsh, Roughan disagrees. "Unpleasant? Probably. Hostile? Possibly. Rude? Not in the walkout scenes we saw. In fact, the striking thing was that Hardaker remained unfailingly professional and polite. He gave that *Sunday* panel a lesson not only on the questions that ought to be asked, but about how to ask them."

That's the thing with Clark. By force of personality, her ability to freeze out journalists who cross her, and her willingness to descend to personal insults, the Prime Minister intimidates the media, and through them the public, into silence.

As noted elsewhere in this book, John Roughan's observation remains valid:

"It took an outsider, unencumbered by our politics, to demonstrate how

242   *NZ Herald*, 17 August 2002, "Clark's easy ride raises fears for vigilant press" http://www.nzherald.co.nz/section/1/story.cfm?c_id=1&objectid=2349858
243   ibid

outrageous her position was and how compliant we [the media] had been."

In considering whether to go back into the valley of the shadow of death that marks any kind of head to head conflict with the Prime Minister, I am also comforted by the fact that Clark herself likes to gossip about others and in fact uses it as a weapon.[244]

"She does like to gossip," Newstalk ZB's Barry Soper told Brian Edwards. "She's a good gossip. There's a lot of gossip around the place…If you really want to find something out you can go to Clark, which is most unlike other PMs…but she'll be calculated."

The Listener's Jane Clifton predicted in her interview for the 2001 biography that Clark's penchant for gossiping about others would eventually come back to bite her.

"I think the gossip is going to get her. I mean, she does gossip, and we love it. It's great. But it's a very fine line, and she's not always going to get away with it…it's dangerous, because there can be a perception of lack of loyalty."

Tom Scott is another quoted in *Helen* who believes the Prime Minister gossips in a deliberate, calculating way.

"She'll chat away in a very gossipy way and reveal quite a lot of information. She has quite a cunning way of embroiling people, giving them information and making them feel part of the circle. And then you don't want to lose access to those phone calls, you don't want them to taper off, so what you do is go with the information you've got. So she's almost handling her own publicity…and all the journalists who take part in that are to a greater or lesser extent compromised, but they also get good information from time to time which they are allowed to use in ways that she proscribes."

In other words, Clark gossips in order to drag journalists into her web and effectively make them do her bidding. You saw specific evidence of this cynical and damaging spin technique in the Doonegate chapter.

Armed with all of this then, and the fact that the Prime Minister, through her PR advisor Brian Edwards, arranged for a carefully crafted version of her life and "those rumours" to be presented favourably in book form leading up to the 2002 election, it's time to tackle the elephant in the room: the sexual politics and sexual orientation of Helen Clark, and their impact, if any, on the policies Labour has forced on New Zealanders over the past nine years.

***

Unusually for a Prime Minister, Helen Clark has never had a real job – at least, not in the outside world. She journeyed straight from high school to university as a student, and on obtaining her qualifications simply stayed on at university as a junior lecturer, thanks to the protective wing of her left-wing mentor, Professor Bob Chapman, who hired her when she graduated.

It was a cloistered, utterly academic existence, peppered with discussion of

---

244 *Helen*, p295

Sartre, Engels and others in coffee bars and meetings of the Princes St branch of the Labour Party. When she wasn't immersing herself in protest politics outside of university, Clark was lecturing on its various themes inside.

There were dinner parties to discuss political issues over and network at, and it was at one of these, in 1977, that Clark met her future husband, the mild-mannered and bearded Peter Davis.

It wasn't, as even Davis admits, exactly a lightning bolt moment.[245]

"Just a lot of interests in common, essentially. In meeting Helen I met somebody who had a rigorous interest in current affairs and politics, and I can't say I'd met anybody before, certainly not in Christchurch, who was interested in those things in the same way. So it was apparent that here was somebody who had travelled and who had an interest in current affairs. So that was the principal common ground".

If that was his test, he could have led a more glamorous lifestyle by dating a *60 Minutes* reporter. But then, who can control intellectual lust?

Ask Helen what attracted her to Peter, writes Edwards, and you get a similar response: "Intellect. Common interests. He had an interesting background, interesting things to talk about. And he was a great reader, very interested in current affairs. So basically common interests in international affairs, policy."

Clark uses the word "interesting" or its derivatives five times in a 32 word passage. Clearly she found Peter Davis overwhelmingly, fascinatingly, irresistibly "interesting", but we're all still none the wiser as to precisely 'why?'. Davis, incidentally, used it four times.[246]

Edwards doesn't press the issue, but some of his observations and comments from other Clark associates are "interesting" too. For a start, despite finding each other compellingly intellectually gripping, it wasn't exactly a *Gone With The Wind* experience.

"Helen and Peter undertook to meet again," writes Edwards. "But as Peter reports, their early meetings were something less than intimate."

"Helen had this strong-willed group around Beresford St – Cath Tizard, Cath's daughters, Ruth Butterworth, and Margaret Wilson. And the way they'd relax at the end of the week was to go around to the Tizards on a Friday evening or maybe a Saturday. In those days they used to do a lot of drinking. Helen doesn't drink much at all now. But that was the way you relaxed at the end of the week. Politics in many ways in those days was lubricated. So that's what we used to do. And some of her friends were involved in local government and local body elections, so we would go out on the odd occasion to restaurants and other places, and little by little had more to do with them and with each other."

---

245 Ibid, p134

246 We do now know, however, that Helen is not "interested" in Peter's musical or television tastes. Davis loves jazz, but "I wouldn't be seen dead at a jazz concert" says Clark. "I hate jazz. I hate all of it." Davis likewise enjoys *The Simpsons*, but tries not to let Clark catch him watching the programme. Doh!

The picture painted in the Edwards book is not so much one of a couple, initially, but one where Peter Davis was gradually permitted to become one of the inner circle of girls:

"He was a dear," tuts Judith Tizard. "I remember her turning up with him at one of these dinner parties – we used to call them 'ladies' nights'. We were shrieking and giggling and gossiping and networking and supporting each other as usual, and Helen turned up with this man, to our vast amusement."

An odd turn of phrase, and it is hard to imagine Margaret Wilson "shrieking and giggling", but Tizard continues:

"He seemed good-natured and tolerant and rapidly proved that he was willing to be teased. No, he was good, he was great.

"Helen said she'd met somebody. I think he was just living up the road in Anglesea Street[247] and was flatting with two women. I can remember being vaguely surprised that Helen was seeing somebody who was as academically flaky as a sociologist," says Judith Tizard.

Cath Tizard remembers Davis as a "slightly bewildered looking fellow" who "wasn't exactly a thrustful conversationalist."

Edwards collects affirmations from each of the women about the status of the Clark-Davis relationship for the official book:

"I think he and Helen are absolutely matched in all sorts of ways," agrees Judith Tizard without further explanation.

"He was very supportive of Helen, there's no doubt about that," says Clark's electorate secretary, close friend and former wife of Jim Anderton, Joan Caulfield. "And they obviously did love each other," she adds.

"I can't say his relationship with Helen was wildly demonstrative," recalls Cath Tizard. "More patting affectionate. And Helen has never been afraid to give Peter a hug in public or that sort of thing."

Except, of course, for the time Clark opted instead to shake husband Peter Davis' hand at the end of her speech to the 2006 Labour Party Conference, rather than a kiss or hug, the exchange caught on a *One News* video.[248]

"I knew that she liked him and he liked her," says Cath Tizard.

Current Labour party president Mike Williams takes a much stronger line than the women:

"Peter just appeared out of the blue. They were obviously always devoted to each other and they've been inseparable ever since. Absolutely normal relationship. You fell in love, you got together."

Absolutely normal and "inseparable", if your definition of both means no

---

247 Property records show that 40 Anglesea Street was purchased by a Raymond Francis Davis in 1966, and sold to a company called Old Town Developments Ltd in August 1976, but with vendor finance via a mortgage provided by Ray Davis. Peter Byard Davis can be seen taking out a caveat over the property in December 1976, and the house was transferred fully into his name in February 1979. Ironically, however, postal records in the Wises Directory for 1976 show the occupier as one Clarke A. Davis. Helen Clark did not meet Peter Davis until early 1977. Go figure.
248 http://tvnz.co.nz/view/video_popup_windows_skin/873521

wedding ring, separate names, separate bank accounts, a splitting of expenses and separate houses in separate names, in separate cities.

After winning selection as Labour's candidate for Mt Albert in April 1980, attention turned to logistics for the upcoming 1981 election campaign and "the rules". Under the electoral rules, a candidate at the time had to live in the electorate they were standing for. As Edwards writes it:

"In pursuit of her goal, Helen decided that she and Peter should move out of Anglesea Street and into the Mount Albert electorate. Peter went along."

Just "when" Peter went along, however, remains unclear.

"There are things where I just trust to Helen's judgment. I can't remember how we identified the Mount Eden house or how long it took or anything for that matter. It was just in the electorate. And frankly, Judith [Tizard's] brother Nigel, who is a builder, always says he virtually had to rebuild the thing. You wonder what the point was in buying it, but it's stood the test of time."

For all of her reading of *Sexual Politics*, *The Second Sex* and so on, Helen Clark showed no sign of financial independence in the purchase of the Cromwell Street property. It was bought in the sole name of Peter Byard Davis on 23 December, 1980, for $40,000. It remains in the sole name of Peter Davis today, although its value is now listed as $740,000.[249]

It is here, however, that murkiness surrounds the whereabouts and abode of Helen Elizabeth Clark. A check of the electoral rolls in 1975 finds Helen E. Clark, student, registered to vote in the Auckland Central electorate, at her student flat at 11 Elgin St.[250] Just six hundred metres away, but across the electorate boundary in the neighbouring Grey Lynn electorate, another Helen E. Clark, student, is also registered to vote there as well, at 3 Browning Street, Grey Lynn.

Neither of the Helen E. Clark, student(s) appears to have shifted address over the next three years, because in 1978, when the electoral rolls closed at the end of July, a Helen E. Clark, student, is still registered at Elgin St, while her mysterious namesake is also still registered at 3 Browning Street.

There is no direct mention in Edwards' book of Clark living at a flat in Browning Street, but a re-check of earlier electoral rolls showed a Helen E. Clark, student, registered to vote at that address for the 1972 election that swept Labour's Norman Kirk to power. No other Helen E. Clark was registered to vote in Auckland city for that election, which is significant because the political Helen E. Clark was standing for the Auckland City Council and needed to have a registered address.

So on the face of the rolls, for three straight elections (72, 75, 78), a Helen E. Clark, student, was registered to vote in the Grey Lynn electorate at the

---

249 Helen Clark has an apartment in her own name in Wellington.
250 Another piece of historical trivia: In March 1977 the Elgin St property was purchased by one Brian James Curtis, contractor. It is impossible to know for sure 31 years later, but this may have been the same Brian James Curtis who later became New Zealand's most wanted criminal in the 1990s after escaping from Paremoremo Maximum Security jail.

Browning Street address. But for the 1975 and 1978 elections, a Helen E. Clark living only a few hundred metres away in Elgin Street was simultaneously registered to vote in the Auckland Central electorate.

The waters of this particular mystery are muddied further however, because despite the electoral rolls, the Grey Lynn seat was abolished prior to the 1978 election.

And here's a further confusing aspect.

According to the official biography of Helen E. Clark, Prime Minister, she vacated the 11 Elgin Street address at the start of 1977 to go and live with Catherine Tizard at Beresford Street in Ponsonby.[251]

"She'd lived in this grotty, god-awful flat, real student dive," Judith Tizard told Brian Edwards. "And it was cold and she always had terrible asthma. She used to get quite ill in the winter. And I said something like, 'Why don't you go and stay with Mum for a while?' because Mum and Dad were living in a three bedroom townhouse with the kids all gone. So I rang Mum and said, 'Helen's looking for somewhere to stay for a couple of weeks, can she stay at your house?' And Mum said, 'Yes, sure'."

Cath Tizard told Edwards Clark was the guest who simply refused to leave.

"Helen moved into the upstairs bedroom and I think from memory it was sort of like the man who came to dinner. She stayed two years…I found that a cheque for board would be put on my dressing table. I don't think we ever formally discussed an amount."

According to the Edwards book, Clark went flatting with Peter Davis at 40 Anglesea Street, Ponsonby, two years later, in 1979. Certainly, after being selected to stand for the Mt Albert seat in April 1980, we know Clark listed her address as Anglesea Street for the purposes of the Auckland City Council local election towards the end of 1980.

So why, in July 1978, was the Auckland Central Helen E. Clark's electoral roll address listed as 11 Elgin Street, Grey Lynn – an address she had left 18 months earlier? This appears to be a breach under the Electoral Act, which says, at s72(7), that temporary digs qualify as a place of residence because "a person who has permanently left his or her former home shall be deemed not to reside at that place, notwithstanding that his or her home for the time being is temporary only".

Technically, if indeed both Clarks were one,[252] Helen Clark was simultaneously registered in 1978 in an electorate that no longer existed (Grey Lynn), and at a house she wasn't living at (Elgin St, Ak Central), while voting from a house she wasn't registered at (Beresford Street, Ak Central)!

In the earlier 1975 election, a politically schizophrenic Helen Clark was

251 *Helen*, p122
252 This would be the same Helen E. Clark who, on 4 December 2007, tried to nail National leader John Key over his electoral address: "**Rt Hon HELEN CLARK**: With regard to appearing in docks, the member is lucky he did not do that himself on his electoral enrolment." Hansard, NZ Parliament, 4 December 2007

standing as a Labour candidate for Piako in the Waikato, whilst simultaneously registered to vote in both Grey Lynn and Auckland Central. Technically, under the Electoral Act, her vote in any electorate in 1975 would have been invalid.

When the main electoral rolls closed again in July 1981, Peter Davis was still registered to vote in the Auckland Central electorate at his 40 Anglesea Street address, while Helen E. Clark was registered to vote in Mt Albert at the Cromwell Street address. There were no other Helen E. Clarks.

Tongues allegedly began to wag in the community, as Clark's official biography makes clear, and very public.

"Rumours that Helen was a lesbian had been circulating for some time and were spread not only by her political opponents, but by some who ought to have been her supporters," writes Edwards.

"In those days," remembers Clark's electorate secretary Joan Caulfield in the book, "she was a young woman, independent, and she wasn't married. And I can remember a Minister, a conservative Labour Minister, referring to her in my presence as 'a barren lesbian'."

This is a subtle twisting of the facts by the Clark camp. Although set in the context of the lead-up to the 1981 election by Edwards, the alleged comment by the Labour cabinet minister must have been made years later, for two very simple reasons: Helen Clark was not even married at this point – no conservative politician would be criticizing her as "barren" when she did not even have a husband. Secondly, Labour was not in power in 1981 so there was no "conservative Labour minister" available to make such a statement. Such a beast did not eventuate until after 1984. And if rumours of Clark's sexuality were still disturbing Labour cabinet ministers in the mid 1980s, then clearly the marriage to Peter Davis in 1981 had done nothing to allay the suspicions of Clark's own colleagues, let alone anyone else.

Helen Clark blames the National Party for rumours about her sexuality, but Caulfield's sources all appear to be Labour people:

"I also heard rumours from a friend of my father's, who lived in the electorate. He said that Helen was a lesbian and Peter was gay and that they were living together for political reasons, to make it look good."[253]

---

253 This particular story simply has not died, as this comment posted to the website of the *Guardian* newspaper in London by a South Auckland health professional this year shows:
"Helen Clark has never been a baby-kisser type of populist. NZ being a small country, it was reasonably well known both inside and outside the Labour party that she is a lesbian. An acquaintance of mine was present at a very discreet Labour Party 'meeting' when she had yet to become cabinet minister, where it was 'suggested' she marry in order to defuse the tabloid press, who had tried and failed to out her, due to her extraordinarily discreet private life. She married a close friend, an equally discreet gay sociologist."
In response to an attack by NZ Labour supporters on his claims, the health professional responded:
"Several of the above posters have serious comprehension problems. Yes, private lives SHOULD be irrelevant. But politics is immensely about alleged 'morality', 'character' etc. Anyhow, I stated my source: a Labour party person who knew that she was advised by the party hierarchy to marry in order to defuse the gay rumours. The background to

Chapter 12

Davis was maintaining two houses at this point however, and two mortgage payments. On August 31st, 1981, he sold the Anglesea Street property, and re-registered as a voter at the Cromwell Street property, on the supplementary roll.

Setting up house within the electorate did not stop the gossip however, and although Mt Albert, a working class electorate previously held by Labour's Warren Freer with a majority of almost 3,000, was probably safe enough for Labour to stand a nanny-goat wearing a red ribbon and still win, Labour's party boss wasn't taking chances.

"Helen's unmarried and childless state was nonetheless of concern to some of her supporters," Brian Edwards writes. President Jim Anderton and Joan Anderton (now Caulfield) raised the issue.

"What happened was that Peter and Helen were at dinner at our place," Caulfield told Brian Edwards. "And Jim brought up the issue of the publicity about Helen and Peter living together and not being married, and what the Opposition would make of that, because New Zealand had always been a very conservative society.

"And I remember Jim saying, 'Well, you and Peter, you should get married. You're living together, so what's the problem?' Not knowing that for Helen it was the last thing she was holding onto that was anti establishment, really."

"I felt really compromised," Helen Clark told Virginia Myers in 1984. "I think legal marriage is unnecessary and I would not have formalised the relationship [with husband Peter Davis] except for going into Parliament. I have always railed against it privately."[254]

And if we revisit Simone de Beauvoir's epic *The Second Sex* for a moment, you'll soon see why:

"Woman, as slave or vassal, is integrated within families dominated by fathers or brothers, and she has always been given in marriage by certain males to other males. In primitive societies the paternal clan, the gens, disposed of woman almost like a thing: she was included in deals agreed upon by two groups."[255]

"Marriage today still retains, for the most part, this traditional form. First, it is forced much more tyrannically upon the young girl than upon the young man. There are still important social strata in which no other vista opens before her; among the workers of the land the unmarried woman is a pariah."[256]

---

this was grounded in the Colin Moyle affair, a Labour minister who was gay, who was hounded by Muldoon for the alleged crime of misleading parliament about his sexuality. Since the Moyle affair, it became internal party policy that high ranking Labour MPs who were gay/bi to 'out' themselves or become Caesar's wife." http://commentisfree. guardian.co.uk/tim_watkin/2007/12/identity_politics.html

254 Clark was also tremendously upset at plans to soften her image. "She had this long, rippling, beautiful hair," recalls Cath Tizard in the Edwards book (p138), "and by the time I'd cut about two inches she was in tears and shrieking at me...the thought of cutting her hair was like cutting a limb off at that stage." She was also reluctant to be more feminine with her clothes, but "once it was explained to her that it was a *tool*, she became very practical about it...she started wearing skirts."

255 Ibid, p446
256 Ibid, p450

This last comment must have been resonating in the young Clark's head on the day of her wedding – she was only tying the knot for political reasons – on the instruction of one of the Labour Party's alpha males, Jim Anderton – soon to desert his own wife.

Whether or not the lesbian rumours at the time were true, certainly in Clark's eyes there was absolutely nothing wrong with homosexuality, and the books she and her circle of friends read reinforced the point. De Beauvoir, for example, who had a string of lesbian liaisons, talked in her book of the kind of woman who wanted to resist male domination. Girls, she wrote, who may not have had much experience of men in their childhoods, often formed very close relationships with very special girlfriends at school or work, relationships that may or may not have crossed over into the physical. This, argued de Beauvoir, was fairly normal.[257]

"In boarding schools and seminaries for young women the transition from intimacy to sexuality is rapid," she writes. "Lesbians are far less numerous in environments where the association of girls and boys facilitates heterosexual experiences.

"Many women who are employed in workshops and offices surrounded by women, and who see little of men, will tend to form amorous friendships with females: they will find it materially and morally simple to associate their lives. The absence or difficulty of heterosexual contacts will doom them to inversion [homosexuality]."

Noting that even a woman with no lack of male contact will "often not be repelled by the caresses of a woman friend", the iconic de Beauvoir draws pen portraits of two types of lesbian: a more masculine, dominant woman, and a softer, feminine woman. Don't be fooled, however, says de Beauvoir, each enjoys the other's charms.

"The woman who turns lesbian because she haughtily declines male domination is often pleased to find the same proud amazon in another… in their mutual embraces each was at once man and woman and each was enchanted with the other's androgynous [male] qualities. On the other hand, a woman who wishes to enjoy her femininity in feminine arms can also know the pride of obeying no master.[258]

"Renée Vivien dearly loved feminine beauty, and she wished to be beautiful… she was proud of her long hair; but she took pleasure in feeling free, inviolate. In her poems she expresses her scorn for the women who in marriage consent to become men's serfs. Her liking for strong drink, her sometimes obscene language, showed her desire for virility.

"The fact is that in most couples the caresses are reciprocal. In consequence the respective roles of the two partners are by no means definitely fixed: the woman of more childish nature can play the part of the adolescent youth associated with

257 Ibid, p437
258 Ibid, p438

the protective matron, or that of the mistress on her lover's arm...all kinds of combinations, transpositions, exchanges, *comédies* are possible."

According to de Beauvoir, lesbianism was not innate, but "a choice" made by and open to women, either with or without a man in their life.

"If the prehensile, possessive tendency remains especially strong in a woman, she, like Renée Vivien, will be oriented in the homosexual direction. Or she will choose only males whom she can treat like women: so with the heroine of Rachilde's *Monsieur Venus*, who buys herself a young man; she enjoys caressing him passionately but does not let him deflorate her.

"Never in the presence of husband or lover can she feel wholly herself; but with her woman friend she need not be on parade, need not pretend: they are too much of a kind not to show themselves frankly as they are. This similarity engenders complete intimacy.[259]

"It is difficult to state with certainty, for example, whether the lesbian commonly dresses in mannish fashion by preference or as a defence reaction. Certainly it is often a matter of spontaneous choice. Nothing is less natural than to dress in feminine fashion; no doubt masculine garb is artificial also, but it is simpler and more convenient...the significance of woman's attire is evident: it is decoration, and to be decorated means to be offered..."Masculine clothing, at first a disguise, becomes a uniform; and under the pretext of escaping male oppression, woman becomes enslaved to the character she plays; wishing not to be confined in woman's situation, she is imprisoned in that of the lesbian."[260]

Remember, this was one of Clark's favourite books, and it clearly raised the option of a woman having a man for appearances, and a close female friend for other things.

In Peter Davis, Helen Clark struck the ideal man: one who always said 'yes'. As Edwards tells it, Davis barely batted an eyelid at being told he would have to marry for the sake of "the Party".

"Peter went along with the decision, as he has gone along with almost all of Helen's decisions since they first began living together."

Davis himself agrees.

"I didn't mind one way or the other too much. But I don't think Helen was too keen. We were involved in this larger game of politics. You were more or less ambushed into it. I didn't really mind. Helen's strong-willed and her whole life has required her to bend that will at certain times. But I think this was probably at a deeper level. It was about identity and what it means to be a woman breaking convention. And maybe in this respect she couldn't break convention entirely. But I don't remember any decision being made about it. In these things, I go along with Helen. If Helen wants to do it, I'll do it."

But a decision was made, albeit very quietly, in early November 1981. A

---

259 Ibid, p440
260 Ibid, p443

wedding would be arranged on 6 November – in only a few days' time – at the Registry Office. The election was only three weeks away, time was of the essence. Significantly, Helen Clark did not invite or tell her closest friend, Judith Tizard, that she was getting married to a man in breach of everything she believed in.

In the Edwards book, Judith clearly still felt the pain in 2001, even after 20 years.[261]

"She didn't even tell me, evil cow. She didn't want to get married. I was aware of that. But she didn't tell me…And I was pissed off with her. I was *really* pissed off with her. We were good, really close friends."

Only the Andertons, Judith's mother Cath Tizard, and Helen Clark's immediate family were aware of the wedding, and even Clark's parents were not on the original list of invitees until Cath Tizard twisted the young politician's arm.

And as for a happy wedding day – forget it. Retired political studies lecturer Ruth Butterworth, a long time friend of Clark's, is quoted remembering the black mood at the "wedding".[262]

"She was resistant up to the last minute. I mean, she was crying on the day. It was just so awful because it was so deeply against her principles. She didn't believe in marriage. It went so deep."

Significantly, Brian Edwards' official biography of the Prime Minister goes out of its way to talk about the rumours surrounding Helen Clark.

"The lesbian allegations persisted: Helen was having an affair with Cath Tizard, which led to the break-up of the Tizard marriage; she was having an affair with Margaret Wilson; her relationship with Peter was a mere sham, designed to conceal the truth that both were gay."[263]

But even more significantly, look at the difference in passion over the issue between Clark and Davis.

"Over the years," said Clark, "you still get the National Party rumour mongering, most-recently that the marriage has broken up. When Peter went to Christchurch they ran that one around. It never stops. I've heard National MPs interject, 'What about your affair with so and so?' They never stop. They're relentlessly personally nasty. The one thing I hate is the National Party. I think they're loathsome people. I do."[264]

Now, contrast Clark's venom with Peter Davis' mild comments:[265]

"I think it could well be that her friends were more upset than us. I don't remember being upset. I remember being a little bit concerned, because it was a little bit extreme. But I assumed that it would die down."

261 *Helen*, p145
262 Ibid, p 148
263 Remember, this showboat was being floated long before any *Investigate* articles – years earlier in fact – by Helen Clark herself.
264 *Helen*, p144
265 Ibid

A couple of things are quite striking in that. Firstly, Davis certainly didn't realize Clark was as angry as she appears in the previous paragraph. Why are he and Clark not singing from the same hymnbook?[266] Or was Clark's fury in her Edwards interview only for "show" – an act?

Edwards doesn't pursue it. Secondly, Davis talks about "her friends" being more upset about it. Not "our friends", but "her friends". It may be insignificant, but he speaks as if he's an outsider in his wife's social circle.

The complexities of the Clark-Davis relationship are hinted at in Brian Edwards' book, but so are the pressures on the couple. Helen for example, was one of the prime movers behind the scenes of the 1985 Homosexual Law Reform Bill, working furiously with her electorate secretary at the time Judith Tizard, to rally support for the law change. Yet the full extent of Clark's involvement is not disclosed in the book, presumably because of the tensions the issue caused with her conservative parents.[267]

"I said to Peter [Davis] one day," exclaims George Clark, " 'I think they should all be drowned or something or other'. And he said, 'George, you are looking at about seven or eight percent of the population'[268]. It's abhorrent to me," George Clark adds. It's worth remembering that he was interviewed for the Edwards book in 2001.

It is time to cover off a relevant issue as well. Helen Clark's book suggests her critics were spreading a whispering campaign that Clark was having an affair with Dame Catherine Tizard, and that this was a factor in the Tizard marriage break-up in 1981.

In 26 years as a journalist, including time at the heart of the political web in Wellington, that is *one* rumour I don't recall hearing. Suggestions of a romance between Clark and Cath's daughter, Judith Tizard, are a different kettle of fish however, but were never referred to in Edwards' book. To this day, I also find it inexplicable that Clark invited Ruth Butterworth, Joan Caulfield and even Judith Tizard's mother Cath to the wedding, but evidently made Cath swear not to tell Judith. Why? Why would you exclude such a close friend, unless it might cause pain?

I wouldn't "out" someone unless it was relevant, but Tizard threw the first stone in a comment she posted on a gay website (Ecoqueer) by trying to insinuate critics of the Civil Unions Bill in 2004 must have been gays who were still in the closet[269]:

---

266 When the *Sunday Star-Times* led with the Peter Davis kissing photo in September 2006, there was widespread fury from commentators and friends on behalf of Peter Davis, but he himself merely shrugged. "Don't worry about it, it's just one of those things", he told a long-time friend, before continuing on a totally different topic, as if nothing had happened. Listener, "The Silent Type", Sep 30-Oct6 2006

267 *Helen*, p184

268 In fact, the actual rate of exclusive homosexuality in the population, established by a British study of more than 20,000 people, is less than 1%. Source: *Eve's Bite*, Ian Wishart, Howling At The Moon, 2007, p101, fn63

269 http://www.stonesoup.co.nz/ecoqueer/archives/003556.html

"I was working in Helen Clark's electorate office in 1984-7," wrote Tizard, "and had to cope with the most amazing anger and abuse from people opposed to the Homosexual Law Reform Bill, who felt free to ring and threaten Fran, Helen and/or me with verbal assault, physical violence or eternal damnation. It was a very weird time and I also got dozens of calls from very frightened people who had been forced to sign the Anti petition as you descibe [sic]. The not-suprising [sic] follow up has been the number of people since who admit to being violently opposed to the reform then who now realise that they are glbt [gay, lesbian, bisexual, transsexual] and that that was why they were so angry and frightened then. I wonder what devils are frigtening [sic] Mr Tamaki?"

Given that Tizard seems happy to fling out innuendo about other people's sexual orientation, it seems to meet the international ethical test for hypocrisy, so let's deal with Judith's elephant. She clearly has spelling issues. She's also bisexual[270]. There, we said it. Homosexuality has been legal for more than 20 years now, and it does seem deeply hypocritical to allow people to be politically active on the point whilst coyly hiding behind "privacy".

Heterosexual politicians get no presumed "privacy" regarding their orientation. How can Labour's gay wing reasonably justify the continued closeting of *any* gay Labour MPs, whilst at the same time helping promote an 'out and proud' message to kids through gay initiatives in schools? As patron of the Auckland Pride Centre, Tizard hosts special events like the Centre's "Coming OUT Day".[271]

The party's gay wing, Rainbow Labour, says in its mission statement that "It exists to influence Labour policy, government policy, and New Zealand legislation to further remove the boundaries and barriers to equality in our lives."

Well, if you want to influence policy and the lives of ordinary voters, at least admit who you are. And since when was being gay in the Labour Party a barrier to advancement?

Tizard has been a constant social companion to Clark over the years, attending opera, classical concerts and theatre performances, as well as all the other things that close friends usually do. As Minister for Auckland, Tizard was perfectly placed to be Mistress of Wine and Cheese as needed.

When former Labour Prime Minister Mike Moore fired shots across Clark's bows in a *Herald* opinion piece last August, one line in the article particularly set tongues wagging:[272]

"Exactly what does the "consort" Judith Tizard and the legion of Ministers outside Cabinet actually do?" asked Moore.

270 Tizard had already been "outed" as bisexual back in 2003 by two gay journalists, Jonathan Marshall and David Herkt
271 http://www.pride.org.nz/Organisation.htm
272 *NZ Herald*, 29 August 2007, "Mike Moore: Return to Muldoonism?"
http://www.nzherald.co.nz/category/story.cfm?c_id=49&objectid=10460368&pnum=0

Commentator Fran O'Sullivan, like many others, read the entrails.[273]

"Clark's office laughed off Moore's searing criticism with a 'that's Mike' rejoinder. Clark said it was 'ridiculous'. But the badinage on the ninth floor of the Beehive – particularly between Clark and her chief of staff Heather Simpson (H2) – will not have been anywhere near as polite.

"The pair retain strong feelings over a 'whispers' campaign that they believe Moore's 'beagle boys' orchestrated against them after Clark's victory. Simpson is in a lesbian relationship. Moore's decision to call Minister for Auckland Judith Tizard Clark's 'consort' will magnify paranoia that there is a subtext to the comments."

Clark has only herself to blame. Tizard's job has always looked like a reward for teacher's pet, and Tizard has consistently ranked close to the bottom of public approval ratings in her portfolio.[274]

The fact that Judith Tizard has the highest domestic air travel bill behind only the Prime Minister has only added to the rumour mill and the criticism:

"Ms Tizard was revealed yesterday by the National Party as the second-highest ministerial spender on domestic air travel[275] since 2000, with a total bill of $337,719," reported the *Herald* in late 2006.[276]

"What on earth *does* she do all day?" queried National's Bill English. "How can she claim that she is extremely busy working for Auckland when, in the last six months, over half of her media appearances have been for arts functions, including attending the same Royal New Zealand Ballet performance of *Trinity* in two different cities?"[277]

Despite being a prolific air traveler, like Clark, and being an appreciative fan of attending the opera, like Clark, attempts to pin down Tizard on her real work have been more difficult. National MP Richard Worth asked under the Official Information Act at one point for "all reports and advice notes she has sent to Cabinet colleagues and officials seeking additional funding for Auckland projects over the past 12 months?" Worth was stunned when

---

273 *NZ Herald*, 1 September 2007, "Fran O'Sullivan: Moore's subtext all about election win" http://www.nzherald.co.nz/category/story.cfm?c_id=49&objectid=10461015
274 *Metro* magazine, March 08
275 Given her high mileage, and her tendency to repeatedly interject National MPs while they are speaking in Parliament, Judith Tizard has been hit with taunts like "get back on your broomstick", to which Tizard takes considerable offence. Tizard shed "crocodile tears" over the broomstick jibe, telling parliament it was an insult to women and witches. However, the Minister's capacity for hypocrisy knew no bounds because in late 2007 she appeared in a gay chat show on Alt.TV, where she proceeded to beat a hanging figurine of a witch on a broomstick, saying the witch's name was "Ruth Richardson" (video can be viewed here: http://youtube.com/watch?v=voaOPR0WwGc&feature=related). The original newspaper story featuring Tizard's outrage on behalf of witches can be seen here: *NZ Herald*, 27 June 2007, "Angry Tizard objects to rivals 'broomstick' insult" http://www.nzherald.co.nz/topic/story.cfm?c_id=177&objectid=10448162
276 *NZ Herald*, 17 Nov 2006, "Frequent flyer Tizard cops flak" http://www.nzherald.co.nz/section/1/story.cfm?c_id=1&ObjectID=10411197
277 ibid

Tizard admitted she hadn't done any reports or notes for her colleagues – so none existed.

New Zealand can thank Tizard for Civil Unions however. While it was ultimately Tim Barnett and later David Benson-Pope who shepherded the legislation through parliament in 2004, it was Tizard who first championed gay marriage back in 1996.

"Judith Tizard announced that she would take a proposal to the Labour Party caucus to support… registration of same sex marriages," reported a gay news website.[278]

"If that's what gay and lesbian people want (the right to marry)," said Tizard, "I don't see why the rest of the community should stop that."

Reading the official Clark biography, it's not so much the Helen-Peter story as the Helen-Judith story. Take the account of what happened when Labour lost the 1993 election under Moore:

"Helen and Judith decided it was time to take a break," writes Edwards, who then quotes Tizard.

"So Helen and I went to Fiji. We had a ball. Just lazed about and snorkeled and read and drank wine and gossiped. And Peter came up and spent three days with us."

Although Clark and Davis had so much in common when they met, it did not include music or leisure pursuits apparently.[279]

"Peter's interests are much more in jazz and contemporary music," Tizard says in the book, whilst Clark was strictly classical and opera. "He likes cricket, he likes music, he likes films. They really enjoyed travelling together, but I think Helen decided she needed to have lots of other things she enjoyed doing too, so she made a conscious effort."

As Edwards puts it, "Helen had decided that politics could not continue to be her sole preoccupation. She needed a balance in her life, other interests and activities outside politics. Judith was one of the earliest to become aware of this change of emphasis.

Judith, of course, had been a confidante since Clark's first days in Labour. When Clark missed out on a cabinet appointment in the 1984 Lange administration, she burst into tears and had a rant to Tizard.

"You know, I don't have to put up with this. I could get a job at the UN. I could get a job at any university in the world," she told Tizard.[280]

Although not, apparently, if the Americans had anything to do with it.

Despite her disappointment over a Cabinet position in the first Lange term, Clark did manage to secure the chairmanship of the Foreign Affairs and Defence Select Committee – a prestige position for an anti-nuclear, anti-US activist. And naturally, paranoia set in.

---

278 http://www.qna.net.nz/news/403.html
279 *Helen*, p229
280 Ibid, p182

"A Government MP known for her strong anti-nuclear stand claims 'American sources' have been spying on her," reported the *Auckland Star* in 1986.[281]

"Mt Albert's Helen Clark says her long distance telephone calls are almost certainly monitored by Americans.

" 'They have surveillance equipment to pick up long distance conversations and I believe mine would interest them'," Clark was quoted as saying. "Sometimes I feel afraid."

Apart from listening in to late night calls between Helen Clark and a mystery woman lawyer who Clark described as a close personal "confidante", it's unclear what significant intelligence the US would have gleaned from eavesdropping on Clark. Clearly, however, she didn't want her personal life messing up her political ambitions.

"Ms Clark," reported the *Star*, "said she has to lead a 'squeaky clean' personal life for fear of being the target of smear campaigns. A spokesman for the American Embassy in Wellington described Ms Clark's claims as 'incredible'."

What's more incredible is the suggestion that Helen Clark was complaining to a major newspaper that she was being forced to lead a "squeaky clean" personal life because of American surveillance. She was after all, ostensibly happily married. Didn't a "squeaky clean" personal life come with that particular territory? What could the Americans possibly glean from Clark's phone calls that could "smear" her personally?[282]

And again, in case I haven't reinforced this point enough, it was Helen Clark putting this in the public domain, not the media. The *Auckland Star* though, like so many other New Zealand media over the years, never pushed Clark for a more detailed explanation.

In the Virginia Myers book, Clark lists a handful of confidantes. Judith and Cath Tizard are both members of that inner sanctum, as is Margaret Wilson and the woman Clark calls "my lawyer friend", as well as Joan Caulfield.

On the other hand, there are very few men close to her. One telling ingredient in the Clark mix appears to be an almost sweeping, stereotypical dislike of men, as she illustrated in the book *Head and Shoulders*:

"I remember being greatly influenced by Kate Millett's *Sexual Politics* and Germaine Greer's *The Female Eunuch* when I was about 20.

"Men in particular lose control entirely. They scream and shout and are personally abusive. It's really quite extraordinary. I never scream and shout, that's not my nature."

Imagine Clark's outcry if a male politician were to make such a generalization: "Women in particular lose control entirely. They scream and shout and are personally abusive…"

---

281   *Auckland Star*, 16 September 1986. Reprinted in *Investigate*, November 2003 issue
282   Clark made the same comment after claims in 2006 that private detectives were stalking her husband, saying she and Davis were being very careful. "It puts restrictions on the little things you do on your own," the *Herald* quoted Clark. No one bothered to ask, "Why?" *NZ Herald*, 22 September 2006, "Detective adamant he didn't follow Davis"

Clark then goes on to detail being bailed up one day at a party by a male colleague from her university days, complaining about what the Government was doing to the country.

"I finally flipped and said, 'Don't you f...ing well speak to me like that! If you knew how many bloody hours a day I worked and now I come to a party at midnight on a Saturday night and have a f...ing fool like you screaming at me about how hard you work!'."

Helen Clark's opinion of men can clearly be seen in the following 1984 disclosure.

"There are colleagues to whom I rarely speak, like Roger Douglas, and it's mutual. What could we say to each other? There are years of very sharp differences of opinion.

"Roger's very intense, and sexist.

"The team which promoted Lange to power is incredibly sexist and I don't see any way that a woman could ever have got admission to it. People like Moore and Prebble can't help appearing sexist. I think that's been a lot of the problem for me.

"Part of my being overlooked for any office is because I belong to another faction in the party, but part of it is also that I'm a woman.

"I think they find most women terribly threatening...I suppress so much. I'm conscious of some of the putdowns and the sexism.

"Discussions around Parliament are entirely conducted in terms of 'he'. The men say it's a generic term, but I don't accept that. Of course it's a put-down!"[283]

Another tell-tale pointer to the Prime Minister's current apparent hostility towards the modern nuclear family can be seen in the way in which she regards mothers.[284]

"I've never had any intention of having a child. I definitely see children as destroying my lifestyle. It's inconceivable that I would become pregnant. I realise my attitude is unusual, but I have other interests which crowd out everything else, and I think I'd go around the bend if my small amount of spare time was taken up by children.

"I was able to develop as a professional person with no breaks in career... I wasn't caught in the trap of the young bride who seems to stop maturing when her kids are born."

That's a pretty stinging slap in the face to more than a million New Zealand mothers – that the Prime Minister thinks women are immature or brain dead because they have kids![285]

---

283 Clark went on to amuse many in recent years by occasionally referring to Speaker of the House Margaret Wilson as "Mr Speaker", before correcting herself.

284 *Head and Shoulders*

285 In fairness to the Prime Minister, her comments betray a subconscious, generalized belief more or less in line with the tone of the various feminist books she absorbed in her youth. When it comes to her own nieces and nephews, however, Clark is by all accounts a fantastic aunt. Thus, a distinction can be drawn between abstract philosophical concepts, and real-life requirements. The abstract philosophical concepts, however,

Clark's hatred of the idea of having children appears almost pathological, and again has worked its way out through her policy agenda. It was Helen Clark who introduced a 1989 law change making it possible for primary-aged schoolgirls who get pregnant to obtain abortions without telling their parents.

When former National Party leader Bill English warned National would challenge the underage abortion provision in the Care of Children Bill, Clark's response was terse:

"I've always believed that in the end it is a woman's right, in line with her own conscience, to determine whether or not she has an abortion and you know that's the view I will hold until I go to the grave."[286]

Perhaps her latent disdain for women with children, matched with Clark's dislike of men generally, have played a role in the Thatcheresque style adopted by Clark.

"One sees men behaving very emotionally around here," she told Virginia Myers, "but they are never portrayed as being emotional. But if women are seen to be emotional they are almost written off as unable to do their job. That's why you have got to toughen up.

"I do see myself as a strong person, with strong opinions. The main block to being a woman in Parliament is not being one of the boys; not being in the networks they operate.

"The women MPs tend to be personally quite friendly with each other, but we're not running networks, we're too busy."

The accuracy of that particular claim from 1984 will be tested later in this book.

So what about Helen Clark herself? What do her friends think of her? One person who's known Helen Clark most of her life[287] has seen the changes in their friend, changes that come with the trappings of power. "Helen got into politics with a deep sense of doing good, and she was happy to be working toward's Labour's common goals," the Prime Minister's long time colleague explains. "She didn't have high aspirations as such. But sometime in the late 80s someone told her that her aspirations should be much higher – that naughty word 'ambition' changes everything, and it changed Helen.

"One of the fascinating things about her is the Jekyll and Hide way she compartentalises her private and public lives. In private, Helen Clark is as honest and straight a person as you could meet. She has absolutely high integrity on an interpersonal basis. She is very loyal to those she cares about, whether they are friends or just constituents in need. I've seen Helen do incredible things for people and they've never even known.[288]

---

impact on Labour's policies.
286 Except Clark is being disingenuous: the Bill allowed schools or clinics to organize abortions, even for 9 or 10 year old children, without parental knowledge. Nine or 10 year olds are not "women", regardless of the biological consequence of statutory rape.
287 Interview with the author, 2003
288 Others close to Clark, interviewed by Brian Edwards, have also described her

"But on the other side of the coin, plug in the public politician and it's like flicking a switch. In her political persona she gets as dirty and dishonest as the best of them. She is ruthless and will spare nothing to get what she wants, politically.

"You can see some of that manifesting now in the sense that her Prime Ministership has become almost dictatorial, almost paranoiac, she is so convinced that her path is the right one and the only one...so obsessed with making sure her plans are secure and cannot be derailed by anyone. She is absolutely driven in the changes she wants to make in our society, and nothing is going to stop her."

Clark's friends also want to clarify those persistent rumours that the Prime Minister is actively gay.

"For some people a physical relationship is very important. For Helen Clark, it isn't. Helen sacrificed a number of things in return for her ambition to achieve high office, and as part of that she has made a conscious decision to live an absolutely squeaky-clean private life where no one can pop up out of the woodwork and kiss and tell. She may have desires, but they're not acted upon.

"And let me say this. Helen and Peter love each other very very deeply. They are deeply committed to each other's happiness, and I would say that they are probably closer than most other married couples. They have and enjoy a very, very strong friendship. Let me repeat the point: they are very, very good *friends*."

Peter Davis, himself, seems to echo this in his 2001 interview with Brian Edwards, when asked what he liked best about Helen.

"What do I like best about her? I think she has enormous depths of human potential that are constantly developing and emerging, and she has the ability to surprise...She is concerned about her family. She wants to know how her nieces and nephews are doing at school, and it's genuine. And she wants to be sure that I'm happy in my work or how my Dad's getting on. Those are the genuine things which at base are what keeps her in touch with why she's in this whole business."

Cath Tizard, interestingly, told Edwards that Clark's sentimentality for family and friends doesn't extend to the wider NZ public.

"I don't think she's sentimental, I don't think she cares in a sentimental way...I don't think she has any sort of bleeding-heart feeling of great compassion for the unwashed masses or even the washed masses. But I think she's very loyal in personal relationships, and I'm sure that she sees what she's given her life to doing as something worthwhile."

So what is it that makes Clark's marriage tick? The signs – even more now than back when *Investigate* first raised the issue in 2003 – suggest Clark is gay. It was common in the seventies for lesbians and gay men to shack up in a "marriage of convenience" which provided the outward appearance of a relationship tolerable to wider society, whilst behind closed doors the couple

---

strong loyalty and generosity at a personal level.

continued their private lives at leisure. There were significant benefits in terms of sharing household expenses, mortgages and the like and indeed many such marriages were long-lasting because the couple became great friends, without suffering the passions and sexual tension of an ordinary heterosexual relationship. In many respects, the shared home was a sanctuary from their individual experiences in the wider world.

As Wikipedia notes, "Oscar Wilde, Cole Porter and Rock Hudson are said to have had marriages of convenience to hide their homosexuality", so Clark and Davis are in good company if theirs is such. Wikipedia also notes that gay marriages of convenience (as opposed to other forms) were often referred to in the gay community last century as "lavender marriages":[289]

"Usually, but not always, both parties are assumed to be complicit in a public deception to hide their homosexuality."

There can be any number of reasons for wanting to enter into a marriage of convenience. In Clark's case it was political. In other cases it can be simply to prevent your own family from speculating.

Which could, of itself, again provide a Freudian explanation for Helen Clark's otherwise inexplicable mission to make gay and lesbian relationships mainstream in the eyes of society and the law: here is a Prime Minister whose own preferences were strongly forbidden when she first entered politics, forced to marry a man for the sake of 'keeping up appearances' and avoiding the kind of political smear campaign that befell two prominent Labour MPs in the 1970s (Colin Moyle and Gerald O'Brien), nursing a deep personal hurt at being "cornered" by society and forced to conform.

Little wonder then that Helen Clark apologised out of nowhere to the homosexual community in the gay newspaper *express* in 2002:[290]

"I would offer my personal apology now on behalf of the Government. It's been disgraceful, of course it has. People have put up with the most appalling discrimination, stereotyping, people have been criminalised. Of course it is dreadful," she said, adding that speculation about her own life had been hurtful.

"But I actually have great faith in the common sense of Kiwis and I think these days most people are going to say 'For God's sake, people are entitled to choice about their life, Helen's made her choice, that's fine with us'."

And it would be, if the Prime Minister wasn't also choosing to use her power and position to force major social change on other New Zealanders by stripping away their own rights to choose, ostensibly to right the wrongs she suffered in her own personal life. By embarking on a very liberal social agenda, the Prime Minister has brought her own background into the equation, given that it now appears to be a significant driving force behind Labour's policy push.

289 http://en.wikipedia.org/wiki/Lavender_marriage
290 *express*, 4 June 2002

The enigma of Helen Clark may finally have been solved – a troubled child of the 60s who now has the power to address the perceived wrongs of her youth. The sickly, bookish archetypal nerd who now has the ability to kick sand in everyone else's faces. Forced to go to church, brought up in a family with strict morals, forced to marry when she didn't believe in it, made to feel a criminal for her sexuality.

Now in her 50s, surrounded by a clique of like-minded individuals, Helen Clark is ramming through legislation to disestablish the bourgeois society she detests.

At least now we know why. As I said earlier, the real issue is not whether Clark is gay. It is whether or not she has told the truth, and whether she has made political capital out of her situation.

Most New Zealanders can understand the plight that Clark found herself in during the 1981 election campaign. It would be one thing to be gay, but quietly marry and say no more about it. But since becoming leader of the Opposition in 1993, she has wheeled Peter Davis out for photo opportunities and used her self-confessed marriage of convenience for political reasons in a wide range of media situations and publicity appearances. In other words, Clark's marriage is not a neutral point of reference, it has become a political weapon that makes a positive character statement to voters.

Back in the mid 90s, Davis was only occasionally spotted with his wife, as a Helen Bain profile piece in the *Dominion* makes clear:[291]

"The man at his neighbourhood dairy calls him Mr Clark all the time, and he doesn't mind – doesn't even correct him. Peter Davis is a man comfortable enough in his own identity to be known as "Mr Helen Clark".

"Dr Davis's identity remains rather a mystery to most. His media profile is so low it's subterranean. He is rarely seen by his Labour leader wife's side at public engagements, and he is certainly not the large and frequent presence that Burton Shipley presents as Prime Minister Jenny Shipley's partner.

"Dr Davis's most public moment was probably that photo in *The Dominion* a few years ago, showing him with Miss Clark, mouths agape, as if they were poised for mutual mouth-to-mouth resuscitation, rather than a kiss.

"He reports that after a rare profile during the last election campaign, "people looked at me in the streets as if they knew me". He seems aghast at the memory. As one acquaintance puts it, Dr Davis is "the master of the shadows", leaving the limelight to his wife…

" 'The media focuses quite appropriately on Helen, not me. She'll tell me when I'm needed and when I'm not'."

In a similar profile piece by Vicki Main for the *Christchurch Press*, the line is also run that Peter Davis won't be trotted out as the trophy spouse:

"Unlike Burton Shipley, the Prime Minister's media-friendly husband, Dr

---

Davis will continue to keep a low profile if Labour wins the election. He will commute between the couple's Mount Albert home and his Christchurch job, making public appearances only when necessary.

" 'She understands that I have my career and she has hers', he says.

" 'She has been more or less accepted as a public figure in her own right, rather than requiring someone hanging on her arm. But where it makes a difference and where it's required, I'll be there'.

"Ms Clark agrees. 'I suspect the public won't see a lot of Peter. The overt presence of the spouse is something much more associated with National governments than Labour,' she says."

A lot has changed in ten years. Ever since Brian Edwards raised the lesbian/gay rumours in the official biography seven years ago, the number of functions attended by both Clark and Davis has grown considerably. There are more photos of them together. Davis is now dragged along to APEC and other such forums, the token male spouse.

TV documentaries have been made on the lines of "at home with the Clarks", but even they have backfired – one visual image captured on video was a memo on the fridge from Clark reminding Peter Davis that he hadn't paid his share of the "expenses".

If – and I remind readers that it is only an 'if' – the Clark-Davis marriage is not a genuine heterosexual relationship, but has been portrayed as such, then again the Prime Minister breaches the hypocrisy test and shows a quite stunning cynicism toward the electorate, as well as having an undeclared personal conflict of interest in shepherding through certain pieces of legislation.

Although her own authorized biography raises the speculation (on a number of occasions in the book) that both Clark and Davis are gay, Clark is on record from late 2006 describing any such suggestions as "lies" and "an outrage". Precisely why Clark was so outraged by the suggestion, when many of her closest friends and staff members are gay and Peter Davis is the editor of a book on homosexuality, is not explained and the question was not pursued by journalists at the time. The protestation seemed overly done, especially given Davis' own shrug of the shoulders approach to it.

Six years ago, after deliberately raising the issue herself, Clark told the gay newspaper *express* that she did not see such allegations as a "smear".

"It's all bizarre," Clark told the paper. "I'm not a lesbian myself, but some of my best friends are, literally. So I can't take it as an insult, because it's not wrong in any way to be lesbian. I'm going to refuse to see it as a smear, because I say, 'If I was [lesbian], so what!'"[292]

So what changed? Or has the Prime Minister's bark in more recent years been part of a deliberate attempt to manipulate the media and massage public

---

292 *express*, 4 June 2002

opinion to get sympathy against what she saw as National Party and media inquiries into her relationship?

As Kiwiblog's David Farrar notes, it is not as if Labour comes to the table with clean hands.

"Actually Labour MPs on a regular basis target National MPs who they suspect may be bisexual with gay taunts about bottoms, pansies, etc etc. The so called tolerance party is far from it. Sheer hypocrisy, considering how much noise they make about the rumours about Clark," said Farrar during a long debate about Clark's sexuality on his blog site last year.[293]

Yet as the Kiwiblog debate shows, the mere thought of discussing the Prime Minister's sexuality, even though she and her own media advisor put the matter on the table, sends people on all sides of the political spectrum into paroxysms of guilt.

Some take the line, "it doesn't matter". Others say so what if the Prime Minister has an open marriage and is bisexual, "that's her business". Strong Labour supporters denounce the discussion as "bigotry". But strip the heat out of the debate, and the guilt, and bring it back to first principles: doesn't the voter have a right to know who their politicians really are? According to overseas ethicists, the answer is yes.

Yet here, despite 27 years in national politics – nine of those as Prime Minister – countless interviews, the occasional TV documentary and an authorized biography, collectively the nation is *still* trying to figure out who Helen Clark really is.

The tongues were really set wagging by Clark and her media advisors – they have only themselves to blame. They are the ones who published the lesbian rumours. They are the ones who chose to then stage-manage Helen Clark and Peter Davis together for what turned out to be an endless series of unfortunate awkward photos with cold, rather than warm, body language between the pair.

The more Clark and Davis try to portray themselves as a regular married couple, the less the nation believes them. Perhaps her biggest mistake was trying to convince the public that what she once openly admitted was "a marriage of convenience" was now a marriage just like everyone else's, for the purposes of projecting a "first couple" image.

For most New Zealanders, marriage is still something sacred in any number of ways, something you enter into voluntarily and wholeheartedly – not something you enter into just to get votes. Clark's contempt for this perception of marriage is plain in her passage of the Property Relationships Act, the Care of Children Act and the Civil Unions Act. Yet she insists on trying to convince a disbelieving public that she shares their values, and her marriage is just the same as theirs.

293   http://www.kiwiblog.co.nz/2007/09/more_on_moore.html#comment-335630

You cannot, on the one hand, boast that you were forced into a sham marriage, and then on the other boast that your marriage has lasted better than other people's.[294] Not unless you are prepared to also fully reveal the core dynamics of your relationship. If you are really just good friends and flatmates lumped together by circumstance, then conceivably you could maintain that for a very long time without friction (particularly if both partners have outside interests), whilst couples who married with passion, sexual tension, an expectation of exclusivity and a desire to have a family are undertaking a very different and more intense journey.

In other words, there is a growing disconnect in the public mind between Clark's public statements and actions in the past, and the way she portrays her relationship now. But more than that, Clark has used alleged rumours about her personal life to play the victim card and gain the sympathy of the media and the public. But there are disturbing discrepancies in Clark's public statements about her life, and unraveling those is where we now head.

---

294 "Ms Clark has freely acknowledged the couple married so their relationship would be electorally acceptable but it has endured where others have foundered." – Donna Chisholm, Sunday Star-Times, 3 Dec 1995, "The various views of Helen Clark"

Crocodile Tears: Playing The Victim Card

Sir Humphrey: "Well perhaps you could advise me, Prime Minister. Particularly if the questions are aggressive."
Jim Hacker: "Oh, the more aggressive the better. That puts the listeners on your side." – **Yes Minister**

THERE IS CERTAINLY EVIDENCE THAT Clark's ploy in playing the victim card is rallying the Left around her. Strident defences of the Prime Minister's heterosexuality have been run by media commentator and one-time Labour electorate volunteer Russell Brown, and also the Green Party's "Frogblog" in a post called "The taunts of homophobes"[295]:

"Not that being gay should ever be seen as a criticism – but, clearly, those who hurl it as an insult think it is politically damaging," agonised Frogblog, overlooking the far bigger issue that it may have nothing whatsoever to do with being gay, and everything to do with being a political hypocrite.

"Perhaps [Brash] needs to remind his minders and MPs in no uncertain terms that Clark's marriage, childlessness and sexual orientation are off-limits. His party has a history of this ugly stuff, and he should be very quick to distance himself from smears of this kind, even if they are coming from National Party members," argued Frogblog.

Unfortunately, the Greens overlook a few salient points. This is, after all, a government that has deliberately turned "out and proud" into a massive political issue, so if there is the merest hint of Labour hiding relevant information then they deserve to be pilloried from here to Christmas. Secondly, if it is OK for Labour's Deputy Prime Minister Michael Cullen to categorise National leader John Key as a "rich prick", and insinuate that therefore he is disconnected from the working classes, how is it any less relevant to question whether a childless politician should be held up as an expert on parenting?

---

295 http://blog.greens.org.nz/index.php/2005/09/04/the-taunts-of-homophobes/

There are many parents who would argue that no politician without children should be permitted to vote on parenting issues, by virtue of their total lack of experience.

As a driving force behind the liberalization of abortion laws and the passage of the anti-smacking laws, Clark's knowledge of parenting is directly relevant to public debate. She is childless by choice, and proud of it. She is not childless because of any medical disability. Helen Clark has paraded her childlessness and commitment to her career as a positive example to women – why should the Greens and Labour be allowed to cordon off this area of Clark's life as out-of-bounds?

Under nine years of Clark government, the State has launched its largest ever assault on ordinary New Zealand families, but the media and the politicians are trying to make voters accept that Helen Clark's personal life and beliefs have nothing to do with this, and should not be factored into the equation.

And if Clark has lied about her marriage, that raises the question of her basic honesty. It has nothing to do with homosexuality, *per se*.[296]

The line that the private lives of politicians should remain "off limits" to voters and the media is a dangerous one, and it needs newsroom editors to be stronger in their defence of basic principles of political accountability.

And where, exactly, is the Prime Minister or Russell Brown's outrage when New Zealand's gay media raise the issue?[297]

"Is she or isn't she?" asks one gay website. "Rumors of lesbianism have hounded Prime Minister Helen Clark for years. While she admits that many of her best friends are lesbians, she denies being one herself. Whatever the case, the political climate in New Zealand appears very sympathetic to GLBT causes. Consider Georgina Beyer, the world's first popularly elected openly transgendered member of parliament. When Queen Elizabeth II visited New Zealand in February 2002, Clark sent Beyer as the official greeter. Clark has also shown solidarity with gays by participating in Auckland's yearly Hero Festival and supporting all kinds of gay rights legislation."

Let's return to the issue of "childlessness", because it is a strong undercurrent. The way Helen Clark tells the story, she was a major political figure in 1981 who everyone was gossiping about. The truth is a little less grandiose. She was a young apparatchik who worked largely behind the scenes in Labour, who had inherited a safe Labour seat vacated by the retiring former cabinet minister Warren Freer. How safe? Well, Freer had entered parliament in 1947, and held the seat with a majority of thousands through every election until his 1981 retirement.

---

296 Members of the public who feel squeamish about asking hard questions should consider this: immigrants to New Zealand are required to tell the truth about their relationships, on pain of prosecution and deportation. How is it OK to demand absolute truth from a lowly immigrant, but not from someone seeking a $300,000 taxpayer-funded salary with perks, and the power to make laws that change your life?
297 http://www.gay-newzealand.com/gay_life.htm

The Brian Edwards book repeatedly builds up a mythology that Clark's childless status was being thrown at her in the 1981 campaign. "Though all these rumours were absolutely untrue, Helen's unmarried and childless state was nonetheless of concern to some of her supporters."[298]

Say what? In 1981, *no one* would have queried Clark's childless status as an unmarried woman.

Or here: "In parallel with the rumours about Helen's sexuality ran the theme that it was somehow unnatural for a 30-year-old woman in a committed relationship not to have children."[299]

Again, say what? The average conservative New Zealander frowned on "committed relationships" in 1981, and frowned even more so on children born out of wedlock. While my generation in the early 80s was beginning to break that mould, it is utter fantasy to suggest that voters were tut-tutting because an unmarried MP shacked up with a man in a "committed" relationship *did not* have children!

Brian Edwards continues the mythology here: "Though they were an irritation, the issues of…marriage and children were not uppermost in Helen's mind during the Mt Albert campaign."[300]

It is hard to see why Edwards pursues this line when it is so clearly wrong. It is also hard to see why Clark, Joan Caulfield and others fuel it, when the timing and context appears impossible. Is it fact, is it fiction, is it part of the living legend of Helen Clark, or just Helen Clark, the carefully crafted and airbrushed brand?

I have searched through the media reports leading up to the 1981 election and, unless I'm mistaken, couldn't find any on Helen Clark being either gay or childless. Maybe within Labour's tribal factions it was an issue, but not for the wider public. Instead, very early on in her political career, Helen Clark made capital out of her childlessness. She was proud of it, and proud of the message it sent to women.

In the aforementioned passage from *Head and Shoulders*, you'll recall Clark saying:

"I've never had any intention of having a child. I definitely see children as destroying my lifestyle. It's inconceivable that I would become pregnant… I think I'd go around the bend if my small amount of spare time was taken up by children.

"I was able to develop as a professional person with no breaks in career... I wasn't caught in the trap of the young bride who seems to stop maturing when her kids are born."

There's nothing ambiguous in that; no lament, no regret. And she was playing to her audience. In the official biography, Helen Clark's close friend

---

298   *Helen*, p144
299   Ibid, p150
300   *Helen*, p151

Maggie Eyre is quoted on Helen's childlessness being an inspiration:[301]

"Meeting Helen was just remarkable for me. Here is a woman who doesn't have children. And, as a childless woman myself, I need a role model like that, it's very important to me...I think women who don't have children need role models out there, so that we don't feel like freaks, we don't feel as if we've missed out, we don't feel that we did it all wrong, that we made a mistake."

In 1995, Clark told interviewer Donna Chisholm that she was proud of not being a mother, and not being like the rest of New Zealand.[302]

"I saw a line in a *Christchurch Press* editorial that New Zealanders like their leaders to be ordinary like them. For God's sake . . . I am not prepared to make myself ordinary. If ordinary means I have suddenly got to produce a household of kids and iron Peter's shirts, I'm sorry I'm not interested."[303]

The first newspaper story after that to raise the issue of Clark's childlessness came in 1997,[304] soon after Jenny Shipley was elevated to the leadership of the National Government. The *Dominion*'s Simon Kilroy, interviewing Labour spindoctors for their take on Shipley, reported that "Political strategists expect National to market Mrs Shipley as the archetypal mainstream New Zealand family woman, and to try to contrast her in the public mind with the childless and academic Ms Clark.

"One said yesterday that National "would be mugs" not to adopt that strategy but cautioned that since the last campaign Ms Clark's image had softened and she was now more warmly regarded by voters."

Now here's the important thing: the "childless" issue was being floated by *Labour* strategists, almost as if they wanted National to run with it.

We already know, however, that Clark was proud of being a career woman, and delighted that she wasn't a mother. So why did Labour care if Shipley posed with her kids? Was Shipley meanwhile supposed to pretend that she *didn't* have children? Wasn't Shipley *equally* allowed to be proud of the choice that she had made, balancing both career and motherhood? Were the public not entitled to contrast the different profiles of each leader?

This, again, was cynical, manipulative dog-whistle politics from Labour – trying to paint their own candidate as the unfortunate victim of a mean and nasty family values National Party.

The next news story to raise the issue of Clark's childlessness was a *North &*

---

301 Ibid, p151
302 *Sunday Star-Times*, 3 December 1995, "The various views of Helen Clark"
303 Instead, Peter Davis was expected to be the housekeeper in the relationship, ensuring that all their beds were made up and the house was spick and span. "Sometimes she would get back from Wellington on Friday and the house would be in less than perfect condition and it would upset her," Davis told Chisholm. "She wanted to put behind her the mess and chaos and conflict of politics and come back to a little oasis. If there were unwashed dishes in the sink, it would detract from that and I appreciate that was quite reasonable so I made a real effort to make sure beds were made and plates were washed and she doesn't have to attend to those things after an incredibly tiring week."
304 *The Dominion*, 5 November 1997, "Battle of female contrasts looms"

South interview with Jenny Shipley published in January 1998. In the context of the magazine probing the differences in background between herself and Clark, Shipley answered:

"The person I am is partly crafted *because* I've been a mother. Anyone who's been a mother knows how to anticipate risk, and that's certainly added a dimension to my life which I couldn't imagine I'd have been able to acquire had I not been a mother. Helen has strengths and weaknesses. I have strengths and weaknesses. The public will decide which of those they prefer," Shipley pointed out.

Now is that really a jibe, or just an answer to a sensitive question? Is it any different from Clark saying "I was able to develop as a professional person with no breaks in career...I wasn't caught in the trap of the young bride who seems to stop maturing when her kids are born."

Both answers are flip-sides of the same coin, surely. Remember, Clark's childlessness was a choice made – she herself says – for political reasons, just like her marriage. When you start to look at the published material, it's as though Clark is wearing the children she never had as some kind of badge of honour, with as much satisfaction as Shipley has in her two real children.

But Helen Clark and her advisors were not content to let sleeping dogs lie. In February 1998, they ratcheted up their spin with an unprecedented personal attack on the children of National cabinet ministers.

As one newspaper editorial warned:

"Labour leader Helen Clark crossed a political Rubicon when, in an interview with *The Post* last Wednesday, she made reference to the behaviour of Cabinet Ministers' sons. It has long been a parliamentary convention in New Zealand that the private lives of MPs and their families are generally off limits. To break this convention is to risk lifting the lid off a veritable Pandora's box of scandal and sleaze."

For those who remember Clark's outrage when her own family circumstances were questioned eight years later, the above should clarify that Clark herself fired the first torpedo in dragging politicians' families through the mud.[305] The *Post* editorial was right – Helen Clark did indeed lift the lid off Pandora's box for the first time in NZ politics.

It happened because Prime Minister Jenny Shipley called for public discussion on whether families – particularly lower-socio groups like those that later spawned the Kahui problem – needed guidance from a proposed

---

305 Doug Graham and Tuariki Delamere did not thrust their own children into the public spotlight either – but that didn't stop Clark from attacking them, then saying to the *Herald's* Leah Haines eight years later (24 September 2006) that the attack on Peter Davis in 2006 marked a new low. "As Clark points out, she has never put him or her parents into the public eye. 'I've never done that because I've always been conscious that politics goes in cycles, and you don't want people to be exposed when there are different things happening'." Evidently, whilst making that statement, Clark had forgotten authorizing a biography to show her in a positive light leading up to the 2002 election, in which several chapters deal with her parents and her relationship with Peter Davis, and the rumours that they were gay.

Code of Social and Family Responsibility. The Code would tell parents drawing government benefits the basic minimum standards that society expected so that kids could have a decent shot at life.

Clearly it was an idea ahead of its time, which we'll return to shortly, but a clause suggesting children should be encouraged not to break the law stung Clark into launching a devastating attack on the children of National MPs:[306]

"Tell that to [National Justice Minister] Doug Graham's son who crashed a ministerial car and ran off," snapped Clark. "Tell it to [Immigration Minister Tuariki] John Delamere's son who was up for cannabis possession."[307]

Clark, however, dug her heels in, and implied Jenny Shipley was a bad mother for having a political career and kids.[308]

"The code [has come] from someone who has left the bringing up of her teenagers to a boarding school. It has all the appearance of someone of privilege telling others how to bring up their children."[309]

Nor were male MPs let off the hook, with another swipe implying the only good politician is a childless politician – anything else is neglect:

"How many fatherless families in the Cabinet?," she asked.

MPs on all sides of the house were aghast at Clark's outburst. If anything starkly epitomized the difference between a parent and a non-parent, it was the Labour leader's willingness to attack children in order to get at their parents and score political points.[310]

"Alliance women MPs have disowned Ms Clark's comments," reported the *Christchurch Press* the following morning. " 'You're on your own on this one, Helen', they said.[311]

"Alliance MP Laila Harre, speaking for her party's women MPs, condemned Ms Clark's 'itemised and personalised attacks' on Government MPs' family lives. Ms Clark had fallen into the Prime Minister's trap, designed to turn New Zealanders into 'moralising, judgmental labellers. The code will not be defeated by attacking the PM for sending her children to a boarding school – or Cabinet members who are divorced'.

---

306 *The Evening Post*, 18 February 1998, "Code could 'blow up' on Government, warns Clark".
307 It was around this time that Clark's moonlight career as an art forger began.
308 This was the same Clark, who in a holier-than-thou moment in 2006, told journalists, "I don't muck-rake. My party has no mandate to muck-rake." – *NZ Herald*, 20 September 2006.
309 *The Evening Post, supra*. Given Clark's support for round-the-clock daycare and greater State control of families, it seems to be a mixed message Clark was sending here, as if the arch-liberal was trying to outflank the conservative by appealing to the ultra-conservative in a mutual tut-tut session.
310 A similar stunt was pulled by the Labour-leaning GayNZ website in late 2007 when it claimed one of Bill English's sons was a homophobe, after trawling through the 15 year old's Bebo site for evidence. The website (run largely by 'childless' people) was pilloried in the media for using children to score political points against an opponent. *NZ Herald*, 26 September 2007, "English: Attack on my son disgusting"
http://www.nzherald.co.nz/category/story.cfm?c_id=107&objectid=10465934
311 The Press, 19 February 1998, "Clark attack on lives of MPs' families raises storm"

"Ms Clark had implied that combining a family and career was irresponsible. 'It's a major betrayal of hard-won representation for women by women in Parliament,' said Ms Harre, a mother of two."

Tuariki Delamere told journalists Helen Clark's comments were despicable, and from the gutter:[312]

"As one of the many parents in this House, I often worry about how my family – my children – will become a target of those people malicious and nasty enough to use our children as convenient political tools, tools that have no way of fighting back. I am so disappointed that Helen Clark is one of those people. As a parent it makes me angry."

Clark, however, was unrepentant, telling the NZPA[313] she stood by her comments, and telling the politicians criticizing her that "people in glass houses should not throw stones".[314]

The proposed Code of Responsibility included references to trying to maintain a healthy lifestyle, which Helen Clark interpreted (deeply ironically it turns out) as an attack by "Nanny State" on people's private lives:

"How many smokers in cabinet?" she challenged. "How many heavy drinkers in the cabinet?[315]

"The Nanny State that preaches to you can have no effect except to stigmatise those who fall through the cracks."[316]

Take that Helen Clark quote from only ten years ago and frame it!

"She wants to busy herself with what goes on in the homes of the nation in areas which families regard as their own responsibility," opined Clark about Shipley, "and I think she's going over a very dangerous line."[317]

Frame that quote as well, from the woman whose government made an art-form out of telling kiwi parents how to raise their kids.

By now, you could probably be forgiven for wondering whether the anti-Nanny State Helen Clark of 1998 was abducted by aliens shortly thereafter and replaced by a shape-shifting lizard who proceeded to introduce the most "Nanny State" government of the modern era. Either that, or Helen Clark was simply a deeply cynical political machine capable of arguing black was white if she thought it would win her votes.

Despite Clark's invoking of the phrase "Nanny State", however, Shipley's views were simply a case of stating the obvious:[318]

"I want to put this to you; at best whether we like it or not, if a child is nurtured

312 Ibid
313 *Waikato Times*, 19 February 1998, "Clark firm in code row"
314 *The Dominion*, 24 February 1998, "MPs say do as I legislate, not as I do"
315 *The Evening Post*, 18 February 1998, "Code could 'blow up' on Government, warns Clark"
316 Ibid
317 *The Dominion*, 30 March 1998, "Shipley's religion-in-schools comments may prove divisive"
318 Jenny Shipley speech, 26 March 1998, "Values, Society & Education"
http://executive.govt.nz/Speech.aspx?type=speech&rid=12934

in a family where they know who they are and they see strong relationships around them, they are so much more likely to do well in the future than a child who sees nothing but destruction and disappointment in relationships.

"So the family institution is unavoidably important even if some struggle to accept that that is fashionably correct," warned Shipley.

"On the issue of education, there are some who have spent a period of time in recent years saying at the risk of offending individual sensibility we should try and be so neutral, to the point that we have created almost an amoral environment where children simply don't know where or from whom they should seek to establish reference points from."

Looking back, and looking at the huge drop in behavioural standards at New Zealand schools over the past ten years, the huge increase in youth crime, and the huge increase in child abuse at the hands of young inexperienced parents who themselves come from broken homes, there are many who would argue Jenny Shipley was right.

She continued:

"We also know that where a child is spiritually nurtured, whether it's Christian faith, the Buddhist faith or any other faith in the world, with a sense of who they are and that spiritual dimension, where that is nurtured, it gives that individual a greater level of confidence, to stand tall knowing who they are.

"So at best, the spiritual dimension is important. Where it is absent it simply leaves a gaping hole that often becomes a vacant space for other values to fill.

"On the issue of cultural dimension, while there are many in the audience more able than I to speak about this, it is certainly my experience as Minister of Social Welfare and Minister of Health that if you are seriously talking about wellness and healing you must recognise who the person is, what their history is and where their future is, and if a person is culturally confident about their history, their whanau and the future, they stand very much taller than those who have no sense of their cultural dimension and depth.

"On the issues of the law, when people do have respect for not only their own space, but where the boundaries are, they not only experience more freedom personally, but they also have more respect for others. Where there is no certainty on those lines, not only is it disappointing for the majority, it can be extremely destructive for the individual.

"While it is sometimes unfashionable, particularly in the media, to talk about the elements that lead to the best chance for children, I believe we know a huge amount about what gives a child the best chance, our society the best chance and our nation the best chance.

"And the only way we will be able to offer that chance to all is if we get off the fence and speak up about that which is best and offers opportunity, rather than almost embracing that which is worst because we are at a loss to know how to fix it.

"We don't help those in trouble by simply trying to confront the majority with that same set of values. In my opinion, the only way we will raise our own horizons is have the debate on what the values should be in our collective interests and benefits.

"To those who are outraged at what I say, I frankly do not apologise. I am sick and tired of those who say that the values debate is too hard. Doing nothing is leading us to a very negative environment and it is my belief many New Zealanders want to do something. They are looking to you as leaders, just as they are looking to me as a leader to try and help find boundaries, lay out pathways and set goals," concluded Shipley.

That was ten years ago. Instead of engaging in the debate, however, Clark and the Labour team played politics and shot it down.

"The Labour Party personalized its campaign against the code of social responsibility yesterday by likening Prime Minister Jenny Shipley to busybody *Coronation Street* character Ena Sharples," reported *The Dominion*.[319]

"Mrs Shipley, who bears a striking resemblance to Ena Sharples off *Coronation Street*," taunted Labour's Steve Maharey[320], "sees nothing wrong with leaning over the back fence and telling the neighbours how to run their lives."

Ah, the irony.

Maharey also tried to hit Shipley's domestic life via a backhand slap, saying Labour was not interested in Mrs Shipley's family "or whatever", but then launching into an attack on her mental state:[321]

"She does not have the capacity to do the job. Mrs Shipley has been elevated above the point where she's coping well."

Yet when one National party grassroots official then sent out a newsletter targeting Helen Clark for looking "so wan and stressed"[322], Helen Clark told the media "the only evidence we have of people running smear campaigns is from the National Party itself."[323]

Pot, meet kettle.[324]

Helen Clark then found herself denying that a photo opportunity at the Beehive featuring her holding babies was a publicity stunt designed to make her appear maternal in the election campaign.[325]

"I have a lot to do with Plunket – I have for years – and they asked me to host the function, which I was very happy to do," Clark told the *Dominion*.

---

319 *The Dominion*, 28 February 1998, "Labour likens Shipley to Sharples"
320 Arguably, Maharey's biggest claim to fame in his political career was infamously being labeled "Smarmy Maharey" as a result of the John Tamihere interview in *Investigate*, April 2005.
321 *The Dominion*, 10 May 1999, "Clark key weapon as Labour guns for Shipley"
322 *The Dominion*, 20 April 1999, "Leaders at centre of mud-slinging allegations"
323 *The Dominion*, 17 May 1999, "Childless focus pathetic – Clark"
324 This is the same Labour Party which, after National MP Nick Smith had a stress-related breakdown, continues to taunt him in the debating chamber to this very day, "Have you taken your pills today, Nick?"
325 Ibid

Obviously if you go to a Plunket function it is packed with babies. The media are going to want to photograph you with babies."

Well, that's not entirely true. Plunket nurses don't tour the country with a van-load of babies at their disposal. The appearance of Clark with specially shipped-in babies and attendant mothers at the Beehive (not a Plunket clinic) for the occasion was definitely a stunt.[326]

National's Treasurer Bill Birch, angered at what he felt was the personal denigration – "or whatever" – of Shipley's domestic situation by Labour, fired back in Parliament.

"She has impeccable credentials to lead us in the National Party," argued Birch. "A farmer's wife, mother of two…she knows what it's like to face high interest rates on farm mortgages and at the same time bring up a young family."

It was a fair comment to make. In repeated media interviews over the years, Clark's subliminal message to women was that they really couldn't have it all, and that career was a better choice than motherhood. Clark repeated this mantra firstly because it reflected her own choices, and secondly because it reflected hardline feminist values and would thus appeal to a core Labour constituency. It was a positive pitch to a defined market.

Shipley on the other hand was being portrayed to women as one who reached the top, even with those family responsibilities. It was also a positive (in the sense of affirmatory) message and pitch, reflecting the core values of hundreds of thousands of women trying to balance career and home life.

"It seems from these early volleys that their personal lives may be fair game," noted Wellington's *Evening Post* in an editorial.[327]

"Thus, the parental status of both women loomed large this week. Miss Clark objects to Prime Minister Jenny Shipley referring to her view of life as seen through the prism of motherhood. National, she said angrily on Monday, had constantly sought to denigrate her as a woman without children. That's silly. Mrs Shipley is a mother – it's one of her frames of reference. To pretend it hasn't affected her opinions would be to paint a falsehood. Equally, Miss Clark and husband Peter Davis have nothing to apologise for – her childless state reflects that of more and more couples for whom parenthood is not or cannot be an option. That each leader's lifestyle describes a different female state does no more than allow voters to use yet another standard against which to judge two competent women."

Well said.

---

326 Whilst happy to bathe in Plunket's reflected glory for the 1999 election campaign, Prime Minister Clark soured her long history with the organization by cancelling funding for the Plunketline service in 2006 in favour of a rival service run by an American multinational. "To be frank, I can't imagine it is the intention of this Government to undermine Plunket and that is what I want to ask the Prime Minister," Plunket president Kaye Crowther told journalists (*NZ Herald*, 10 April 2006). But Clark did indeed pull the plug. Ironically, it is now National that is promising to restore 24 hour Plunketline coverage for mothers
327 *The Evening Post*, 20 April 1999, "Contrasting home lives of the party leaders"

In hindsight, Labour's bleating about Clark's choices being somehow off-limits was little more than an attempt to muzzle debate and limit voter focus purely to the issues Clark preferred. It has largely worked, because discussion on whether a childless Prime Minister can truly appreciate the dynamics faced by parents has been deemed "politically incorrect" in the news media today.

Which is incredible, given that Clark's authorized biography dwells on the subject:

"Helen has been consistently unapologetic on the subject," writes Brian Edwards.

"I never wanted children," Clark says in the book. "I could not have done what I've done with my life, professionally, in terms of pleasure or travel, if I'd had children. It was a very deliberate choice and I'll never regret it. You've just got better things to do with your life, unimpeded."

You can almost imagine Gollum, from *Lord of the Rings*, agreeing with Clark about disposing of any distractions in his pursuit of the ring of Power: "Nassty, horrible ~~rug-ratsss~~ hobbitses".

"If indeed there is such a missing dimension," continues Clark to a question about whether she's missing out, "I'm very happy to have it missing…As for the suggestion that it's unnatural for a woman not to have children, that argument assumes that we are born to reproduce. That used to be our fate; it was never our choice."

Now there's a line that could have been written by Simone de Beauvoir or Germaine Greer!

So next time you see an Oscar-winning performance from Helen Clark on how everyone has been so mean, you can rest assured it is all for show, aimed directly at the lizard brains of 100,000 Labour-voting mums (and media commentator and former Labour party pamphlet boy, Russell Brown) – a naked and cynical bid for sympathy. Meanwhile at home, watching it on TV, Clark will be laughing her head off (as indeed evidence emerges later in this next chapter).

But the personal attacks by Clark on the families of opposition MPs came back to haunt her in 2006, when her own family situation was again thrust into the spotlight by virtue of a very strange set of circumstances and massive bungling by the PM's media team. It became widely known in the media and elsewhere as, "the Peter Davis incident".

The Peter Davis Incident

Sir Humphrey: "If there had been investigations, which there haven't, or not necessarily, or I'm not at liberty to say whether there have, there would have been a project team which, had it existed, on which I cannot comment, which would now have disbanded, if it had existed, and the members returned to their original departments, if indeed there had been any such members."
– Yes Minister

IN JUNE 2006, A CHAIN of events was set in motion that culminated in a massive media uproar. It began with a letter to *Investigate* magazine, and cc'd to Britain's *News of the World* and the *San Francisco Chronicle*, which we reported on in the magazine:

A strange thing happened on the way to this edition going to press. We received an unsigned letter purporting to have originated within the Police, suggesting Prime Minister Helen Clark's husband Peter Davis had been in a spot of bother in San Francisco recently and needed some assistance from NZ authorities.

The letter alleges "the whole incident has been hushed up". So far, so good. *Investigate* initiated inquiries in the United States, asking guarded questions of both the Los Angeles NZ Consulate, and the after-hours duty officer at the NZ Embassy in Washington DC. The official in LA seemed genuinely unaware of the incident:

"Peter Davis? I actually don't know that name."

"Prime Minister's husband!" we reminded her. We could hear her blush over the phone, but it was an easy enough mistake to make. She said she wasn't aware of the incident but suggested Washington might know.

The voice of the Washington official (it was 6pm in DC) grew distinctly shaky when we raised it, and suggested we call the Ministry of Foreign Affairs in Wellington.

So we did. We left a phone message with the Ministry's Consular Desk that gave no details of the incident at all, but simply said, "Please call Ian Wishart back at *Investigate* magazine" with our phone number.

Only 20 minutes later, we received the following phone call from MFAT official Brad Tattersfield, who wasn't the person we'd left a message for:

Investigate: Hi...Ian Wishart speaking

MFAT: Yeah, it's Brad Tattersfield from MFAT here, following up on a message you left.

Investigate: Yes, I'm just seeking information on an incident involving Peter Davis where he needed some police assistance to get out of San Francisco recently.

MFAT: We have no information on that, *I'm advised that the incident didn't happen.*

Investigate: Who advised you?

MFAT: The Prime Minister's Office.

Investigate: (in surprised tone of voice): But I haven't rung the Prime Minister's office yet!

MFAT: Well, they know you are making inquiries, and they've advised me that the incident did not happen and to refer you there.

Investigate: Who in the Prime Minister's Office?

MFAT: Their press people.

Investigate: But I haven't rung them.

MFAT: Well I don't know, all I know is that they contacted us a few minutes ago.

Naturally, we were stunned. How could the Prime Minister's Office have known what we were calling about before we even phoned them, and why had they contacted MFAT to head us off at the pass with "the incident didn't happen" before we'd given details of what the "incident" was?

We fired through a call to the PM's office demanding an explanation, but soon afterward the phone rang again with MFAT's Brad Tattersfield again:

MFAT: Look, just to get things clear on this. We, in Foreign Affairs, became aware of your inquiry via our Consul-General in LA. We got a message from them, they contacted our consular division."

Investigate: Your specific comment to me was the PM's office had advised you?"

MFAT: Yeah, no, I got my wires crossed there, they hadn't advised us, but what did happen was when I called them they said that they were aware of it, they were aware of your inquiry. Now you'd have to ask them how they were aware of it. I don't know the answer to that."

Investigate: I hadn't rung anybody in NZ at all. I find it bizarre that the PM's office can know what I'm inquiring about."

MFAT: Well, as I say, you'll need to ask them. I spoke to David Lewis. As to how he would know that, you'd need to ask him.

Investigate: What time did you speak to David Lewis?

MFAT: Just before I spoke to you.

Investigate: And you initiated the call to the PM's office?

MFAT: That's right, yeah.

Investigate: Why did you initiate the call to the PM's office?

MFAT: Because, ah, to let him know that you may be contacting them.

Investigate: Why?

MFAT: Because that's what we do in government.

It was a mite presumptuous of MFAT to assume we'd be calling the PM's office before we had a confirmed story, but here's the irony: when MFAT rang to say "Wishart's on to you", the PM's office replied, "We already know". We finally got through to David Lewis in the PM's office four hours after first calling Los Angeles:

Investigate: How on earth did you guys find out about my inquiries this morning?

PM'S Office: How? How did you find out about what you're inquiring about? If you're making inquiries of government departments about matters to do with the PM's office, the PM's office would probably be informed.

Investigate: The curious thing is that Brad Tattersfield assures me that you knew before he told you.

PM'S Office: Before he told me, yes.

Investigate: So who told you?

PM'S Office: I'm not going to name individuals, I don't have to subject myself to your inquisition.

Investigate: So as to the substance of the issue, seeing as you're aware of what I'm asking about, what's the Prime Minister's response?

PM'S Office: I have no knowledge of the incident.[328] We're making inquiries to see if there's any veracity at all to what you're suggesting.

If there was genuinely no truth to the reported incident involving Peter Davis in San Francisco, one would have expected LA, Washington, MFAT and the PM's office to yawn quietly and ignore it. Instead, Wellington was a hive of activity and intrigue with official denials being prepared before we even told them we were investigating, and a direct hotline to the PM's office that appeared to bypass ordinary MFAT channels with lightning speed. For an outfit protesting innocence, they were all acting as guilty as hell. One moment denying an incident had ever taken place; four hours later saying they were "making inquiries" still.

As we go to press, we still can't tell you the full detail of the San Francisco allegation, or even whether it happened. What we can say is that our own inquiries have stepped up a notch, both here and overseas, because of the apparent sensitivity to it in Wellington.

---

328 I had been prepared to believe that perhaps *Investigate* had caught the tail-end of an already-circulating rumour, but according to this response the PM's media team knew absolutely nothing of the rumour. Which made the massive behind the scenes activity so bizarre. Why go to such trouble when Clark could have said, "no, it never happened"?

***

The whole thing reeked of butt-covering by officials, but I failed to comment on one further curiousity at the time – the role of the LA consulate. Although we'd contacted three NZ diplomatic posts in the US, only LA reacted by making an instant phone call to the Prime Minister's office in Wellington. Yet LA was the office that had told *Investigate*:

"Peter Davis? I actually don't know that name."

In the wake of that story, the magazine received further contact from others who'd heard whispers of a similar incident. We ran a follow-up in the next issue:

JULY ISSUE – More evidence is emerging about a mysterious "incident" involving Prime Minister Helen Clark's husband in the United States. But the more that comes to light, the more it appears the Beehive is in damage control mode – even though no media organization has yet published the full details of the alleged "incident".

Both the Prime Minister's Office and the University of Auckland are evading direct questions about the movements of Helen Clark's husband Peter Davis, as the mystery over an alleged incident involving Davis in the United States deepens.

Last month, *Investigate* broke the story of how Davis had apparently required NZ Police assistance while in the US, possibly in San Francisco.

After last month's issue was printed, but four days *before it went on sale*, we received a new tip from a man with further specific details of an incident involving Davis, and advising the source of the story was a Judge.

On the strength of that new information, *Investigate* phoned the Prime Minister's Office again that morning querying whether Davis had been involved in an incident in either San Francisco or Los Angeles, or anywhere else in the United States. We also asked when Davis had last been in the US. What we received back at the end of the day was an answer specifically relating to Los Angeles *airport*, even though we had not restricted our question to the "airport":

BEEHIVE RESPONSE, Monday June 12, 5:19pm
In response to you asking if the PM was aware of an incident occurring at Los Angeles airport involving Peter Davis and requiring intervention by NZ government personnel, a spokesman for the PM said: "Not as far as we are aware."

David Lewis
Chief Press Secretary
Office of the Prime Minister
Wellington, New Zealand

What, we wondered, did that mean? Was the PM's spokesman not aware whether the PM was aware of the incident? Or did he mean that he himself wasn't aware of the incident? Naturally, we fired off another request for clarification:

INVESTIGATE QUESTION, Monday June 12, 6:40pm

Hi David

Thanks for your answer, but it really is not definitive enough.

Whether or not the PM's *spokesman* is aware of an incident is, with the greatest respect, irrelevant. Nor did it address my questions as to the temporality of Mr Davis' US travel.

I expect the Prime Minister to be fully briefed on any undue event that befalls her husband, therefore I would expect the PM herself to know categorically whether an incident of any kind occurred in any place.

Accordingly, I'll rephrase my questions to make a direct answer easier.

These are questions specifically for the Prime Minister to answer in the first person.

1. When was Peter Davis last in the United States?

2. What was the date of the last occasion he exited the continental US via either San Francisco or Los Angeles (please specify the date applicable to each city)?

3. What status of NZ passport did Mr Davis last travel to the US on: ordinary private; government official; or diplomatic?

4. Is the Prime Minister aware of an incident where her husband required either NZ police or Foreign Affairs assistance to liaise with any Federal or State authorities in the US on his behalf, or indeed to assist in his repatriation to New Zealand?

5. Can the Prime Minister categorically state that at no time in the past year has Peter Davis required New Zealand consular, embassy, or NZ governmental assistance of any kind whilst in the United States?

6. If he has required assistance of any kind, please specify the date and nature of assistance provided by any New Zealand official.

Regards

Ian Wishart

BEEHIVE RESPONSE, Tuesday June 13, 1:59pm

1. When was Peter Davis last in the United States?

Professor Davis is a private citizen. We have no comment.

2. What was the date of the last occasion he exited the continental US via either San Francisco or Los Angeles (please specify the date applicable to each city)?

Professor Davis is a private citizen. We have no comment.

3. What status of NZ passport did Mr Davis last travel to the US on: ordinary private; government official; or diplomatic?

When Professor Davis travels with the Prime Minister, he does so on a diplomatic passport. Otherwise, he does so as a private person on his own passport. His official trips are on the public record.

4. Is the Prime Minister aware of an incident where her husband required either NZ police or Foreign Affairs assistance to liaise with any Federal or State authorities in the US on his behalf, or indeed to assist in his repatriation to New Zealand?

No.

5. Can the Prime Minister categorically state that at no time in the past year has Peter Davis required New Zealand consular, embassy, or New Zealand governmental assistance of any kind whilst in the United States?
We are not aware of New Zealand government assistance.
6. If he has required assistance of any kind, please specify the date and nature of assistance provided by any New Zealand official.
See above.
David Lewis

INVESTIGATE QUESTION, Tuesday June 13, 2:58pm
Hi David

Your answer to question 5 requires further clarification because of the use of "we" and the imprecision of the reply.

Surely, the PM is in a position to know one way or the other or to seek definitive confirmation from officials.

Accordingly I re-submit Q5 for a definitive personal answer from the PM on an issue of fact.

I also add a Question 7 which asks:

Q7: Is *any* official in the Prime Minister's office or her secretariat aware of an incident where her husband required either NZ police or Foreign Affairs assistance to liaise with any Federal or State authorities in the US on his behalf, or indeed to assist in his repatriation to New Zealand?

Yours sincerely
Ian Wishart
PS: Also, can you please confirm that the Prime Minister has *personally* seen my questions to date and *approved* all answers?
Regards
Ian W

BEEHIVE RESPONSE, Tuesday June 13, 3:15pm
Ian, with due respect, you've now asked the same question three times. I don't intend spending my days replying to the same questions rephrased slightly. I've told you we are not aware of any incident. That means we have no knowledge of any incident as described. If you have some other information you'd like to put to the PM, do so. Until then, have a nice day.
Regards
David Lewis
Chief Press Secretary
Office of the Prime Minister

And as pointed out, those answers that have been given are vague. Take our Question 4 and Lewis' response:

"4. Is the Prime Minister aware of an incident where her husband required either

NZ police or Foreign Affairs assistance to liaise with any Federal or State authorities in the US on his behalf, or indeed to assist in his repatriation to New Zealand?"

"*No.*"

On the face of it, it appears to be a clear answer that the Prime Minister is unaware of the incident. But if Clark hadn't even seen my question, then the answer only means that the PM's spokesman is saying she is not aware. And the PM's spokesman could be wrong. Perhaps Clark is aware but hasn't discussed it with her media team. How would he know if he hasn't asked her, and if he has asked her why is he refusing to confirm that?

That refusal to answer specific questions could indicate two things: firstly, that Lewis and the PM's media team are deliberately trying to shield the Prime Minister from the questions so she can deny responsibility for misleading answers when the full story emerges. Although *Investigate* specifically requested personal answers from Clark (who's on record accusing the magazine of refusing to give her ministers the chance to comment) all of the emails have ultimately been sourced as "a spokesman for the PM". *Investigate* even has a taped conversation with Lewis where we ask at one point: "Who's this answer from, the Prime Minister?", and Lewis replies: "A spokesman for the Prime Minister".

Investigate understands Lewis, who took over as chief press secretary after long-time staffer Mike Munro quit after the election, has previously gone out on a limb for his boss, even at the expense of his own family relationship – parliamentary insiders say Lewis took the fall for Clark over Speedogate, causing immense stress in Lewis' personal life.

By issuing vague denials in his own name, although worded as if Clark has approved them, Lewis gives Clark the chance to deny making the statements down the track.

As you can see, Lewis has pointedly failed to confirm that Helen Clark has even seen *Investigate's* questions about her husband, let alone approved the answers.[329]

Secondly, by refusing to answer more direct questions the PM's Office is fuelling suspicion within the wider media that an incident has indeed taken place, and that the silence is effectively a case of 'neither confirm nor deny', in the hope that media interest will die down.

Nor is the PM's Office prepared to seek reports from Ministry of Foreign Affairs and Trade or Police as to whether any assistance has had to be provided to Davis, preferring to rest instead on the "not as far as we are aware" answer – "we" being the PM's media team.

In the US political scene, such vague answers are called "plausible deniability" – they're constructed in such a way that if the truth does emerge then people further down the food chain take responsibility.

---

329 A similar stunt was pulled in Paintergate: Clark was deliberately not shown the list of police questions, and instead allowed her legal advisors to draft responses as they saw fit. In PR terms, this is called "arms-length".

Regardless, a newsletter of the Sociological Association of Aotearoa, which Davis is a member of, confirms that he attended the annual conference of the American Sociological Association in Philadelphia late last year.

Investigate's two published articles on the alleged "Peter Davis incident" were based on information from separate sources and our own tete a tete with the Prime Minister's office. Having worked as a cabinet press secretary, I was well aware that media advisors wouldn't hesitate to adopt "Yes Minister" tactics to obfuscate or avoid answering direct questions without qualifications.

Some people think *Yes Minister* was a comedy. When I worked in Mike Moore's office in 1986, we regarded it, undeniably, as a documentary:

Jim Hacker: "Yes or no? Straight answer."

Sir Humphrey: "Well Minister, if you ask me for a straight answer, then I shall say that, as far as we can see, looking at it by and large, taking one thing with another in terms of the average of departments, then in the final analysis it is probably true to say, that at the end of the day, in general terms, you would probably find that, not to put too fine a point on it, there probably wasn't very much in it one way or the other. As far as one can see, at this stage."

In David Lewis' case, there was a clear refusal to remove the arms-length "protection" offered by her media team, and let Helen Clark answer the questions under her own signature. Whether that was a tactical decision by her media team in this particular instance, or a blanket policy that applies to most media queries, I don't know. What is now abundantly clear is that it backfired hugely on the Prime Minister by adding to the impression of evasiveness. Instead of quelling what had now become a nationwide whispering campaign, the Prime Minister's refusal to divulge Davis' travel schedule, or "categorically state" that there had been no incident, merely added fuel to the media fire.

It's not as if our question was not plain:

"5. Can the Prime Minister categorically state that at no time in the past year has Peter Davis required New Zealand consular, embassy, or New Zealand governmental assistance of any kind whilst in the United States?"

Yet the response was qualified. It doesn't say there was no assistance. It merely says the PM's media team *are not aware of New Zealand government assistance.*

Let's get this in perspective. The Prime Minister's Office has a Prime Minister in it. We were not asking her media team – we were asking her! The question we were asking related to the Prime Minister's husband. In any normal, functioning kind of Prime Minister's Office, the PM would categorically know whether any incident involving her husband had taken place. The answer would not need the fudging of the above response.

Furthermore, the PM's Office had insisted throughout that it was "making inquiries", yet the record later shows it made no inquiries of other government agencies, or even of Davis or Clark, as far as we can tell. In short, there was good reason for us to believe the PM's Office was lying.

In hindsight, I lay the blame for everything that followed directly at the feet of the PM's media advisors. For the first six years of her administration, the highly experienced and well-regarded Mike Munro – an ex-*Herald* gallery reporter – had been in charge of media manipulation for Clark. But when Munro quit after the 2005 election, it all turned to custard for Helen Clark. Suddenly, all the gold she touched turned to crud, as crisis after crisis blew up around her.

John Tamihere had kicked it off with his stream of consciousness interview with *Investigate* in April 2005, and then David Benson-Pope stuck his foot in his mouth after being caught stuffing tennis balls in a student's mouth. David Parker had a meltdown soon after. Through all of it, the Clark media team led by David Lewis and Kathryn Street did not seem to have Munro's *Rumpelstiltskin*-like ability to make crises disappear.

Helen Clark, the brand, is a creation of her media advisors. In the days when she led the Labour Party her way, she took it to an all time low in the polls and as Opposition Leader herself ranked only two percent in the preferred Prime Minister stakes. It wasn't until Brian Edwards, Judy Callingham, Maggie Eyre and her parliamentary press secretaries took control and rebuilt Helen Clark that she became Labour's six million dollar woman.

But when the maestros departed and left the Prime Ministerial remote control to their disciples, short circuits resulted.

Putting my own Beehive spindoctor hat on, the best way to deflate the rumours surrounding Peter Davis in the US would have been to acknowledge them early at a news conference, and deny them. End of story. Hiding the Prime Minister behind a raft of carefully worded answers that did not address the questions was a red rag to a bull. It looked highly evasive, and even other media were picking up that vibe.

Not only that, it allowed a massive whispering campaign to gain further momentum.

The *Herald on Sunday*, *Sunday Star-Times* and other papers and TV stations were all chasing the story by now. One newspaper asked *Investigate* if the magazine would be prepared to share the costs of a US private investigator who claimed to have found a document verifying the story but wanted an exponentially large US-dollar price for it. We declined.

Oddly, our own investigations with US authorities could not find any evidence that Peter Byard Davis had *ever* entered the US on any occasion. Given that it is a matter of public record that he has, this only added to the sense of intrigue surrounding the alleged story.

But something else was up. Video footage of an election night kiss involving the Prime Minister's husband and a mystery man was sent to an Auckland man who alerted *Investigate* to it. The footage had screened on Paul Holmes'

Prime TV 2005 election wrap-up – repeatedly – enough to spark discussion on talk radio and blog sites like Kiwiblog.

It also dovetailed with some information provided to the magazine about Clark and Davis' wider circle of friends, and provided *Investigate* with an opportunity to remind readers we were still seeking further information.

We slotted it in as a minor update in the magazine, which had been set down as the "smoking gun issue" owing mostly to a series of stories based around guns – a new twist on the John F Kennedy assassination, a special report on fighting in the Middle East, an investigation of the Rex Haig murder conviction case where we named a new suspect and a Mark Steyn commentary entitled, "How the West was lost". The Peter Davis kiss photo was a final addition to a series of front cover "smoking guns".

Had things gone according to plan, nobody would have batted an eyelid. *Investigate* readers would have seen the Peter Davis photo and our request for further information in the context of our ongoing battle with the PM's office, and life would have proceeded as normal. Unfortunately, just after the *Investigate* issue had gone to press, all hell broke loose in Wellington.

Labour was already being seriously wound up by taunts that it was "corrupt" over the pledge card scandal, so when TV1 news ambushed Clark in early September with a question about the rumours surrounding her husband she gave them a withering look that, by rights, should have killed them on the spot. Some commentators have speculated this was the straw that broke the camel's back and saw Labour unleash Benson-Pope and Trevor Mallard for a pre-emptive strike against National Leader Don Brash.

Mallard's challenge in the debating chamber just days later for Brash to talk about his "affair", amid cat-calls referring to "Diane" and "the Business Roundtable" – made Brash's position untenable. The irony was that rumours about Trevor Mallard having an affair were already doing the rounds at this time.

Helen Clark seemed to revel in Brash's matrimonial distress, telling reporters "I'm looking forward to the first question in Parliament about integrity."[330]

Asked if she would rein Mallard in, Clark told journalists essentially that Brash had brought it on himself, and Labour had nothing to do with it.

It was too late for us, meanwhile, to alter the magazine. It was already printed and being distributed – heading straight into a warzone.

That Sunday, New Zealand woke to the news that Peter Davis was "not gay". This was probably a source of confusion to most people, given that the only media up until that moment in time to ever suggest Peter Davis was gay was in fact Helen Clark's own biography by Brian Edwards. *Investigate* had not suggested Davis was gay either, but it didn't stop an over-eager *Sunday Star-Times* from going for the Doctor – Doctor Ian Scott that is, the man in the blue suit who'd been pictured kissing Peter Davis. Scott is indeed gay, but was at pains to tell the newspaper Davis was not; effectively, a "some of my best friends are not gay" defence.

The *Star-Times* had purloined the *Investigate* photos and run them themselves.

The fallout from the publication was immediate, with a seemingly furious Prime Minister Helen Clark telling journalists the suggestion that Davis was gay was "drivel". She also, initially, called the contact between the two men a "hug".[331]

"I would describe him [Scott] as being one of an inner circle of Auckland friends whom we have, and all of them will be falling over themselves laughing today at this kind of rumour," Clark snarled. "My husband was not particularly happy with Ian's hugging of him at the time, but that happened and there is nothing more to it."

If Clark had stopped there she'd probably have been OK, but her next comment has again succeeded in undermining the credibility of her entire explanation.

She added that Ian Scott was "reasonably boisterous and drunk" at the time[332], which is a bit concerning and seems extremely unlikely given that Scott was the Deputy Chair of the anti-booze Alcoholic Liquor Advisory Council (ALAC) at the time. He was also listed as a medical consultant to the Community Alcohol and Drugs Service (CADS) in Auckland, and takes an active role in helping addicts recover.

Was Helen Clark seriously expecting New Zealand to believe the Deputy Chair of ALAC was rolling around her campaign rally out of his tree? More importantly, if her allegation was not true – if she was in fact making this up on the hoof – then how much of the rest of her statement to the media might be untrue as well?

In her absolute public outrage, had Clark cleverly realized she could manipulate public sympathy and shock her critics into silence? Was she merely adopting the old political weapon of attack being the best form of defence?

Under further questioning, the PM then changed the initial reference to a hug by conceding the two men *had* kissed on the mouth, but she then claimed Peter Davis was "disgusted" by the kiss from one of his oldest gay friends.

Not only was there no sign on the video footage of Davis recoiling from the kiss, there is nothing in the body language of the two men to support the Prime Minister's claim. While none of this proved that Davis was gay, it was materially at odds with the Prime Minister's public statements – a conflict of evidence. Additionally, the "homosexual panic" defence drew immediate fire from blog commentators:

331 http://www.sfbaytimes.com/index.php?article_id=5512&sec=article
332 *The Independent*, UK, 19 September 2006, "Dirty Politics: sex and smears down under" http://www.independent.co.uk/news/world/australasia/dirty-politics-sex-and-smears-down-under-416569.html

"Well I must say that if I were gay I would be pretty upset at Helen for the way she handled that situation. Peter was 'disgusted'… so if I were gay I'd be classified as disgusting now?," exclaimed one person on David Farrar's Kiwiblog.[333]

"Disgusted that a friend (long term friend who was open about his sexual orientation) kissed him. So let me see, it's cool to have gay friends, it's cool to pass legislation that allows gay people to associate and form legal unions, it's cool to have anti discrimination laws for sexual orientation but her husband is suddenly 'disgusted' by it…

"Get real…If he is disgusted by homosexual behaviour then being married to a Labour PM and having gay friends around must be a living nightmare for the poor wee sausage."[334]

Again, the circumstantial evidence suggests Clark deliberately lied to the media in a desperate attempt to deflect attention from her relationship. It is simply not credible that a champion of making homosexuality legal, of giving same sex couples marriage and property rights, and whose 2IC, Heather Simpson, appointments secretary, and press secretary Kathryn Street were all lesbian, and who attended the civil unions of gay male friends, could use the word "disgusted" at the idea of a gay kiss and mean it.

If Clark was not telling the truth about Ian Scott, the deputy chair of ALAC, being drunk, and she was not telling the truth about Davis being "disgusted", then was she telling the truth when she denied they were gay? It was a denial that ran around the world, even featuring on America's *David Letterman* show with a walk-on of a woman purported to be "New Zealand Prime Minister Helen Clark, ladies and gentlemen", followed a little later with "10 signs that your husband is gay…"

Clark didn't help her cause, either, by being hypocritical over the issue of personal attacks. The Don Brash "affair" had been publicized by David Benson-Pope and Trevor Mallard. Clark suddenly did an about-face and told journalists in the wake of the publicity about her husband that she would rein Mallard in.

This was, of course, the same Clark who only a couple of days earlier had smugly stated: "I'm looking forward to the first question in Parliament about integrity." Now she was singing a different song:

"I don't muck-rake. My party has no mandate to muck-rake[335]…Personal

---

333   http://www.kiwiblog.co.nz/2006/09/corrupt_vs_cancerous.html#comment-235485

334   There's another angle to this as well. If Don Brash and his wife had won the election that night, and his deputy Gerry Brownlee had rushed from the audience to kiss Don Brash on the mouth, what might have been the reaction, both of Brash and the media? We know Ian Scott kissed Davis on the mouth, because Helen Clark has confirmed it. The circumstances of "why" remain unanswered, and the only answer offered – that the Deputy Chair of ALAC was drunk – is highly unconvincing. In this case, Clark's answers raise even bigger questions about the truthfulness of her responses. But her "outrage" appears to have deflected any further media digging.

335   Except for when she launched an attack on the children of National and NZ First

attacks form no part of Labour's strategy. That's where Trevor was out of line.[336]"

So far, so good. But her next comment was a pearler:[337] "But I can't state too strongly that Labour regards Dr Brash as a corrosive and cancerous person within the New Zealand political system."

So much for a moratorium on personal attacks.

But more skullduggery on the *Investigate* article was about to emerge. It was Helen Clark's office that had tipped news media off about the *Investigate* story – before the magazine was even published! An *Investigate* magazine news release responding to a Beehive attack on the magazine detailed the developments:

"*Investigate* has published photos of Peter Davis taken on election night, as part of the magazine's wider investigation into whether Mr Davis was involved in an incident in the United States. Because of stonewalling by the Prime Minister's office and a refusal to answer specific questions, the magazine has been forced to commence a wider-ranging investigation into Mr Davis' background and events leading up to the alleged incident.

"Contrary to idle speculation about Mr Davis' sexuality in the Sunday papers, the photos have been published without comment by *Investigate* with a request for further information, and people can make up their own minds about the magazine coverage, once they've actually read it.

"Personally, we were as stunned as everyone else to see the magazine emblazoned across the front of a Sunday broadsheet in a typefont comparable to "CHURCHILL DECLARES WAR!", on the basis of an otherwise innocuous publication in the magazine.

"If the Prime Minister wishes a swift resolution to this, given her erroneous claims in the past that *Investigate* never seeks her comment, she should front up with the information the magazine is seeking, without restriction. Instead, even though the magazine has asked, she refuses to provide it.

"What I will say, for the record, is that *Investigate* has not spread any detail of the alleged incident involving Peter Davis in the US, mainly because until it is proven or disproven it is defamatory, and also because we had been trying to trace the source of the rumour – something that becomes almost impossible once the entire population have heard of it.

"As a result of our initial stories – and prior to the rumour becoming widespread – *Investigate* has been provided with an amount of detailed information about Mr Davis both overseas and in NZ which requires further investigative work.

"For the first time tonight, we can reveal that at no point has *Investigate*

cabinet ministers. *NZ Herald*, 20 September 2006, "Mallard says he will do his bit..."
http://www.nzherald.co.nz/section/1/story.cfm?c_id=1&objectid=10402159
336 *NZ Herald*, 21 September 2006, "Nothing personal, but Brash is cancerous, says Clark"
http://www.nzherald.co.nz/section/1/story.cfm?c_id=1&objectid=10402288
337 Ibid

ever tried to pitch this story to other media, and in fact that it is other media (including every Sunday newspaper) who have for weeks been pestering *Investigate* for an exclusive preview when the story breaks.

"After the Brash story broke this week, *Investigate* received this email from the editor of a Sunday paper: "Hi Ian, Sorry to be a pain, but I just wondered if we could touch base over the Davis story. I have been contacted in the last five minutes by a source who has put down a marker regarding any allegations/rumours. Basically, it was making clear that the Prime Minister was ready to sue if anyone stepped out of line and also indicated that they very much expected you to be running a story in the issue of the magazine appearing on Monday. If you could spare five minutes to talk that would be great. Regards,"

"My question to bloggers, the media and the public is this: why was the Prime Minister's office tipping off the media about a forthcoming issue of *Investigate*? Methinks they doth protest too much. Again, some straight answers to straight questions – rather than vague denials – from the Prime Minister would be helpful.

"Meanwhile, the record will show that we have continued to be politely circumspect in our dealings with media queries like the one above, as this email to the editor shows:

"As you can appreciate it is all extremely sensitive at the moment. *Investigate* broke a story in its July issue that it was checking reports of an incident involving the Prime Minister's husband, Peter Davis, in the US. In the process of trying to confirm whether an incident had happened, *Investigate* was stunned to learn that the Prime Minister's Office was aware of our inquiries before we'd made any phone calls in New Zealand. Contradictory statements issued by Ministry of Foreign Affairs and Trade and the PM's office further raised our suspicions.

Since then, the PM's office has refused to answer straight questions, or confirm that the Prime Minister will take direct responsibility for the answers given. Additionally, fresh information regarding the alleged incident overseas has been supplied to the magazine, information which we are working through in NZ and overseas.

Because of the volume of information, and the names of specific people that have been passed on, we are now fully engaged in a thorough and ongoing investigation. Regards, Ian

Then there was this email from the *Sunday Star-Times* to *Investigate*: "Hi Ian "The tomtoms are beating about Monday's mag, saying you are going the whole hog on the Peter Davis story, including the allegations that he was involved in [deleted] in the US and [deleted]. Also the story about the kiss from the blue man in a suit. We've also heard that you have backers who've organised a war chest to fight any defamation allegations. Obviously the timing is ripe. "Can you confirm/comment? "Donna Chisholm | Deputy editor | *Sunday Star-Times*"

And our response was:

"Hi Donna "thanks for the heads up... "There will be a further development in Monday's *Investigate*....but we have not finished our ongoing inquiries into the whole incident. I would describe Monday's release as an evolution of the investigation, rather than its resolution."

To which Donna replied: "Will be keen to see it! Any comment on the goss that you've got wealthy backers and a war chest!?"

As is now apparent from the PM's statements today, it appears this was spin being run from the Beehive. I was unaware at the time and I responded:

"I forgot to add – I am unaware of any "backers" for a defamation case. *Investigate's* position is that it prefers to publish material that is factual and correct and therefore can withstand a defamation action. That is why our investigation into the substance of the Peter Davis incident is taking time...because we want to make sure that when we do publish that it is solid. The facts at present are that the PM's office has refused to answer straight questions on the matter – causing us to investigate further both in New Zealand and overseas."

Donna's final message to me was: "Well if you do stack it up, it will be a real coup..."

This is typical of the approaches I have repeatedly had from the news media over the weeks. Again, at no time has *Investigate* sought publicity. The 'Smoking Gun' cover was merely a play on words based on the JFK headline, the How The West Was Lost headline, the new info on the Rex Haig murder case and of course our request for info on Peter Davis.

MEDIA RELEASE ENDS

The incident left both *Investigate* and the *Sunday Star-Times* licking their wounds, but Clark on the other hand suddenly seemed absolutely delighted, and barely able to suppress her glee.

In a perceptive article by the *Herald on Sunday's* Leah Haines, you get a strong sense that Clark almost planned the whole thing, and that her outrage the week before was yet another Oscar-winning performance to bring the punters on side:[338]

You couldn't shut the taxi driver up when he heard I was off to see Helen Clark. "I think after the last week they're in for another term after this one, eh?" The Nats had gone too far this time. "You can throw words like corruption around, that's OK, but," he tut-tutted, shaking his head in disgust, "with all this stuff about her husband. Well, that's just not on."

But the driver's belief that National is the one bagging her husband Peter Davis, when in fact not a public word has been uttered by National to deride the professor, is just what Labour would have him believe.

These are murky days. If politics was a hand-knitted jersey, it would be so fiercely spun as to be a matted mess at the bottom of the washing machine. They are days of private eyes and mudslinging, where all sides are claiming the moral high

---

338 *NZ Herald*, 24 September 2006, "I always keep a sense of humour - Clark"
http://www.nzherald.co.nz/index.cfm?objectid=10402666

ground and we, the public, are left wondering what on earth is really going on...

...Clark casually plonks herself down on a black leather chair opposite me, offers a wide, self-conscious smile, and skews the coffee table so her knees are facing mine.

She's normal. She's nice. She has sparkly eye make-up on and a blue plastic bracelet given to her by someone at a shopping mall this morning. Clark Of The People. But not Clark unmasked.

The blueberry muffins, which sit uneaten and unoffered on the other end of the coffee table, are a clear indication that this, like the muck-raking and political attacks of the past week, is all about business.

This is not a woman who "lost it", as some suggested when she lashed out and called Don Brash "cancerous" and "corrosive" last week.

Somewhere, among all the mud and the muffins, is a masterly plan.

Nevertheless, it can't have been an easy week for Clark – having her intensely private husband dragged into the fray, and even having to defend her ageing parents from prying media calls.

"Oh," she booms, when I ask if she's feeling OK, or if she is feeling terribly stressed. Then she laughs, one of those deep "He, he, he, he" kind of laughs. "I always keep a sense of humour."

There's a sharp contrast, too, behind her televised comments on how "creepy" it was being allegedly stalked by an Auckland private detective hired by the Exclusive Brethren, and her confessional tone in the Leah Haines interview:

"I keep a little corner of my life that I'm not followed in," she explains, "unless it's by the Exclusive Brethren," at which she laughs so heartily that she makes a huge snorting noise...

...She knew it was all on when the first article appeared last week about the showdown in the National caucus over Don Brash's alleged affair.

"I rang my husband and said 'I feel now that there will be retaliation. I think we have to steel ourselves for the rumour mill which has been building up a head of steam to erupt around us'. And that proved to be prophetic."[339]

Sure enough, early that Saturday a photographer sprung Dr Davis as he meandered to the letterbox to get the paper.[340]

The next day, he was splashed over a Sunday newspaper's front page. Clark instantly blamed the National Party, while mounting a ferocious defence of her husband.

...Which brings us to today. Does she think we really have entered a new era

---

339 Which backs up the earlier suggestion that the Prime Minister's Office was fuelling the media fire.
340 Notice here how Clark subtly skips the in-between bits, where her office was ringing around the Sunday papers, suggesting *Investigate* might have something on Clark's husband next week. Reading the newspaper interview, you wouldn't even know Clark's office had a role in it.

where politicians' personal lives have become fair game for public consumption, or is this just a blip in time? "The widespread view among the commentariat," Clark laughs heartily again, "which I share, is that it's not an issue unless it is in stark contradiction to the public pose someone has adopted. That's when the media will move in. Because they see hypocrisy."

Does she think Brash brought the media attention about his affair on himself when he issued a press release saying he was going home to work on his marriage? "I wouldn't want to go down that track. I think when you're in a leadership position in a political party, the chances are, if you're not purer than driven snow, it's going to come out sometime."

That's a shame, I say, because it makes for a boring Parliament. She laughs. "Well, it might. But I think it's a discipline we accept in these positions."

Apart from her strange and discordant boast that she is "purer than driven snow" Clark, in a roundabout way, agrees that scrutiny comes with the territory, and makes it sound like a game of cat and mouse. There were certainly shades of cat and mouse in a further round of email exchanges with the Prime Minister's office, which *Investigate* reprinted in its Letters pages with the headings as they appear below:

YES, PRIME MINISTER?
Dear Ian,

We have no reason to believe there is any truth or substance in the implications in your questions. In any case, the answers to all the questions is no.

We cannot regard you as an objective journalist and henceforth we'll treat your requests for information on the same basis as we do any other partisan figure.

David

David Lewis

Chief Press Secretary

Office of the Prime Minister

NO, PRIME MINISTER!
Dear David,

You seem to forget the years I was hated by National for the Winebox coverage, and also in fact our publication on the eve of the 2002 election of documents linking the Business Roundtable to National.

But then again, that's selective memory from the ninth floor.

I make no apologies for catching the Prime Minister and her team in continued acts of dishonesty. It's my job…

…There will, at some point soon, be some fresh questions.

Regards

Ian

YES, PRIME MINISTER? II
Dear Ian,
You sound like David Brent [of *The Office*].
regards
David Lewis
Chief Press Secretary
Office of the Prime Minister

NO, PRIME MINISTER! II
Yeah...I thought some of his quotes were quite *apropos*:
"If at first you don't succeed, remove all evidence you ever tried."
"If you can keep your head when all around you have lost theirs, then you probably haven't understood the seriousness of the situation."
"If your boss is getting you down, look at her through the prongs of a fork and imagine her in jail."
"When confronted by a difficult problem, you can solve it more easily by reducing it to the question, "How would the Lone Ranger handle this?""
Take your pick...
Cheers
Ian

YES, PRIME MINISTER? III
"Is your work done? Are all pigs fed, watered and ready to fly?..."
David Lewis
Chief Press Secretary
Office of the Prime Minister

NO, PRIME MINISTER! III
Scheduled for take off around the same time the words "integrity" and "Labour" can be used in the same sentence without causing guffaws of laughter.
Regards,
Ian

Hard on the heels of this very public questioning of the Clark-Davis marriage, however, the Prime Minister couldn't help herself when she appeared at the annual Big Gay Out festival in Auckland's Pt Chevalier just a few months later in February 2007.

Delivering a speech to thousands of gay attendees, with Judith Tizard at her side, Clark summed up her message, captured in a YouTube video watched by thousands[341]:

---

341   http://www.youtube.com/watch?v=jIVuhEfHElQ

"Georgina [Beyer] has done a wonderful job on behalf of the Rainbow communities," exclaimed Clark, "I want to register how important she has been to us!"

"It's wonderful to come along and celebrate the Big Gay Out. It's been an amazing day. Judith and myself we've been to Waiheke, we've been to the Philharmonia concert, we've started a women's fun run, we're ending up here. It's great to see the crowd, great to see the pride, because that's what the Hero festival is all about. It's about pride in who *we* are!," she exclaimed, punching the air for emphasis.

On the internet, bloggers and other commentators immediately seized on the "we" comment, asking whether it was merely the royal "we", or whether the Prime Minister was quietly outing herself, while others speculated it was an attempt to get gay voters to empathise with her by fuelling speculation.[342]

"What will be fatal for Clark is the revelation (if true) that her marriage is in fact a marriage of convenience in which she entered specifically to project an image which belies the reality of her life," wrote blogger Adolf Fiinkenstein from the blogsite *No Minister*. "Sadly, such a perception fits in quite nicely with the lies and deception she has adopted so willingly for so many other issues. She deserves all the innuendo she gets."

"The issue is not Clark's sexuality," he continued. "It is her capacity to lie about it if she thinks a few lies will win some votes. There is substantial rumour and strong 'circumstantial evidence' that both she and her husband are homosexual. I couldn't care less if they are homosexual but I do care if they deceitfully put across the notion they are not."

Of course, it is a matter of public record confirmed by the Prime Minister herself that Clark's marriage was definitely a marriage of convenience, but she is now on record denying the gay rumours.[343]

There's one final thing I'll say on this point. Two years ago, I pointed out to journalists that we were still investigating the various claims and innuendo surrounding the US incident and another that allegedly took place in New Zealand. I refused to stop investigating just because of political correctness, and I've kept an open mind through the investigation. But if the evidence really did exist, I think it would have turned up given the blowtorch we used to verify it one way or the other. Whilst I cannot explain the strange behavior of the PM's Office and the Ministry of Foreign Affairs, I personally don't believe the innuendo. I think Davis has been unfairly pilloried, perhaps because of the deeper issues regarding the Clark marriage that we've already touched on.

You are entitled to debate whether the Clark marriage has been presented

342 http://nominister.blogspot.com/2007/07/rise-of-sexless-marriage.html
343 A gay *Investigate* reader, furious with the magazine for running the Peter Davis photo, recanted his fury a few months later after returning from a business trip to Wellington. In a discussion about the scene in Wellington, his taxi driver matter of factly claimed that he often ferried Peter Davis "and his partner" around as well.

honestly to the public, because the Prime Minister herself put that ball in play. But please don't cling to the rumours that have circulated about Davis. I've seen no hard evidence to support them, and I'm now of the view that utter stupidity in her media team was the biggest factor in allowing those rumours to get way out of hand, by not answering straight questions when they had the chance.

To recap some of the major points in the last couple of chapters, then: Firstly, Helen Clark was the first politician to declare open season on the private lives of MPs' families, and made no apologies for doing so. Secondly, Helen Clark appears to have been shedding crocodile tears about the "childless" issue in a cynical bid for voter sympathy. Thirdly, the Prime Minister's seems to play both sides of the gay coin for similar effect. Fourthly, maybe we all underestimated the artist in Clark after all.

Finally, let's not forget that, in the lead-up to the 1999 election, Labour misled voters by claiming to be anti-Nanny State and anti government interference in private lives.

But was Labour really anti-Nanny State and government interference in people's lives, or was that simply another carefully-crafted electioneering slogan for 1999? To get a sense of Labour's hidden agenda for the Clark years, we return to the political climate the Prime Minister cut her teeth in – the "Women's Lib" movement of the early 1970s.

The Velvet Revolution

Sir Humphrey: "The interview was over. We were just chatting, harmlessly."
Bernard Woolley: "Harmlessly?!"
Sir Humphrey: "It was off-the-record!"
Bernard Woolley: "It was on the tape!!" – **Yes Minister**

IT USED TO BE SAID the hand that rocks the cradle rules the world. Now, people whose hands have never been near a cradle are deciding what's best for children, and the country. If one thing could be said to have defined the Helen Clark Labour administration, it would be the introduction of sweeping social reforms.

Armed with academic theories and left-wing ideology, the payoff for many groups who supported Labour during each election campaign has been to see various pet projects bulldozed through the legislative process regardless of public opposition.

Before addressing any of those in this book, however, it is worth taking a trip down memory lane, because none of these sweeping reforms were dreamt up overnight. What I wrote in 2005, on the eve of a major feminist conference, has probably been thrown into even sharper focus by the passage of the anti-smacking laws since then, and it forms the backbone of the following narrative.

***

Veni, vidi, vici. I came, I saw, I conquered. When Julius Caesar uttered those immortal words 2055 years ago, he was speaking militarily. When hundreds of women from around the country gathered for a national conference in mid 2005 to mark the 30th anniversary of the 1975 United Women's Convention in Wellington, Caesar's words could aptly have been re-applied to an entirely different battle, a battle for hearts and minds rather than land.

At no time in the past three decades has that battle been cast in sharper relief – particularly after Labour MP John Tamihere's decision to throw open public debate about the capture of policy and governmental power by Labour's lesbian/feminist wing.

Back in the mid 1970s, only four women were in parliament. Today, there are 34 – if you count Georgina Beyer – and as Tamihere pointed out women now have their hands firmly on the levers of political, judicial, constitutional and economic power.

But there's a twist to this Cinderella story, a quirk of irony that few have fully appreciated. Back in the 1970s, one of the primary complaints of the women's movement was the existence of a male old boys' network that didn't choose the best *person* for the job, only the best *man* for the job. Three decades later, men's groups are now making similar complaints, in reverse.

Has New Zealand lurched from one unfair power to extreme to the other? And if so, did it happen by accident?

The woman who organized the 2005 women's conference – former Labour cabinet minister Margaret Shields – clearly doesn't think so:

"In the early 1970s a small group of women within the NZ Labour Party decided that enough was enough," Shields posted in an internet forum called "The Women-Power Network" back in 1999.

"We began the reorganization of the Women's Section of the Party so that it could become an agent of change; through organising and encouraging and training women to take a larger, more strategic role in politics.

"It is not an accident that now the Prime Minister of New Zealand and the Leader of the Opposition are both women."

John Tamihere, too, doesn't see the power shift as a coincidence.

"You see, these people think in timeframes of ten to 15 years, it's only bastards like me that struggle through the current term. So when you're positioning for high places, they're thinking that far ahead," Tamihere argues.

"They don't have families. They've got nothing *but* the ability to plot. I've gotta take my kid to soccer on Saturday, they don't. So they just go and have a *parlez vous francais* somewhere and a latte, whereas we don't get to plot, we're just trying to get our kids to synchronise their left and right feet. They don't even think about that.

"I've got a fifteen year old whose testosterone's jumping and he's scrapping around at school. Now they don't have that, and because they don't have that they're just totally focused. You've also got a fully paid organization called the union movement, who can co-opt fully paid coordinators. These people just never sleep."

If Tamihere and Shields are correct, then the sweeping social policy changes manifested by Labour have their roots deep in the distant past, in "sleeper cells" of "change agents" drafted into the Party with one goal in mind.

Back in 1973, the feminist movement organized its first-ever United Women's Convention, to mark the 80th anniversary of women getting the vote in 1893.

As well as today's household names – Helen Clark, Margaret Wilson, Marilyn Waring, Silvia Cartwright – nearly two thousand other women, from varying walks of life, turned up. And among those watching with more than a little interest, feminist and then-communist, Kay Goodger.

Goodger, who now incidentally rejects the radicalism of her youth,[344] nonetheless authored and co-authored in 1973 and 1974 a series of documents for New Zealand's Socialist Action League which set out a long term plan for changing the face of New Zealand society.

"Many women, as they become interested in women's liberation, realise that a new kind of society must be built if we are to achieve freedom from our oppression as a sex…whether this will involve a socialist transformation of society is at present a subject under discussion among feminists," she wrote.

"The new feminist movement is characterized by its deep-going challenges to every aspect of women's oppression…The once-sacred 'family' is being questioned and the philosophy that 'biology is destiny' emphatically denied."

As signaled by Goodger, an aspect of New Zealand society to come under sustained attack from the radical feminist wing over the next three decades was the traditional family. If the family could be crushed, broken down, sidelined as irrelevant or portrayed as no better than other methods of child-rearing, radical feminism could set the agenda for centuries to come.

"Where else in the world do Amazons rule?," lamented John Tamihere at his now-infamous lunch.

The Socialist Action League's plan in 1973 was for a utopian future 'Amazonia' reflecting what she believed had been a reality in the past.

"The oppression of women began with the origin of the patriarchal family, private property and the state. Anthropological evidence [not cited] has shown that in the primitive communal society, women held a respected and important position. The basic economic unit was the maternal gens or clan, in which the family as we know it did not exist. In this clan, goods were shared among members equally.

"Women…were not tied to individual men economically, nor was there any compulsion to remain with one sexual partner."

But then, claimed Goodger, the bad old days arrived when men mysteriously wrested power from the matriarchs and "introduced" the so-called "family" where "monogamy…was strictly enforced" and families had their own houses and own possessions. Thus, the world abandoned Amazonian communism, she wrote.

---

344 Don't be harsh on Goodger. We can all say and do things in our youth that we later wince at. One of the first groups to spring to her defence when this article first appeared was a men's group who said they'd been treated very well in their professional dealings with Goodger in recent years. The cold hard reality however is that writings can encapsulate the thoughts of a generation, and take on a life of their own as a manifesto of future goals that young disciples will work towards. In that sense, the Socialist Action League documents certainly did become the blueprint for infiltration of the Labour Party and the implementation of long-term, society-changing strategies

"Today, the nuclear family unit remains as the basic economic cell of class society...The family also serves to perpetuate capitalist rule by inculcating in children the values of the private property system.

"Obedience to authority is first learned in the family.

"Acceptance of the hierarchical, exploitative and alienating social relations within capitalism depends considerably upon the tremendous influence of the individualistic, patriarchal family.

"With its thrust against the family institution, the women's liberation movement is profoundly revolutionary," wrote Goodger.

She then called on radical feminists to do all they can within political parties, government departments and communities to target and eliminate institutions like the traditional family.

In her 1973 analysis, Goodger correctly identified that New Zealand's establishment would not just throw their hands up and say "fair cop, guv", when faced with the demands of radical feminism. So instead, she argued for a series of smaller steps, none of them big enough to wake up the slumbering majority against them, but each step big enough to achieve irreversible change, particularly in the attitudes of the wider public.

Did the Socialist Action League plant the seeds now growing in Labour's social policy advice units? If Prime Minister Clark's calls for a massive increase in government childcare facilities and more women in the workforce is any indication, the answer must be yes.

Back in 1973 Goodger wrote that the family would suffer a body blow if women could be freed from having children. Rather, as in Soviet Russia, the state should play a bigger role:

"The concept that society as a whole should take the responsibility of caring for children is embodied in the demand for government-financed, 24-hour, community-controlled childcare centres. This demand opens up the possibilities of replacing the family institution."

Goodger also reinforced that whoever rocks the cradle and educates the children defines what and how future generations think:

"The fight for equal opportunity is also taken up in the education system, around demands such as for an end to discrimination against women in the schools and universities, for opportunities to enter all fields of education, for women's studies programmes to teach the truth about women throughout history, and for birth control information and contraceptives to be freely available for all students.

"Because of the key role played by students and young women in the feminist movement as a whole, action on campuses and in the high schools can play an important part in helping to spark struggles by other women.

"Action to win control of university and high school facilities to benefit women, such as use of classrooms and the library for women's studies, provides an example for the general fight to win control of the resources of society away from the ruling class and its apologists.

"In addition, the campuses can serve as vital organising centres for the feminist movement."

As with much Marxist rhetoric, however, it ignored inconvenient realities. The demand for more female teachers, for example, glossed over the fact that – even back then – more than three-quarters of all teachers were women in 1972. Thirty-three years later, men are almost extinct as teachers.

Selling the message in a sugar-coated way to women was also seen as important by Goodger back then, with her comment that women pushing for the "right" to exterminate unwanted fetuses should join forces with women seeking taxpayer-funded childcare, as a means of uniting women who may have different views under a common socialist banner.

"The real meaning of sisterhood becomes clear at such times," she wrote.

Despite that, Goodger argued that merely capturing people's hearts and minds didn't go far enough, that "the sisterhood" had to take control of the Government from within.

"The deep roots the [Labour] party has in the working class, through the unions, makes it objectively an ally of the women's liberation movement. Feminists working within the Labour Party can do much to further the cause of women's liberation."

Again, John Tamihere's account of what has happened to Labour eerily reflects that 1973 plan of action.

"Oh yeah, there's definitely a 'machine' all right. It's formidable. It's got apparatus and activists in everything from the PPTA all the way through. It's actually even built a counterweight to the Roundtable – Businesses for Social Responsibility. Its intelligence-gathering capabilities are second to none."

Having those activists in place, with the power to write laws and decide what children will be taught in schools, is a dream come true for what Opposition MPs are calling "the lesbian/feminist cabal" running the Labour Government.

Goodger, again surprisingly prescient back in the seventies, realised that more liberal sex laws would help bring down the hated family unit.

"[The family] moulds the behaviour and character structure of children from infancy and throughout adolescence, disciplining them and teaching submission to established authority. The family represses sexuality, discouraging all sexual activity which is not within marriage.

"Our goal must be to create economic and social institutions that are superior to the present family institution."

As part of the list of "demands" that the Sisterhood would work towards over the next thirty years, wrote Goodger in 1973, were

• Abortion to be free and on demand
• Sex education and birth control 'integrated into the education system at all levels' and readily accessible through 'government-financed clinics.

The government should initiate a public education campaign to overcome ignorance, fears and illusions...'
- An end to coercive family laws
- De facto marriage should be considered to have the same status, legally and socially, as marriage by legal contract
- 'The rearing, social welfare and education of children should become the responsibility of society, rather than individual parents...All laws enforcing individual ownership of children should be abolished.'
- 'All discrimination against homosexual men and women should be outlawed...laws should be repealed'
- 'All laws victimizing prostitutes should be abolished'
- 'Paid maternity leave of 12 weeks with no loss of job or seniority should be available'
- 'The government should provide the finance for free child-care centres, open to all children from early infancy for 24 hours a day'

Thirty years later, abortion is now free and effectively on demand. Sex education is now introduced at pre-school level as part of the government early childhood curriculum. Laws introduced by Labour in 2002 have given de facto relationships the same legal status as marriage, and extended to gay couples by the Civil Unions Act in 2005. The Care of Children legislation introduced by Labour in 2004 strips families of the 'ownership' of their offspring in favour of the wider community. Biological parents become merely "guardians".

Anti-smacking legislation that came into effect in 2007 and which encourages schools and other government agencies to report cases to CYFS, has further emphasized the State's stranglehold on a generation of kids.

Prostitution has been legalised and the number of children engaged in prostitution has increased dramatically – presumably a result of families no longer being "sexually repressed".

Paid maternity leave is in, and Helen Clark's government implemented 20 hours free daycare for every child, last year.

In short, an agenda written by an offshoot of the Communist Party in 1973 has been met in full by the women it infiltrated the Labour Party and public service with all those years ago.

One of those women is Margaret Shields, a former Minister of Customs in the 1984 Labour Government of David Lange. Shields' biggest claim to fame back then was perhaps her insistence that she could see a phallic symbol in a glass of liquor on the rocks used in a magazine advertisement, in much the same way as kids see the shapes of animals in the clouds.

It fell to Shields to organize the 2005 conference, and although now well clear of national politics, she proudly retains her membership of "the Sisterhood", based on her advice to a woman overseas recently.

"We need to find ways of 'making it for a purpose', and supporting women who have made it into the executive wing. If women do not support other women we can hardly expect men to do so![345] Moreover, support is a two way street. The fervour with which women scrutinise and criticise women who are in positions of influence is, at times, terrifying. It says a great deal about the pent-up desires of women for a better world but fails to acknowledge the real difficulties for one woman, or a small minority of women in a sea of men.

"We need to make sure that we have mechanisms and networks to support those lonely women who are in positions of authority. They need to be kept in touch with the organisations from which they have come. Especially, if they are in the political arena, they will find their life very difficult unless they have trustworthy support networks to provide the encouragement and reinforcement to stick with some of the issues that fired them up in the first place."

In comments analogous to Tamihere's rage against the 'Machine', Shields confirms the web that exists within Labour:

"The systems that work best to keep women leaders going are, in fact, informal networks of old friends who can be trusted to tell the truth out of kindness rather than malice and who are there when life is really tough. It is important to remember that no minority group can win without compromise and trade. Women in power are seldom a majority.

"Don't expect the world to change overnight because one woman became a manager or a member of parliament. However, if you work with her she may be able to make a real difference over time especially if she knows which are the critical issues and has a group around her to help support a shared long term strategy.

"Yes, we can make a difference but sometimes we need patience and sometimes we need to find more subtle ways of achieving our goals."

Those "subtle ways", advises Shields, include disguising the real reason for taking a particular position on an issue:

"To give but one small example, I never talk about equality in decision-making as a human rights issue – although it undoubtedly is. Instead, when working in developing countries, in particular, I always approach the question of inclusion of more women in decision-making as an issue of commonsense – to avoid the problems of things not working properly because all experience has not been brought to the table. Most men (and women) accept that logic whereas they will rail against the idea of 'human rights'."

Writing in 1979, feminist author Christine Dann also talked of this method of persuasion, taken to a new level, and fine-tuned by the thought-police of communist China:

---

345 Hardline feminist rhetoric, like hardline neo-Nazi rhetoric, is ultimately tribal – "My group is better than your group!". What on earth is wrong with encouraging people to support an idea on its merits, rather than supporting it because a woman said it? Or a man?

"Which brings me to a second major radical feminist organising method – consciousness-raising. As pioneered by radical feminists Kathie Sarachild and others, consciousness-raising is used by women as an extremely effective way of making the vital connections between their personal lives and political oppression. The technique has been used before principally by the Chinese in the 'speak bitterness' campaigns they conducted among the peasantry.

"In consciousness-raising a group of people who are dissatisfied with their lives as women (or workers, or blacks) meet to find out what is wrong, work out why it is wrong, and consider ways in which wrongs can be righted. Once a group establishes trust, so that everything can be discussed freely, consciousness usually rises fast. Participants come to realise that problems which the dominant ideology characterises as personal (lack of beauty, money, security, employment etc) are not a result of personal inadequacy at all, but are due to deliberate political manipulation.

"As each woman tells a similar story of abortion and contraception problems, as each worker repeats familiar tales of boss trouble, personal histories take on political significance. A good consciousness-raising group does not stop at the level of heightened awareness, but goes on to study and discuss the reasons for and the mechanisms of oppression, and to take part in actions and groups which aim to end it."

Dann describes the technique as "vital" if socialism wants to control New Zealand society and thought.

While feminism has achieved some very worthwhile goals for New Zealand society as a whole, simply swapping a political patriarchy for a matriarchy doesn't achieve balance.

On the other hand, to see what has happened to New Zealand society and politics in the past three decades as merely a 'Marxist revolution without the blood' is to miss a lot of the subtleties entirely. As Dann wrote before it happened, "If we learn anything from revolutionaries such as Mao it should be to break the rules of revolution as successfully as he did. To show as little respect for Mao and his ideas as Mao did for the Comintern and the theories of the Russian experts on revolution. To place more confidence on the insights and experience of the radical women of New Zealand today than in the words of 19th Century European men."

In other words, the radical feminist agenda was to take Marxism further than even Marx envisioned. To re-educate women, and through them, change the world: an iron fist inside a velvet glove revolution. A very female coup.

The Bold And The Dutiful:
Clark's Powerbase

Sir Humphrey: "I knew about it."
Bernard: "Then why are you aghast?"
Sir Humphrey: "I'm aghast that it got out." – **Yes Minister**

QUAINTLY, TWO DAYS AFTER FIRST being elected to Parliament in 1981, Clark was asked whether NZ was ever likely to have a female prime minister.[346]

"I can see a time when we will have a woman Prime Minister. But for it to happen without it being an 'odd' thing, we'll need more women members. Many people in the electorate have said that Ann Hercus would make a wonderful Prime Minister."

Twenty-seven years later, Prime Minister Clark has now assembled a network of very powerful women. Most of her key advisers are female. Three of her most senior aides, including Heather Simpson and chief press secretary Kathryn Street[347], are lesbian.

When she finally came to power in 1999, Clark's friend Margaret Wilson was promoted to Attorney-General. Wilson, a law graduate, was there when Helen Clark was first elected to Parliament in 1981, as the *Auckland Star* noted at the time.[348]

"On Sunday, while a former university colleague, law lecturer Margaret Wilson, fielded non-stop phone calls, the fledgling MP relaxed over coffee after her first official engagement."

Dame Silvia Cartwright – an otherwise relatively undistinguished judge whose biggest claim to fame was the feminist cause-celebre heading the first

---

346 *Auckland Star*, 30 November 1981, Helen Clark interview
347 Kathryn Street, formerly National Radio's parliamentary reporter, is also the partner of Labour MP Maryan Street. The identity of the third aide is not relevant to the story.
348 *Auckland Star*, 30 November 1981

Cervical Cancer Inquiry in 1988 – became Clark's pick for Governor-General. Cartwright boasts in her CV of her strong work on "women's issues" both in New Zealand and for the United Nations.

"Since 1993, she has been a member of the United Nations committee monitoring compliance with the United Nations Convention to Eliminate All Forms of Discrimination Against Women (CEDAW)."

Cartwright's husband Peter became the Government appointee heading the powerful Broadcasting Standards Authority, which regulates what broadcasters are allowed to say, and he also serves on the Film and Literature Board of Review regulating censorship issues.

It's been a long time coming, but Helen Clark's 1970s vision of a socialist revolution is coming to pass as trusted friends take up network positions. One of her philosophies is to attract people who can shield her, allowing her to disengage from controversy.

The late Revenue Minister, Trevor de Cleene, who served in the Lange administration above Clark hinted at his protege's "power of one" mentality.

"One cannot be a supreme individual," he remarked wryly in 1987, after noting that Clark had reined herself in enough to become a Cabinet team player. But clearly the words "team" and "Clark" are not synonymous: 21 years after de Cleene's comments, Clark is no longer just one among many, she arguably *is* the Labour Government. No longer confined by the constraints of more senior colleagues, Clark has used the past nine years to bring long repressed plans to fruition.

Again, Clark foreshadowed the existence of her own hidden agenda way back in that 1984 book:

"If anything, I hold my views more strongly than ever, now," she wrote. "But it makes me more cautious, more inhibited. I've learned survival skills."

And those survival skills clearly included learning to keep her mouth shut, as a 1987 *Auckland Star* report noted:

"Clark, who says earlier remarks were taken out of context and sensationalised, now says she sees no problems remaining faithful to the rule of collective responsibility, which stops her from publicly criticising Cabinet decisions.

" 'I think that when you accept a role of working within any institution, as I have, you accept that you are not a free agent,' she says. 'I accept the constraints as the price of working within the system'."

Although Clark has, on occasion, tried to pass off the comments she made in 1984 as "taken out of context", she nonetheless told interviewer Karren Beanland – herself a future Labour Government press secretary – in 1987 that she still stood by "that interview".

But by 1987, having gained her toehold in Cabinet at last, Helen Clark was wasting no time getting her networks going.

"She is still suspicious enough of existing Parliamentary power groups," wrote Beanland, "to have surrounded herself by her own people as Ministerial support staff. Labour activist and feminist Sandi Beattie is one."

"My thinking," said Clark at the time, "is that it is important for Ministers to have independent staff, people who are independent of the department and in a position to offer advice from a different perspective. I am not going to fall into the *Yes Minister* syndrome."

The *Dominion Sunday Times* also deduced some serious networking was underway as early as 1987.

"She works within the structures of the Party, building support and influence...the pattern of quietly and deliberately building an organisation around her can already be seen."

Helen Clark has been the engine room behind Labour's internal politics since 1993 (and in fact her influence extends much earlier given her place on the party's ruling council in the 80s). So what legacy has she given Labour? What fresh blood does she bring to the table through the networks she has set up?

Commentator and die-hard Labour man Chris Trotter argued two years ago that Labour was effectively now ruled by three groups under Clark's changes:[349]

The departure of its ideologically sophisticated activists left Labour profoundly vulnerable. It quickly became prey for a motley collection of identity politicians (gays, lesbians, ethnic and religious minorities), trade union time-servers and technocratic careerists...

...What does remain alive and well in the Labour Party is intolerance and repression. The splits to Left and Right have engendered a siege mentality that continues to focus the party's attention on the stultifying qualities of loyalty and obedience. Rebels and visionaries need not apply when it comes to choosing and ranking Labour candidates.

What leads to selection is a talent for representing (or winning patronage of) at least one of the three dominant Labour Party sectors: the affiliated trade unions, the Women's Council, and the gay and lesbian-dominated Rainbow Council.

As a couple of unsuccessful, non-union, heterosexual male candidates only half-joked after one selection meeting: "We'd have had a better chance if we'd got up on the stage and kissed each other!"

While Labour's MPs continue to be chosen by dogmatic second-wave feminists, gay and lesbian campaigners and ideologically inert trade union officials, there is little prospect of encountering the inspirational leadership needed among Labour's backbenchers.

Trotter's argument, whilst described as simplistic by Labour Party activist Jordan Carter,[350] nonetheless forced the latter to admit there was more than a little truth to the feminists, gays and union leaders claim:

"What is true is that many (but certainly not all) current party activists and

---

349 *Dominion Post*, 2 June 2006, "Chris Trotter column"
350 http://jtc.blogs.com/just_left/2006/06/the_call_of_the.html

prospective candidates are from the union, women's or rainbow sectors," said Carter. He disagreed however that these lobby groups were putting their own people and interests first:

"What is not true is that these are simply interest groups. In the Labour Party's sectors, the Labour Party and the broad social democratic programme come first. The "interest" comes second."

According to Carter, however, feminists, gays and unionists now "are" the Labour Party. That's what you are voting for because that's who the membership are:

"It's also worth noting that Trotter seems to romanticise the mass-based party which has, largely, passed away. The reason sectors in Labour have grown more active is because they are parts of social networks which people seem to enjoy spending time with. They are more real and relevant to people's political lives than sitting down with a dozen other people from your suburb in a conventional party branch."

It is Clark who has dominated Labour. It is Clark's core networks that now dominate candidate selection and policy development.

Eight years ago, commentator Colin James predicted what would happen if Clark's networks got their tentacles into the civil service – they would destroy it:

"This government came into office suspicious of a public service it saw as dedicated to a policy direction, established after 1984, which it wanted to "correct". The Treasury had, it worried, colonised much of the public service and those colonies would have to be neutralised or extirpated."[351]

As James points out, Labour's answer was to boot senior civil servants out of Cabinet meetings, and to appoint a new layer of politicized Ministerial advisers who would in effect run the show, reducing civil servants to "factotums, expected to run errands to order".

"Rewind to the late 1980s and Clark's tenure of the health portfolio," noted James in 2000. "Departmental director-general George Salmond retired in frustration as many decisions were made inside Clark's office, where Heather Simpson had Clark's ear and the department did not.

"Simpson is still Clark's chief adviser. Self-effacing, affable, very intelligent, intensely loyal, this one-time academic economist is a central figure in the Clark-Anderton administration. She has Clark's absolute trust. Her writ, which she exercises only in Clark's service, runs wide.

"Clark herself is very controlling, delegating only to ministers she fully trusts. This is a very centralised, top-down government. Senior public servants are having to earn its trust.

"Mistrust is not good for morale. Equally bad has been the high-profile attacks by Clark on salaries and 'waste'.

"The message to a bright high-flyer is to acquire a monkish disposition

---

351 http://www.colinjames.co.nz/management/Management_column_May_00.htm

and see labouring in the public's interest as reward in itself – or head for an Australian consultancy.

"Given that public servants are these days expected to carry the can when things go wrong, only the idealistic or the second-rate will be there a decade's time. Capacity for first-class policy development will not be there. It barely is now.

"For the moment this doesn't matter to the government. But after some time in office it will need new ideas, especially in social policy. For that it will need world-class analysis which overworked mates in ministers' offices will not be up to. There will be only the public service to turn to."

As this book has shown, Labour's core networks of "feminists, gays and union leaders" have indeed infiltrated the upper echelons of the public service – the rise of Karen Sewell (whose pedigree draws on all three groups) from principal of a failed ultra-liberal high school to Secretary of Education being a classic example.

It reinforces the existence of, and fulfillment, of the Socialist Action League agenda spelt out in the last chapter. So how did Clark manage to pull it off? By learning to bide her time, and hold her tongue.

Clues to Clark's approach again emerge in her 1984 interview where she says:[352]

"I think I deal with conflict reasonably well now. And I'm smarter at handling pressure. I won't engage if I don't feel like it."

Clark says she goes so far as not to listen to answerphone messages at night in case one of them is abusive or negative and "I'll lie awake thinking about it."

"When I get an abusive letter I fire it in the bin. I won't lose any sleep over it. I try to put a private area around myself, a *cordon sanitaire*, so that I have some space between myself and what's going on."

In charge of Clark's cordon sanitaire now is Heather Simpson.

One of seven children, born in 1953, Heather Madge Simpson grew up in the deep south, Waikiwi near Invercargill. She trained as an economist at Otago University, joining Labour in the early 80s and standing as a candidate for the southern seat of Awarua in the 1987 election. Back then, Simpson appeared to support the policies of Roger Douglas.[353]

"The Labour government in the past three years has been prepared to take many of the hard decisions which most people have known had to be taken but which previous governments have continually postponed," she said in one campaign interview.

It was during that campaign that she first appears to have met Helen Clark, and the pair very quickly struck up a friendship, with Clark hiring her as a personal assistant and policy advisor when she was elevated to cabinet in 1987.

352 *Head and Shoulders*
353 *National Business Review*, 23 September 1994, "Trusted lieutenant keeps low profile in Labour party"

According to former Labour colleagues, she quickly developed a reputation:[354] "That was when Simpson's reputation as The Groke[355] started. She was the gatekeeper hired to challenge the bureaucracy, fend off the lobbyists and fight for her minister. Many went unhappy from her door."

Simpson is notorious for refusing media interviews, and she hated being centre of attention when former cabinet minister John Tamihere outed her in 2005.

"The first and only time this reporter met Helen Clark's executive director Heather Simpson, she shooed him away with the warning, 'Oh no, oh no'," wrote journalist Graeme Peters nine years ago.[356] "It was a fitting introduction to a person famous among journalists as an avoider of the media spotlight. Despite her reputedly huge influence over the new Prime Minister, Ms Simpson won't return reporters' phone calls, give interviews or make herself available for photographs."

The *Dominion's* Helen Bain had similar problems.[357]

"Heather Simpson, Labour leader Helen Clark's executive director, is so determinedly low-profile that despite working in Parliament Buildings for the past three years, as Ms Simpson does, I have no idea what she even looks like…Parliamentary staff who have the advantage of having actually sighted her say she is ginger-haired and stocky, and her clothing was described rather uncharitably by one observer as 'utilitarian'."

Graeme Peters records that Simpson, even by 1999, had built "enormous, some would say undue, influence over the party, its leader and policies. She runs Clark's office and as such is the most senior person on Clark's four person management committee comprising spindoctor Mike Munro, troubleshooter Tony Timms and programme organizer Dot Kettle."

Carolyn "Dot" Kettle, then in her early to mid 30s and a former lawyer turned speechwriter for Helen Clark, reports to Simpson, said Peters. "Simpson is reputed to have written most of Labour's policy."

"They run that office like a university staffroom," one Labour colleague remarked of Clark and Simpson in 1999.[358]

The *Herald's* Audrey Young, in a profile written after the last election,[359] says Simpson "is much more than Clark's right-hand woman with her boss's total confidence and trust. She is her proxy."

With a relationship that close, Simpson's divergence into criminality with the pledge card overspend, and her interference in the Ministry for the

354 *Sunday Star-Times*, 22 October 2006, "The H-Bomb"
355 Look it up, I had to! "The Groke" is a character in Tove Jansson's "The Moomins", variously described: "The Groke is a very frightening creature. It moves very slowly but never seems to stop in that it pursues relentlessly whatever prey it has set its mind on… Whenever the creature is near, the air is chilled. Fires are quickly extinguished and everyone starts to feel their blood go cold", or like this: "Nobody is sure exactly what the groke is. She is a mysterious, solitary, hairy beast, who stands in the forest and howls".
356 *Evening Post*, 14 December 1999, "Helen Clark's inner circle"
357 *The Dominion*, 20 November 1999, "Powers behind the scenes"
358 Ibid
359 *NZ Herald*, 8 October 2005, "Clark's No.2 piecing together a government" http://www.nzherald.co.nz/section/1/story.cfm?c_id=1&ObjectID=10349268

Environment, raise serious questions about how much Clark knew and had secretly authorized.

"She also oversees policy development and strategic direction and regularly meets political advisers'" continues Young. "And where there's trouble in Government you'll find Simpson. Clark has the reputation of closely following ministers. She does that through Simpson. If there are major problem areas, say the Foreshore and Seabed court decision, or the spending at tertiary institutions, or III systems, or funding of wananga, she will take close interest.

"She knows of everything going through the Cabinet and attempts to remove the knotty problems at Cabinet committee stage. While she is held in awe by many in the party, one former colleague is reported as saying she likes people to be afraid of her, but doesn't respect anyone who is."

With Clark at the head of her team, it adds up to a seriously tight five. Munro's departure, now filled by press secretary Kathryn Street, means that three of Clark's closest advisors are gay. As are Clark's closest friends. Unwittingly joining the dots in Labour's Rainbow Connection, Graeme Peters identifies Margaret Wilson and Judith Tizard as "her two closest personal friends", adding that Tizard and Clark were flatmates together as well.

It is Clark's advisory team who screen all media and political flak, carefully ensuring that the Prime Minister is isolated from anything negative. Under the expert guidance of Mike Munro in the first two terms, the PM's team developed a list of journalists who they "trust" will ask the Prime Minister only soft questions, while other journalists are blacklisted, regarded as too "dangerous" to be allowed near the PM for interviews.

Likewise, when hard questions are being asked in Parliament's debating chamber, the Prime Minister is often noticeable by her absence.

All of this, a carefully stage-managed almost Presidential governmental style, has contributed to the Prime Minister's dream run in the opinion polls for most of her term, and her reputation as a leader "clearly in control".

But there are other allegiances at work within Labour – an almost united opposition to the idea of anything "higher" than Clark in the pecking order.

When Helen Clark's new cabinet was sworn in after her 1999 election win, a surprising new precedent was set: an almost total refusal by the Clark cabinet to swear allegiance on the Bible.[360]

"Only two of 25 MPs made ministers yesterday used the Bible to swear their oaths at Government House in Wellington," reported the *Herald*.

"The Alliance leader and Deputy Prime Minister, Jim Anderton, and Maori Affairs Minister Dover Samuels placed their right hand on the Bible to swear their oath of allegiance to the Queen, ending in the familiar phrase 'so help me God'.

---

360 *NZ Herald*, 11 December 1999, "Only two choose to swear on Bible"
http://www.nzherald.co.nz/section/1/story.cfm?c_id=1&objectid=105159

"All the others in the Labour-Alliance Coalition, including Prime Minister Helen Clark, solemnly affirmed their intent instead, without reference to God."

In other words, fewer than 10% of the incoming Labour cabinet acknowledged the existence of God, in a country where, at the time, more than 70% of citizens believed in God. One can debate the merits of belief in a different forum, but one can't deny that the cabinet's collective lack of belief played a substantial role in the Government's approach to its far-reaching social engineering agenda.

It is, if you like, an extension of the "Nanny State knows best" philosophy. The *Herald's* John Roughan touched on the dangers of an atheistic State in a *Herald* commentary last year.[361]

"Atheism, humanism, rationalism, call it what you like, is a conviction that offers nothing beyond the reach of human knowledge, when there plainly are such things…a politician who admitted he or she was an atheist…would be declaring a fearful conceit that no power is beyond them."

The feminist wing of the Labour Party, if it nurtured any notional religious beliefs at all, would be most closely allied to New Ageism and Wicca (witchcraft in the old tongue), and the Rainbow wing would be similar in outlook. There is no inherent barrier between trade unionism and Christianity – the latter having a strong social justice role and many older unionists remain strong in the faith. But with 30% of New Zealanders expressing New Age/Wicca beliefs, those people would find a natural home supporting Labour, which explains why, despite Labour's apparent godlessness comparative to its citizens, it still rates.

Much of Labour's policy, as you've now seen, has been inspired by its gay/feminist wings, and the "smash the family" agenda it inherited from the Goodger documents. If you want to see these networks in action, a good starting point is then-Governor General Dame Silvia Cartwright. It was she who, on 16 June 2002, became the first big gun to advocate a ban on smacking.[362]

"There is a contradiction in the way we look at the assault of another person, and the way we look at the physical discipline of children. It is unlawful to slap another person's face, but not unlawful to do the same to your child . . . We need candidly and honestly to search our souls about all acts of violence and the way we deal with each other . . .And we must examine our laws to see whether they are capable of delivering a society which is safe for all children."

Cartwright has no children, and raised a strawman argument – because few parents slap children's faces as a form of discipline. But it was emotive, and it created headlines, not least because Governors-General, being unelected figureheads, are supposed to stay out of the political arena.

361   *NZ Herald*, 13 January 2007, "John Roughan: Atheism scary in its sheer conceit"
362   Speech to the Save The Children AGM, 16 June 2002. The Alliance's Laila Harre had raised it earlier, but with little response.

As the first ripple in the pond, however, it soon spread.

One of Clark's pet issues, as you've seen, was how outraged she felt at having to get married. The very word, with all of its connotations of coupledom, was anathema to Clark back in 1981.

Little wonder perhaps that 20 years later, Labour under Clark rushed to implement the de-facto Property (Relationships) Act in 2001 giving effective marital status to any relationship, gay or straight, of three years' duration or more. Wedding rights without the wedding.[363]

Critics, however, were quick to note that the State was screwing around with people's domestic relationships, by automatically turning de-facto couples into married couples in the eyes of the law.

The irony that a woman who hated being "forced" to marry then went on to forcibly "marry" thousands of people in de-facto relationships is lost on Clark.

That "waving the magic wand" approach to the exercise of power appears inbuilt with the Prime Minister, who confesses she sees herself as a big-picture decision-maker:

"With the decisions being made, I don't want to be the one who implements them. I move onto the next thing. I like to see myself more as a decision-maker than as someone who works out the details."

Ironic, then, that Clark once decried such a dictatorial style.

"I've never believed in the magic wand theory of political change," she told the *Dominion Sunday Times* in 1987, "where your government came in and it somehow magically did everything you thought that it ought to. Life's never been like that and it never will."

Back in 1987, however, Clark was probably lamenting any chance of "magically" doing everything she wanted. She was, after all, a fringe-dweller in the halls of power and – some argue – a sellout to her socialist roots:

"Douglas bought Clark off," argues David Lange in his autobiography, *My Life*.[364] "She responded by putting her head down. I do not remember her buying into any fight we ever had in cabinet. She was by her own account a survivor: as long as her paddock had a good sole of grass the firestorm could consume the rest."

In Brian Edwards' book, Lange refers to Clark being promoted to Cabinet post 1987 because she had failed to rock the boat in the first term and thus, "got through quarantine". Lange paid tribute to Clark's ability to keep her agenda hidden.[365]

"We live in an age where instant gratification is deemed to be a political necessity, where the next public opinion poll is critical, where the three year

---

363 It was certainly an "agenda" issue for Clark. The possibility of exactly this law change had first been mooted by her associate Judith Tizard in 1995. The Dominion, 12 July 1995, "Outside the marriage cordon"
364 *My Life*, by David Lange, Penguin paperback, 2006, p253
365 *Helen*, p190

electoral cycle is where you either haemorrhage or triumph. And here we've got a woman who is almost Chinese in her approach to time.

"She actually has an agenda," added Lange in the 2001 interview. I don't know the detail of that agenda today. But it will be there. And it will still be maturing."

It's amazing what seven years can reveal in terms of agenda.

Elsewhere in his own book, Lange argues Clark protests too much about her gender being an issue.[366]

"Clark was a silent attendant at caucus. She has spoken of the troubles she faced as a woman in the caucus of those days but she did not help herself by her association with Anderton and his cohort, which made her an object of suspicion and resentment and added to the difficulties routinely met by women members."

The relationship between Clark and Labour's hard left that Lange raises is an interesting one. Clark's hackles raise at comparisons with communist philosophy, but she chose interesting friends and causes.

In Washington in the 80s, the future NZ Prime Minister's nickname was "Red Helen", a moniker earned not just from her anti-nuclear stance but also her decision to support the communist Government in Nicaragua in 1986. The then Labour Party president, Margaret Wilson, was also chairing Labour's Nicaragua Support Committee, and both she and Clark detoured to the communist nation to pick coffee beans in support of the regime, while en route to a meeting of the globalist group, Socialist International, in Peru.

In January 1987, Margaret Wilson visited Moscow in the company of Labour Party officials Tony and Alison Timms, and MP Fran Wilde. A *New Zealand Herald* report during the tour records Wilson as stressing "the importance of direct public contacts [between NZ and Soviet Russia], especially since the middle classes in New Zealand lack objective information and are heavily indoctrinated."

For some inexplicable reason, however, the Helen Clark publicity machine has turned her socialist leanings into another victim card to play. Brian Edwards spins it for her:

"Helen's association with Jim Anderton and the intellectual left of the Labour Party also provided ammunition to those who wished to disparage her. To them, she was a socialist, a friend of the Cubans and Russians, a communist. Fay [Clark's aunt] recalls listening to Parliament on the radio one day and hearing the Prime Minister, Rob Muldoon, refer to the Member for Mt Albert as a communist: 'And I was really upset, because I knew she wasn't a communist'," Fay told Edwards.

And in a *Salient* student newspaper profile in 2003, Clark was even retreating from the label "socialist":[367]

---

366 Ibid, p148
367 *Salient*, issue 22, 2003. Helen Clark profile by Michael Appleton

"We start talking about her early involvement in politics during her time at Auckland University, and I suggest that she probably would have been called a socialist back then. She frowns, for she's not a great fan of the s-word (perhaps because of its Soviet connotations), and says matter-of-factly: 'I think I've always been a social democrat'."

Which makes this report by New Zealand journalist Bernard Moran fascinating:

"When Filipino Intelligence officers raided an underground safe house in Manila on the night of March 24, 1988, they not only captured leading hard liners of the Communist Party of the Philippines New Peoples' Army, but also 97 computer discs.

"I have in my possession," continues Moran, "a photocopy of a three-page document from one of those discs. It is headed 'Workshop 1: Party to Party Relations, June 13, 1986'.

"It deals with overseas work and those who are in consultation with the International Department of the Communist Party of the Philippines (CPP). On page three, line eight, Helen Clark is listed as the 'individual link' for New Zealand."[368]

It could have been, and possibly was, some oik Filipino communist's fantasy list. Then again, maybe someone Clark had met in Nicaragua had punched her name in as a worthwhile member of the Vast Left Wing Conspiracy. Remember, Clark was not a major international player in 1986, although as we've seen she certainly was paranoid that the CIA was eavesdropping on her phone calls.[369]

But perhaps it was indeed more tangible than that. In the Brian Edwards book, Clark says she was in the Philippines prior to this period.[370]

"I chaired the Foreign Affairs and Defence select committees and I travelled quite widely. I mean, there was nothing to do at home... *I went to the Philippines to watch a general election*...I went to the Socialist International Congress in Peru in 1986."

Clark's trip to the Philippines is glossed over in one sentence, but clearly she met people, stayed with people and built her international network. The circumstantial evidence, then, appears to suggest Clark was a New Zealand contact point for the Filipino Communist Party. There is absolutely no doubt, despite her reticence however, that Clark is a one-world, socialist government gal. Her membership of international socialist organisations stretches back to the 1970s and appears to continue to the present.

Clark appears in a photo of the 1998 "leadership" of the so-called "Global Progress Commission" – a world government wing of Socialist International. The Global Progress Commission's mission statement – drafted with Helen

368 Cited in *Investigate*, November 2003 issue
369 *Auckland Star*, 16 September 1986, "Americans tap my phone"
370 *Helen*, p183

as one of its international advisers – has much to say on the need for world government.[371]

"Globalisation is an irreversible phenomenon of our time. We have entered a New Age based on the globilisation of the world economy, and the Left cannot approach this reality in a Spirit of rejection.

"Globalisation creates the possibility of opening up a new frontier of development, where old dogmas are no longer of any use."

Among "fundamental questions" that the Global Progress Commission hopes to provide answers to: "What can be expected from coordinating economic policies or from a world economic government?

"We do not want nationalist, populist, bloated States...the social legitimation of political power involves the role of the State with regard to citizens' welfare, educational opportunities, health, pensions and access to all the other social rights and public services – in short, social cohesion policies."

The GPC fervently believes the State, exemplified by a powerful parliament operating beneath a collective world government organisation, offers the best solution for public welfare and human progress.

"Civil society without effective political institutions creates a void which gives opportunities to the demagogues who promise to exclude the intermediaries like the parliament...or to lay the groundwork for what is called a people's democracy (or the saviour of a nation, which is even worse).

"Whenever the emotions of the people rock the ship of state, the political parties turn into a stabilising element and guarantor of [the State's] continuity."

It is, in effect, a not-so-secret society of international socialist leaders who each pledge to lend assistance and support to other members when their respective peasants get restless – assistance which even the Global Progress Commission admits is controversial.

"Because of our supporting political parties, we are accused of interfering in the internal affairs of other countries."

Another organisation with similar objectives is Parliamentarians for Global Action, also a vehicle for Clark's international aspirations. Labour MP and Deputy Speaker Ross Robertson served on the 15 member executive committee of the New York-based PGA, and Labour's Harry Duynhoven also has an official role. The PGA was formerly known as Parliamentarians for Global Law.

The Left, it seems, networks incredibly well. Certainly, there is good first hand evidence of 1980s Soviet communist infiltration of both the peace movement in New Zealand and the Labour Party, according to Moran and researcher Trevor Loudon.

The pair this year broke a major story that ran in Australia's *National*

---

371 The source documents were removed from the internet at some point after this issue was publicized in the November 03 issue of *Investigate*

Observer and here in *Investigate*.[372] This particular excerpt outlines how communist Russia used trade union leaders Jim Knox, Ken Douglas and others to reach deep inside New Zealand's political heart:

By late 1986, the NZ peace movement contained 367 disparate groups; this in a population of under 4 million. One thousand, or 20%, of NZ doctors belonged to the International Physicians for the Prevention of Nuclear War (IPPNW). Town councils voted to become nuclear free, erecting notices at their boundaries that one was entering a nuclear-free zone. By 1987, 70 percent of New Zealand's population was living in such zones.

New Zealand was heralded as a shining example to the world. Its homegrown peace movement had triumphed, and is still giving most New Zealanders a sense of pride in their non-aligned status. They have created their own destiny.

However, previously untold evidence indicates that the anti-nuclear movement served the strategic interests of the Soviet Union. New Zealand was specifically targeted in a clandestine political operation, designed to remove it from the Western Alliance.

In the late 1970s, policy makers in the International Department of the Soviet Communist Party, the CPSU, developed doctrine about exploiting what they termed the "correlation of forces" within a particular country to achieve a specific outcome. This implied expert direction of the "correlation."

A key force to be "correlated" was the New Zealand trade union movement. It would be helpful at this point to outline the changes that were occurring. Tony Neary (now deceased), the Irish leader of the Electrical Workers Union, chronicled the infiltration in a paper he gave at a conference in Washington DC, in March 1987, organized by Owen Harries under the auspices of the Hoover Institute.

Neary claimed that the Soviet Union – through one of its main front organizations, the World Federation of Trade Unions (WFTU) – had successfully infiltrated the New Zealand trade union movement and changed its direction.

He noted that until the mid-1970s, there was a good working relationship between the NZ Federation of Labour (equivalent to the ACTU) and the United States labor federation, the AFL-CIO. The change began in May 1979, when Jim Knox was elected FOL president and regular visits by NZ trade unionists to the Soviet Union and other Eastern bloc countries commenced.

By 1986, known Communists from the Moscow-aligned Socialist Unity Party (SUP) and the Maoist-leaning Workers Communist League (WCL), along with their sympathizers had considerable control in seven of the eight largest trades councils (branches of the FOL), covering 70 percent of the FOL membership.

Bill Andersen, president of the SUP and the Auckland Trades Council, attended the Twenty Seventh Congress of the Communist Party of the Soviet Union (CPSU) in March 1986.

---

372 *Investigate*, April 08, "Red Squares"

Joint communiqués signed by Jim Knox on behalf of the FOL and by the heads of visiting Soviet delegations had been adopted by delegates at the 1984 and 1985 FOL conferences.

Behind Jim Knox was Ken Douglas, the affable, competent and powerful general secretary of the FOL and chairman of the SUP. In 1986, he took two months "sick leave" in the Soviet Union. That year, Jim Knox also visited the Soviet Union where, according to the Soviet news agency TASS (February 22) he pledged to "pool efforts in the struggle to prevent a new war with which the imperialist states, above all the United States administration, threatened mankind." He also said: "Soviet peace initiatives are highly appreciated in New Zealand and are supported by broad sections of the population."

TASS (February 1985) quoted Knox as saying that "contacts between the trade unions of New Zealand and the USSR grow stronger from year to year. New Zealand trade unionists follow with interest the Soviet people's strides and come to see for themselves that the socialist system acts in the interests of the working people."

A vignette from that era, illustrates the relationship. Each year, the Soviet embassy in Wellington invited delegates from the FOL conference to an embassy function. During the 1986 conference, most delegates attended this reception. To emphasize the importance of the NZ-USSR relationship, Jim Knox at the conference warmly presented the Soviet delegates with large expensive sheepskin rugs.

The American guest from the AFL-CIO, received a small brown paper parcel. Knox from the rostrum told delegates that the parcel contained a book on New Zealand, but when the American visitor opened the paper, he found a small cheeseboard. The New Zealand *Herald* reported that "it was a case of hard cheese for the American delegate."[373]

Tony Neary had considerable public respect for his lonely struggle, but his criticisms of Soviet trade unions as mere appendages of the State were rejected within the FOL. He was regularly accused of seeing "Reds under the bed", to which he responded:

"In the New Zealand trade union movement, those who mutter about Reds under the beds must be joking. The Reds are already in the beds and have been there for some years. By now they are sitting up and getting breakfast brought in."[374]

The "Reds" were the Socialist Action League (Trotskyites) and the Socialist Unity Party.

TESTIMONY OF A FORMER SOVIET INTELLIGENCE OFFICER
Oleg Gordievsky, an officer of the Soviet security service, the KGB, was appointed in 1985, the resident designate at the Russian Embassy in London, responsible for intelligence gathering in Britain. From 1974, he had been working as a long-

---

373   Tim Donoghue, "Hard Cheese," NZ Herald, May 23, 1986, p.8
374   Anthony Neary and Jack Kelliher, *The Price of Principle,* Harlen Publishing, 1986, p.206

serving undercover agent for the British Secret Intelligence Service (MI6), until his formal defection in 1985.

He recalled: "KGB activity in Australasia was increased as the result of the election of David Lange's Labour government in New Zealand, on an anti-nuclear programme in 1984. The (KGB) Centre was jubilant at Lange's election.."[375]

Gordievsky visited New Zealand on four occasions from 1986 onwards to brief the Security Intelligence Service on Soviet clandestine activities in the region. For years, he said, New Zealand:[376]

"...had been under massive propaganda and ideological attack from the KGB and the (Soviet) Central Committee, and the ruling Labour Party had seemed unaware of the extent to which the fabric of their society was being damaged by subversion...

"In its attempts to draw New Zealand into nuclear-free activities, the Soviet authorities had made tremendous efforts to penetrate and strengthen the Labour Party, partly through the local Party of Socialist Unity (in effect the Communist Party of New Zealand) and partly through the Trades Union Congress."

Gordievsky alleged that the New Zealand and Australian communists were being run by the International Department of the CPSU. He said:[377]

"I know the situation in New Zealand very well; only 500 members of the Socialist Unity Party, but they are invaluable because each was ready to do something. It was like the KGB had 500 agents in the country."

Gordievsky added: "Plus some of them penetrated the trade unions, and then they penetrated the left wing of the NZ Labour Party."[378]

Their aspirations were spelt out in a Socialist Unity Party Auckland Regional Newsletter, dated 12th November, 1980.

"To date in the region the Peace Council[379] has made good progress among trade unions, but more effort must be made to build on this and take the peace question to the factory floor.

375 Christopher Andrew and Oleg Gordievsky, *KGB: The Inside Story of its Foreign Operations from Lenin to Gorbachev* (London: Hodder&Stoughton, 1990), p.513
376 Oleg Gordievsky, *Next Stop Execution: The Autobiography of Oleg Gordievsky* (London: MacMillan, 1995), pp.356-6
377 Gordievsky, quoted by Greg Ansley in the *New Zealand Herald*, 15th October 1990. (Ansley was quoting interviews that Gordievsky had given to Australian journalist James O'Brien, which had appeared in the *Melbourne Herald Sun* and *Brisbane Courier Mail*.)
378 Ibid
379 The "Peace Council" here refers to the New Zealand Peace Council for World Peace (NZCWP), the SUP-controlled affiliate of the Soviet-run World Peace Council. The NZCWP later became the Peace Council of Aotearoa/NZ. *Investigate* magazine clashed heavily with the Peace Council in early 2007 over its ongoing role in compromising news media through "the Media Peace Awards". These "awards" sponsored by the "Peace Foundation" provide money to journalists whose stories are most in line with Peace Foundation ideals. Sadly, the awards are entered by many mainstream media, including both TV channels, as well as *North & South, Metro* and the *Listener* and various newspapers. No journalist should be receiving money or an "award" merely for reflecting the worldview of the donor. It is an utter corruption of journalism and part of the reason mainstream media are utterly compromised on some major issues. Those who take part should hang their heads in shame. See http://www.thebriefingroom.com/archives/2007/08/the_rise_of_the.html

"Also needed now is to broaden the Peace Council into other areas of the community, join up prominent personalities including MPs, increase church involvement, university involvement, other peace groups, community clubs etc.

"Here branches and comrades can act as catalysts. We must be extremely careful that in building the Peace Council, it does not become overburdened with 'SUP' people, or be labeled as just another 'SUP' front.[380]

"If our Party is working correctly, only a few comrades, reporting back to the Region and Branches, and taking forward issues from the same sources, are necessary to ensure effective involvement in the Peace movement. The broadest possible base is needed if we are to make the Council effective."

In July 1980, Labour Party Council member and unionist Allan O'Neill, claimed that the Socialist Action League and Socialist Unity Party were infiltrating the Labour Party. "It appears to be a new tactic of these political organizations to get their members into the party, to incite from within and push their own political dogmas."

Other Labour figures made similar accusations, but nothing was done. By the early 1980s, the SUP had gained control of the Federation of Labour and most of the major unions in the engineering, dairy, hotel and transport industries.

These unions were affiliated to the Labour Party and enjoyed block voting rights at Party conferences. Every financial member of an affiliated union was counted as a member of the Labour Party. This gave affiliated unions thousands of votes each, which when coordinated guaranteed the SUP's ability to choose the Labour Party's president, executive, policy council – and to influence policy on that council.

Understandably, the SUP took advantage of this preferential system, so that through the mid to late 1980s, the majority of Labour Party senior officials were SUP sympathizers or secret members. The same infiltration was occurring at branch level, ensuring that the SUP became the leading power bloc in the Labour Party.

SUP members studying at the Lenin Institute in Moscow during the early 1980s were drilled extensively by their Russian tutors on the advantages to the Soviet Union that could accrue from the election of a Labour Government in New Zealand.

On the 6th June, 1984, SUP National Secretary George Jackson, addressed a meeting of the Party's Hamilton branch. He explained the rationale for

---

380 In what appears to be either another blatant piece of disinformation from Helen Clark, or evidence of incompetence as Labour's spokeswoman on peace issues (and few people would call Clark 'incompetent'), Clark told journalists during a visit to Masterton in 1987 there was no truth to suggestions of communist infiltration of the Peace Movement. "She said that among the thousands of supporters of peace there might be 'one or two' people with communist leanings". She added there was "no proof" of anything more. As an integral member of the Peace Movement, a member of Socialist International, and a leader who appears to have been a contact point for the Communist Party of the Philippines, I believe Clark must, again, have been lying to the news media. NZ Herald, 28 May 1987, "Libya 'variation on red scare'" supporting Labour in the upcoming national elections. According to a Party document, Jackson stated that:

"The Federation of Labour and Combined State Unions, later joined under the Council of Trade Unions banner, have more influence on the Labour Party than for many years. And the trade union structures have the ability to transform economic campaigns to political campaigns."

NEW ZEALAND ACTIVISTS TRAINED IN MOSCOW

We now come to the previously untold story of how the SUP was itself infiltrated by a humble truck driver, who was later selected to attend a specialist course at the Lenin Institute in Moscow.

John Van de Ven, a Dutch immigrant resembled the mythical tug boat captain, stocky, powerfully built, full of restless energy. He chain-smoked thin cigars.

In the late-1970s, Van de Ven worked as a tanker driver for Mobil and belonged to the Wellington Drivers' Union run by Ken Douglas. Van de Ven raced through his delivery rounds and received several warnings that his speed was upsetting the union's workplace rules. Undeterred, he raced on until called into the union office and forthrightly informed that if he didn't play by the rules, he would lose his union card and not drive trucks in Wellington again.

"I was mad at being treated like this," Van de Ven told the authors. "So I decided to get even. I had no firm plans, but I knew the union was run by the SUP and so I thought that if I can get in – then sometime down the track I'll get even. It was as simple as that."

Van de Ven went to the union and performed obeisance. He apologized for his misdemeanors and offered to assist with menial tasks, even hand out copies of the SUP newspaper, *Tribune*. After a year's probationary period as a model unionist, his talents were recognized. Drivers' Union official and senior SUP member, Richie Gillespie took him aside and said the union had big things planned for him, if he could prove himself.

Fortuitously in 1977, Van de Ven discovered a legitimate grievance over tyre safety issues on the tankers. When the company refused to make the changes, he led a prolonged strike that paralysed petrol supplies for weeks around the lower half of the North Island. Finally Mobil capitulated and conceded that the Drivers' Union, not the company, must have the final say on safety issues.

Ken Douglas, impressed with Van de Ven's leadership, personally invited him to join the SUP. In 1978, he joined the Porirua branch and studied Marxist-Leninist theory under a secret member (who was later appointed to senior positions in business). Within two years he took over the Porirua branch chairmanship and in 1981, was the SUP candidate for Porirua at the General Election.

Still on course to get even, he contacted the Security Intelligence Service (SIS), who asked him to stay in place. He was put on the payroll, assigned a handler and given the code name "Joe Martin".

Van de Ven's common sense and "street smart" talents were recognized with selection for further training in Moscow from 29th October, 1983 to February 12th, 1984. The course had been shortened because of the developing situation in New Zealand. He noted that their passports had to be surrendered and were not stamped so as to leave no record of being in the USSR.

He went with three other SUP members and one month later they were joined by Bill Andersen, George Jackson and Marilyn Tucker (all SUP Central Committee members).

"On arrival in Moscow," recalled Van de Ven, "we were quarantined for medical checks over four days and given new identities. I became John Van, Jim Thompson became Jimmy Brown, Allan Ware – Allan Wolf, Peter Devlin – Peter Jay."

"This took place in an old mansion near Moscow. The ten acres of woodland was surrounded by high walls so that nobody could look in or out. After that, we were transported in a mini bus with black-curtained windows to the Lenin Institute for Higher Learning in Prospect Leningradski, across the road from Metro Aeroport, an underground station."

"There were 3,500 communists from all over the world, being trained five and half days a week, according to the requirements of their home country. We were assigned three tutors who were specialists on New Zealand. They were a (first name unknown) Venediev, who lectured on the National Question (racial manipulation) and trade unions. He was also a staff member of the World Marxist Review. Other tutors included Bella Vorontsova (doctorate in history) and Eduard Nukhovich (doctorate in economics), both of whom visited New Zealand to liaise with SUP branches."

"Peace was high on the agenda. As one tutor told us: 'We have many clever people in the Soviet Union, but no one has even been able to come up with a weapon potentially as powerful as the Peace Movement.'"

Van de Ven was told that the reason for the "condensed" 13-week course was that Yuri Andropov had initiated a strategy for taking a social democratic country out of the Western Alliance, by utilizing the "correlation of forces" provided by the Peace Movement.

New Zealand was given a high priority by the Soviets, for its strategic propaganda potential. The Soviets prioritized countries according to their strategic interest. The UK, Chile, Argentina and South Africa were Category One. Tiny New Zealand was in Category Two – alongside the then Soviet client-state India.

The particular circumstances of New Zealand with a national election in late 1984, was seen as providing a suitable testing ground for this strategy. If it worked as intended, then the concept could be applied to countries like Denmark for example.

There were two key aims:
• To get rid of ANZUS
• For the Labour Government to steer through Parliament, Nuclear-Free legislation

Van de Ven described the techniques of the strategy as "brilliant", which when applied within the trade unions, the Peace Movement and the Labour Party, worked as intended. "Our role was to influence and steer the Peace Movement, not by taking the top jobs, but to be done in such a way that the top people in the various peace groups were seen as reasonably responsible by the average New Zealander."

"So our training consisted of being able to train lesser known communists, secret members, sympathizers and fellow travelers, to take over these groups, unite them, but never take the leading roles. My own role was as a 'nuts and bolts' technician."

The overall project director was Gennady Yannaev, an engineer by training and later a leading member of the 1991 coup that overthrew Mikhail Gorbachev. Van de Ven got on well with Yannaev, and was several times invited to his home for meals and drinks. He found Yannaev a dedicated and honest communist, who frequently vented his disgust at the corruption within the Nomenklatura. He was informally questioned about the other members of the New Zealand delegation and Bill Andersen and Ken Douglas.

In 1985, with the Labour Government in power, the SIS released John Van de Ven. A personable, talented man with considerable drive, he became successfully self-employed. Due to circumstances unrelated to his undercover work, he gassed himself in his car in April 1992.

If you listen to Helen Clark's version of events, she was instrumental with Margaret Wilson in getting the ANZUS alliance destroyed. Lange in his autobiography disputes that, claiming it was his decision. Either way, however, there is no doubting the power of grassroots political activism, possibly helped along by the Soviet Union, in getting the anti-nuclear issue addressed.

But while Clark may have considered herself "red" in Labour's traditional socialist fashion, traditional Marxists like Waikato's Philip Ferguson reckon Labour is a whiter shade of pale pink. "The Labour Party in NZ is now the party of capitalist modernisation," Ferguson posted in a Marxist newsgroup in 2002.

"This is why it pursues a fairly neo-liberal economic lie, combined with political correctness and 'respect for difference' as its ideology. It 'modernises' NZ by incorporating it more in the world economy, arguing for free trade and so on, while removing old, non-market barriers to discrimination in NZ (eg liberalising laws on homosexuality, being very politically correct in relation to race and so on) and thus tying into it a layer of career-women feminists and Maori, while working class women and working class Maori continue to languish at the bottom, oppressed not by formal discrimination but by the free play of the market.

"Thus when [commentator Paul] Harris talks of Labour being a coalition of unionists, feminists, Maori and progressive capitalists, this is one thing he is largely correct on. (He's mistaken when he throws in the poor and also not to mention that the Maori he is talking about are middle class).

"But what is significant about this coalition, is that it is overwhelmingly middle and upper class. The Labour feminists are all people like former governor-general Cath Tizard, current attorney-general Margaret Wilson, academics like Helen Clark, lawyers like Lianne Dalziel, etc etc etc. The Labour Maori big names are business managers. The Labour gay and transgender MPs are all solidly middle class as well.

"Indeed, it's interesting to see where someone like Helen Clark hangs out. Last week she was on the catwalk at the Wearable Art Awards, dressed up in some silly creation.

"Some other week, she is hanging out with the film industry set. Another week she is off mountain-climbing in Japan. Another week, she's making a wildlife doco in Canada. People like her are part of the artsy fartsy 'creative industry' set, and that's where they hang out. They have no organic connection at all to the working class.

"The largely parasitic artsy fartsy brigade (and the eejits who teach labour studies in universities) love Helen because she is the liberal middle class personified. She is them. There is not the faintest whiff of anything proletarian off her and her coterie atop the Labour Party."

Daphna Whitmore – another leading New Zealand Marxist writing in their newsletter, *The Spark,* in 2002, is also scathing of the Clark/Wilson power axis.

"What is there to distinguish Margaret Wilson and Helen Clark from any pro-imperialist leaders? Take their stance while at a social democratic convention in Peru in 1986. While the conference was on, over 300 political prisoners and prisoners of war were massacred. Clark and Wilson were the New Zealand Labour Party delegates. This gathering of Labour parties from around the world praised the social democratic president, Alan Garcia, for his 'handling of the situation'."

Damned if you do, damned if you don't. But don't be fooled into thinking that the fact that the really hard Left don't respect her makes Clark and her beliefs "harmless" in the grand scale of things.

The Power Of One

Sir Humphrey: "There are four words you have to work into a proposal if you want a Minister to accept it."
Sir Frank: "Quick, simple, popular, cheap. And equally there are four words to be included in a proposal if you want it thrown out."
Sir Humphrey: "Complicated, lengthy, expensive, controversial. And if you want to be really sure that the Minister doesn't accept it you must say the decision is 'courageous'".
Bernard: "And that's worse than controversial?"
Sir Humphrey: "(laughs) Controversial only means this will lose you votes, courageous means this will lose you the election."
– Yes Minister

HELEN CLARK'S FATHER, HOWEVER, WOULD undoubtedly be pleased that the hardline communists don't like his daughter. Whatever issues the young Helen Clark had with her parents, George Clark told journalists in 1989 when Helen became Deputy Prime Minister that "political differences have never caused any sparks in the Clark family".

George Clark, then 67, said he wasn't impressed that the media had tagged his daughter as "dull and boring".

"It simply isn't the case – she's led a varied and interesting life and anyone who talks to her will find out she's far from boring," he told the *Herald*. He did, however, suggest that his daughter still had some growing up to do:

"In my opinion, in life you should start off being a socialist and get more conservative as you get older."

When asked if he expected the Deputy Prime Minister to follow that path, his response was blunt: "Everybody changes."

The jury is still out on that one. Despite being a key player in the burgeoning student protest movement in the early 1970s, Clark "felt that I was beating my head against a brick wall. There was a certain gratuitous pressure in going out on large marches, but it wasn't going to change Government policy."

Flash forward to October 2003 and look at Helen Clark's response to the news that 40,000 New Zealanders had taken to the streets calling her a "dictator" on the GM issue:

"I've been on larger marches than that."

She used the same line to mock marchers against the Electoral Finance Bill.

In another ironic touch of Clark's ivory tower worldview, she added that GM protestors weren't listening to assurances from science that GM is safe:

"There's (a saying) 'none so deaf as those who do not want to hear'."

Little wonder then that a woman who quickly realised peaceful street marches were a waste of time when matched against the unbridled power of the New Zealand Government, now pays little attention herself to the will of the people.

Even so, the Prime Minister's "arrogance" – as the protestors label it – stands in sharp contrast to her feelings when she was just a backbench Labour MP in the Lange Government:

"You can become very callous when you exercise power," she wrote in *Head and Shoulders* in 1984, "and I have to check myself against that...In the end it's how the person in the street feels about you and your efforts that counts."

But what happens when you marry an "I know best" attitude to some of Helen Clark's other personal baggage? Back in 2000, just after Labour took power, journalist Bernard Moran foreshadowed some of what New Zealand was likely to see from the new Labour Government.

"Amending the Education Act to make sex education compulsory and remove parental rights to withdraw children from such classes. This is a follow on from the new health curriculum introduced this year, which affirms homosexuality and fails to address marriage in a substantial or positive way.

"In 1989, Helen Clark successfully introduced an amendment enabling female minors to have abortions with full confidentiality and without parental consent. In 1990, she achieved the repeal of the law forbidding access and instruction in contraceptives to under 16s."

Moran also suspected in 2000 that legalisation of prostitution was on the cards, a prediction finally realised in 2003.

Clark has mastered the manifestation of real power – by changing the system from within, irrevocably. And she has used her networks and supporters to do it, as an Act newsletter on the abolition of the Privy Council five years ago and Labour's takeover of the justice system pointed out.

"In cabinet Margaret Wilson has a paper to replace the present Deputy Commissioners on the Environment Court with her own political appointees. The Deputy Commissioners are appointed for five years and work with the Court to assist the judges.

"*The Letter* understands that the officials had recommended that most, if not all, the Deputy Commissioners be reappointed. But that does not fit with Margaret Wilson's plan to reshape the courts to her radical agenda.

"What sort of people will Wilson appoint? She has already appointed as a Deputy Commissioner a former Alliance candidate. Another appointment is a former Christchurch Labour city councillor who is costing the Court a fortune, as he cannot hear cases in Canterbury for conflict of interest reasons. Let's remember Joris de Bres was Margaret Wilson's personal choice, as was Ella Henry (the Human Rights Commissioner who thinks traffic tickets are issued because she is Maori), and triple-dipper Susan Bathgate.

"Margaret Wilson in her 'academic' writing has opined that the reason NZ has not become a true socialist state is because the Left has not replaced the "capitalist" legal structures. To achieve her vision of an Aotearoa Socialist Republic with the Treaty of Waitangi as the constitution, courts must be restructured and what better way than to replace the "colonial" Privy Council with a NZ Supreme Court – one where she and Helen Clark pick the judges."

Clark once remarked that she hadn't come this far "to be burnt out in a hail of gunfire". Loosely translated, she'll bide her time and when she's tough enough she'll strike back. Tolerance is a word to Clark, not a belief system.

As one of her friends indicated earlier in the book:

"You can see some of that manifesting now in the sense that her Prime Ministership has become almost dictatorial, almost paranoiac, she is so convinced that her path is the right one and the only one..so obsessed with making sure her plans are secure and cannot be derailed by anyone. She is absolutely driven in the changes she wants to make in our society, and nothing is going to stop her."

Another to pick up that vibe was *Salient's* Michael Appleton, in that 2003 interview:

For all she talks about tolerance, it is quite clear that she is a very intolerant person. She's intolerant of people who have different political views from hers, she's intolerant of ministers whom she perceives as incompetent, and she is intolerant of journalists who criticise her.

When I ask her what sort of leader she is, her reply illustrates the paradoxical way in which she likes tolerance as a philosophical concept, but not as a political practice. She says of herself: 'Firm, not afraid to lead on key issues. A front foot leader on issues. Leave people in no doubt about where you stand. Endeavour to deal with people fairly. Not tolerant of silly attacks or nonsense. Yeah, I think providing firm direction, a clear set of policies, signal what you're going to do, get out there and get on with it, matter-of-fact, no messing around. Pragmatic. Practical.'

Clark is broadly intolerant of anything that gets in her way politically. During the last election campaign, when Nicky Hager released his book *Seeds of Distrust* about the potential release of sweet corn contaminated with genetically-engineered material, Clark let rip at the Greens. 'I am sickened at the way these allegations have been levelled at me personally and at the Government and its officials in general. I am going to sing from the rooftops that this is a very dirty campaign where the Greens and their supporters have descended to the gutter of the National Party.'

When Corngate was brought back into the spotlight this month by a select committee inquiry, rather than debate the issue on the facts, she refused to testify in front of the committee, and instead got stuck into her opponents, accusing Jeanette Fitzsimons and Nick Smith of 'colluding' in an attempt to smear her good name. 'I sometimes wonder whether I'm a victim of my own success as a popular and competent Prime Minister.'

But vitriol is how Clark commonly responds when attacked. When TV3's John Campbell confronted her with the corn allegations during the election campaign, she was quick to turn on him. She called it 'despicable' and 'unethical' journalism, and referred to him as 'that little creep'. In March 2001, she called former National MP Wyatt Creech a 'scumbag' and a 'sleazeball' for having raised the issue of a potential conflict of interest involving Clark's husband. In July 2001, she labelled John Yelash a 'murderer' after he claimed her government had asked him to find 'dirt' on former Maori Affairs Minister Dover Samuels. Anyone – no matter whether they are attacking her from the left or the right – who has slightly different view to her on race relations is labelled a 'racist'. And, any ministers of hers who do anything slightly daft – Marian Hobbs or Dover Samuels, for example – get 'flicked', as she has so eloquently put it.

Indeed, while the Prime Minister might be trying to bring about a tolerant society, she is doing so in a way that bears all the hallmarks of intolerance: she is unwilling to debate her opponents on any great number of issues because she believes she holds the one and only acceptable view.

This might seem a rather tangential discussion: so, the Prime Minister is an intolerant person? So what? Well, scholars of leadership often speak of how well a leader's message 'fits' with their actions. That is, does the leader personify the message they are espousing? A good example of a leader embodying his message was Former US President John F Kennedy. JFK spoke a number of times about building a more tolerant society. So what did he do when Ban The Bomb protestors turned up outside the White House in 1962? He sent out coffee and doughnuts to help them through the rainy afternoon, and invited the protest leaders into the White House to discuss their concerns with him. Afterwards, he said his actions were driven by a belief that dissent and debate were healthy parts of the democratic process.

Can anyone imagine Clark acting similarly? Not likely, because doing so would actually imply that a decision she had made was in any way debatable, a view to which she is not willing to subscribe. She seldom bothers showing up to Parliament anymore (her attendance record this Parliamentary term is worse than any other prime Minister in living memory), and she tries valiantly to dodge any questions thrown her way during Question Time. All of which illustrates that she believes her decision-making is above debate.

And, sure enough, when protestors against the government's 'fart tax' turned up at Parliament recently, Clark didn't reach out *à la* JFK. Instead, she insulted their intelligence by saying, 'Government policy is based on substance, not hot air. It's [the protest] an ill wind that blows no good.'

Previous New Zealand governments have been turfed out when there has been a great difference between the rhetoric and the reality. The Fourth Labour Government was tossed out because, while David Lange said in 1987 that it was time for the country to have a cup of tea (that is, the costs to social cohesion outweighed the benefits of continued reforms), his government decided instead to just keep on going. The Bolger Government became breathtakingly unpopular in its first term because its caring rhetoric aimed at the elderly was not matched by action. And now, while Clark talks the talk of a tolerant society, not since Robert Muldoon has New Zealand had a leader so intolerant of anyone who questions her as Clark.

Clark's determination to change the world, one icon at a time, can be seen in her approach to a wide range of issues.

ON DEFENCE: Scrapping the strike power of the Air Force, for example, was an action that far exceeded her election mandate merely to cancel an order of US F16 fighter jets destined to replace the Skyhawks. It was also a fundamental constitutional change – a unilateral government action that affected the balance of the armed forces and their ability to respond to any threat, and it was done without any public consultation, and without any defence "white paper" analysis on how New Zealand could defend itself from, for example, a regional conventional conflict in Asia which might put Auckland and Sydney within strike range of hostile aircraft.

There was an implicit assumption that the United States might come to the rescue in any such conflict, but given the US performance in Iraq that shouldn't have been taken for granted on the grounds of either effectiveness or likelihood. Additionally, although Clark declared New Zealanders to be living in "a benign strategic environment", the events of 9/11 and Bali that followed, plus growing unrest in the Philippines and Indonesia, suggest stability in the region cannot be assumed as a given.

Ditching air defence without boosting surface to air missile defences (New Zealand effectively has none) still leaves the mainland vulnerable. At a tactical level, if New Zealand ground troops were deployed either locally or in Australia, a lack of air support would also leave them prone to hostile aircraft, particularly in the absence of a credible SAM capability.

This was, however, the same Helen Clark who two decades earlier had been a prominent anti-military protester, so there was a philosophical driving force behind the gutting of the Air Force strike wing.

That same philosophy has seen Labour courting the Chinese, there have been far more top level political and military visits by the Chinese to New Zealand than there have from the US or Britain.

At the same time, New Zealand's blue water navy has been reduced to fisheries patrol work, and whilst the Army has 105 LAV3 armoured personnel carriers they are more suited to civilian crowd control than serious military intervention, nor are they as versatile off-road as their predecessors.

ON OUR CULTURAL HERITAGE: The Clark administration wasted no time abolishing regal honours such as knighthoods, again without any attempt to gain consensus from the wider public. Coupled with the unconstitutional haste and shortcuts of due process in scrapping the rights of citizens to appeal to the Privy Council, it can be argued that the Government has breached constitutional conventions – no longer seeing itself as a caretaker of the country's traditions and mores, but as supreme ruler and judge of what New Zealanders are, and are not, allowed to value.

ON POLITICALLY-CORRECT THINKING: And it's permeating through the media and wider society. Take TV One's recent "scoop", just as this book was going to press, about National MPs Lockwood Smith and Maurice Williamson allegedly "not believing in climate change", as if it was now a hanging offence.

There is something dangerously Orwellian about "right-think" and forcing everyone to pretend they believe or suffer the consequences. Helen Clark's UN-backed agenda for introducing "Alliance of Civilisations" policies into schools, with government-approved "religious education" for all students, again screams "Thought Police".

People have a basic human right to their own beliefs and opinions. As Thomas Jefferson once said, "legitimate powers of government reach actions only, and not opinions".

Both fascist and socialist States last century tried to re-educate their populations to accept new belief systems. Look at the carnage that resulted.

I raise this not as a personal argument, but an academic one. A Government is representative of the people, but it can never truly speak for all the people. There are many who did not vote for Labour (around 60% of voters at the last election). Traditionally, there has been a difference between general policy and constitutional policy. No one argues that an elected Government can change general laws by virtue of a vote in Parliament. The bigger question is whether mere election gives a government greater power to tinker with the very fabric of the country.

The first radicals to try this in modern times were members of the Lange administration, but even then they did not assume and exercise the power Clark claims to herself. State asset sales, whilst highly controversial, still underwent due process via parliamentary debate and scrutiny. Scrapping the airforce strike wing, on the other hand, did not.

In an editorial on a proposed revamp of oaths and affirmations four years ago, the *Herald* expressed unease with Labour's "we know best" approach:[381]

"Quite simply, the dumping of traditional honours has deprived the awards of their ability to inspire, even though the dedication and service of the recipients is no less remarkable. The introduction of the New Zealand Order of Merit and, more recently, the axing of knighthoods have succeeded only in downgrading the recognition of our highest achievers. A significant loss, and no gain, has resulted from the removal of a vestige of our history.

"In its framing of the review of oaths and affirmations, the Government again finds problem with that past. 'Some of the oath provisions on the statute book ... use old-fashioned and unduly complex language,' says Justice Minister Phil Goff. Partly in that context, a Government working group will look at oaths taken by new citizens, public office holders and some state sector employees. But, more controversially, it will also consider whether the present oaths 'adequately reflect the values and beliefs important to New Zealand in the current age'.

"This should set alarm bells ringing. The Government is only too happy to nominate what it believes should be New Zealanders' values and beliefs – no matter what the public really thinks. There was never popular pressure to abolish knighthoods; they went because the Government deemed them to be a relic of the British class system. Likewise, there was no public mandate, and only a razor-thin parliamentary majority, for the scrapping of the Privy Council and establishment of a local Supreme Court. An overwhelming majority wanted a referendum on the issue. The Government deemed the country ready for its own highest court. Another vestige of the past disappeared.

"The Government denies, of course, that this all amounts to an imposition of republicanism by stealth. Yet the lack of popular endorsement for its policies leaves little room for interpretation."

When Helen Clark infamously tried to sit down before Queen Elizabeth at a state banquet, having also refused to allow Grace to be said for the nominal head of the Church of England,[382] it was Clark's personal baggage being played out in public, but without any recognition by Clark or Labour that just because they believe something and have a 51% majority does not give them a mandate to trample on the views of the other 49%. So much for tolerance.

Yet when the same Helen Clark can be seen wearing a Muslim hijab[383] – the antithesis of everything feminism stands for – you can see the chameleon emerge from the politician.

The decision by Labour and the Greens to ram the anti-smacking laws down parents' throats, changing generations of largely successful child-rearing simply

381   *NZ Herald*, 1 January 2004, "Editorial: Public must have say"
382   *NZ Herald*, 25 March 2002, "Poll shows, 'she who wears the pants'..."
http://www.nzherald.co.nz/section/1/story.cfm?c_id=1&objectid=1291509
383   *Investigate*, March 2007 issue

because the flower-power baby-boomers had a problem with authority figures, is another perfect example. More than 80% of the country are opposed to childless party leaders and university academics telling them how to raise kids. Karen Sewell, who now runs the Ministry of Education and who was an early advocate of anti-smacking laws, helped run one of New Zealand's worst high schools where the response to student discipline issues was simply to tell kids that school was largely optional: "if you don't want to be in class, don't come".

Imagine the reaction from Labour if the country treated its law changes the same way: "if you don't like the laws, don't obey them". No fault, no penalty.

The argument raised against smacking was allegedly one of equality – that if you can't smack a stranger on the street why should you be allowed to slap your child's leg? It was far too simplistic an analysis.

When police arrest people, they physically assault them in the process. They grab them, they cuff them, sometimes they hurt them – all of it far more painful and traumatic than a slap on the hand. Why does the State have the power to assault people in the process of enforcing order? Because at the end of the day, it has to.

Perhaps the most telling factor, however, are the crime statistics released just as this book was going to press. In 2007, violent crime committed by 10 to 13 year olds rose a whopping 30%, to more than 1,200 offences. Violent offences involving 14 to 16 year olds have risen by 47% since Labour came to power in 1999.

Sadly, all of these kids have received most or all of their educations under Labour party policies, and during a period of heavy advertising and promotion to abolish smacking as a form of discipline available to parents.

Individually, you can separate out any one of these "Nanny State" issues and possibly make a passable (I won't say compelling because I don't believe the merits are that good) argument in favour of reform in a particular area. But taken collectively, as repeated instances of "we know best" arrogance and in the face of widespread public disapproval in some instances, there's a growing suspicion that Labour has had a deliberate, creeping agenda for massive social reform in New Zealand, and that none of these things have happened by accident.

A government that considers itself above the law – even if it believes it has good motives – is a government out of control, especially in a country with such a fragile constitution as New Zealand.

"A Constitution is a human habitation," wrote a prominent New Zealand law professor 28 years ago. "Like a city, it may preserve its life and beauty through centuries of change. It may on the other hand become either a glorious ruin from which life has departed, or a dilapidated slum that no longer knows the great tradition of its builders."[384]

---

384 Professor R Q Quentin-Baxter, 1980, "The Governor General's Constitutional Discretions: an essay towards redefinition" (1980) 10 *Victoria University of Wellington Law Review*, 290.

Twenty-one years ago, Justice Minister Geoffrey Palmer warned in the second edition of his book, *Unbridled Power*, that there's a fine line between democracy and a benevolent dictatorship.

"A concentration of power in one group or one person always presents dangers.[385] ...The division between formal legal powers and the actual exercise of political power adds to the confusion. For example, no one doubts that Cabinet is a vital actor in our system of government. Yet it is almost unknown to the common law and to statute. In law, it is no more than an informal committee. It operates according to a series of conventions which the law does not enforce.[386]

"Constitutional changes should not be embarked on lightly. They concern the framework of rules within which the whole community must function. No rules are more fundamental than these; none of greater importance."[387]

Sir Geoffrey Palmer argued strongly in 1987 that scrutiny by an aggressive news media was important to keep governments on their toes.

"A key vehicle for public opinion acting as a check upon government is the news media. The ways in which news is reported, editorial opinion is expressed, television and radio current affairs programmes are handled all affect the capacity of the public to probe and question the decisions of government.

"The knowledge that such scrutiny will occur acts as a constraint upon the making of the decisions themselves. How potent a force the media can be in alerting public opinion to the actions of government depends on many factors. It is fair to say that while the media in New Zealand functions as a reporter of events, the capacity to probe and question is less highly developed. And the amount of probing which the media can do is shaped by how much the public is interested in the fruits of that sort of journalism. If people do not buy newspapers which undertake that task, or do not watch the television programmes which do it then less investigation will be undertaken."

But Palmer, even back in 1987 when the media had more staff and more competition, was concerned that journalists did not have the balls to really challenge strong political leaders.

"Certainly it cannot be asserted in New Zealand that the activities of the press and the electronic media have reached the stage where they can be regarded as the fourth estate of government, with a vital role in checking the power exerted by the government. Such a claim is often made for the press in the United States, and the history of that country is not short of examples to support such a claim. But any politician will tell you the media is important. Politicians have a love hate relationship with the media, which is reciprocal. There is tension in the relationship. But each needs the other.

---

385 *Unbridled Power*, Geoffrey Palmer, Oxford University Press (second ed.) 1987, p5
386 Ibid, p4
387 Ibid, p1

"How a group of senior politicians drawn from both sides of the house view the news media can be seen by examining the report of the *Standing Orders Committee of Parliament* which reported in July 1985:

" 'It is absolutely basic to the parliamentary system that the work of Parliament is done in public. The reporting of debates in the house is concentrated far too much on dramatic incidents, with little attention being paid to issues being debated and arguments being adduced. Press statements and speech notes are used as source material without analysis or balance. The reporting of select committees is even more inadequate. Many are not reported at all and there is a tendency to rely on written submissions only'.[388]

"One of the problems with our system of government," continued Palmer, "is that much of politics tends to be seen as theatre or entertainment. The media and the public tend to view it as a game and the politicians as players. Trivia and posturing often attract attention. Matters of substance are too often ignored by the media."[389]

Twenty years later, have things improved?

A growing concern in Western democracies has been the rise of "presidential" Prime Ministers.

"The charge has sometimes been made," writes Palmer, "in the United Kingdom and in New Zealand, that government by cabinet is in eclipse. What we have now, it is said, amounts to a presidential system with the Prime Minister as president. R H S Crossman described in 1963, a phenomenon he called prime ministerial government. Lord George-Brown's statement about why he resigned from Mr Harold Wilson's Cabinet in 1968 echoes the same theme: 'I resigned on a matter of fundamental principle, because it seemed to me that the Prime Minister was not only introducing a presidential system into the running of government that is wholly alien to the British constitutional system… but was so operating it that decisions were being taken over the heads and without the knowledge of ministers, and far too often outsiders and his entourage seemed to be almost the only effective 'Cabinet' '.[390]

"The ability of the Prime Minister to command media attention is a most important source of his or her power. Much of the Prime Minister's power will always depend upon personality and temperament… Cabinet government is based on teamwork – it is not and should never become presidential government," warned Palmer 21 years ago.

It is a symptom of "boiling frog syndrome" – where the water warms so slowly that the frog doesn't realize it is being cooked until it is too late – that we don't remember how much we have lost, until we look back.

In 1951, for example, it was accepted that just because New Zealand was

---

388 First report of the standing orders committee, July 1985. Appendix to the journals of the House 1984 to 1985, i.14, p11
389 *Unbridled Power*, p17
390 *Cabinet Studies: A Reader* by V Herman and J E Alt, London, 1975, p103

a civilized country, this did not mean a government could not become dangerous in the future. Legal commentator D J Riddiford argued strongly that New Zealand needed, "a necessary safeguard against a single assembly seizing excessive power, and against the further danger of an ambitious politician, through his dominance over his party, becoming a dictator. Lust for power being a fundamental human passion, the menace of despotism is always present."[391]

There is no doubting that Helen Clark is powerful, and that she has used her force of personality to achieve a range of policy developments, but recent polls have been sending Labour analysts an unmistakable message.

Coupled with the dishonesty and corruption of the political and legal system that many savvy observers are already noticing, and last year's revolt over the anti-smacking laws, Labour, the Greens, NZ First and United Future's decision to ram through the draconian Electoral Finance Act on Christmas Eve last year is shaping up as the issue that may cost Labour this election – the straw that finally broke the public's back in terms of tolerance.

Given what you're about to read in the next chapter, even Sir Humphrey might look at the EFA and say to Helen Clark with a wry smile, "That was *very* courageous, Prime Minister".

---

391 "A Reformed Second Chamber", D J Riddiford, 1951, 3 *Political Science* 23

The Rise Of Queen Helen

"You know the PM's motto: In defeat, malice; in victory, revenge."
– Yes Minister

AS NEW ZEALAND LURCHES TOWARD a crucial election, the impact of draconian new electoral laws is starting to be felt. Labour used a pamphleteering drop by seven members of the 7,000 strong Exclusive Brethren church in the 2005 election, as an excuse to draft high-impact gagging laws.

Critics will undoubtedly debate for years to come who the real target of the law was. The Prime Minister and her front bench repeatedly argued it was to stop people like the Brethren influencing elections. But the law as it was passed has no real effect on the Brethren. What it does impact is ordinary New Zealanders who, thanks to the unprecedented legislation, lost their automatic right to free speech for one year in every three.

The intent of the new law may have actually been to intimidate grass-roots critics of the government into silence.

So how has it all come to this? How, in the space of nine years, have we come to the point where laws similar to those in use in communist China have been introduced in the West? Although some other countries have electoral spending laws, none go so far as New Zealand, particularly in the area of restricting ordinary people's freedom of speech.

Part of the blame can be sheeted home to Governor-General Anand Satyanand, in my view. According to one distinguished constitutional expert, the New Zealand Governor-General still has the power to step in if a Prime Minister oversteps her boundaries:[392]

"The bond of mutual confidence between the Governor General and the Prime Minister requires that each should bring to the attention of the other any

---

392 Professor R. Quentin-Baxter, 'The Governor-General's Constitutional Discretion: An Essay Towards a Redefinition', 1980, 10 *Victoria University of Wellington Law Review* 314-315

circumstance which he believes may lead to a departure from constitutional principle, or to a situation of crisis or emergency; and each should inform the other of any development in his knowledge or assessment of the position. The Prime Minister has a duty to ensure the information available to the government is at the Governor General's disposal."

It is Professor Quentin-Baxter's next paragraph that I believe applies to the outrage of the Electoral Finance Act:

"If the Governor General is of the opinion that a course of action, proposed by the government and opposed by segments of public and Parliamentary opinion, raises a question of constitutional principle and is not merely a matter of policy to be determined from time to time by the government in power; that the proposed course of action was not, before the most recent general election, a normal or foreseeable consequence of the present government's assumption of office; and that these considerations are not outweighed by the present or pending emergency; he may so inform the prime Minister. In that case, it shall be the duty of the prime minister either to defer or modify the proposed course of action in conformity with the Governor General's opinion, or to tender his resignation, or to advise a dissolution of Parliament."

Based on that analysis, our current Governor-General had a legal duty to tell the Prime Minister she was making major constitutional changes without a mandate. Clark then had a duty to either defer, modify or resign. But that phone call was never made.

As Geoffrey Palmer commented on the Professor's conclusions,[393] "Appearance is important in convincing citizens of the integrity of their political institutions. The ultimate referee, when the chips are down, should not belong to one of the teams playing the game. In highly exceptional circumstances the Queen's representative can act as protector of the Constitution. We should strive to keep the office free from political controversy and appoint people who enjoy broad support throughout the community."

Another supposed check on Executive Power is the role of Parliament's Speaker. Thirty years ago, standards of accountability were ruthlessly enforced:[394]

Rt Hon We Rowling: can the Minister indicate whether the delay referred to was based on negligence or unwillingness to act?

Hon David Thomson: the right Honourable gentleman, can have his prurience satisfied in the report of the commission of enquiry.

Speaker: "Order!... I require, the Minister to withdraw his comment, because it infringes standing order 80, which states that answers shall not contain argument or controversial matter. All that is required of the Minister is to give the answer to the question. He will withdraw his last comment."

---

393 *Unbridled Power*, p32
394 *New Zealand Parliamentary Debates*, vol. 433, p3042

Now, contrast that 1970s demand for non-controversial answers with current practice, where the Speaker, Margaret Wilson, opts not to intervene when Ministers digress away from providing answers, into merely baiting:[395]

Simon Power: Can the Minister confirm that when Burton was transferred from hospital, following the amputation of his leg, he had already managed to obtain a knife and assault a guard as they were loading him into the van, and how does exposing the public to the risk of someone Mr Matthews describes as being "an extremely dangerous individual" on five 9-hour road trips fulfil the Department of Corrections' stated intention that he should be held "in the most secure facility available"?

Hon Phil Goff: Firstly, he was held in the most secure facility available. Secondly, unlike under a National Government—when the rate of escapes was six times higher than it currently is—when this Government keeps people in custody and transports those people, there is a far better chance that they will stay in custody than when there was the ludicrous situation whereby the National Government allowed people simply to walk away from prisons that sometimes did not even have fences around them.

Or perhaps this from Michael Cullen, who clearly even fails to address the question:

Hon Bill English (Deputy Leader—National) to the Minister of Finance: Does he agree with recent media reports that fixed 2-year mortgage rates are likely to exceed 10 percent?

Hon Dr Michael Cullen (Minister Of Finance): If we had a National Cabinet with Roger Douglas in it, I am sure that would be very likely. Luckily, the combination of the two together is a self-controlling prospect.

Hon Bill English: Does he agree with recent media reports that fixed 2-year mortgage rates are likely to exceed 10 percent?

Hon Dr Michael Cullen: My previous answer referred to a hypothetical future, which is unlikely to happen; I am sure, indeed, that it will not happen. The member, like many others, is referring to other possible hypothetical futures.

Nowhere, in that exchange, was the substance of English's question even addressed. Sir Geoffrey Palmer, in 1987, noted that standards had already fallen in the time that he had been in Parliament. Arguably, today's Cabinet divulge very little of substance via questioning in parliament, because they simply string out a series of dodgy answers until the opposition parties have used up the limited amount of questions they are allowed to ask.

"The way in which the speaker discharges the responsibilities of the office is an important influence on setting the standard of debate in regard to both its propriety and its relevance to the matter being discussed," Palmer argues.[396]

Failings of the existing checks and balances aside, I believe you can pinpoint the wider problem to a constitutional dilemma that has had considerable discussion behind the scenes, but almost none in the daily media. *Investigate* first raised it all the way back in February 2000 – the theory that New Zealand's current political system is, to put it bluntly, technically illegal.

Novel and crazy as it sounds, here's how the argument goes.

Constitutionally, New Zealand was clearly once a lawful British colony – a far-flung suburb of London governed ultimately by Westminster, acting via a colonial government. If you can imagine a picture of a tall tree, with the main trunk representing Great Britain, you'll follow what I am saying here. One of the major branches of this tree represents the New Zealand colonial government, elected by the Queen's subjects in New Zealand but ultimately getting its constitutional support and authority from the main trunk: Great Britain.

OK, so what happens when New Zealand declares itself independent from Britain? In legal terms, the colonial politicians sitting on New Zealand's tree branch begin sawing the branch off that they are perched on. At the moment they finally cut the ties to Britain, the branch drops to the ground, unsupported.

This is because, in constitutional law, the branch (New Zealand) is no longer connected to the tree (Britain). But here's where the problem arises. The New Zealand colonial government did not originally gain its absolute authority to rule from New Zealand voters, but from an Act of the British Parliament. It was the British Parliament who created a subordinate parliament for New Zealand. New Zealand voters could choose which politicians sat in it, but they could not choose to make a change in the parliamentary system itself. So, when the NZ politicians sawed off the tree branch they were sitting on by declaring independence in 1986, they lost their right to govern that very day.

In legal terms, the colonial government that finally severed ties with England had no legal powers to continue governing without an immediate fresh election, not just to let voters choose between one party and the other but, more substantially, to get voters to ratify the new constitutional position.

In New Zealand, this was not done at the time of independence from Britain, and has not been done since. Instead, the administration in power the day before independence was the same administration the day after, as if they had miraculously remained sitting in thin air, next to the tree trunk, whilst the branch supporting them crashed to the ground.

If the tree doesn't do it for you, try an electrical analogy. The New Zealand Government is a giant light bulb whose wires track back to a power supply

---

396 *Unbridled Power*, p122

in England. When the plug is pulled (independence) the lights go out for the Government. To plug the lights back in, the New Zealand Government and political system has to find another power source for its authority to govern – the people.

At the heart of the issue is the essence of independence. The British Crown cannot make a colonial *government* independent, it can only grant independence to the entire colony. It is then the responsibility of the entire colony to decide how it will handle its newfound independence, what political system it wants and so on. For example, the parliamentary system set up for colonial purposes might not be ideal for an independent nation. Independence is not a mere rubber stamp in a bureaucrat's journal – it is a fundamental shift, a constitutional earthquake if you like, that changes the entire power base of a nation.

In most countries – East Timor being a recent example in our neck of the woods – independence is marked by the lowering of the colonial flag, and then a referendum to ratify a new constitution. Such constitutions usually acknowledge the supreme sovereignty of the people, who then delegate certain powers to an elected government to exercise on their behalf.

This is actually a very important point. Such a constitution sets out in legal terms that the "people" call the shots, and "government" is their servant – not the other way around.

What happened in New Zealand's case was actually quite sinister, in constitutional terms. Instead of the New Zealand people gaining independence, the process was hijacked – the colonial government actually seized for itself the absolute power previously reserved to the British Crown.

One evening, the citizens went to bed acknowledging the King of England as sovereign, and the next morning they awoke to the news that the crown had passed to the Government in Wellington, without a vote. Suddenly, we all woke up with a new master: the Wellington political machine, unleashed for the first time, and hiding behind the mask of "the King of New Zealand".

Ostensibly, this feat happened in 1947, when New Zealand ratified the British Statute of Westminster Act from 1931 granting the colonies independence, but in truth the stunt was not finalized until the Lange administration introduced the Constitution Act of 1986, and the Imperial Laws Application Act of 1988. Arguably, 1986 is the year New Zealand finally became independent from Britain.

It was this constitutional sleight of hand, successful only because of the political ignorance of most New Zealand citizens, that has turned the New Zealand government into one of the world's most powerful, in terms of what it is allowed to do to its people.

Former Labour Prime Minister Sir Geoffrey Palmer – the man in fact responsible for the 1986 Constitution Act – laments in his book *Unbridled Power* the dangers of concentrating so much power in the hands of so few:

"A concentration of power in one group or one person always presents dangers," he writes[397], citing a passage from judicial icon William Blackstone in 1765:

"In all tyrannical governments, the supreme magistracy, all the right both of making and enforcing the laws is vested in one and the same man, or one and the same body of men; and wherever these two powers are united together, there can be no public liberty."[398]

In light of Labour's apparent control of the police force, there is room for cynicism here in NZ.

"In some other countries," continues Palmer, "notably the United States, people tend to regard government as a necessary evil, which should use and be invested with powers to the most limited extent possible. New Zealand, almost since its beginning, has never followed that view. To New Zealanders, the government is a friend. It does things for them which they want done. Governments in most countries look after things like law and order, taxation, the army, navy and air force. The New Zealand government does much more, as do countries which have developed a welfare state. With the demands which have been made upon government in New Zealand, it is hardly surprising that we are a highly regulated and much governed society. In recent years there has been a realisation that we went too far.[399]

"A British minister, Richard Crossman, once wrote: 'the modern state, with its huge units of organization, is inherently totalitarian, and its natural tendency is towards despotism. These tendencies can only be held in check if we are determined to build constitutional safeguards of freedom and personal responsibility'.[400]

Of course, in New Zealand the government wasted no time in scrapping some of those safeguards, once it had gained legislative independence. One of the first to go was New Zealand's Upper House, a low-rent equivalent of Britain's House of Lords. Most western democracies have a second chamber so that massive changes rammed through Parliament can be corrected or even vetoed if necessary. In the US, Congress must get its proposals past the Senate and past the Presidential veto as well. In Australia's federal system, Parliament likewise reports to a Senate. It is not a perfect system, but it is better than having absolute power hinge on a one vote majority in Parliament.

"New Zealand passes too many laws and passes them too quickly,"[401] acknowledges Palmer. "In 1977, B Manning, a respected American authority, wrote 'hyperlexis is America's national disease – the pathological condition

---

397 *Unbridled Power*, Geoffrey Palmer, Oxford University Press (second ed.) 1987, p5
398 *Commentaries on the Laws of England*, W Blackstone, reprint of 1st ed, London 1966, vol 1 p 142
399 Palmer, supra, p7
400 *Socialism and the New Despotism*, R H Crossman, London 1956, p24
401 Palmer, supra, p139, citing Manning, B, 'Hyperlexis: Our National Disease', 1977, 71 *Northwestern University Law Review* 767

caused by an overactive lawmaking gland'. But in no United States legislature, and there are 51 of them, is it so easy to pass statutes as in New Zealand. All but one of them have two houses; all have legal restrictions upon what they may pass laws about; *and in none* does strong party affiliation influence legislation to the extent it does in New Zealand.

"In all the countries mentioned the opportunities for holding up legislation are greater than in New Zealand as, with the exception of the State of Queensland and Nebraska, all have two houses in the legislatures. In all countries, the scrutiny is likely to last longer and be more searching than it is in New Zealand," warns Palmer.

Parliament's website actually reveals exactly how the New Zealand Government was granted independence, rather than the people, with this sequence of events[402]:

• In 1857 responsible government was consolidated and more than nominal independence from Britain achieved when the British Parliament passed the New Zealand Constitution Amendment Act. This gave the New Zealand Parliament authority to amend all but a few entrenched sections of the New Zealand Constitution Act 1852.

• Although the change in the designation of New Zealand – from the "Colony of New Zealand" to the *Dominion* of New Zealand" – took effect on 26 September, 1907, complete autonomy in New Zealand's foreign affairs was not obtained.

• The Governor-General continued to: be appointed by Britain; act as both representative of the British Government as well as the sole official representative of New Zealand views to the Imperial government; be the only person to hold the official coding ciphers; exercise sole discretion over which material and despatches were to be passed to the New Zealand government.

• New Zealand acquired the right to conduct its own international trade negotiations independently of Britain in 1923. It exercised this right for the first time in 1928, when it signed a trade treaty with Japan.

• Before the Statute of Westminster Act 1931 – and arguably until the New Zealand Parliament passed the Statute of Westminster Adoption Act in 1947 – the New Zealand Parliament was not a sovereign parliament, it did not have the capacity to make all law, (such as legislating extra-territorially), and there were some laws that it could not unmake.

• Full New Zealand sovereignty can be dated to 1947 – both in terms of gaining formal legal control over the conduct of its foreign policy and the attainment of constitutional and plenary powers by its legislature.

• In passing the Constitution Act 1986 (effective 1 January 1987), New Zealand "unilaterally revoked all residual United Kingdom legislative power."

---

402 http://www.parliament.nz/en-NZ/PubRes/Research/Papers/9/1/8/00PLLawRP07041-New-Zealand-sovereignty-1857-1907-1947-or-1987.htm

New Zealand, as of 1987, is a free-standing constitutional monarchy whose parliament has unlimited sovereign power.

King Charles I was the last British monarch to enjoy "unlimited sovereign power", yet by some freak constitutional powerplay New Zealand's politicians have managed to channel the ghost of Charles I, by giving themselves the same unlimited power the former monarch had.

Because of Helen Clark's supreme position at the top of the political food chain, whilst in office she executes what the New Zealand Government's own website acknowledges is "unlimited sovereign power". Critics challenging the title of my book should be realizing the errors of their assumptions by now.

As you can see from the bullet points above, none of this happened in a vacuum. It happened incrementally, each a small step that did not alarm the natives (you and I). Had the NZ Government tried to do all of it at once the public would have recognized it as the declaration of independence it clearly was, with all of the legal implications. Instead, by making a small change here and a small change there, New Zealand's unwritten constitution underwent death by a thousand cuts, and with it the rights of the people.

Nor am I a lone voice. In an analysis of the incredible powers another strong Prime Minister, Rob Muldoon, gave himself, Victoria University's Deborah Shelton came to the view in 1980 that an "alarming" chasm was opening up between what governments were allowed to do in theory, and what they were actually doing in practice.[403]

"The conclusion that cannot be avoided is that the coherence of the constitution is breaking down. There are two possible responses to this collapse of coherence; either to allow the gap between theory and practice to widen even further, paying lip service to the theory when it is convenient, or, as has become more frequent, repudiating the theory because of the divergence in theory and practice.

"The other alternative is to formulate a constitutional theory and practice that reflects the expectations and understandings of New Zealand society and government and that attempts to control these new powers of the executive through the democratic process."

But such misbehavior is a natural outcome of such a political coup.

To understand my point, look again at the revolution that tipped King Charles Stuart I out of power. The British parliament of the day, representing the wealthy landowners and barons whose tithes kept the King afloat, were getting sick of the King's actions of absolute power against them. When push came to shove, the Parliament, essentially representing the wider British people, claimed sovereignty itself and executed the King – after a bitter civil war.

This was as close as you were going to get in late Middle Ages Britain to

---

403 "Government, the Economy and the Constitution" by Deborah Shelton, unpublished LL.M. thesis, 1980, cited at *Unbridled Power*, p166

a referendum. When Parliament later agreed to re-establish the monarchy under Charles II, it was on Parliament's terms, not the new King's.

So *Britain's* parliamentary system has a clear public mandate, via revolution, from the British people. Where is the clear public mandate for a continuation of the colonial political system in New Zealand, manifested in the absolute power of the New Zealand parliament?

We might not have wanted our government to have "unlimited sovereign power". Just because the British people gave their parliament tough powers doesn't automatically mean the NZ people are subject to the same conditions.

Can anybody explain how it is that the British people (the authentic constitutional root of parliament's power in the UK) can grant "independence" to New Zealand, but essentially dictate the terms by giving the New Zealand government even greater powers over its people than the British government has? In a real sense, the British parliament did not grant the New Zealand *people* "independence" at all, but merely set up a new monarchy in New Zealand (hence the need for niceties like the Royal Titles Act referred to earlier), with "unlimited sovereign power", and none of the protections for citizens enjoyed by most modern democracies.

Helen Clark has jokingly been referred to as "Queen Helen". In truth, she actually is. She has more power than Queen Elizabeth or George Bush have in their own countries – her powers cannot in fact be constrained by the NZ public short of a civil rebellion – unless she and her government voluntarily "assent" to be bound by a referendum. She is the power behind the facade throne of the New Zealand monarchy – Elizabeth II may be monarch in title, but the NZ Prime Minister is monarch in fact.

Twenty-nine years ago, Court of Appeal president Sir Owen Woodhouse made a similar kind of comment, openly comparing New Zealand prime ministers to "the Stuart Royal executive":

"Within a few decades there has been a major movement in the distribution of state power, in favour of the Executive and at the expense of Parliament... As a matter of historical interest, all this may be compared with the effective powers of the Stuart Royal executive.... the nebulous conventions presently relied upon in this country to protect the basic rights of individuals and control an abuse of power are outside the function of the judiciary and have no support other than goodwill and trust."[404]

The scrapping of the Privy Council and the introduction of the Electoral Finance Act show that "goodwill and trust" are useless against a rogue Prime Minister.

When have the New Zealand people ever had a proper vote on what kind of political system they want? The politicians argue that by having elections every three years, they removed the need for an independent referendum on

404 "Government Under the Law", Owen Woodhouse, the 1979 J. C. Beaglehole Memorial Lecture, *Council Brief* (Nov. 79) p8

the political system. But when you look at that claim more closely, you begin to see its weaknesses.

The election we have every three years is limited in scope. You can choose between Tweedle-dum and Tweedle-Dee, but you have no say in the rules that define how these people get elected. You have no ability, for example, to prevent the government from making sweeping constitutional changes without a public referendum. That's because our "unwritten constitution" does not give you that power.

Yet, if a vote had taken place in 1986, when we finally became independent, it might have been a check and balance that voters supported as part of a new constitutional framework. Instead, Labour, NZ First, the Greens and United Future (Peter Dunne's volte-face – choosing to vote against the Electoral Finance Act on its final reading – was a cynical stunt, in my view, allowing United Future to have appeared to listen to public anger, yet rest comfortably knowing the Bill would pass) have railroaded the rights of ordinary voters to speak out in election year.

In hindsight, these are the kinds of messes that independence and constitutional referendums are designed to clean up – they set the rules moving forward. In New Zealand, voters were never given that chance.

It is the abuse of this power that has led directly to the kind of governments New Zealand has suffered since the mid 1970s, and the political crisis our country now finds itself in.

Queen Elizabeth is used as a kind of political glove-puppet by the New Zealand Government – dragged out here every so often to engender warm fuzzies among her loyal subjects who don't realize how dangerously powerful Her Majesty's Government has actually become.

Of course, like much of *Investigate* magazine's work as a journalistic canary down the political mineshaft, many of our colleagues in the mainstream media simply looked blankly at us when we broke this constitutional crisis story in February 2000, only three months into Helen Clark's reign. The media simply didn't, or couldn't, understand the significance of the story.

Internationally, it was different. WorldNetDaily – one of the top-ranked news sites in the world -gave it a front page lead on its website, causing a massive traffic spike on the *Investigate* site. The reason they paid attention was because the same Mickey Mouse constitutional process had been used for Australia and Canada – none of the big-3 former British colonies arguably had a valid government.

All three had been granted "independence" from Britain by what New Zealand constitutional lawyer Philip Joseph describes as "an ongoing gift". We are the only three countries in the entire world to have utilized the process.

"Unlike all the other more newly emerged Commonwealth countries which have become sovereign," argues Joseph, "these three old colonies acquired full powers of legal continuity through an ongoing gift of legal powers from Westminster to the countries concerned."

Except, of course, for one rather major sticking point: You can cut the ties strand by strand in a long slow process if you like, but the day you cut the final strand is still the day the Parliament in power ceases to be valid and the lights go out.

By definition, there can be no other outcome if you are being given true independence.

To his credit, Philip Joseph admits that although his views are shared by mainstream constitutional lawyers in New Zealand, their views may be proven wrong at the end of the day. The reason for the long slow process, he told *Investigate*, was that it allowed Westminster to grant independence in a "gentle" fashion.

"It never properly tells us when we exactly became an independent sovereign nation," Professor Joseph says, "and insofar as we trace our powers through this continuity line back to Westminster yes, it is a problem."

Mark that admission on your calendar – Joseph is widely regarded as one of *the* top experts in the field.

Tony Angelo, a constitutional law expert at Wellington's Victoria University, wondered whether the colonial government would have had the power to protect its own claim to sovereignty with some kind of transitional mechanism.

"If you wanted to argue the case, you'd say that on that date [of final independence], when the cut-off comes, that there has been an implicit affirmation or reaffirmation of certain rules as the laws of this 'newly independent state'."

Overseas constitutional writers don't buy the argument. Australian Ian Henke, for example, told the magazine that John Howard's government slipped a special question into its major referendum on whether Australia should become a republic in 1999.

There were only two questions in the referendum: the first asked whether Australia should become a republic. The second is slam-dunk proof that the Australian politicians were aware their parliamentary system is technically illegal. Specifically, that second question asked Australian voters to ratify a new preamble to the *existing* Australian constitution. The new preamble would have read: "*We the Australian people commit ourselves to this Constitution*".

Those who have followed the past few pages will instantly see the significance of this. John Howard wanted voters to ratify and approve Australia's *existing* (illegal) constitution, which would then have given legitimacy to the parliamentary system. The Australian government recognised (but did not and has not admitted so publicly) that "the ongoing gift" from Britain was illegal. There is no other reason for getting voters to agree that "we the… people commit ourselves" to the Constitution.

If some kind of magic "affirmation" of powers from Britain to the Australian federal government had been valid, the referendum question would have been unnecessary.

However, because Australians did not like the form of the republic being offered to them – the President of Australia would have been "appointed" by Parliament's existing politicians, not elected by the people – they voted "No" to both questions.

But doesn't a government have the lawful authority, while it is becoming independent, to simply ignore its population and say, 'We know what's best because we're the Government'?

It is certainly a line that has been used repeatedly by Prime Minister Helen Clark, who once famously declared that her government would never be dictated to by referenda; loosely translated, this means "we don't give a hoot what the public say".

Ian Henke rejects the "Government knows best" excuse.

"Of course not, because 'lawful authority' in independence, comes from the people. It is the only place lawful authority can come from."

Canterbury University's Philip Joseph agrees, saying the Government cannot claim a constitutional mandate simply because it was voted in during an election.

"That's too mechanistic, in a sense. You've actually got to go back to the fundamentals: what gives them the right to be there to begin with, to actually put policies to the people?"

Although this interview with Joseph ran eight years ago, right at the start of the Helen Clark years, the scandal surrounding the passing of the Electoral Finance Act at Christmas 2007 illustrates the dangers of letting a rogue government go unchallenged on seemingly minor points. As the old saying goes, "give 'em an inch and they'll take a mile!".

A constitutionally unlawful government, which has no mandate to make major constitutional changes, goes on to ban free speech for one year out of every three in the face of massive public opposition, giving New Zealand the most draconian gagging laws in the Western world and trying to embed a political system that makes it harder for voters to get rid of the existing politicians. The same constitutionally unlawful government also wants to create taxpayer funding of existing political parties, if it wins this year's election.

Think how different New Zealand might be today if this issue of the Clark government's legitimacy had been nipped in the bud way back in 2000?

During our 2000 interview with Philip Joseph, he acknowledged the extremely serious implications of our questions: that what we were challenging was not whether a particular law was constitutional or not (which has been ruled on many times in the past), but a much bigger challenge: if the entire legal and political system has not been lawfully constituted, no national court can possibly rule on it. It becomes an issue only the people can ratify.

"I take your point on what you are saying," says Joseph, "and at this point you do step beyond the 'safe' parameters of constitutional analysis.

You are actually asking now: what are the bases of a people, of a state, of a constitution?"

As *Investigate* magazine reported in 2000, leading British constitutional law expert, Professor D P O'Connell, argues that transfers of sovereignty *must* be marked by a break in legal continuity. Which never happened in New Zealand or, for that matter, Australia, which had also enacted constitutional change with its 1986 Australia Acts, ending Britain's ability to pass laws for Australia.

As if on cue, a year after our publication, Australian constitutional scholar Anthony Dillon presented an academic discussion paper[405] for lawyers and judges, now posted on Australia's federal court website. He, too, identifies a matter of hot debate across the Tasman – whether the Australia Acts of 1986 were a declaration of independence, and if so where sovereignty should lie – with the people or with Parliament?

"If one adopts the view that the Australia Acts created a void[406] in constitutional authority, it might well be necessary to discern an 'alternative'… local legal constitutional source.[407] After all, it is recognised that our legal system (and arguably constitution) must have a legal *fons et origo* (source and origin). However, popular sovereignty [vested in the people] is only one possibility, it is not the 'default setting'," argues Dillon.

"Others include authority derived from a divine being, or from the State itself, or from indigenous-non-indigenous reconciliation…"[408]

There are some deeply troubling claims in there – particularly the idea that sovereignty can pass from one master to another, British parliament to NZ or Australian parliament, bypassing the people entirely. Should sovereignty ever vest in "the State"? George Orwell's Big Brother was an example of State power gone rogue.

Dillon takes a closer look at the popular sovereignty argument in Australia:

"In spite of the Australia Acts' limited mandate, many sponsors of popular sovereignty have cited their passage as the decisive and defining moment for the ascendancy of popular sovereignty and the acquisition of autochthony [pronounced *or-tok-thonnee*, it means "true independence"]. Mason CJ [chief justice Sir Anthony]] in *ACTV* was emphatic that 'the Australia Act 1986 (UK) marked the end of the legal sovereignty of the Imperial Parliament *and* recognised that ultimate sovereignty resided in the Australian people'.[409]

"On one level it is difficult to dispute the first proposition of Mason CJ's statement. However, does it necessarily follow that the beneficiary of this relinquishing of sovereign power is the Australian populace and not the

405 http://www.austlii.edu.au/au/journals/FedLRev/2001/10.html
406 http://www.austlii.edu.au/au/journals/FedLRev/2001/10.html#fn39
407 http://www.austlii.edu.au/au/journals/FedLRev/2001/10.html#fn40
408 http://www.austlii.edu.au/au/journals/FedLRev/2001/10.html#fn41
409 http://www.austlii.edu.au/au/journals/FedLRev/2001/10.html#fn52

Australian parliaments? Where is it recognised that this redistribution of Westminster sovereignty should become the property of, and 'embedded in'[410] the Australian people?"

Noting that the Australia Acts make no reference to the people of Australia, Dillon tends to the view that the Australian Parliament had the power to assume sovereignty for itself, without asking the public first.

"....Daley has argued, '[t]o the extent that British parliamentary sovereignty impaired popular sovereignty before 1986, s 15 of the Australia Acts appears to have transferred that power not to the people, but to the Commonwealth parliament'.[411]"

This, naturally, is the default position we find ourselves in here in New Zealand. That the 1986 Constitution Act effectively declared independence from Britain, but that power was seized at that precise moment by the Lange Labour government, aided and abetted by the Bolger-led National opposition which did not truly understand the legal significance of what was taking place, and arguably would have supported the entrenching of political sovereignty anyway.

In both Canberra and Wellington in 1986, the two Labour parliaments were sailing into uncharted waters in the most audacious expedition of political piracy ever carried out in the British Commonwealth. For all of their banana-republic appearance, the Fiji coups have nothing on this.

Describing the myth of "continuing sovereignty" as "suspect" and "divorced from reality", Dillon adds, "As Marshall has noted: '[W]e are operating at the untested limits of the traditional doctrine'.[412]"

Now *that's* an understatement!

"According to the strict view," continues Dillon, "to achieve autochthony [true independence], nothing less than a contrived *break in legal continuity* will suffice.[413] This is usually undertaken by adopting new constitutional arrangements in a manner unauthorised by the pre-existing constitution. When an offspring initiates such a break (no matter what view the traditional theory takes of the parent's powers), such action may prove to be legally decisive. This is because the offspring has repudiated the very source of its autonomy. A revolutionary shift...occurs and the validity of the new constitutional order cannot be traced by a 'stream of authority' back to the parent."

All of which reinforces the points made by *Investigate's* article eight years ago. A constitutional change is an earthquake, not a rubber stamp by a bureaucrat and a prime minister.

Dillon adds weight to the belief that New Zealand became independent as recently as 1986.

---

410   http://www.austlii.edu.au/au/journals/FedLRev/2001/10.html#fn53
411   http://www.austlii.edu.au/au/journals/FedLRev/2001/10.html#fn67
412   http://www.austlii.edu.au/au/journals/FedLRev/2001/10.html#fn91
413   http://www.austlii.edu.au/au/journals/FedLRev/2001/10.html#fn114

"So too, some New Zealand commentators (but especially F M Brookfield) have been able to discern a discontinuity by 'disguised revolution' in New Zealand's 1986 independence arrangements."

So there appears little doubt that New Zealand became independent in a "disguised revolution" only 22 years ago, but with no referendum. No one asked the public's permission.

In sharp contrast, Anthony Dillon argues there needs to be a future referendum in Australia to clean up that country's constitutional shambles.

"If Australians were of a mind to institute a 'technical' break in legal continuity, the following course might be undertaken. James Thomson cites Geoffrey Sawer as suggesting:[414] 'Perhaps the best way of dealing with this is to put to the people as a constitutional amendment a declaratory provision stating that the sovereignty of the United Kingdom Parliament ends on a named future date *and* is replaced by that of the Australian people.'

"This sort of proposal has a great deal to commend it. Had such a proposal been put to the people and accepted to take effect from 3 March 1986, the constitutional arrangements of Australia (in respect of *grundnorm* and autochthony issues) might no longer be in such hot academic debate. In the end, however, the *Australia Acts* alone could only achieve so much. By section 1 [of the Australia Acts] the sovereignty of the United Kingdom Parliament was brought to an end, thereby fulfilling the first proposition of Professor Sawer's proposal ... Moreover, the failure to invest legal sovereignty democratically in the Australian people makes contestable the identity of the true beneficiary of the power formerly exercised by the United Kingdom Parliament."

I want to interrupt here. Note that last comment well – Britain's failure to expressly vest sovereignty in the people is what allowed the New Zealand and Australian Parliaments to seize it. Dillon, however, still has hope of a democratic solution:

"However, this does not mean that Australia cannot adopt such a course even today. A plebiscite (then referendum) question could include a declaratory provision similar to that suggested by Professor Sawer, along with a Constitution Alteration Bill for Australia to become a republic. The declaratory provision should assert that 'all the prerogatives of the Crown and the sovereignty of the Queen are transferred to the people'.[415]"

In other words, Dillon recognises that only a popular vote can ratify what has been done.

Hopefully, if you were labouring under any false illusions that New Zealand's constitutional crisis was an *Investigate* "beat-up" (as the Prime Minister is fond of calling our stories in the hope of throwing the public off the scent), the testimony from leading constitutional experts on both sides of the Tasman has put paid to any doubts. If you take nothing else away from

---

414 http://www.austlii.edu.au/au/journals/FedLRev/2001/10.html#fn132
415 http://www.austlii.edu.au/au/journals/FedLRev/2001/10.html#fn133

this book, at least go away with the realisation that the absolute power of the Helen Clark years was exercised illegally, and both Clark and Attorney-General Margaret Wilson knew as early as mid-2000 the full extent of their problem.

Every rogue law enacted by the Clark government against the wishes of the public over the past nine years is a further case of the Prime Minister rubbing voters' noses in her power.

In early 2001, *Investigate* published its final major story on New Zealand's constitutional crisis, because we'd reached the limits of trying to get a sensible response out of the government:

Unlike other news media, who have reported frequently on the willingness of the Prime Minister to be interviewed at literally a moment's notice, *Investigate* was asked to submit all questions in writing to the PM's Chief Press Secretary, Mike Munro. The magazine refused to do so, but did provide the generalised questions listed above [the same arguments you've just read] in a fax to another of the Prime Minister's media advisors, David Lewis, who also asked for printouts of all the articles that *Investigate* has published on the issue. Two days after receiving that information, Lewis advised that "the Prime Minister will not be making any comment on New Zealand's constitutional position, so there will not be an interview."

If the Government has evidence that it is constitutionally lawful, it apparently is not able to share that evidence with the public.

The Prime Minister and Attorney-General did not opt to clarify the country's constitutional problem. If *Investigate's* research had been demonstrably wrong, don't you think they would have done so? The evasiveness did not sit well with former Governor-General Sir Paul Reeves either, who after reviewing the points made by the magazine, said it was time for the Government to come clean.

Former Governor-General Sir Paul Reeves says it's time for the Government to come clean on New Zealand's constitutional position, following a refusal by the Prime Minister to deny that her Government may be illegal. The question of whether New Zealand has an unconstitutional Government, unable to enforce laws or collect taxes, has taken an intriguing new turn with the Prime Minister's reluctance to clarify the issue, and it is a debate that is giving the former Governor-General cause for concern.

"Ultimately any Government needs to have the assurance that it has a mandate from the people to do whatever it is doing," Sir Paul Reeves told *Investigate*. "I'm not in a position to say whether New Zealand is legitimate or illegitimate, but what I am wanting to say though is New Zealand bloody-well ought to be legitimate, if we ain't!"

In a move reminiscent of equestrian Mark Todd's handling of the drug scandal, the New Zealand Government has taken a similar "neither confirm nor deny" stance on questions of its own lawfulness...

The allegation against the Government is relatively simple to understand: it is legally impossible for sovereignty to pass from the King or Queen of England to the New Zealand Government: the Government is not the Queen's "subjects", the people are, and only subjects could be given independence.

Yet the New Zealand Parliament, in the 1986 Constitution Act, now claims to hold absolute sovereignty over all New Zealanders.

"You end up with the Government saying 'We are the Crown'," says Sir Paul Reeves, "and that's a very interesting development, I think...how did that happen?"

In a report that even the *Listener* admits could equally refer to the New Zealand situation, British constitutional expert Jonathan Freedland writes: "The British system is the very opposite of the Americans': power flows from the top down, not the bottom up. The Government is in charge, and the people are its servant.

"A Prime Minister can act like a king because (s)he has inherited a king's powers. This is not rhetoric but constitutional fact: the bulk of the royal prerogative has been handed from the palace to Downing Street. The result is a British premier who enjoys powers that scholars freely describe as absolutist, with only the most meagre restraint.

"But what makes the executive's power truly extraordinary is that it appoints the judiciary and, armed with a parliamentary majority, controls the legislature – giving it the power to write the very law of the land".

If the Government had been hauled to account over its constitutional status back in 2000, the Electoral Finance Act would not now prevent you from speaking your mind. If Helen Clark had been prosecuted for art forgery, she would not have taken the chance, through Heather Simpson, to steal $800,000 of taxpayer funds for use in private Labour party campaigning. It is unlikely the anti-smacking laws would have been rammed through. If David Benson-Pope had been forced to resign for misleading Parliament in 2005, he would not have been able to damage the career of Madeleine Setchell in 2007 and have been caught lying again.

If David Parker had been made to take the rap for deliberately signing false company documents in 2005, he would not have been at the centre of taking unconstitutional shortcuts and interfering in the integrity of the public service in 2007.

And on it goes.

People wonder why *Investigate* covered some of these stories. Hopefully the answer is blindingly obvious to you now: Leopards don't change their spots. Character flaws tend to remain character flaws, without some kind of major intervention. A Prime Minister with a total disregard for constitutional law, or in fact even the criminal law, will keep committing crimes or breaching the rules as long as she or he can get away with it. It is not rocket science.

This is not an exhaustive biography of the Clark administration – it would be closer to 700 pages if it were – but I have tried to concentrate on some of the main skirmishes and controversies, whilst compiling in one location fresh biographical data as well.

People will undoubtedly query, why some events and not others? I will undoubtedly keep answering, space restrictions. At nearly 150,000 words, this is already a weighty enough tome. Why have I not focused on Clark's positive achievements? Firstly, Labour has an army of media spindoctors churning out the good news about Clark 24/7/52. I saw no need wasting valuable trees copying their efforts. Secondly, the good news has already been preached in her first biography. Thirdly, I wanted to measure her administration not against policy wins/losses, which is a subjective measurement, but more against the way Labour did business, which is objective. It is the latter standard that journalism aspires to in its role as a check and balance on the Executive. There can be different opinions about the merit or success of a policy, but when you measure a Government against illegality and corruption, the benchmark is the law, not whether you like the administration or not.

And the law is interesting. The definition of corrupt is probably a good place to start. When I did the Winebox Inquiry, legal submissions were made on what constituted corruption. Lawyers went scurrying for the most part to dictionaries and the like:

cor-rupt[416] (ke-rupt) *adjective*
   1. Marked by immorality and perversion; depraved
   2. Venal; dishonest: *a corrupt mayor*

cor-rupt-ed, cor-rupti-ing, cor-rupts *verb, transitive*
   1. To destroy or subvert the honesty of integrity of
   2. To ruin morally; pervert
   3. To taint; contaminate

The Compton's Reference Collection adds the definition, "deteriorated from the normal or standard", while the Collins English Dictionary says corruption involves "dishonesty".

A more sophisticated analysis comes from imprisoned Burmese opposition leader and Nobel prize winner, Aung San Suu Kyi, whose definitions of corruption became part of the official record at the Winebox Inquiry:

"It is not power that corrupts but fear. Fear of losing power corrupts those who wield it, and fear of the scourge of power corrupts those who are subject to it.

---

[416] *American Heritage Dictionary*

"Most Burmese are familiar with the four *a-gati*, the four kinds of corruption.

"*Chanda-gati*, corruption induced by desire, is deviation from the right path in pursuit of bribes, or for the sake of those one loves.

"*Dosa-gati* is taking the wrong path to spite those against whom one bears ill-will, and *Moha-gati* is aberration due to ignorance.

"But perhaps the worst of all is *Bhaya-gati*, for not only does *Bhaya*, fear, stifle and slowly destroy all sense of right and wrong, it so often lies at the root of the other three kinds of corruption.

"Just as *Chanda-gati*, when not the result of sheer avarice, can be caused by fear of want or fear of losing the goodwill of those one loves, so fear of being surpassed, humiliated or injured in some way can provide the impetus for ill-will."

In looking back over the revelations of *Absolute Power*, ask yourself whether any of the actions of the Helen Clark government fit any of these definitions. If they do, then you have found proof of Lord Acton's truism: "Power tends to corrupt, absolute power corrupts absolutely."

Finally, Sir Geoffrey Palmer's voice from the past offers hope; that where the public decide enough is enough, they can demand change:[417]

"The question of political will is an important one in all parts of constitutional reform," Palmer wrote in 1987. "No written constitution, Bill of Rights or second chamber can be introduced unless public opinion sees a definite need for such institutions. The public demand will need to be clear as such changes do not appeal to politicians, especially those who happen to make up the government at any time. Any of the changes involves a reduction in the power of government. The record of governments voluntarily relinquishing power is not one to inspire confidence that change will occur unless politicians feel politically at risk."

And that, in the end, may be Helen Clark's real legacy to history – that by her actions (with the total support of her MMP coalition partners) she has provoked New Zealanders so much that they demand, and force, change.

---

417 *Unbridled Power*, p236

Index

Index

Index